Existence and Enlightenment in the *Laṅkāvatāra-sūtra*

SUNY Series in Buddhist Studies

Kenneth K. Inada, Editor

Existence and Enlightenment in the *Laṅkāvatāra-sūtra*

A Study in the Ontology and Epistemology of the Yogācāra School of Mahāyāna Buddhism

Florin Giripescu Sutton

STATE UNIVERSITY OF NEW YORK PRESS

Published by
State University of New York Press, Albany

Printed in the United States of America

For information, address State University of New York Press, State University Plaza, Albany, N.Y., 12246

Library of Congress Cataloging-in-Publication Data

Sutton, Florin Giripescu, 1947-
Existence and enlightenment in the *Laṅkāvatāra-sūtra*: a study in the ontology and epistemology of the Yogācāra school of Mahāyāna Buddhism/ Florin Giripescu Sutton.
p. cm.—(SUNY series in Buddhist studies)
Bibliography: p.
Includes index.
ISBN 0-7914-0172-3. — ISBN 0-7914-0173-1 (pbk.)
1. Tripiṭaka. Sūtrapiṭaka. *Laṅkāvatāra-sūtra*—Criticism, interpretation, etc. 2. Yogācāra (Buddhism) I. Title.
II. Series.
BQ1727.S86 1991
181′.043—dc19

89-4347
CIP

10 9 8 7 6 5 4 3 2 1

To the memory of
LINDA WARREN,
who showed me the depths of *duḥkha,*
and to
CAROL DOROTHY HEIL,
the avatar of womanhood
who brought me to the heights of *sukha,*
the two extraordinary women
whose life essence
nourished the writing of this book.

yathā hi grantho granthena yuktyā yuktis tathā yadi /
ato yuktir bhaved yuktir anyatha tu na kalpayet //

As the text (is completed) by reason,
So is reason (revealed) by the text;
Therefore, let there be reason,
Let there be no other discrimination than reason.

Laṅkā X, gātha 883

Contents

Foreword

Dr. Sutton has written a striking book, which is the first systematic work on the subject since D. T. Suzuki's path-breaking work on the *Laṅkāvatāra Sūtra*. It sets forth a radically different view from Suzuki's: it sees that the Yogācāra was not a subjective idealism. In this, Mr. Sutton's analysis is attractive, for it enables him to do full justice to the dialectical-critical nature of Yogācāra. The result of a systematic understanding of the *Laṅkāvatāra Sūtra* places it in relationship to some key Western philosophical and psychological ideas—to the linguistic analysis of Wittgenstein, the dialectics of Hegel, the depth psychology of Freud and Jung, the Humean flux and Kant's critical stance. But he also emphasizes the soteriological flavor of Buddhist thought. He points out that the idea that Yogācāra is 'consciousness-only' refers to its spiritual practice, not to its metaphysics, which has room for a theoretical realism, not unlike Kant's ideas of a world 'out there' of things-in-themselves, inaccessible to perception and beyond narrow conceptualization. He also emphasizes the closeness of Mādhyamika and Yogācāra approaches: for Yogācāra too, he argues, rejects a specific philosophical point of view, in favor of a dialectical relativism. He concludes that the Yogācāra wisdom may help to enlighten our planet and encourage tolerance. I agree. It conduces to an attitude of mellowness in relation to transcendental and absolutist claims, without abandoning the essence of contemplative religion, which is wanting in many areas of secular and religious thought.

Ninian Smart
J. F. Rowny Professor of Comparative Religions
Department of Religious Studies
UNIVERSITY OF CALIFORNIA, SANTA BARBARA

Preface

This is an interpretation of the Mahāyāna Buddhist world of ideas and spiritual aspirations, as it appeared toward the end of its Indian phase, before its further expansion beyond the land of its birth into China, Korea, and Japan. Our focus is the Yogācāra philosophy, as reflected primarily in that fourth-century creative synthesis called *The Visit to Laṅkā.* This is perhaps the least explored, and certainly the most controversial, school of philosophical Buddhism, in spite of the enormously influential role it played in the subsequent development of Buddhism, especially in the Zen schools of China and Japan.

During the last half century since the publication of Professor Daisetz Teitaro Suzuki's outstanding *Studies in the Laṅkāvatāra Sūtra,* "One of the most important texts of Mahāyāna Buddhism, in which almost all its principal tenets are presented, including the teaching of Zen" (London: 1930, reprint in 1968), there have been to my knowledge only three book-size studies of this school, and a handful of scholarly articles. The first of these three books, Aśok Kumar Chatterjee's *The Yogācāra Idealism* (Varanasi: 1962), made no attempt to reinterpret critically the groundwork laid by Professor Suzuki's initial interpretation of the school as an "absolute idealistic monism." The two subsequent books, however, can be said to represent major steps away from this traditional interpretation, which was almost unanimously, and perhaps too uncritically, embraced by the students of this school, from both East and West, for an amazingly long time.

Janice Dean Willis' study *On Knowing Reality* (New York: 1979) contains a brief yet insightful introduction to her translation of the *Tattvārtha* chapter of Asaṅga's *Bodhisattvabhūmi.* In this introduction she characterizes Yogācāra as "a kind of nominalist philosophy" (p. 36) which underscores "the ordinary being's chief delusion," that is the error of confusing the naming of objects with the objects themselves. Although she attributes the "mistaken" interpretation of the Yogācāra as absolute idealism to the misleading literal translation of the key notion of "Mind-only" (Citta-mātra), Willis' makes a distinction between the early writings of the two masters of the school, Asaṅga and Vasubandhu, and the writings of the "later historical and philological period," particularly the *Laṅkāvatāra-sūtra* (pp. 25, 31, 36) where, she claims (unfortunately without adequate documentation), the terms "Conceptualization-only" (Vijñapti-mātra) and "Mind-only" (Citta-mātra) are employed "in senses that seemingly deny the existence of external objects altogether" (p. 36). To be fair, however, one should also note that she does not exclude the possibility (first suggested by the great medieval master Tsoṅ-kha-pa) that most of the "idealistic" proclamations of the sūtra were intended in a "provisional sense" only, in order "to divert sentient beings from their preoccupation with materialism" (p. 32).

The third and latest book-length attempt to re-interpret the school of Yogācāra, Thomas A. Kochumuttom's *A Buddhist Doctrine of Experience* (Delhi: 1982) is, in author's own words, "an invitation to a re-evaluation of the traditional interpretation" (namely in terms of realistic pluralism, n.n.), "rather than a categorical rejection of it" (p. xvi). Based upon his translations of Vasubandhu's four essential works (*Madhyāntavibhāga-kārikā-bhāṣya, Trisvabhāva-nirdeśa, Triṃśatikā,* and *Viṃśatikā,* the last two being traditionally grouped together as the *Vijñapti-mātratā-siddhi*), Kochumuttom's invitation to re-interpret Yogācāra as a return to the realistic pluralism of the early Hīnayāna Buddhism is, admittedly, a half-hearted one, neither convinced nor convincing (see pp. xvi, xxi, and 232f.). Although he acknowledges the fact that "Vasubandhu's understanding of reality defies all descriptions, because for him reality is ineffable (*anabhilāpya*)" (pp. xxi & 224f.), Kochumuttom allows himself to fall too easily into a classical dualistic trap, that very trap that the Buddhists themselves were taught to avoid. For, just because there is no justification in the writings of Vasubandhu (and, one may add, of other Yogācāra writers as well) for a belief in monism and in an "absolute mode of existence in terms of consciousness," as the author rightly observed, it does not necessarily follow that he, Vasubandhu, believed in the opposite extreme, that of "realistic pluralism," as the author would like to conclude—I think—on the rather weak and arbitrary ground that "an assumption of plurality of beings does not contradict any part of the texts" (p. 229).

My answer to Kochmuttom's interpretation of the Yogācāra is threefold. First, many Yogācāra texts, and the *Laṅkāvatāra-sūtra* in particular, repeatedly deny that a plurality, or multiplicity of beings can be admitted, in the ultimate sense. To wit, here is just one quote from *Laṅkā* III: 154, verse 32:

> Multiplicity (of dharmas) is produced from the habit-energy of discrimination; it is born of mind, but it is called among the people as (something) external (to the mind)—this I declare to be nothing but mind (*citta-mātra*).

Second, and related to the first, all Buddhist schools agree that everything is temporary, nothing is permanent. All dharmas are transient (*anitya*). Therefore, pluralism can be admitted only in the immediate, not in the ultimate sense. Third, and most importantly, it is quite possible, in my opinion, to consciously refuse to be hemmed in by any one-sided philosophical view and embrace, instead, a transcendental position to any and all conceptualizations about reality, as the Yogācāras (and the Mādhyamikas before them) have done, on purely epistemological, but also on spiritual grounds, as we shall see. This is the conclusion that I arrived at from my reading of the *Laṅkāvatāra-sūtra*, the text that most authors have perceived to express the alleged idealistic monism of the Yogācāras in its strongest terms.

To summarize, the difficulty of placing the Yogācāra school within the larger perspective of Buddhist doctrinal history revolves around two crucial issues: first, the paradoxical language of the texts belonging to this school (especially the *Laṅkāvatāra-sūtra*), which avoids expressing a definite philosophical position regarding Reality, on account of its transcendence of conceptual language; and second, the controversial interpretation of the central tenet of the school, Citta-mātra (or Mind-only). This concept has been taken to be either an outright denial of external Reality, or a formula indicating the essential role of subjective factors in cognition and the limitations of conceptual thinking, as well as a metaphor for the primacy of *Yogic* meditation over philosophical speculations about the nature of Reality itself. If interpreted ontologically, as a denial of an intrinsically objective Reality, the Mind-only doctrine would, indeed, place the Yogācāra school alongside other idealistic orientations in Indian philosophical history. If interpreted epistemologically, however, this doctrine would represent a powerful critique against (a) the objectification of language, (b) the artificiality of dualistic logic, and (c) the type of conventional knowledge derived from both.

This kind of knowledge, according to the Yogācāra Buddhist, the philosophical meditator, is really no knowledge, since it can only provide the delusion of facticity, or the "Suchness" of things, tainted as it is by the subjective factors of perception and biased judgment. True knowledge, on the other hand, can only be attained within the context of the *totality* of human existence, that is to say in the direct experience of life, which transcends verbal categories, dual logic, and a pseudo-ontology based upon the reification of thoughts and ideas (including the idea of Mind-only itself!).

Now, in order to reach the core of Yogācāra thought, I have made use of the following methodological approaches, either individually, or in various combinations, as the topic required: the text-critical (philological), the Buddhist-hermeneutical (philosophical), the historical, the psychological, and the sociological methods. Structurally, the study is divided into two major sections—each with a general introduction—and a final overview. Each of the two major sections contains several topical chapters organized in such way that, together, they afford the reader a systematic and comprehensive grasp of the Yogācāras' metaphysical system—their epistemology and soteriology.

Looking back, however, one has to admit that the immensity of the project seemed overwhelming at times, since even for more seasoned scholars the difficulties of interpreting such a text as the *Laṅkāvatāra-sūtra* are enormous, especially when one takes into account the complex and unsystematic nature of this ancient and esoteric work. In addition, the textual difficulties seem to be compounded for someone who is not as familiar with the living Buddhist tradition as one who grew up in the Buddhist world might be.

And yet, in spite of these caveats, the world of ideas waiting to be discovered is so rich, so original and fascinating, and so little has been written about it in recent years that, enormous as the challenge has been, it has certainly been worth the effort. Consider, for instance, the mere fact of discovery by the West of the existence of a distant and exotic culture, such as happened with Zen Buddhism following the military occupation of Japan at the end of World War II—a discovery that, surprising as it may seem, has since enriched our own freedom and civilization.

For, if civilization represents the maximum of human freedom, and freedom means the maximum of existential options to choose from, then learning about a different mode of existing in the world, and of interpreting human experience, will make us aware of our own self-imposed limitations and stimulate self-reflection. And that in itself may help bring about the fostering of a new, intellectually coherent worldview, consistent with our diverse experiences, a real necessity in a culturally divided world which still lacks a common basis for a mutually acceptable dialogue.

This kind of cognitive integration will bring to the fore once again the original meaning of the word *religion*,—from the Latin *re-ligāre*, 'to tie, to connect,' or reconnect with the 'other', with the past, the present, and hopefully, the future—which is, in more ways than one, related in meaning to the word *education*—also from the Latin *e-ducāre*, 'to carry through, to direct, to lead toward, to provide a compass, a guidance through a multitude of seemingly disconnected ideas or events.' And that is precisely what this book attempts to do, namely to bring about a systematic coherence in the 'forbidden forest' of exotic Buddhist ideas, and to try to put them in the larger perspective of a possible world history of religious philosophy.

Therefore, for those who feel attracted by the history of human thought in general, and are intrigued by the questions raised by the Buddhist way of interpreting the world in particular, I sincerely hope that their investment of time and effort will be rewarded with sufficient food for thought to keep them nourished for some time to come, in whatever spiritual journey they have undertaken. This in itself would constitute a special reward that would meet and even exceed the author's highest aspirations.

INTRODUCTION

0.1. The Purpose of the Study, and the Significance of the *Laṅkāvatāra-sūtra* within Buddhist Doctrinal History

The scope of this study is to investigate some of the essential ideas of the last creative phase of Indian Buddhism, namely the Yogācāra school, as presented in one of its earliest and most influential texts, the *Laṅkāvatāra-sūtra*.[1] The school of Yogācāra, which is sometimes referred to as the idealistic school of 'Consciousness-only' (Vijñāna-vāda), represents not only the highest point of Mahāyāna philosophy, but also a unique attempt to synthesize the best elements of both Mahāyāna and Hīnayāna doctrines, as one author puts it.[2]

The credit for this accomplishment goes usually to the two illustrious patriarchs of the school, the half-brothers Asaṅga and Vasubandhu, who initially followed the Sarvāstivāda (Hīnayāna) tradition. They lived some time between A.D. 359-450 in the north-western region of Gandhāra which has been, since the time of Alexander the Great, under strong Graeco-Roman influence, shown —according to certain writers—by the presence of Manichaean and neo-Platonic elements in their works.[3] It is important to note, however, that these two brothers were rather late converts to, and interpreters of, a religious system which was already in existence all over India, not only in the northern regions, but in the more remote coastal areas of the South, as well.[4]

Indeed, the findings of many scholars seem to converge toward a common belief, namely that between 100 B.C. and A.D. 200, the bulk of Mahāyāna Buddhist literature developed around the Āndra district of Southeast India, which was an apparent Mahāsaṅghikan stronghold.[5] The most renowned Mahāyānist, Nāgārjuna (c. A.D. 150-250), the founder of the Mādhyamika school, was also born in the Āndhra district (near Śrī Parvata or Śrī Śailam) and lived most of his life there, according to his biography translated by Kumārajīva, in the fourth century.[6]

Aside from his own works, which influenced all subsequent Mahāyāna literature to some degree, he greatly contributed to the spread of the *Prajñā-pāramitā* corpus of writings among the Mahāsaṅghikan circles throughout the South. What all these early Mahāyāna scriptures had in common was a certain doctrinal core, at various levels of development, which revolved around such concepts as universal Voidness, a transcendental Buddha, the Bodhisattva stages, the Essence of Buddhahood, an intrinsically pure Mind, etcetera.[7] While there was no doctrinal agreement among the various Mahāsaṅghikan subsects (such as the Ekavyavahārika, Lokottaravāda, and Kukkuṭika), these concepts are found in the texts they all quoted: the *Avataṃsaka, Mahāparinirvāṇa, Śrīmālādevī, Vimalakīrti, Suvarṇaprabhāsa, Prajñāpāramitā,* and others.[8] The close doctrinal affinity between some of these texts (*Avataṃsaka, Śrīmālādevī, Prajñāpāramitā* with regard to the Citta-mātra, Tathāgata-garbha, and Śūnyatā concepts, respectively) and the *Laṅkāvatāra-sūtra,* indicates in all likelihood a common cultural milieu, to say the least.

The very title of the text which constitutes the subject of this work (*Āryasaddharma-laṅkāvatāronāma-mahāyāna-sūtram,* or "A Mahāyāna scripture, called 'The descent into Laṅkā,' containing the noble orthodox teaching of Buddhism") suggests either South India or Ceylon as its origin. According to an old Pāli legend, dear to the southern Buddhists, the Buddha is said to have visited the island of Laṅkā three times during his preaching career. On the other hand, the name *Laṅkā* may also be taken in the metaphorical sense to symbolize a magical place (either a solitary island in the middle of the ocean, or a citadel on the peak of Mount Malaya) where beings larger than life, such as an omniscient, transcendental Buddha and the many-headed king of the *rākṣasas,* Rāvaṇa, meet for the purpose of hearing the doctrine of Enlightenment, as laid out in the first chapter of the book.[9]

The southern origin of the text may also be inferred from the fact that its first translators into Chinese, Dharmaraksha and Gunabhadra, came from central India, and were Law-Teachers of the *Tripiṭaka,* the southern (Theravāda/Hīnayāna) canon, who had—just like the two brothers in the North, Asaṅga and Vasubandhu—only recently joined the ranks of Mahāyāna converts.[10]

Conversions such as these were by no means uncommon, especially when southern Buddhists travelled to northern monastic centers of learning.[11] For example, the Tibetan historian Tāranātha (Kun-dga'-sniṅ-po) mentions among the twelve *Tāntrika* teachers of Vikramaśīla in the eighth century a certain *ācārya* called Laṅkājayabhadra (or Jayabhadra from Laṅkā, or Ceylon; Tibetan: Laṅkārgyal-bzaṅ). Having become a *bhikṣu paṇḍita*, versed in all the Śrāvaka *Piṭakas*, he went to Magadha, where he became a Mahāyānist and Tantric scholar, particularly of the Guhya-tantra school. Then he went back to the southern town of Koṅkana, where he preached Guhya-tantrayāna before finally establishing himself as the Tantra-ācārya of Vikramaśīla.[12]

By that time (seventh-eighth century), the monastic university of Vikramaśīla (in the area of modern Bihar) had already become the hub of Buddhist missionary activity, as well as learning. It was from such places of high learning that the teachings of the Yogācāra school were first taken into China by the second (actually the first) *Ch'an* Patriarch, Bodhidharma, in the fifth century, and to Tibet by Padmasambhava in the seventh century, where it has survived up to modern times as one of the main strands of Tibetan Buddhism.

According to Chinese tradition, Bodhidharma is said to have received the teaching of the Laṅkāvatāra (later known as the Ch'an) school, directly from Guṇabhadra, the second of the four known translators of the *Sūtra*, and the alleged first patriarch of the school.[13] He is also believed to have written a commentary on the *Laṅkāvatāra-sūtra*, the *Leng-chia yao-i*, also known as *Ta-mo lun*.[14] Unfortunately, the life of Bodhidharma is shrouded in mystery—due partly to the scarcity of reliable evidence, and partly to the mythological embellishments added in later periods—as is the possible use of the *Laṅkāvatāra-sūtra* in the early history of Ch'an.[15] According to J. R. McRae, the following is known from Chinese sources:[16]

> He was a native of South India, a Brahmin by birth and perhaps a member of the ruling family of some unknown and probably minor principality. He was a Mahāyānist and a meditation instructor who focused his proselytic efforts on the Lo-yang area. Other than these few remarks and what may be inferred from his *EJSHI* [*Erh-ju ssu-hsing lun* or *Treatise on the Two Entrances and Four Practices*, McRae's abbreviation, n.n.], nothing else can be said about him with any certainty.

As far as the transmission of the *Laṅkāvatāra-sūtra* itself, and the role it played in the subsequent development of the school, McRae points out two separate issues, namely (1) whether or not Bodhidharma and/or Hui-k'o (his first disciple and the second patriarch) actually used the *Laṅkāvatāra-sūtra*, and (2) the connection between this text and the Ch'an tradition descended from him.[17]

To answer the first question, McRae analyzes three references to the *Laṅkāvatāra* found in Hui-k'o's biography, as preserved in

Tao-hsüan's *Hsü Kao-seng-chuan* (*Biographies of Famous Buddhist Monks*, or *HKSC*, in short). For their relevance to our study, let us reproduce them here (in McRae's translation), as follows:[18]

> [1] In the beginning *Dhyāna* Master (Bodhi)dharma transmitted the four-fascicle *Laṅkā(vatāra Sūtra)* to (Hui)-k'o, saying: "this *Sūtra* is the only one that is suitable for China. If you base your practice on it you will attain salvation." (Hui)-k'o single-mindedly imparted the mysterious principle (of the *Laṅkāvatāra* to his students) just as it had been explained before (by Bodhidharma).
>
> [2] At the end of each of his sermons, (Hui)-k'o said: "(The understanding of) this *Sūtra* will become superficial after four generations. How utterly lamentable!"
>
> [3] Therefore the Masters Na and (Hui-)-man always carried the four-fascicle (version of the *Laṅkāvatāra Sūtra* as the "essential (teaching) of the mind" (*hsin-yao*). They preach and practice it at every occasion, never varying from (the true understanding thereof) that had been bequeathed to them.

One can glean from these statements that the *Sūtra* was held in high regard during the early stage of its transmission into China. However, according to McRae's findings, "These three short statements appear quite out of context in the *Hsü Kao-seng-chuan*," and they may have been interpolated into the text of Hui-k'o's biography along with other biographical materials.[19]

Therefore, McRae concludes, the first issue cannot be definitively resolved, because "there is no direct evidence to suggest that Bodhidharma and Hui-k'o did in fact use the *Laṅkāvatāra*." Indirect evidence would suggst that interest in the *Laṅkāvatāra* peaked sometime between the sixth and seventh centuries, but waned after a short period. While it is conceivable, McRae argues further, that Bodhidharma and Hui-k'o were among the first Buddhists in China to make use of the text, it is quite certain that a final blow to its popularity was incurred by the career of Hsüan-tsang, who refused to permit lecturing on previously-translated scriptures, specifically the *Laṅkāvatāra*.[20]

As far as the possibility of a real connection between the *Sūtra* and the later Ch'an tradition of the North is concerned, and of its use by the *Dhyāna* Masters of the North as a justification for the idea of sudden Enlightenment, after thoroughly researching the evidence,

McRae concludes:[21]

> . . . The connection between the *Laṅkāvatāra Sūtra* and the Northern School during the early eighth century was equally tenuous. Although this scripture apparently had some kind of mystical appeal to the followers of early Ch'an, there is no evidence that its contents had any impact on the development of the School.

However, our contention is that the impact of the text should not be judged exclusively by the specific references to it found in the works of one author or another, nor by the continuity of a single idea, such as that of sudden Enlightenment.

Rather, the *Sūtra*'s influence should be judged in the context of the number of characteristic concepts it had in common with other related texts, as we have previously pointed out. That would explain why so many different schools of thought claimed relation to, and derived authority from the *Laṅkāvatāra-sūtra*. Since this text represents an attempt to gather many of the concepts floating freely, so to speak, in the South Indian Buddhist cultural milieu (such as Tathāgatagarbha and Ālaya-vijñāna, Śūnyatā and Dharmadhātu, Self-lessness and Self-realization), its insights and solutions fueled the inquisitiveness of the Chinese mind for a much longer time and at a much deeper level than the texts themselves would allow us to infer. One cannot but agree with Suzuki's assessment in this respect that "It it difficult to say how significant these characteristics of this text were to the earliest Ch'an figures."[22]

More recently, another scholar, Bernard Faure, after an impressive investigation of the lineage and doctrine of the northern Ch'an, gives us a more committed assessment, which concurs with the broader view regarding the influence of the text in China and beyond (see below). He says:[23]

> The heterogeneity of the *Laṅkāvatāra* thus allowed quite different currents of thought to harken back to this sūtra. While a master of the tradition of Hua-yen like Li T'ung-hsüan (635-730) could characterize it by the Yogācāra theories such as the "five dharmas"(*pañca-dharma*), the "three Self-natures" (*tri-svabhāva*), the "eight *vijñāna*s" and the "double absence of Self" (*nairātmya-dvaya-lakṣaṇa*), a representant of Ch'an like Yung-ming Yen-shou (904-975) retains of it only the emphasis given to *"the spirit of the Buddha's words."*

According to Faure, the divergent trends with regard to practice (sudden or gradual Enlightenment), just as those with regard to doctrine, can also be traced back to the *Laṅkāvatāra*. He continues:[24]

> On the practical level, the *Laṅkāvatāra* provided the adepts of Ch'an with the notions of "suddenness" or the "dhyāna of the Tathāgata." Kuna Hōryu had already stressed that this sūtra was not as "gradualistic" as Shen-hui and his heirs proclaimed it to be. Hence, it is possible that the "masters of the northern dhyāna," amongst whom Chih-i, the patriarch of the T'ien-t'ai school, criticizes the excessive "suddenness' [doctrine, n.n.], and who claim their lineage from the *Laṅkāvatāra*, are none other than the disciples of Bodhidharma. For Yanagida, the Ch'an of Bodhidharma and of Hui-k'o—whose *Sequence to Biographies* points out the specifics—is doubtless the "dhyāna of the Tathāgata" as defined by the *Laṅkāvatāra*.

In conclusion, Faure aptly points out, all these divergent trends betray the myth of a purely spiritual search ("le myth d'un Ch'an 'angelique'," perpetuated by Suzuki and others), the search for a transcendental Truth uncontaminated by its relation with the molding agents of history, political and otherwise.[25] Indeed, one can say that, from the larger, historical perspective, dichotomies such as orthodoxy and heterodoxy, northern and southern, sudden and gradual (Enlightenment), reason and faith, scriptural knowledge and mystical insight, by themselves, prove the relative nature of any 'transcendental Truth' held by one school or another, at one time or another, based upon this text or the other.

Furthermore, it is important to remember in this context that there was another school in the study of the *Laṅkāvatāra-sūtra* beside the one transmitted by Bodhidharma and his followers of the northern (Ch'an) school of Buddhism. This was the school known as Yogācāra idealism, based upon Asaṅga's *Mahāyāna-saṃgraha*, whose lineage is still traceable today.[26] Since this school revolves around the *garbha* theory, as well as the system of the Eight Vijñānas (especially the *Ālaya-vijñāna*), the *Laṅkāvatāra* has been used as one of its central authorities.[27] When these two concepts (Garbha and Ālaya) became combined under one theory of Citta-Mātra, as taught in the *Avatamsaka Sūtra*, the *Laṅkāvatāra* was even more eagerly sought by the followers of both schools.[28] Some of the commentaries on the treatise written by Asaṅga were in fact the work of obscure Zen Masters, such as Ch'ien and Shih.[29] Jikidō Takasaki's opinion is relevant in these matters and well worth quoting:[30]

> The *Laṅkāvatāra* is actually a collection of various theories among Mahāyāna Buddhism, among which the *garbha* theory, and the Vijñānavāda are prominent, and these two are combined under the theory of *cittamātra* taught in the *Avataṃsaka*. Later Vijñānavādins regarded the *Laṅkāvatāra* as one of the authorities, but in China it was respected by the followers of the Avataṃsaka school as well, because of its exposition of the *cittamātra* and *garbha* theory. This is quite significant for determining the fate of the *garbha* theory, to which we will refer at the end of this introduction.

His assessment supports the point that the influence of the text went beyond its immediate transmission and use by a narrow circle of early followers of Bodhidharma's teachings.

Now, the first Chinese translation of the text is, unfortunately, lost, but we do know that it was done in A.D. 420 by Dharmaraksha, whose title was: "Master of the Law, Teacher of the Tripiṭaka, of Central India." It had four fasciculi and bore the simple title, *The Laṅka-Sūtra*. The second translation (which is, in fact, the first extant one), also in four fasciculi under the longer title, *The Laṅkāvatāra-Treasure-Sūtra*, was done by Guṇabhadra, as mentioned, in A.D. 443. Two more translations from "the same text" were subsequently attempted: one by the northern teacher Bodhiruci (criticized by Fa-tsang) in A.D. 513, and the other by Śikshānanda, between 700-714, with a preface by the Empress Tse-t'ien Wu-hou (and revised by Fa-tsang and others). These last two versions had, respectively, ten and seven fasciculi.

It was the fourth and last translation, entitled *The Mahāyāna Laṅkāvatāra Sūtra*, that was considered by Suzuki to be the best of all the Chinese versions, being the product of cooperative effort by both Chinese and Indian scholars.[31] However, the only extant commentaries by Chinese and Japanese scholars are based upon the older, and shortest translation in four fasciculi attributed to Guṇabhadra. One of the two extant Tibetan translations was also done from Guṇabhadra's version of the original Sanskrit. The origin and date of the other is, unfortunately, quite obscure.[32]

Most commentaries still extant are in Chinese, none in Sanskrit. There are altogether fifteen works dealing with the subject of the *Laṅkāvatāra-sūtra* in Chinese: two of the T'ang dynasty, four of the Sung dynasty, seven of the Ming dynasty, and two of the Ch'ing dynasty. One of the T'ang commentaries has received special attention among Japanese scholars. It was written by Fa-tsang as a comprehensive introduction to the study of the *Laṅkāvatāra* and it represents, in Suzuki's opinion, the "most valuable literature ever written in connection with the sūtra."[33]

Incidentally, in as far as the Ch'an patriarchal tradition is concerned, one should also be aware of the occasional substitution of names, especially in Tibet, where, for instance, the lineage of a fifth century Kashmiri monk, Dharmatrāta, becomes Bodhidharma's lineage, while Bodhidharma himself becomes known as Bodhidharmatrāta. In China, too, the names of the early translators (Bodhiruci, Guṇabhadra and Bodhidharma) were often confused and biographical details easily transferred.[34]

In Japan, the *Sūtra* was known and studied from the Nara era in the eighth century, when owning or copying a Buddhist text was considered a deed of merit. However, it was not until the fourteenth century that the first commentary was written by a Zen monk called Kokwan Shiren (1278-1346). In this eighteen-fasciculi work, entitled *Butsugoshinron* (or, "Treatise on the Essence—or Heart—of the Buddha-teaching"), he undertook a division of the *Sūtra* into eighty-six sections, according to various topics that he distinguished in the text. Since he was also the author of a thirty-fasciculi history of Buddhism, known as *The Genko Shakusho,* his authority was respected by successive commentators, who maintained his topical division of the *Sūtra* as a useful frame of reference in analysing its contents. Thus, Tokugan Yōson's commentary, written in 1687, is considered to be an improved and expanded version of Kokwan's work.

A third Japanese book on the *Laṅkāvatāra* is *Ryōgakyō Kōyoku* by Kōken, mentioned by Seigai Omura and Gisho Nakano in the *Explanatory Notes* to the *Nihon Daizōkyō* (completed in 1921).[35] In addition, more recent Japanese studies are also referred to by Suzuki in his *Studies,* p. 65. They are: Sogen Yamakami's Japanese rendering of Śikshānanda's translation of A.D. 714 (the T'ang version in seven fasciculi); Shōshi Mitsui's brief exposition of the *Laṅkāvatāra* teaching; and Hōkei Idzumi's Japanese translation of the Nanjio edition of the Sanskrit original, which was used also by Suzuki for his own English translation.[36]

Aside from the Nanjio edition, which is the most complete and therefore most widely used one today, there are two other Sanskrit versions of the *Laṅkāvatāra-sūtra*. The first was issued by the Buddhist Texts Publishing Society with an introductory note by Dr. Kaikyoku Watanabe entitled "Concerning the Original Text of the *Laṅkāvatāra* and Its Chinese Translations." The editor, the Reverend Shōshi Mitsui, also included a free rendition of the contents, referred to above. His edition was superseded by the Nanjio text of 1923, which mentions it as one of the sources consulted.[37]

A more recent edition, entitled *Saddharmalaṅkāvatārasūtra*, (Darbhanga: 1963), was put out by P. L. Vaidya, with an Introduction by S. Bagchi. Although I did not consult it during the writing of this book, it does not seem to add further material, since it is based on the same manuscript (No. 3 from the Buddhist Sanskrit Texts in the possession of the Asiatic Society of London) which was used, among other sources, by Nanjio.

In Nepal, the *Laṅkāvatāra* is still used as one of the nine principal Mahāyāna texts (the *Nava Grantha*) of Newari Buddhism. Along with the *Gaṇḍavyūha*, it represents the quintessential teachings of the Yogācāra school in what is, in fact, the last authentic survival of Indian Mahāyāna Buddhism.[38]

Now, the relation between the *Laṅkāvatāra* and Zen (Ch'an) may be summarized thus: Bodhidharma brought from southern India the mystical outlook propounded by the *Ekayāna* school with its stress on meditation (*dhyāna*).[39] There is good reason to believe that he either knew about the *Sūtra* before returning to China, or he became acquainted with it from the writings of Guṇabhadra. At any rate, once familiar with the contents of the text, he felt inclined to emphasize its experiential, mystical side, rather than its doctrinal and metaphysical aspects. It is highly probable that certain statements found in the text caught his attention and guided his teachings. Such statements are found in abundance throughout the *Sūtra;* here are a few samples from chapter III, pages 194-97:[40]

> Mahāmati, words (utterances) are dependent on letters, but meaning is not. (p. 194, ll. 1-2)
>
> Mahāmati, a son or a daughter of a good family who conforms himself/herself to the letter (*vyañcana*) will ruin his/her (understanding of) the ultimate truth/reality, and will cause (others) to fail to recognize (the truth, *paramārtha*). (195, ll. 1-3)
>
> Therefore, Mahāmati, let son or daughter of a good family take good heed not to get attached to words as being in perfect conformity with meaning, because (the meaning) of truth (does not come) from the letter.
>
> You must not be misled by looking at the finger-tip. For instance, Mahāmati, when someone with his finger-tip points something to somebody, he (the latter) may mistake the finger-tip for the things to be pointed at. (196, ll. 4-8)

This is explained at length in the following paragraph (197, ll. 1-8):

> Mahāmati, the meaning is pure [*vivikta*, lit., kept apart, separated, abstract, clear] and is the cause of Nirvāṇa. Words [*ruta*, utterance] are tied to discrimination [or imagination, *vikalpa*] and are the vehicle of transmigration (Saṃsāra). Moreover, Mahāmati, meaning is attained from the accumulation of much learning; and this much learning, Mahāmati, means to be experienced with meaning and not to be skillful with words.
>
> Then, to be experienced with meaning means (to have) a view which is not at all affected by any philosophical school, and which will keep not only yourself but others as well from falling away (from truth). So is said, Mahāmati, that much learning is (conducive to) true meaning.
>
> Therefore, let those (possessing much learning) be honored by him who is longing for meaning, while those acting in the opposite way to this, namely those who are attached to (the idea) that meaning is the same as the words, they are to be disregarded and shunned by truth-seekers.

The emphasis on the spirit rather than the letter of the scripture is very concisely expressed in the following verse which, perhaps, gave currency to the celebrated metaphor and most frequently quoted word of wisdom in the entire history of Zen Buddhism:[41]

> As the immature observes the finger-tip and not the moon, so indeed those who cling to the letter (*akṣara*) do not see my truth [or essence, *tattva*].

Statements such as quoted above may very well have influenced Bodhidharma's general frame of interpretation of the Buddhist texts, including the *Laṅkāvatāra*, which in our time led Buddhologists like Suzuki and others to draw the following retrospective assessment:[42]

> (If) all religious experience requires its intellectual interpretation, Zen, too, must have its philosophical background, which is found in the *Laṅkāvatāra* . . .
>
> . . . The transcendental intuitionism of Zen and the teaching of Pratyātmagatigocara in the *Laṅkāvatāra* were what connected the two so closely.

If one accepts Suzuki's interpretation, the next step would be to say that whatever attracted a religious virtuoso like Bodhidharma to the study of this sūtra—be it the abandonment of reason, or mystical experience—proved to be tantamount to "attaining the unattainable" for the great majority of his followers. This might explain why the study of the *Laṅkāvatāra-sūtra* after Fa-ch'ung (who was contemporary with Hung-jen, the fifth patriarch of Zen Buddhism), gradually fell into neglect, being replaced by that of the *Vajracchedikā*, a sūtra belonging to the *Prajñā-pāramitā* literature. Whether this change was due to textual and doctrinal difficulties, as Suzuki suggests,[43] or on account of the preferences and idiosyncracies of one master or another, as Bernard Faure discovered,[44] it is a complicated and difficult issue to decide, especially when, regretfully, one does not have access to the Chinese and Japanese sources. According to Suzuki, in the Preface to the Chin-shan edition, (Sung dynasty, 1085), Su Tung-pei wrote the following:[45]

> The *Laṅkāvatāra* is deep and unfathomable in meaning, and in style so terse and antique, that the reader finds it quite difficult to punctuate the sentences properly, not to say anything about his adequately understanding their ultimate spirit and meaning which go beyond the letter.
>
> This was the reason why the sūtra grew scarce and it became almost impossible to get hold of a copy.

What both Faure and Suzuki seem to suggest is that once Zen became popular outside the small circle of early followers of the *Laṅkāvatāra*, the pressure to favor the larger body of *Prajñā-pāramitā* literature, rather than relying exclusively upon a single authoritative text, increased.[46] In addition, the growing belief that for those endowed with unusual sharpness of mind, Buddhahood could be attained through a flash of insight, triggered by a mere gesture or pithy utterance, contributed to a general attitude of aloofness from all the written scriptures, characteristic of the late Zen followers.[47]

0.2. Dating the Text: Problems of Form and Interpretation

Ascertaining the date of the *Laṅkāvatāra-sūtra,* as of many other Mahāyāna texts, is a very hazardous endeavor. One thing that can be said for certain, is that it was written before the first (reported) Chinese translation of A.D. 443. Beyond that, one has to rely on inferential judgement. In such a case, we are faced with two kinds of evidence from which one may infer, rather than ascertain, the date of the scripture; these are: external and internal.

As to the *external* evidence, if one first accepts the common supposition that the *śāstras* came after the *sūtras,* then, one would be inclined to think that the *Laṅkāvatāra* was written before the major commentarial works of, for instance, Vasubandhu, who in his *Vijñaptimātratā-triṃśikā* treats of the same concepts found in the *Sūtra,* without, however, referring to it explicitly.

It is important to note that it was not until the works of Sthiramati and Dharmapāla that the *Sūtra* was first quoted with explicit mentioning of its name.[1] Therefore, one cannot discard the possibility that, regardless of the order in which they were written, both the *Laṅkāvatāra-sūtra* and the commentarial works of Asaṅga and Vasubandhu made use of the same disparate source materials circulating among the Mahāyāna Buddhists. The problem is compounded by the uncertainty regarding the dates of Asaṅga and Vasubandhu themselves.

In a 1982 article, entitled "Sources of the *Laṅkāvatāra* and its position in Mahāyāna Buddhism," Jikidō Takasaki juxtaposes the opinions of two noted Japanese scholars regarding the possible dates of Asaṅga and Vasubandhu, and accordingly, the date of the *Laṅkāvatāra.*[2] Thus, the late Dr. H. Ui ascribed to Asaṅga the date of 300-380, and, to his younger brother Vasubandhu, 320-400. Since neither mentioned the *Sūtra* by name, he assumed that the *Laṅkāvatāra* must have come into existence toward the end of the fourth century A.D.[3] The late Dr. S. Yamaguchi, however, having examined the Tibetan translation of the *Vyākhyāyukti* (attributed to Vasubandhu), and found a series of verses identified with vv. 135-7 in the *Sagāthakam* chapter of the *Laṅkāvatāra*, concluded that at least some portions of the *Sūtra* might have been known to Vasubandhu (assuming that the attribution referred to above is correct).

Consequently, two possible scenarios may be considered regarding the date of the text: (a) to suppose that the *Laṅkāvatāra* was compiled in the early half of the fourth century, or even earlier; or (b) to admit that Vasubandhu lived approximately between 400-480 (as it is generally assumed today), and, therefore, to accept that the *Sūtra* was gradually put together over a period of time stretching from the last part of the fourth century into the first half of the fifth century. According to Takasaki, this latter hypothesis seems to have been favored by Dr. Yamaguchi, although it was not clearly stated in his original article.[4]

Takasaki himself affirmed on two different occasions that the *Sūtra* was compiled after Vasubandhu.[5] His evidence, however, is based almost entirely upon an internal criterion which (impressive as it may seem) is, according to Suzuki, "more or less of the character of an ingenious surmise."[6] The internal criterion invoked in asserting the date of the *Laṅkāvatāra* is the identification of Ālaya-vijñāna (the Repository-of-impressions) with Tathāgata-garbha (the Womb-of-Buddhahood), a novel idea which is not found in the works of Asaṅga and Vasubandhu. On the other hand, neither the Tathāgata-garbha theory, nor the Vijñapti-mātra (or Citta-mātra, Mind-only) concept was known to the famous Mādhyamika philosopher, Nāgārjuna. Therefore, the *Laṅkāvatāra* appeared after these writers had produced their works.

In addition to these important doctrinal differences, other *internal* criteria may also be considered. In the above-mentioned article, Takasaki further outlines an impressive array of evidence by which the date of the *Sūtra* may be judged. The evidence is grouped roughly under three headings, as follows:

(1) Proper names of sūtras, of *personae*, and of historical persons (e.g., the *Mahāparinirvāṇa sūtra*, Ch. 8, p. 258, v. 16; the *Śrīmālādevī-sūtra*, Ch. 6, pp. 222-23; and the *Nāgāhvaya-sūtra* (= *Nāgārjuna-sūtra*), *Sagāthakam:* 286, v. 165, respectively);[7]

(2) Idiomatic initiating phrases, such as *yad uktaṃ bhagavatā* (lit., "that was spoken by the Lord," or "thus spake the Lord"), and others, which seem to refer to previous (Hīnayāna or Mahāyāna) works, according to the respective contents of the particular passage thusly introduced (e.g., the expression *avacanam buddhavacanam*, "Buddha's word is a silent word," or "Buddha's word is a No-word," a cliché

commonly found in the Pāli *Nikāyas* and the Chinese *Āgamas*, as well as in the Sanskrit *Prajñā-pāramitā* literature; the Tathāgata-garbha theory alluded to in the *Śrīmālādevī-sūtra* and in the *Tathāgata-garbha-sūtra*, or the expression *vijñaptimātrāvasthāna*, "Abiding in imagination only," whose complete explanation is found in the treatise of thirty verses, the *Vijñaptimātratā-triṃśikā* of Vasubandhu);[8]

(3) Technical terms, or key words indicating a system of doctrines (e.g., Yogācāra-vijñānavāda, Mādhyamika, the Bodhisattvas-Mahāsattvas, the Pratyekka-buddhas, the four kinds of Śrāvakas, and the theory of the Eight Vijñānas contrasted with the traditional Abhidharma theory of the Six Vijñānas, etc.).[9]

After marshaling all these data, however, Takasaki seems to have changed his conclusion when he says that:[10]

> . . . the *Laṅkāvatāra* was not acquainted with the developed Vijñānavāda established by Vasubandhu and that probably the *Laṅkāvatāra* is located a bit earlier than Vasubandhu.

In this conclusion, he is in agreement with David J. Kalupahana, who says the following:[11]

> The *Vijñaptimātratāsiddhi* of Vasubandhu represents a systematization of the metaphysical Idealism embodied in the early Yogācāra texts like *Saṅdhinirmocana-sūtra* and *Laṅkāvatāra-sūtra*, but there is no fresh evaluation of the ideas found in these early texts.

Moriz Winternitz, on the other hand, favors a later date for this important sūtra, when he says in his *History of Indian Literature*, vol. 2 (Calcutta University: 1933), pp. 333-37, that:[12]

> We could infer that Chapter X was written not long before A.D. 513. The philosophy of the Vijñānavāda, which is taught in all the parts of the *Laṅkāvatāra*, coincides with the doctrines of Maitreya-nātha, Asaṅga, and the *Mahāyāna Śraddhotpāda*, which may be ascribed to the 4th century A.D. at the earliest. It is, therefore, probable that the *Laṅkāvatāra*, even in its earliest form, was not in existence more than 50 or, at its very most, 100 years before A.D. 443.

He seems to base his judgement upon the general structure of the text, which reflects its historical development. Inconclusive as the internal evidence appears to be, in the light of Takasaki's analysis (and Suzuki's words of caution), I personally feel inclined to follow the structural approach, suggested by both Winternitz and Suzuki. The latter was the first to point out that the *Sūtra:*[13]

> . . . is just a collection of notes unsystematically strung together, and, frankly speaking, it is a useless task to attempt to divide them into sections, or chapters (*parivarta*), under some specific titles.
>
> . . . If this, however, is to be done successfully, the whole arrangement as it stands of the paragraphs must be radically altered; and this redaction is possible only by picking up and gathering together cognate passages which are found promiscuously scattered throughout the text, when for the first time a kind of system would be brought into the text.

Suzuki (and others) also noted that the extreme sections of the text (i.e., the first and the last three chapters) are clearly incongruous with the main body of writing (chapters II-VII of the Nanjio edition), and therefore, they must have been added at a later date. For the reader's convenience, I shall give first the chapter headings, as found in the Nanjio edition:

I. "Chapter One Known as Rāvaṇa-invitation" (*rāvaṇādhyeṣaṇāparivarto nāma prathamaḥ*), pages 1-21;

II. "Thus (ends) Chapter Two Known as the Collection of All the Dharmas in the Thirty-six Thousand (ślokas) *Laṅkāvatāra*" (*iti laṅkāvatāre ṣaṭtriṃśatsāhasre sarvadharmasamuccayo nāma dvitīyaḥ . . . parivartaḥ*), pages 22-135;

III. "Thus (ends) Chapter Three on Impermanency in the *Laṅkāvatāra*, a Mahāyāna Sūtra" (*iti laṅkāvatāre mahāyānasūtre 'nityatāparivartas tṛtīyaḥ*), pages 136-210;

IV. "(Here ends) Chapter Four on Realization" (*abhisamayaparivartaś caturthaḥ*), pages 211-16;

V. "Thus (ends) Chapter Five on the Permanency and Impermanency of the Tathāgata" (*iti tathāgatanityānityatvaprasaṅgaparivartaḥ pañcamaḥ*), pages 217-19;

VI. "Thus (ends) Chapter Six on Momentariness" (*iti kṣaṇikaparivartaḥ ṣaṣṭhaḥ*), pages 220-39;

VII. "Thus (ends) Chapter Seven on Egolessness" (*iti nairmāṇikaparivartaḥ saptamaḥ*), pages 240-43;

VIII. "Thus (ends) Chapter Eight on Meat-eating from the *Laṅkāvatāra* which is the Essence of All the Buddha-teachings" (*iti laṅkāvatārāt sarvabuddhapravacanahṛdayān māṃsa-bhakṣaṇaparivarto 'ṣṭamaḥ*), pages 244-59;

IX. "Thus (ends) Chapter Nine Known as *Dhāraṇī* in the *Laṅkāvatāra*" (*iti laṅkāvatāre dhāraṇī parivarto nāma navamaḥ*), pages 260-63;

X. "Thus (ends) the Mahāyāna Sūtra Called the *Ārya-Saddharma-Laṅkāvatāra*, here completed with the Verses" (*ity āryasaddharmalaṅkāvatāro nāma mahāyānasūtraṃ sagāthakaṃ samāptam iti*), pages 264-376.

Now, the first discrepancy to strike the reader of this *Sūtra*, is the random alternation between prose and verse sections. Scrutinizing the text from various angles, Takasaki set forth the hypothesis that the verses represent the original form of the *Sūtra*, which was later expanded through numerous prose commentaries interpolated by various compilers.[14] With the help of the section division first attempted by Kokwan Shiren in his fourteenth-century edition, Takasaki separated the prose sections which stand independently from those which are related in content to the verses present in both the main body and the verse section, *Sagāthakam*. Thus, he arrived at the conclusion that the independent prose sections are of later origin than those accompanied by verses similar in content.[15]

Another criterion employed by Takasaki to peel away the layers of the text is the reference to the 108 questions (*praśna*) and statements (*pada*), all denied (Ch. II, gāthas 12-59 and pp. 34-37). This preliminary outline of the topics, however, is not borne out by the main body of the *Sūtra*, where the term *aṣṭottaraśata* appears only three times and is used rather loosely. Of these three instances, only the first (*aṣṭottare nirābhāsapadaśate*, II: 97, 1.3) may refer to the 108 clauses in the introductory section, since their common referent is the imaginary nature of all concepts. The second instance refers to magical formulae (*'syāṣṭottaraśatābhimantritena*, IX: 261, l. 14), while the third indicates philosophical doctrines (*aṣṭottaraṃ nayaśataṃ*, *Sagāthakam*: 306, v. 317).[16]

The disconnection between the different sections is also shown by the fact that, in all, there are fewer than 108 topics treated in the main text, while important subjects (such as the system of the Eight Vijñānas) are not even mentioned in the initial 108.[17] Most significant, however, is the contrast between the mythological character of the *Rāvaṇa* chapter, with its heavy borrowing from the

Rāmāyaṇa epic, and the deeply philosophical nature of the rest of the text.[18] J. W. Hauer believed that the first chapter was without doubt the oldest, since it is the only one taking place in Laṅka, from which the entire sūtra takes its name."[19] That this is not necessarily true is shown by the fact that the Guṇabhadra translation of A.D. 443 already bore the title of *The Laṅkāvatāra-Treasure-Sūtra,* although the *Rāvaṇa* chapter, as well as the *Dhāraṇī* and the *Sagāthakam* chapters, were missing.[20]

Hauer is quite convincing, on the other hand, when, considering the differences in style and content between chapters, he classifies the *Sūtra* into five sections or layers, to which he ascribes different time periods, as follows:[21]

(1) Chapter I, the *Rāvaṇa* chapter (which he believes to be the earliest): standing on its own, with no connection to the rest of the *Sūtra,* it lays the basic mood (*Grundton*) for the appreciation of the novel Yogācāra philosophy in broadly acceptable mythological terms, typical of its time;

(2) Chapters II-VII, as the exposition of the uniqueness of the Mahāyāna world of ideas: hang together as the main body of the text to which the rest of the chapters were added at different times. While the introductory section seems to be older, these two strands were obviously written before A.D. 443;

(3) Chapter VIII, on the prohibition against eating meat, shows the Mahāyānists' defensiveness in the face of the early encroachment of Tantric elements (such as eating meat, drinking wine, etc.). It may have been written shortly before A.D. 443 (?), since it was included in Guṇabhadra's translation.[22]

(4) Chapter IX, the *Dhāraṇī* chapter, despite being only three pages long, introduces a full-blown Tantric world of magical spells and rituals. Its sharp contrast to the main ideas of the text (such as Citta-mātra or Mind-only) is clearly revealed in the last sentence, which states (X: 263, ll. 1-2):

> imāni bhavatā mantrapadāni bhāṣitāni rākṣasānāṃ nivāraṇā-rtham//
>
> These magic phrases are given by the Blessed One to guard against the (hindrances of the) Rākṣasas.

But, if all ideas about the world are mere mental constructs, of what use are mantras against something which is characterized as nothing but imagination? (Time frame: A.D. 443-513).

(5) Chapter X, the *Sagāthakam,* consisting of 884 verses, attempts to review the entire content of the *Sūtra* (minus the Tantric elements).

According to Hauer, however, it represents "a grandiose monotony on the principle of 'Nothingness' (*Nichtsein*)," from the 'absoluten Negativismus' to the 'individuellen Idealismus.' It was appended as the last layer of the text, shortly before A.D. 513, the date of Bodhiruci's translation (supra, p. 7). As Takasaki suggested, it may have developed independently from the same source materials as the main text, until they were finally combined by an anonymous compiler into one volume.[23] While over two hundred gāthas may be found elsewhere in the *Sūtra*, 680 are completely new, dealing mainly with refutations of various doctrines, especially those held by the Sāṃkhya philosophers.[24]

Now, as already mentioned, the only English translation to date is that of Suzuki (1932), which was followed by an index of technical terms, with their Chinese and Tibetan equaivalents (1933).[25] These, along with the extensive explanations and glossary found in his earlier *Studies* (1930), have been immensely helpful not only in guiding my steps through the slippery field of Buddhist Sanskrit, but also for inspiring my thoughts through the arcane and lofty heights of Mahāyāna philosophy and religion. In so far as the quality of Suzuki's translation of the text is concerned, I shall let the author speak his own mind:[26]

> As regards the English translation of the Sutra, I have decided after much hesitation to send it out to the public with all its many imperfections. It is a bold attempt on the part of the translator to try to render some of the deepest thoughts that have been nourished in the East into a language to which he was not born. But his idea is that if somebody did not make a first attempt, however poor and defective, the precious stones may remain buried unknown except to a few scholars, and this perhaps longer than necessary. And then things develop. As it is illustrated in the long history of the Chinese translations of the Buddhist texts, there must be several attempts before the work assumes something of finality.

The present work is precisely such an attempt to expand and build upon the foundation laid down through his efforts. Any self-avowed imperfections notwithstanding, my debt of gratitude to Professor Suzuki for making available to the Western reader the complete knowledge of this text is in no way diminished, for without his lifetime contribution, I would hardly have dared to study, let alone venture to fathom the depths of this important Mahāyāna treatise.

Sharing a common fascination with the metaphysical heights

of the Yogācāra philosophy, however, should not stop us from critically assessing Suzuki's interpretation of the text, especially in regard to some of the most crucial concepts of the School found in the *Laṅkāvatāra*, such as Citta-mātra and Tathāgata-garbha. Consequently rather than duplicate Suzuki's good work (which would not have served any purpose), or retranslate the entire text (an awesome and forbidding task, given the dimensions of the manuscript), I selected only those essential concepts which define the distinct contribution of the *Laṅkāvatāra-sūtra* to the development of Yogācāra thought—concepts which Suzuki has either insufficiently treated (such as Tathāgata-garbha), or insufficiently understood (such as Citta-mātra, or Vijñapti-mātra, which he mistakenly interprets as expressing the rejection of the external, objective world as an illusion produced by the mind: *lokaṃ vijñaptimātram*).[27]

It seems that there has been a general following of Suzuki's initial explanation of these terms found in the *Sūtra*, which has led to the overall assessment of the Yogācāra philosophy not only as the school of Mind-only (which *it is*, in the sense of Yoga practice), but also as the school of radical Subjective Idealism à la Bishop Berkeley (which *it is not*, as we shall see).

It is true that one of the ten essential teachings of the Yogācāra school, as given by Asaṅga in his *Mahāyānasaṃparigraha-Śāstra*, proclaims that "the objective world and the subjective ego are only manifestations of the universal Consciousness (Ālaya)."[28] But without going too far into detailed explanations (which will be given in the course of this study), let us say briefly that the term *ālaya* (or *ālaya-vijñāna*) is primarily a psychological one, having the general meaning of "abode" (as in Himālaya, the "abode of snow") or "receptacle" (here, of perceptions; the equivalent of the Western notion of the subconscious, as it were).[29]

Therefore, Asaṅga's statement has an epistemological, rather than an ontological, import, and here the confusion begins. For, when read in the context of Yogācāra epistemology, which is closely related to and based upon the practice of meditation, the words *objective world* should be taken to infer "as erroneously perceived, and subjectively interpreted as such," on account of imagination, discrimination (*vikalpa*), and mental habits or memories (*vāsanā*). Also, 'Universal Consciousness' is best understood as the consciousness which is common to all men, and, in this sense, universal (i.e., the subconscious in its most basic, or pure state, the 'Ālaya'), rather than some universally present 'stuff', 'entity', or 'substance', existing independently (*svabhāva*), outside the realm of human mental activity. This meaning is clearly conveyed by the following verse from the

Laṅkāvatāra-sūtra (III: 186, v. 77):

> vikalpamātraṃ tribhavaṃ bāhyam arthaṃ na vidyate/
> vikalpaṃ dṛśyate citraṃ na ca bālair vibhāvyate//
>
> The triple world is nothing but imagination: the external object(s) does not exist; it is the discrimination (which) sees multiplicity (of objects); but this is not understood by the immature.

0.3. Methodology and Outline of the Study

The Sanskrit version upon which the present study is based, represents in fact a reconstruction (by several scholars, English and Japanese) of the (lost) original from a number of more or less complete copies found in Nepal circa one hundred years ago.[1] According to Bunyiu Nanjio, the editor of this Sanskrit version, the Nepalese manuscripts were carefully checked (with the help of another Japanese scholar, Dr. Unrai Wogihara) against an earlier Indian edition of the *Laṅkāvatāra-sūtra*, the Tibetan translation, and the three extant Chinese versions of the text.[2] Thus, all possible variants and corrections were carefully incorporated either into the text itself, or into the numerous footnotes. This gives the reader a number of options in the reading of a difficult word or turn of phrase in Sanskrit, which can be quite helpful in clarifying certain obscurities in the development of a philosophical argument. I have taken advantage of such options only where the meaning of the text could be made clear by a simple substitution of a case ending, gender, or diacritical mark, as suggested in a footnote by the editor himself, according to one or another version of the text, as indicated. In addition, I have also separated the independent syntactic constructions in accordance with current practice, which greatly facilitates the reading of the text, especially when this text is written in the so-called Buddhist Hybrid Sanskrit, characterized by strings of long compounds and a scarcity of verbal forms.

In the elaboration of this study, however, my main concern was not so much with textual issues, as with problems of meaning and interpretation. Therefore, I have given this study a topical format, better suited to the purpose of isolating the main strands of philosophical discussion pursued in the text. Given the nature of these topics, I have alternately, or simultaneously, used several hermenuetical approaches. As appropriate, historical, philosophical, logical, psychological, and sociological concepts have been made use of, not to supplement, but rather to *complement* the primarily linguistic orientation of this investigation into Yogācāra thought. I have tried (if not always successfully) to keep my personal speculation to a minimum, relying instead on authoritative explanations found in other related texts, as well as on the competent opinions of various specialists in Buddhist Mahāyāna doctrine.

Of the latter, most helpful were the works of Daisetz Teitaro Suzuki, the great teacher and popularizer of Zen Buddhism in the West, whose translation of the *Laṅkāvatāra* in its entirety, along with his *Studies*, provided the inspiration and the starting point for my own study. His contribution to an emerging philosophical world culture was acknowledged by the most original and influential European philosopher in our century, Martin Heidegger, with the words: "If I understand this man correctly, this is what I have been trying to say in all my writings."[3]

Furthermore, of great assistance to my understanding of the wondrous mind of the fourth century Indian Buddhist in general, and of the *Laṅkāvatāra* world of ideas in particular, were the writings of several other great scholars of Buddhism, past and present, such as those of F. Th. Stcherbatsky, Jikidō Takasaki, David J. Kalupahana, and Alex Wayman.[4] Their investigations of different facets of Buddhist philosophy as presented in the *Laṅkāvatāra* and other related texts have much enriched our knowledge of a fascinating system of thought that is yet to receive the scholarly attention and effort it fully deserves.

I have divided my study in two major sections. Each attempts to bring into focus one important aspect of Buddhist thought expressed in the *Laṅkāvatāra:* the first, its ontological position, or worldview, and the second, its epistemological, or rather gnoseological position. In a way, they are complementary, for one is expressed in terms of the other; in other words, one presupposes and even reinforces the other. Many ideas presented in the *Sūtra* may be taken one way or the other (such as Citta-mātra, or Ālaya-vijñāna), since either their meaning and significance vary contextually, or they may overlap. Taken together, they give an idea of the way in which the Yogācāra Buddhist perceived his relationship with, or thought about, the world.

His thought, was informed however, by an ultimately religious purpose, which in Buddhist terms is freedom from suffering (*duḥkha nirodha*), or Self-realization (*Pratyātma-gocara*). This soteriology is evident throughout the *Sūtra*, so that no matter where one begins to inquire, analyzing one concept or another, eventually one is led to the recurring motif of Self-realization, or Buddhahood. All concepts are, in the last analysis, according to the *Laṅkāvatāra*, nothing but artificial constructs, made of Mind-only (Citta-mātra), the purpose of which is to teach the adept the primacy of personal experience over the empty speculations of various theorists and philosophers, Hindu as well as Buddhist. It is for this reason that my initial plans to add a third section on ethics and soteriology (which would have completed the ideological triad which informs any religious system) were dropped. Indeed, in as far as the *Laṅkāvatāra-sūtra* is concerned, the importance of practice, in terms of ethical development and the attainment of Self-realization, is so pervasive and implicit in the treatment of every topic under discussion, that a separate section would only have repeated what has already been said over and over again.

This fact, however, should not be taken as an indication that the text by itself can replace the personal training and spiritual guidance of a competent teacher of meditative practice. For the *Laṅkāvatāra* was originally intended to complement not supplant the direct communication between a spiritual guide, the Master, and his pupils, the religious disciples.

The role of the religious scholar, the historian of religion, on the other hand, is (or should be) strictly limited to the interpretation of the text in the light of his linguistic, historical, and philosophical expertise. The latter, in particular, should be used cautiously, and only on corroboration with other authoritative textual material collected from both within and without the Buddhist tradition.

It is from this theoretical standpoint that I wish to approach the exegesis of a religious text such as the *Laṅkāvatāra*, as well as the criticism of its interpreters, whether Buddhist or otherwise. It is my aim to clarify the ideas presented in the text itself, and render them comprehensible to the contemporary Western reader, and not to pass judgment upon the religious value (or lack thereof) of those ideas in the life of any living being, Buddhist or non-Buddhist. This, of course, should not stop anyone from assessing the role these ideas have played in the lives of the historical communities from which they arose, nor should it inhibit us from reporting their impact upon past and present cultural phenomena and historical events. Admittedly, the task of the cultural historian, the critic of ideas, is a delicate, even a dangerous one at times, steering, as he must, between a necessary measure of objective reporting and his own and others' personal convictions and life experience.

Bearing all this in mind, I shall now describe how I have structured the wealth of ideas scattered rather amorphously throughout the ten chapters of the *Laṅkāvatāra-sūtra*.

Part One, on the **ontology** of the Sūtra, contains, after the opening introductory section, three chapters on three different doctrines dealing with various aspects of Being: its *inner* essence, and its *outer* manifestations in time and space. The initial introductory section (ch. 1.0.) is an atempt at placing the Buddhist view of the world within the larger spectrum of possible ontological interpretations available in both Eastern and Western religio-philosophical traditions. In final analysis, they can all be reduced to two fundamentally opposite points of view, namely: philosophies of 'substance', of immutability, and of Being, on the one hand, and philosophies of 'process', of dynamic change and transformation, and of Becoming, on the other. The essential core of Buddhist philosophy belongs to the latter, but the process of clarification and the debates related to these issues went on for many centuries, within the Buddhist philosophical circles.

The reason for this becomes obvious if one considers the implications of this choice for the achievement of the main goal of religious pursuit: liberation, or salvation, from the unsatisfactoriness of human condition, or existence. The simple fact is that while, in religious systems which adopt a static ontology of Being, as a given, once and for all, salvation tends to depend on *who* you know (i.e., the Supreme Being, the Creator, the Law-Giver, the Lord God, etc.), in religions where the dynamic ontology of Becoming prevails, salvation depends on *what* you know. Knowledge (Greek: *gnosis*, Sanskrit: *jñāna*) becomes the main vehicle for the universally coveted goal of spiritual freedom.[5]

And yet, that does not necessarily mean that those who know most become saints, while those who are ignorant remain the sinners in Buddhism. For, in the word of continual Becoming, knowledge, too, can become a hindrance to salvation. Concepts and ideologies can also be oppressive and non-conducive to liberation (just like external tyrants), especially when one considers the inescapable fact that they are all tied to artificial dichotomies of thought, and to the conventionality of language. Consequently, in the ultimate confrontation with an ever-changing Reality, knowledge, too, has to be transcended, according to Buddhism.

Thus, knowledge for the Buddhist practitioner represents only the first step toward Self-realization. The second, more decisive step is its application, and the third, and most important one, is its transcendence in the final act of Enlightenment. Therefore, one can safely say that for the Buddhist practitioner, Self-realization equals Self-transcendence (i.e., going beyond the Self and what belongs to the Self: knowledge, memories, attachments of all kinds).

This act is truly a change in ontological status, a change of one's being, and of one's existence. Hence, the *practical*, experiential character of Buddhist ontology in general, and of the Yogācāra philosophy, in particular.[6]

Furthermore, this emphasis on practice and spiritual experience also explains why the dominant discourse in the *Laṅkāvatāra-sūtra* is *descriptive*, rather than *prescriptive* (as is the case with most other religious texts). The *Sūtra* merely describes the general direction of one's spiritual striving, and the conceptual frame needed to get from here to there, without ascribing ultimate ontological validity to any of the concepts discussed, which, according to the text, are to be regarded as mere didactic tools, to be used and eventually discarded at the appropriate time in one's spiritual development when their usefulness has come to an end.

Finally, one can also say that the philosophy of the Yogācāras is truly *ontology*, not metaphysics, in the older Aristotelian sense, since it is content to *describe*, without commitment, the nature of Reality of Being. It does not make apodictical claims about the ultimate ontological status of the existential entities under discussion, or about the relations between them. For, according to all Yogācāra texts, all things exist interdependently, and all notions about them are nothing but artificial constructs of our own mental imagination.

Bearing all this in mind, here is how the ancient Buddhists have conceived the structure of the surrounding world. In order to express the essential nature of Being, the Yogācāras developed the original theory of **Tathāgata-garbha** (ch. 1.1.). A careful treatment of its historical roots is given together with the threefold meaning accepted by the *Laṅkāvatāra* and other related texts (such as the *Śrīmālādevī*, the *Ratnagotravibhāga*, and the *Tathāgata-garbha*). It will be shown that, unlike its historical precedents (i.e., the Vedic Hiraṇya-garbha and the Upaniṣadic Ātman), the Tathāgata-garbha is nothing more than an impersonal principle, whose value is primarily didactic (rather than purely ontological).

This chapter is further subdivided according to the three different meanings of the concept, given alternately in the text, namely: Tathāgata-garbha as the essential, supramundane, pure *dharma* (which represents a vague Buddhist echo of the Upaniṣadic Ātman); Tathāgata-garbha the Embryo-of-Buddhahood (which parallels the Vedic 'Golden Egg', Hiraṇyāṇḍa, used interchangeably with the 'Golden Womb', Hiraṇya-garbha, in the *Ṛg-veda* 10. 121. 1); and Tathāgata-garbha as the Womb, or Matrix-of-Buddhahood, identified with Ālaya-vijñāna on account of its peaceful and receptive qualities, in sharp contrast to the constant turmoil of the other, evolving Vijñānas (*pravṛtti-vijñānas*).

The second chapter (ch. 1.2.) provides an in-depth survey of the Yogācāras' notions of Self, the paradigmatic manifestation of Being *in time*, as it were. While the focus is on the theory of the **Five Skandhas** (the personality aggregates), it includes a brief overview of the Ātman controversy in Buddhism, prior to the *Laṅkāvatāra-sūtra*. The necessity of such an overview becomes obvious if one considers the fact that the exposition of the Self concept in the *Laṅkāvatāra* has a pronouncedly polemical character, primarily directed against the Hindu-Brahmanic view of Self, and it continues an age-long debate regarding the specific nature of non-Self (Anātman), within the Buddhist community (*saṃgha*).

Within the Skandhas chapter, this historical overview is followed by five other subsections. The first two of these are mainly descriptive, dealing with the two types of aggregates described in the *Laṅkāvatāra:* the formative (*rūpa*) and formless (*nāma, arūpin*) elements of personality. The next two subsections revolve around the relation between the Skandhas and the total personality, when regarded from the point of view of (a) the empirical self (*pudgala*), and (b) the trans-empirical, or transcendental Self (i.e., the Tathāgata, as the realized being, the Buddha, the Enlightened One). And finally, the sixth subsection of the Skandhas chapter points out that according to the *Laṅkāvatāra-sūtra* no metaphysical theory (including that of the five personality aggregates) is adequate to represent Reality, and therefore, all that can be said about the manifestations of Being *in time*, is that "the Tathāgata, or Self, is neither the same, nor different from the Skandhas." This represents the quintessence of the Buddhist theory of Indeterminacy (*Avyākṛta*), which is in fact a denial of metaphysical dualities (such as 'sameness' and 'otherness'), otherwise known as "Śūnyatā," or "Voidness."

The third, and last chapter dealing with ontological questions (ch. 1.3.), introduces the *spatial* manifestation of Being, as symbolized by the broad technical term **Dharmadhātu**, or the "Realm-of-the-existential-elements." This concept designates the totality of all possible worlds, both real and ideal. Therefore, along with the physical, cosmic universe, it also includes as its equivalents the Buddhist notions of *Tathatā* (Suchness), *Buddhatā* (Buddhahood), *Śūnyatā* (Voidness), *Dharmatā* (Realm of Religion), *traidhātuka, tri-bhava* (Triple World), or *trikāya* (Three bodies), *Paramārtha* (Absolute Truth), *Bhūtakoṭi* (Limit of Reality) and *Nirvāṇa* (Extinction). As the extension of Being *in space*, Dharmadhātu represents the metaphysical complement of the Five Skandhas, which are the extension of Being in time, and therefore, its impermanent aspect. But Dharmadhātu (or its synonyms, Tathatā, Śūnyatā, etc.) is also similar to the Five Skandhas in that it partakes of both the physical, or objective, and the spiritual, or subjective, sides of existence. Being heavily pregnant with soteriological meanings, the term *Dharmadhātu* may also be rendered as the "Sphere-of-religion," as in the older Pāli scriptures.

The conclusion of this section points out that the writer's division of the *Laṅkāvatāra-sūtra's* description of existence into three ontic categories, corresponds to Maitreya's (the founder of the Yogācāra school) threefold characterization of the nature of Being, as follows:[7] (1) Always non-existing (i.e., Tathāgata-garbha); (2) Existing, yet not from the absolute point of view (i.e., the five Skandhas existing only in the relative sense, being dependent upon external causes and conditions); and (3) From the absolute point of view, existing and yet non-existing (i.e., Dharmadhātu which symbolizes the Absolute Reality of the universal Law, Dharma, and of the state of Suchness, Tathatā, and Voidness, Śūnyatā, of the physical universe, and which is yet non-existing as the representation of the illusory phenomenal world, or as the summation of all the metaphysical worlds concocted by human imagination, Vikalpa, Vijñapti-mātra, or Citta-mātra).

Part Two, which presents the **epistemological** concepts elaborated in the *Sūtra*, has five chapters. First (ch. 2.0.) comes as an introduction to, and a historical review of, the most fundamental tool of logical analysis in Buddhist epistemology, the tetralemma (*catuṣkoṭi*), or the four logical alternatives (all denied). They are: (1) Affirmation; (2) Negation; (3) Conjunction of both; and (4) Disjunction (i.e., neither affirmation, nor negation, hedging). By denying the absolute validity of each of the four alternatives, Buddhist epistemology in general, and Yogācāra thought in particular (having as its cornerstone the doctrine of Mind-only), can be regarded as: (a) a radical critique of any form of philosophical dogmatism, and (b) a ruthless exposure of the relativity of knowledge, on account of its conditioning by the subjective aspects of cognition (e.g., selective perception, memory of past experience, and arbitrary judgment).

In addition to the subjectivity of the process of cognition, the inherent limitations of language, based upon metaphorical imagery and dual categories (such as high and low, this and other, good and bad, Saṃsāra and Nirvāṇa, etc., all having a tendency to be reified, or objectified, in the minds of most people) also render any claim to absolute validity of a given point of view, or philosophical position, absolutely baseless and utterly untenable, under close scrutiny. Hence, the apparent irrationality, or paradoxical nihilism, of certain Mahāyānist concepts, such as the Relativity (or Voidness) doctrine of Nāgārjuna, or the Mind-only doctrine of the Yogācāras.

According to the statements made by their proponents, however, as preserved in authoritative texts, such as the *Mūlamādhyamika-kārikās* of Nāgārjuna and the *Laṅkāvatāra-sūtra,* these concepts are not to be taken literally, but rather as meditational tools for the purpose of liberating the mind from the fetters of dogmatising, conceptualising, and absolutising. Incidentally, the Buddhist tetralemma dialectics not only precedes the two best known dialectical formulations used in the West (i.e., the ancient Aristotelian dilemma and the more recent Hegelian triad) but also supersedes them in its completeness and its consistent application throughout the first thousand years of Buddhist ratiocination, and even beyond.

Now, the following four chapters, each devoted to one of the original Yogācāra constructs, are conceived as exemplifications of the four limbs of the tetralemma logic, the paradigmatic formula of Buddhist epistemology. The first, and most important such construct, **Citta-mātra** (ch. 2.1.), holds a central position in the *Laṅkāvatāra,* and it is still considered to be the hallmark of the Yogācāra school, which is sometimes referred to as "the School of Mind-only." Obviously, it can be regarded as a strong, positive affirmation of the existence of Mind, and 'affirmation' is the first limb of the tetralemma. Unfortunately, it is also the most misunderstood of all Yogācāra concepts.

Beginning with Professor Suzuki's interpretation, most scholars of Buddhism mistook the Citta-mātra concept (whose origins can be traced to the purity of mind sought after in the process of meditation) to mean a cognitive statement regarding the ultimate nature of the world (i.e., made of 'mind-only'). Hence, the prevalent misconception of the Yogācāra school as a school of radical, Subjective Idealism.

Our contention, however, is that (a) historically speaking, the term arose from a specific practical context of Yogic meditation (whence the name of the school, *Yogācāra,* or "Yoga-practice"), and (b) philosophically, and in accordance with the explanations given in the *Laṅkāvatāra,* Citta-mātra refers to that fundamental epistemological error committed by those who fail to distinguish between a philosophical system which purports to describe the world (when, in fact, it merely makes statements *about* it), and the nature of the world *itself.* For, ultimately, all speculative statements are "nothing but the mind (or thoughts)," while the world cannot be described in words.

Now, when the compound is taken apart, three meanings for the *citta* appear in the discourse of the *Laṅkāvatāra-sūtra.* The first designates the empirical mind, or the conscious activity of the ordinary self. The second may be identified with Ālaya-vijñāna, or undefiled Tathāgata-garbha (when taken as *essence*); as shown, it refers to the transcendental Self, or the Unconscious in its original state (i.e., untainted by *kleśas,* the adventitious defilements accrued as a result of good and evil action, or *karma*). The third, and most elusive meaning, seems to indicate the idea of a universal Mind, projected upon the world at large (vide: the equation between *tribhava* and *citta*). It is the cognitive equivalent of Tathāgata-garbha, when taken to mean either the universal womb, in which all beings are included, or the *essence* of all dharmas (or existential building blocks). A modern approximation may also be found in the Jungian concept of the Collective Unconscious, remote as it may be from the cultural point of view.

There are two reasons why this third meaning of *citta* cannot stand by itself (apart from the first two) as a denial of the external world as such: First, it is, in the final analysis, a psychological construct rather than an ontological assessment of Reality beyond the mental realm of cognition, and second, like any construct, its spurious nature is due to artificial discrimination (*vikalpa*), based upon conventional language and error (*bhrānti*), both removed from Reality as such. Consequently, it can neither affirm nor deny the existence of the external world (*bāhya*). Ultimately, it is "merely one's own mind" (Citta-mātra) reflecting itself in verbal projections (see *Laṅkā.* III: 208; ll. 16-17).

This, indeed, represents the most important epistemic thesis of the Yogācāra philosophy, namely that every statement about the world is a *metaphorical* statement, a mere representation of it (Vijñapti-mātra) which tells us more about our own mind, our own tainted perceptions, reasoning, and memory of past experiences and habits (*vāsanā*s), than about the external Reality as such (Tathatā). Thus, the statement "Mind-only" (Citta-mātra) is not a prima facie description of the world and its essence, but a characterization of all our statements *about* the world and their unavoidable limitations. I venture to call this thesis, so insisted upon in the *Laṅkāvatāra-sūtra,* the 'epistemological reduction of the Citta-mātra doctrine.'

The details of this cognitive process are spelled out in the next chapter (ch. 2.2.) on the five Epistemic Categories (**Dharmas**), the three Modes of Cognition (**Svabhāvas**), and the attainment of Superior Knowledge (**Āryajñāna**). Since it is beyond empirical cognition, I call this transcendental state, the state of religious wisdom, of Gnosis, or simply, the state of *No-mind.*[8]

According to the *Sūtra*, there are five steps in the accumulation of knowledge.[9] They are described as follows: first, there is the mental propensity to substitute a name, or a symbol (*nāma*) for the object itself, which leads to the recognition of the object in its particularity, but also places the subject one step away from its object, that is, from Reality in its immediacy. The subsequent recognition of the object is the 'Sense-perception' (or 'Appearance', *nimitta*). Together, these two steps, or categories of cognition, constitute a highly contrived mode of cognition, based upon the imagination (of various terms and their recognition), and therefore called "False- (i.e., mediated) knowledge" (*parikalpita-svabhāva*).

The next step in the hierarchy of Epistemic Categories is based on discrimination (*vikalpa*) between qualities of various objects. Therefore, it is designated as a 'relative' mode of knowing Reality (lit., "cognition of existence depending on another," or *paratantra-svabhāva*), in contrast to the 'absolute', or 'perfect' knowledge (lit., "cognition fully developed, perfect, true to existence," or *pariniṣpanna-svabhāva*), designated by us as 'Gnosis'.

The last two Epistemic Categories fall under this absolute Mode of Cognition. They are called "Right-knowledge" (*samyagjñāna*), and "Suchness" (*tathatā*). While both are transcendental to empirical cognition, the former represents the synthesizing function of the mind, the awareness of common patterns between phenomena, while the latter conveys the supreme cognitive ability to see through the veil of delusion, into the pure essence of Reality, thereby causing an ecstatic state of joy (*pratimuditā*).

The third chapter in the second half of our study (ch. 2.3.) further expands the investigation into the cognitive theories developed by the Yogācāras. The emphasis is placed here on the general theory of consciousness, known as the psychological system of the **Eight Vijñānas**. It will be shown that, while there are several usages of the term *vijñāna*, it was the meaning of 'perception', or 'sense-consciousness', which caused some Western scholars to call this school *Vijñānavāda*, or the "School of Representation (-only)." As a rather sophisticated map of consciousness which, for the first time in history, erects a complex psychological system on the purely empirical basis of observation and experience, this theory admits two broad divisions of the states of consciousness: on the one hand we are offered seven *dynamic* states of consciousness, impelled by constant interaction with the external world through the five senses and the power of will (which can be either conscious, or unconscious, i.e., *via* impulses), and on the other hand, the text speaks of a *static* repository (Ālaya-vijñāna), where all sense-impressions are stored for future retrieval. These two functionally, but not structurally, different types of Vijñānas are constantly compared with the agitation of the waves, when blown by the wind of the senses, on the surface of the deep and tranquil waters of the ocean of consciousness.

While strictly speaking a psychological theory, the Vijñāna system attempts, from the epistemological point of view, to integrate the two different cognitive modes, namely the empirical, concrete, accumulative, discriminative mind, on the one hand, and its opposite state of *No-mind*, on the other. The latter represents the intuitive, abstract, spontaneous, wholistic, and transcendental aspect of mentation, which is said to be free from one-sided attachments and dualistic logic.

If the *Mind-only* doctrine stands for the *affirmative* mode of the Buddhist fourfold dialectic (tetralemma), and Transcendental Gnosis (Āryajñāna) for its *negation* (No-mind), then the system of the Eight Vijñānas (states-of-consciousness) illustrates their *conjunction* into an organic, functional unity, consistent with the inner, psychological experience. But, to become fully aware of this fundamental unity one has to realize, according to the *Sūtra*, an inner revolution (*parāvṛtti*). That is to say, a process of reversal (*vyāvṛtti, parivṛtti*) is needed in order to return the wave-like agitation of the seven *pravṛtti-vijñāna*s back to the profoundly peaceful state of the Repository-of-impressions (the eighth state, Ālaya-vijñāna). However, according to the text, the Vijñānas do not completely vanish from sight, since they do not really exist in or by themselves, apart from Ālaya. In other words, *Mind* and *No-mind*, like all other dualities, co-exist interactively, co-dependently, like two sides of the same coin.

Therefore, it is further pointed out that all such distinctions are mere conventions, similar to the images appearing in a mirror, in a vision, or a dream, without real existence outside the mental realm (Citta-mātra, Vijñapti-mātra). Thus establishing the ultimacy of the inner experience over the external world (*pratyātma-āryajñāna* or *gocara*), the author(s) of the *Sūtra*, the Yogācāra Buddhist, is in fact making a powerful statement regarding the objective *limits* in knowing the truth about the external Reality. The far-reaching implications of this epistemological position, and its soteriological value, will be fully explored in the fourth and last chapter of this study (ch. 2.4.), the chapter on **Causation (Hetu-pratyaya**, causes and conditions).

In this chapter, which is both historical and doctrinal, the writer presents the Yogācāra Buddhist's epistemological dilemma vis-à-vis the question of how one can know the truth in a world characterized by change and impermanency. The issue of causality is crucial in answering this question, for, if we know how things are derived from one another, we may also know which things are primary and which are secondary, and perhaps arrive at the first cause, the creator, the atom, and so on. However, the frame of mind from which the author of the *Sūtra* begins his inquiry into the issues related to Causation may be summarized by the disjunctive formula: *Neither this, nor that . . .*

Now, the Yogācāra view of causality is the product of criticism, integration, and synthesis of the early ideas regarding the problem of change, of origination and disappearance. Therefore, this chapter opens with an attempt to explain, albeit briefly, how the Buddhist ideas of causality have gradually expanded from the early, purely psychological notions (such as the Chain of Causation) regarding the origins of pain, old age, and death (i.e., the original meaning of Dependent Origination, *paṭicca-samuppāda*) to the Mahāyāna view of Causation as a cosmic philosophical principle. Thus, it is pointed out that the idea of Causation in the Pāli *Nikāyas* was not only thoroughly internal and subjective, but also simple and linear, of the type "A causes B," or "whenever A is present, B is present" (*imasmiṃ sati idaṃ hoti, Majjhima-Nikāya* 1.264).

The later Mahāyāna view of Determinism, to which the author of the *Laṅkāvatāra-sūtra* subscribes, is, however, not only complex, but even paradoxical at times, challenging one's common sense assumptions and logic. Its essence is expressed by the concept Hetu-pratyaya, which includes both a causal nexus and causal conditioning through a multitude of factors and relations. No single factor or one-sided relation will do: *Neither this, nor that* . . . All factors interact with and feed on one another. This is the Mahāyānist view of Causation. But since in Buddhism, philosophy is always intermingled with religion, there is another, religious perspective on Causality.

From this religious point of view, the Yogācāra Buddhist *denies all four possibilities* of Causation: namely that things originate either from themselves (i.e., internal causation), or from another (i.e., external causation), from both (self and other), or from neither. Such a radicalism is, admittedly, intended to discourage the Buddhist adept from pursuing the intractable complexities of the infinite *net* (as opposed to the *chain* of primitive Buddhism) of causal factors and relations. The theoretical and practical consequences of this fact are investigated in the subsections of this chapter.

First, a *theoretical* basis is implicitly laid down for a truly monistic view of the universe. Having decided that no entity has independent existence (*niḥsvabhāva*), or egohood (*nairātmya*), the ancient ontological duality symbolized by the two terms Saṃsāra and Nirvāṇa is replaced in the *Laṅkāvatāra-sūtra* by all-inclusive concepts such as the "Womb-of-Buddhahood" (Tathāgata-garbha), the Repository-of-impressions" (Ālaya-vijñāna), and Mind-only (Citta-mātra). (However, it should be noted that in the *Laṅkāvatāra-sūtra*, these Yogācāra concepts are used synonymously, with minor differences of meaning depending on the context). Furthermore, at a closer look, it becomes obvious that the older, ontological duality has merely been replaced with a new, epistemological duality, that of the relative and absolute points of view regarding Causation. This duality will become more clear in later scriptures, which speak specifically of "conventional" and "absolute" truths (*saṃvṛti-* and *paramārtha-satya*). Thus, instead of the phenomenological duality of subject and object, one defines Reality in terms of lower (philosophical) and higher (religious) points of view.

On the *practical* side, two important consequences are noted: (a) the use of the theory of Causation as a teaching device, in order to help the novices rid themselves of the attachment to the illusion of permanence, Original Cause, Creator, time, atom, Self, and other (than Self); and (b) the denial of the idea of Causality itself which brings about absolute freedom from *all* cognitive associations—thereby closing the gap between the inner and outer realities—and, ultimately, the cessation of affliction. In that consists the soteriological value of the theory of causation, from the Yogācāras' point of view. These two practical consequences constitute the topics of the two subsequent subdivision of this last chapter.

An *excursus* is also inserted between them, highlighting Nāgārjuna's thought in respect to Causation. Its purpose is to point out the similarity, if not absolute identity, between the Yogācāra and the Mādhyamika schools, in that regard.

* * *

In concluding this introductory section, let us reiterate our statement of purpose. This work is an attempt mainly to clarify and systematize the *Laṅkāvatāra* world of ideas, which, after half a century of virtual neglect following Suzuki's brilliant studies, now require reevaluation in the light of modern scholarship. At a time when the exchange of all sorts of ideas between different cultures has become the hallmark of our century, it is highly imperative that we are careful to set these ideas in the right historical and cultural perspective.

Thus, at the end of this book, the reader may be surprised to learn, among other things, that the Buddhists elaborated the first empirically based system of depth psychology (two millenia before Freud), that they understood the Self as a psycho-physical combination, or stream of events, rather than a fixed entity (long before David Hume's 'bundle of perceptions' shocked Western consciousness), that the Buddha and his followers used dialectical logic skillfully from the sixth century B.C. onward (before Zeno, Socrates, Aristotle, and Hegel did so in the West), and that by applying it with remarkable thoroughness in the fields of perception, language analysis, and religious philosophy, they established the limits of reason and of language in understanding and expressing Reality (many centuries before Kant and Wittgenstein discovered those limits). Thus, one may add, the Buddhist philosophers made a remarkably creative and original contribution on the long and arduous path to the liberation of humanity from the shackles of intellectual dogmatism and absolutism of every kind.

For all these reasons, it is the writer's hope that this and other similar studies of Buddhist philosophy, will help to settle the Yogācāra school of thought in its proper place, not only vis-à-vis the Asian cultural world (Japanese Zen culture is only one of its heirs), but also within an integrated, global history of man's intellectual discoveries, religious and non-religious. With its ruthless analysis of the inherent limitations of language, logical reasoning, and knowledge, Yogācāra thought could at least make a contribution in revealing the importance of subjective factors in the cognitive process, which has only recently begun to be given its due, and long-awaited, recognition.

Part One:

CONCEPTS OF BEING

1.0. The Nature of Buddhist Ontology

General Considerations

The importance of the contribution of Buddhist thought to the universal cultural history of man has often been understated. Not only is the Buddhist religion one of the oldest religions on earth showing a continuous development over the course of twenty-five hundred years, but it is also the first to claim as its scope the whole of mankind, thereby asserting for the first time, in both theory and practice, the universality of man, beyond all cultural, spatial, and temporal boundaries.

In addition, it also gave rise to the first attempt to formulate a systematic psychology, based on empirical experience as well as rigorous introspection. The spread of the written word on a wide scale, as well as the beginning of a truly refined Indian art, can also be traced to the Buddhist milieu. In China, the invention and growth of the technique of printing with wooden blocks was a direct consequence of Buddhist missionary fervor. Indeed, the oldest preserved book is a Buddhist text printed in 868.[1]

Overall, the height and depth of Buddhist ethics, metaphysics, and logic, attained in the savant works of the most prominent expounders of the Buddhist cultural tradition, are only now beginning to gain the recognition they deserve, and their eminent place in the universal history of ideas is increasingly acknowledged. In this context of growing recognition of the originality and profundity of Buddhist insight into the nature of inner and outer realities, one is forced to consider the fact that Buddhism was the first religio-philosophical system to assert and demonstrate, with great argumentative power, the ever-evolving nature of Reality, in both its subjective and objective aspects.[2]

True, both the early Pāli texts, as well as the later commentarial literature, portray the Buddha as a great ethical teacher pointing toward the escape from suffering for all mankind. Practical matters of discipline, nonattachment, and freedom from all passions were his most important concerns. And yet, in spite of this emphasis on salvation and his disdain for all philosophical speculation, he could not avoid building his own metaphysical system. For, any ethical formulation (since it cannot float in the air all by itself) presupposes, and indeed requires an underpinning worldview, an ontological vision to support it, that is to give it cosmic stability and validation.

This inescapable fact was intuitively felt by the Buddha Śākyamuni when he declared ignorance as the root cause of suffering. Having done this, the question arose as to what constitutes the nature of ignorance—the dispelling of which would bring about the longed-for end of suffering—and the corollary of this question, the whole issue regarding the accumulation of the right kind of knowledge which would destroy ignorance, the root cause of suffering. Hence the elaboration of the specifically Buddhist world-view, which takes the idea of Impermanence (Anitya) as its corner-stone—a dynamic view to be sure—in which everything flows from one state of Being to the next, in a continuous Chain of Causation (Pratītya-samutpāda). The other two essential marks of existence (*bhāva-lakṣaṇam*): non-Self (Anātman) and suffering (Duḥkha) follow logically from the first.[3]

Since the only continuous thing in the world around us is change, and the same can be said about ourselves as fragile and perishable beings subject to birth, old age, sickness, and death, pain becomes a universal characteristic of animate existence. The only escape from the Saṃsāric 'Wheel of Becoming' is through the proper understanding of, and inner detachment from, the idea of permanence, either in its positive aspect (i.e., world substance, personal Self, space, Causation, Nirvāṇa), or in its negative interpretation (i.e., total denial of the reality of the world, of the personal Self, Non-Causation, No-Liberation, and so on).

Although the dogmatic formulations vary considerably from one school to another, these issues constitute the common thread running throughout the development of the Indian phase of Buddhism and beyond. Thus, from the Realistic Atomism of 'primitive' Buddhism (which took the dharmas as the irreducible 'elements of existence'), to the Dialectical Relativism of the Śūnya-vādins, and the Nominalism of the Vijñānavādins, the Buddhist view of Reality clearly posited itself against the static, unchanging Hindu-Brahmanical worldview (which regarded the unity of the Brahman-Ātman polarity as the underlying Essence of Being, both cosmic and personal), thereby affirming a more complex and radical view of human personality and of its relation with its cosmic environment. This view, although less amenable to clear-cut explanations based on the dual system of logic (i.e., the "either/or" system applied to the reality of Being and Non-Being being replaced by the fourfold negative alternative, the *catuṣkoṭi* logic), had the advantage of turning the transiency factor—the stumbling block of any ontology—into an organic component of a truly dynamic concept of Reality, in which 'change' (i.e., 'Becoming') is as important, if not more so, as 'Being.'

Now, there are two general types of religio-philosophical systems: the 'substance' and the 'process' varieties, that is, philosophies of Being on the one hand, and Becoming, on the other. Examples of the first are—in the West—the philosophies of Parmenides, Aristotle, Descartes, Leibniz, Spinoza, Locke, and Kant, and—within the Indian context—Jainism, Sāṃkhya, and Vedānta. Examples of the second are—in the West—Heraclitus, Henri Bergson, Alfred North Whitehead, and—on the Indian stage—Buddhism.[4]

It has become customary in the last three hundred years of Western philosophical history to substitute with increasing frequency in discussions regarding the nature of Being and Becoming the term *ontology* for the older (Aristotelian) term *metaphysics.* The term *ontology* was first suggested by the French Cartesian philosopher Joannes Claubergius (or Clauberg, 1622-65) in a posthumous edition of his *Elementa Philosophiæ sive Ontosophia,* which was first written and published in 1647.[5] Just as theology is said to be the science (*logos*) about God (*theos*), argued Clauberg, so *ontosophy,* or *ontology* should be the name for the science about Being in general (*on*).

The term caught on, and the major thinkers of subsequent centuries gave it both prestige and specificity of meaning. Kant, for instance (1724-1804), called ontology "the science of the general attributes of all things" which, he wrote, "can teach us nothing about things as they are in themselves, but only the a priori conditions under which we can know things in our general experience, i.e., principles of the *possibility* of experience" (my italics).[6] Ontology represents the main subject matter of Hegel's (1770-1831) *Science of Logic,* in which the title of the first section defines logic as "The Doctrine of Being."[7]

In our own time, the great existentialist philosopher Martin Heidegger (1889-1976) writes in *Being and Time* that the only fruitful approach to the general notion of Being (*Sein*) can be made through an existential description of the particular being of man (*Dasein*), and that the "*Fundamental ontology,* from which alone all other ontologies can take their rise, must be sought in the *existential analytic of Dasein.*"[8]

For Heidegger, philosophy—and, one can also add, religion—is first of all ontology, that is to say a statement about the mode in which Being (*Sein*), or Existence (*Existenz*), constitutes itself in the world of phenomena (*Dasein*), and the task of ontology is to clarify the meaning of this constitutive structure of Being. In *Being and Time* (p. 13), Heidegger says:

> Basically, all ontology, no matter how rich and firmly compacted a system of categories it has at its disposal, remains blind and perverted from its ownmost aim, if it has not first adequately clarified the meaning of Being, and conceived this clarification as its fundamental task.

Like the modern phenomenologists, the Buddhist philosophers did not hold universal categories as real, for, in their view, it was the individual phenomena alone which accounted for the manifestation of Being in the world. According to the *Avayavinirākaraṇa* (*Six Buddhist Nyāya Tracts*, Bibliotheca Indica, Calcutta, 1910), individual atoms continually rise into being and die the next moment, while the appearance of "wholes" is only an illusion. Only the constituents exist, and not the constituted. In a discussion regarding the "Ontological Problems on which the Different Indian Systems Diverged," Surendranath Dasgupta writes (in *The History of Indian Philosophy*, Cambridge: 1963, vol. 1, 165):

> Buddhism holds everything to be momentary, so neither cause nor effect can abide. One is called the effect because its momentary existence has been determined by the destruction of its momentary antecedent called the cause. There is no permanent reality which undergoes the change, but one change is determined by another and this determination is nothing more than "that happening, this happened."

Specifically referring to the Vijñānavāda ontological position, as reflected in the *Laṅkāvatāra-sūtra*, Dasgupta further proceeds to offer this view of the system (*History*, 147):

> All phenomena both being and non-being are illusory (*sadasantaḥ māyopamāḥ*). When we look deeply into them we find that there is an absolute negation of all appearances, including even all negations, for they are also appearances. This would make the ultimate truth positive. But this is not so, for it is that in which the positive and negative are one and the same (*bhāvābhāva-samānatā*). Such a state which is complete in itself and has no name and no substance had been described in the *Laṅkāvatāra-sūtra* (p. 70) as thatness (*tathatā*). This state is also described in

> another place in the *Laṅkāvatāra* (p. 78) as voidness (*śūnyatā*) which is one and has no origination and no essence. In another place it is also designated as *tathāgatagarbha* (p. 80?).

His view is essentially correct, providing that one bears in mind the important qualifying fact that the specific categories elaborated and presented in the Buddhist texts (such as Tathatā/"Thatness," Śūnyatā/"Voidness," Tathāgata-garbha/"The Essence-of-Buddhahood") are never purely and solely ontological (in the sense in which it is understood in Western philosophy), but they also carry psychological, epistemological, and even soteriological connotations, each in various proportions, as the case may be.

Therefore, it is sometimes with difficulty, and never with absolute certainty, that the distinction between the ontological, epistemological, or soteriological concepts can be made. This will become clearer by means of illustration. In *Laṅkā* III: 176-77; ll. 19-20, 1-4, for instance, the following questions (named the "indeterminables," or "inexplicables," *avyākṛtam*), are asked:

> Moreover, O Gotama, is everything determinable? (Or) is it all indeterminable? Is there a self? Is there no self? Does the world exist? Does this world not exist? Is there another world? Is there no other world? And is another world existent or non-existent?
>
> Is there liberation? Is there no liberation? Is it all momentary? Is it all non-momentary? Are space, cessation (of rebirth) without premeditation, and Nirvāṇa, O Gotama, created or uncreated? Is there intermediate existence? Is there no intermediate existence?

In replying to these questions, the author rejects both alternatives, positive as well as negative, as extreme views held by the worldly philosophers who tend to dichotomize Reality into neatly separated categories which, subsequently, become reified, or objectified, thus taking on a pseudo-ontological life of their own. The importance of this phenomenon, that is, of the interaction between concepts and the intrinsically objective Reality, is underscored in Yogācāra Buddhism by the doctrine of Mind-only, or Imagination-only (Citta-mātra, or Vijñapti-mātra).

Along with a cluster of related concepts (e.g., Voidness, Suchness, multiple Causality, the Relativity of things), this doctrine in particular brings to the fore the role of subjective factors in defining Reality, the delusion of the "facticity" of things, and the limitations of cognition in general, when judged against the background of the totality of human experience. It makes one aware and appreciative of the multiple shades and nuances of truth, and of the ever-shifting relationships between language and what we decide to call at a given moment "the intrinsically objective or identifiable Reality," which has always been a matter of convention, or consensus among philosophers (*Laṅkā* III: 177; ll. 5-16):[9]

> I (then) said this to him, Mahāmati: "If so, O brāhman, this is merely materialism, brāhman. It is not mine, brāhman, this is your worldly philosophy. I, O brāhman, explain that in the triple world, the cause of evil is due to the habit-energy of imagination and erroneous thinking since beginningless time. Discrimination, O brāhman, develops from the lack of awareness that there is nothing (to be discriminated) but what is seen in one's own mind, and not from the perception of external object(s). According to the philosophers there is a triple concordance between the objective (world), the (five mediating) senses, and the (subjective) Self, (but) such (a view) is not mine.
>
> O brāhman, I am neither (an adherent to) the school of Causation, nor to the school [or doctrine] of No-causation, except that having understood through meditation that the (duality of) subject [grasping, *grāhya*] and object [grasped, *grāha*] is merely (due to) imagination, I teach the (doctrine of) Dependent Origination. And yet, this is not perceived by you, nor understood by others who are beset by (their) attachment to (the idea of) Self and its continuity. Mahāmati, cessation, space, Nirvāṇa exist in the manner of name (only); as realities, they are unascertained. Hence, the question of whether they are created (or not) is likewise [or, once again unobtainable, superfluous, futile, pointless]."

These lines express the fundamental concern with the establishment of a valid ontological basis for the essentially pragmatic process of liberation. The key concept here is the idea of Dependent Origination (*pratītya-samutpāda*) which is skillfully employed to demonstrate the insubstantiality of both the external Reality (*artha, dṛśya*) and the empirical Self (*ātman*). Such a view, then, would imply the continuity between all (apparently isolated, or independent) events and/or entities. Consequently, even the boundaries set up by the common-sense philosophers between the subject (inner reality), the object (outer reality), and the intermediary realm of the senses (which partakes of both), are rejected as the illusion of the 'threefold relation', or concordance (*saṃnikarṣa-trayānām*). Thus the *Laṅkā* II: 80-81; ll. 14-17, 1-3 further explains:

> By this is meant that all existing (things) are to be regarded as forms born of a dream or a vision, and they are not produced from self, other, or both, (which are) non-existent (*abhāva*).
>
> Having understood that the non-evolving of the Sense-perceptions (*vijñāna*s) is due to the seeing of the non-existence of the external world, which is merely in accordance with one's mind, considering the triple world as arising from the causal conditions, from imagination, and from a complex network [lit., implacable multitude, *akūṭa-rāśitva*] of causal factors, they (the Bodhisattvas) find that by means of non-recognition of all *dharma*s, external and internal, which are beyond [recognition, or description], and from learning that there is nothing (to be seen as) self-nature, and in desisting from the views (regarding) birth, they (the Bodhisattvas) obtain the recognition that things are unoriginated, which is in accordance with (the view) that one's own existence, (as well as) the elements of existence (*dharma*s), etc., are an illusion (*māyā*).

However, one important fact needs to be emphasized at this point. This and other similar passages found in the *Laṅkāvatāra*, where the nature of existence seems to be equated to that of a dream (*svapna*), or an illusion (*māyā*), are not to be taken to mean an outright denial of Reality as such. The fault lies not in the external world per se, but rather in our own mind, with its self-deceptive proclivity of discrimination (*vikalpa*). This is made very clear in the following lines (*Laṅkā* II: 52; ll. 1-3):

> Mahāmati, body, sensory-enjoyment, and habitat have their existence only when measured by imagination. The hare's horns neither are, nor are not; there can be no discrimination (about them)! So it is, Mahāmati, with all things: their coming forth (into being) neither is, nor is not. One must have no discrimination (about them)!

The truth about Reality can be seen only when the mind relinquishes its obstinate habit of perception through contrasting categories, or opposite polarities, which are mutually definable, their illusory (independent) existence being mutually conditioned. Thus the *Laṅkā* II: 54; 125 and vv. 127-28:

> The visible (world) is not found (as such); the multiplicity (of things) arises from what is seen in the mind (only). Body, sensory-enjoyment, and habitat betray [or, are declared to be, *khyāyate*] our own subconscious [or, Repository-of-impressions, *ālaya-vijñāna*].
>
> Long and short, etc., come into existence bound up with one another; when existence is asserted, there is non-existence, and where non-existence is presented, there is existence.
>
> When analyzed down to the atom, there is indeed not even a form [or substance, *rūpa*] to be discriminated (as such); what can be established is merely the [truth, effect, or impact of the] mind (only); which does not please the heretics [i.e., the Sāṃkhya philosophers].

This conclusion leads us to the following observations which, without being new, will help us set the philosophy of the Yogācāra school, as presented in the *Laṅkāvatāra-sūtra*, within the proper hermeneutical perspective.

The Practical Aim of the Yogācāra Philosophy

First of all, the entire thrust of the discourse in the *Sūtra* is directed, as we have already pointed out, toward a practical, rather than a theoretical aim. This is referred to throughout the text as the "inner truth of noble Self-realization" (*svapratyātmāryagatigocara*). In view of this aim, the method of analysis of the nature of Reality is decidedly empirical, or practical in intention. Of course, given the transcendental nature of the goal, this sort of empiricism has quite a different meaning from what is commonly understood in the West. However, considering the important role played by intuition in any introspective activity, be it psychological or spiritual in nature, one can safely speak of a Buddhist empiricism, at least at the level of intent, if not of actual and consistent application.[10]

Another interesting fact worthy of consideration here is the decidedly *descriptive* approach (as opposed to *prescriptive*, the dominant form of discourse in religious texts), which is, most probably, a direct consequence of the practical orientation of the Yogācāra school, referred to above.

In the *Laṅkāvatāra*, the issues are presented as answers to questions raised by the disciple Mahāmati, as we have seen. Sometimes, these answers are aphoristically short, and sometimes they are elaborated and extensive, but their appeal is rarely authoritative, never revelatory, and most frequently challenging one's capacity of reasoning and understanding. As we have pointed out in relation to the above quotations, and as we will see in the subsequent analyses of specific topics, the author(s) of this important Mahāyāna sūtra approaches the philosophical concepts as objects of reflection, as didactic tools for use in the teaching of Buddhist novices, and consistently refuses to commit himself as to their ultimate ontological validity.

Consequently, and now we come to our third observation, one can say that the philosophical concepts presented in the *Laṅkāvatāra* are truly ontological in their essential nature. This is especially true if we take the term *ontological* to mean something quite different from the older Aristotelian term *metaphysical*, in the sense that, while metaphysics is the science that makes *existential* assertions about different kinds of entities and the relations between them, ontology merely *describes* such entities and relations, without deciding whether they actually exist.[11] Then one can further say that the Buddhist worldview, as presented to us in the *Laṅkāvatāra-sūtra*, is remarkably consistent, and also unique, in abstaining from metaphysical commitment regarding the ultimate existential Reality of the Mahāyāna entities and constructs it discusses.

This singular feature (among the Mahāyāna corpus of literature) is brought about through the persistent application of two key Buddhist concepts: the 'Middle Way' between extremes, and its corollary, Dependent Origination. Thus, whether it is the Tathāgata-garbha idea (here regarded only as a teaching device, as a stepping-stone toward the understanding of the difficult to grasp non-Self, Anātman, doctrine), or the Five Skandhas (personality aggregates), the Dharmadhātu, or the realm of Nirvāṇa, the discussion invariably ends with a forceful rejection of both extreme views regarding their existence (*sat*), or non-existence (*asat*), as we have pointed out in the passages quoted above.

Now, in our presentation of Yogācāra ontology, as described in the *Laṅkāvatāra-sūtra*, we have selected three concepts out of a large number of qualifying choices, too cumbersome to be analyzed within the space of a single book. For one thing, many of these Mahāyāna ideas are quasi-synonyms, their meanings overlapping, or at least interlocking, e.g., *Dharmadhātu* (Absolute Realm), *Dharmakāya* (Body-of-Law), *Dharmatā* (Religious Realm), *Tathatā* (Suchness), *Śūnyatā* (Voidness), *Tathāgata-garbha* (Essence-of-Buddhahood), *Buddhatā* (Buddhahood), *Āryavastu* (Noble Realm), *Ālaya-vijñāna* (Repository-of-impressions). The three pivotal concepts (which are in themselves complex ideological constructs made up of a number of subordinate ideas, or levels of meaning) are: **Tathāgata-garbha**, the **Five Skandhas**, and **Dharmadhātu**. The choice is not altogether arbitrary. Aside from the fact that they all play a major role in the development of Mahāyāna thought in general, and that of the Yogācāra school in particular, they represent three paradigmatic categories which inform any ontological system, as explained by Edmund Husserl in his fundamental book *Ideas: General Introduction to Pure Phenomenology* (London: 1931, reprint New York: 1962).[12]

Naturally, every transcendental ontology sets out to describe, first and foremost, the nature of the 'Essential Being'. In Buddhism, this is the paradigm of the Enlightened Being, the Buddha who has transcended all conditioning, or—as is the case in the later, Mahāyāna, stage of development—the abstract transcendental principle of Buddhahood, called by its various names: *Buddhatā* (Buddhahood), *Tathatā* (Suchness), *Dharmatā* (Lawfulness), *Śūnyatā* (Voidness), et cetera. In a substantial portion of the Yogācāra literature, the *Laṅkāvatāra-sūtra* included, this abstract cosmic 'substance,' impregnating, but also enveloping the universe, as it were, is referred to as **Tathāgata-garbha**, the "Essence-of-Buddhahood."

This abstract, transcendental Buddha-nature can be both static, receptive, and unmanifested, as well as dynamic, active, and manifested. Although, as we shall see, it is said to be beyond both Being and non-Being, its outer, manifested aspect can make it available in temporal and spatial dimensions. One can say, therefore, that the system of the **Five Skandhas**, or the "Five Personality Constituents," represents the most significant form of Tathāgata-garbha's manifestation *in time*, that is in the external world of Becoming, to which the transient human personality conspicuously belongs.

The other fundamental dimension of the structure of Being, in its outer, manifested form (that is to say, immanent rather than transcendent), is its extension *in space*, illustrated here by the concept of **Dharmadhātu**, the "Realm-of-the-existential-elements," as it were. According to its usage in the *Laṅkāvatāra-sūtra*, as explained by D. T. Suzuki, it expresses "the most comprehensive view of the universe, including not only this visible sense-world, but all possibly conceivable ideal worlds."[13]

With the risk of repeating what I have already stated, it is important to keep in mind, however, that when it comes to Buddhism, any attempt at systematic categorization will be just that—an attempt, for the mere purpose of clarification, ridden with a degree of artificiality extrinsic to the nature of Buddhism, which is practical in method and religious in purpose. Having said that, I can also add that for a work such as this, even given these unavoidable limitations, my ontological categories are not as neat and homogenous as delineated above, for they constantly interact with other related concepts, crisscrossing various levels of existence: inner and outer, physical and ideal, temporal and spatial.

I shall now proceed with the topical investigation of the threefold ontological structure as presented in the *Laṅkāvatāra-sūtra,* namely the essential nature of Buddhahood (Tathāgata-garbha), and its personal (the Five Skandhas) and cosmic (Dharmadhātu) manifestations.

1.1. The Threefold Meaning of Tathāgata-garbha and its Relation to Ālaya-vijñāna: the *Essence* of Being

Preliminary Considerations

The Tathāgata-garbha concept is one of the most widely discussed in the Mahāyāna literature, and like the Citta-mātra principle—its epistemological counterpart in the Yogācāra school—has engendered a broad range of scholarly interpretations and comments regarding its meaning and significance. However important this may be, I will not attempt to review here the relevant literature regarding the meaning of the term *garbha,* since (a) it has been done elsewhere in great detail, and (b) it falls beyond the limited scope of the present work.[1] What I intend to pursue in this section is the hermeneutics of the concept, as it appears in the *Laṅkāvatāra-sūtra* (using both philological and historical approaches, when appropriate), in the hope that more light can be shed on its multiple and complementary levels of meaning, and on its relation with other, parallel, metaphysical constructs, both Buddhist and Hindu (e.g., *Ālaya-vijñāna,* the Repository-of-impressions, and *Ātman,* the Self, respectively).

In reviewing the various renditions of the term *Tathāgata-garbha* provided by the translators and the interpreters of the essential Mahāyāna texts, one is impressed by the fact that these authors, as a rule, tend to opt for a single meaning disregarding all other possible meanings which are embraced in turn by other texts and by their respective translators. To limit the discussion to the texts just quoted above, Takasaki, for instance, in his *Study of the Ratnagotravibhāga,* uses the expression "The Matrix of the Tathāgata," while Hideko and Alex Wayman, in their joint translation of the *Śrīmālādevī-sūtra,* prefer the opposite term "Embryo of the Tathāgata." When Suzuki, on the other hand, undertook the difficult task of translating the *Laṅkāvatāra-sūtra,* relying mostly on Chinese sources, he decided to maintain the expression in its original Sanskrit form, although he indicated his preference in his *Studies,* where he says that it represents the "womb where the Tathāgata is conceived and nourished and matured."[2]

Having considered the different contexts in which the expression appears in the *Laṅkāvatāra,* however, and bearing in mind the various meanings attributed to *Tathāgata-garbha* by noted authorities who studied the related texts, I came to the conclusion that no one consistent rendition would accomodate all situations encountered in the text. For instance, we will find that quite often *Tathāgata-garbha* is used with a sense resemblant to the Hindu *Ātman,* that is, as an underlying ontological Reality, or essential nature behind phenomena.

This can be said to attribute a passive, or static, quality to the *garbha* element in the compound. An opposite meaning is distinguishable when the Tathāgata-garbha is said to evolve, or be set in motion, along with the personality aggregates (*skandhas*), elements (*dhātus*), and bases (*āyatanas*). In such a case, the meaning of *garbha* is very appropriately rendered by the words "embryo," "germ," or "seed," which suggest a dynamic, active sense. A third possible, intermediate, meaning—rendered by the words "womb," "matrix," or "receptacle"—as something potentially active but dormant (like a seed or an embryo) is conferred by Tathāgata-garbha when explicitly equated with Ālaya-vijñāna, a situation uniquely evidenced in the *Laṅkāvatāra-sūtra.*

Although it is not always easy to extricate these three distinct meanings, I believe it is well worth the effort for the sake of rendering more precisely the complex soteriology advanced in this important Mahāyāna sūtra. Such an approach not only does justice to the subtlety of the Yogācāras' metaphysical thought, but it also resonates with similar uses of the term in parallel texts, the closest doctrine being the *Śrīmālādevī-sūtra.* A. Wayman, who first translated this scripture into English (from Tibetan, Chinese, and Japanese sources, and some Sanskrit fragments) with the collaboration of his wife, Hideko Wayman, has subsequently come to a more nuanced interpretation of the Tathāgata-garbha concept. This appears in his 1981 article on "The Title and Textual Affiliation of the Guhyagarbha-tantra," where he states (p. 4, n. 5):[3]

> Accordingly, it appears that all three senses of the word *garbha* are alluded to in a passage of the *Śrīmālādevīsiṃhanāda-sūtra;* cf. the translation of Alex Wayman and Hideko Wayman, *The Lion's Roar of Queen Śrī-Mālā* (New York, 1974), p. 106, where, however, the translators can now acknowledge, by reason of the present information of three kinds of *garbha,* that they

wrongly translated the word *garbha* each time as 'embryo'. It would be just as wrong, of course, to translate it each time as 'womb'. The passage can now be understood this way: "Lord, this Tathāgatagarbha is the Illustrious Dharmadhātu-womb (first kind of *garbha*); the Dharmadhātu-embryo (second kind of *garbha*); the essential of supramundane *dharma* and the essential of the intrinsically pure *dharma* (third kind of *garbha*)."

Such a flexible interpretation not only does justice to the various nuances of meaning found in the texts, but is also in full accordance with the commentarial tradition. Louis de La Vallée Poussin, for instance, in the *Vijñaptimātratāsiddhi* quotes the work *Buddhatāśāstra* (belonging to the Chinese canon and attributed to Vasubandhu) as saying that the word *garbha* has three meanings: *garbha* which is enveloped (*saṃgṛhīta*), *garbha* which is hidden, and *garbha* which is enveloping.[4] Based on these three meanings, according to the *śāstra*, all beings can be considered to be Tathāgata-garbha: first, because they are included in Tathatā (the "thusness" which is the nature of the Buddhas); second, because Tathāgata is not manifest in beings, but is concealed in them; and third, because all qualities of the Buddha (i.e., the thirty-two marks of the Superman, *dvātriṃśanmahāpuruṣalakṣaṇarūpadhārin*) are present in every sentient being, albeit in potential, or embryonic state.[5]

In addition, Vasubandhu also explains (following *Śrīmālikā*) that the Tathāgata-garbha is of five kinds, namely: 1. *tathāgata-garbha*, where *garbha* has the meaning *svabhāva*, "nature," which comprises all dharmas (except Ātman), the realm of the Tathāgatas; 2. *saddharma-garbha*, which means the cause (*hetu*) of all good dharmas, corresponding to the nature of the Tathāgatas; 3. *dharmakāya-garbha*, which has the sense of attainment, or mastery (*adhigama*, *pratipatti*); 4. *lokottara-garbha*, where the word *garbha* is taken as "reality" (*tattva*); and 5. *prakṛtiśuddha-garbha*, which implies that the originally pure, true essence of all dharmas is secretly concealed, as the inner nature of the Tathāgatas.[6]

In his *Study on the Ratnagotravibhāga* (p. 25, n. 44), Jikidō Takasaki also agrees on the possibility of interpreting the compound *Tathāgata-garbha* from three different angles, or points of reference. He says:

> The word *tathāgatagarbha* is interpreted in the *Ratna.* in three ways, namely: 1) *tathāgatasya ime garbhāḥ sarvasattvāḥ*, (p. 70. 17); 2) *tathāgatas tathataiṣāṃ garbhaḥ sarvasattvānām*, and 3) *tathāgatadhātur eṣāṃ garbhaḥ sarvasattvānām*. They correspond to *dharmakāya*, *tathatā*, and *tathāgatagotra*, respectively.[7]

He further explains these three correspondences thus: 1) "the Absolute Body (*dharmakāya*) of the Tathāgata penetrates all living beings;" 2) "the Tathāgata, being the Reality (*tathatā*), is the undifferentiated whole;" and 3) "there exists the Germ of the Tathāgata (*tathāgatagotra*) (in every living being)."[8] In a subsequent footnote (p. 198, n. 9), Takasaki gives the textual basis for his interpretation, which consists of the following three sentences: 1) (*sarvasattveṣu*) *tathāgata-dharmakāya-parispharaṇārtha;* 2) *tathāgata-tathatā-'vyatirekārtha;* and 3) *tathāgata-gotra-saṃbhavārtha,* where the term *saṃbhava* would mean, according to him, the idea of 'origination,' or 'manifestation,' as in the expression *trividha-svabhāva* of *tathāgatadhātu.*[9]

Takasaki's interpretation of the threefold meaning of the Tathāgata-garbha comes close to the similar division of the term given in the *Buddhagotraśāstra,* as pointed out first by Poussin (see above reference to the *Buddhatāśāstra*), namely: 1) *tathāgata,* as *garbha* in which *sattvas* are 'enveloped'; 2) *garbha* in which *tathāgata* is 'hidden'; 3) *sattvas* possessed of *garbha* of *tathāgata,* that is, of *garbha* 'enveloping' *tathāgata.*

The first one, says Takasaki, shows the "all-pervadingness of *dharmakāya,*" the second should be applied to *samalā tathatā* ("Reality mingled with pollution") in the sense of *sarvakleśa-kośopagūḍho dharmakāyaḥ* ("the Absolute Body is concealed by the cover of all defilements"), and the third "shows the existence of *gotra* among *sattvas*".[10] Bearing this in mind, we shall now see what, if any, similarities to such theories can be found in the *Laṅkāvatāra-sūtra,* and consider their implications.

Tathāgata-garbha as Essential, Supramundane, Pure Dharma, and its Contrast with the Hindu Ātman

Although it is not clear how many monks of the Mahāyāna schools came from the upper strata of Indian society, it is widely believed that many were educated people, which, at that time, meant that they were familiar with the general philosophy of the Vedas and the Upaniṣads. The latter, as well as the earlier Pāli scriptures concur in giving this impression. In an article entitled "The Background of Early Buddhism," J. W. de Jong gives the following assessment:[11]

> It cannot, however, be doubted that the majority of the monks belonged to the upper strata of society, the castes of the brāhmans, the kṣatriyas and the rich merchants. It should, of course, be remembered that conversions among the upper

classes usually attract more attention. But in the case of Buddhism it can safely be assumed that the information given by the texts faithfully records the true facts. For Buddhism is an aristocratic doctrine of deliverance, making high ethical and intellectual demands.

Starting from this premise, it should not be too difficult to admit the possibility that a number of Hindu-Brahmanical ideas, both new and old, found their way into the communities of Buddhists which were in constant movement across the Indian subcontinent, and that when carefully scrutinized, these ideas may be traced back to their original forms, lurking just beneath their newly adopted Buddhist garb.[12]

To the extent of my knowledge, this possibility has not yet been fully investigated in regard to the Tathāgata-garbha concept. Its sudden emergence in certain Mahāyāna texts poses a theological problem not only in respect to the early Hīnayāna nominalism (i.e., the doctrine of the individuality and impermanence of all phenomenal dharmas—*anitya*—and of their composite nature—*anātman*), but also in relation to other Mahāyāna schools, such as the Mādhyamika and Śūnyavāda, which—as is known—reject all physical and metaphysical entities outside the realm of Dependent Origination (*pratītya-samutpāda*).[13]

Thus, in apparent contradiction to these most basic Buddhist ontological principles, the entity called "Tathāgata-garbha" is described in the *Laṅkāvatāra-sūtra* with the following words (II: 77-78; ll. 13-18, 1):

> At this time, Mahāmati, the Bodhisattva, the Great Being, said this to the Lord: "Now the Blessed One mentions the essence-(*garbha*)-of-Buddhahood (*tathāgata*) in the scriptures. And verily it is described by you exactly as pure, free from error, clear primary substance (or fundamental form, *prakṛti*) endowed with thirty-two (characteristic) marks (of excellence), hidden in the body of every being like a gem (*ratna*) of great value enwrapped in a dirty cloth, enveloped in the raiment of the personality aggregates, of elements and bases, and soiled with the impurity of false imagination, of delusion, hatred and passion, being also described by the Lord as eternal, auspicious, firm and constant."

For the puzzled disciple, such a characterization is tantamount to the re-acceptance of the discarded Hindu notion of the underlying metaphysical entity of the universe, the Ātman. To dispel his doubt and confusion, he further questions his Master (II: 78; ll. 1-4):

> Is not this teaching regarding the essence-of-Buddhahood similar to the Ātman doctrine of the philosophers, O Blessed One? (For) the heretics also, O Lord, do teach the doctrine of Ātman as being an eternal Creator, unqualified, omnipresent and imperishable.

However, the reply seems to indicate that the Tathāgata-garbha is taught as an impersonal principle, whose value is primarily *didactic* (rather than ontological), for the purpose of dispelling the fear inspired in immature minds by the all-to-radical doctrine of Egolessness, as an intermediary step toward its deep comprehension, as it were. Thus the *Laṅkā* II: 78; ll. 5-18:

> The Lord replied: "Not at all, Mahāmati, my 'Essence-of-Buddhahood' is not equal to the Ātman doctrine taught by the heretics. For what the Tathāgatas teach, Mahāmati, is the doctrine of Essential Nature of Buddhahood having the meaning of being devoid of will-effort, ineffable, unborn, Nirvāṇa, Reality-limit, Voidness.
>
> The Tathāgatas, the Arhats, the Fully-enlightened Ones, teach the doctrine pointing to the Essence-of-Buddhahood for the purpose of making the immature cast aside all trace of fear due to (the teaching of) Selflessness, and (for the purpose of realizing) the state of non-imagination and non-discrimination.
>
> But, Mahāmati, (I hope that) the present and future Bodhisattvas, the great beings, would not become attached to the (idea of) Selfhood. Mahāmati, as a potter makes various vessels from a mass of clay of one sort through the combination of effort, thread, water, stick and manual skill, likewise, Mahāmati, the Tathāgatas preach the doctrine of Selflessness of *dharmas*, which removes the traces of every imagination, by various combinations of skills and means, with insight; so, either through the teaching of the Essence-of-Buddhahood, or through the doctrine of Selflessness, like the potter, in various ways, they teach through synonyms, figurative expressions and terms.
>
> Because of this reason, Mahāmati, the teaching of the Essence-of-Buddhahood is not the same as the doctrine of Selfhood (Ātman) of the philosophers!"

The comparison with the potter, who makes use of all resources at his disposal for the purpose of achieving his goal, clearly indicates the author's emphasis upon a combination of skills, means, and insight (*prajñā-upāya-kauśalya-yoga*) that is essential in the process of teaching difficult-to-understand doctrines, such as that of Selflessness (Nairātmya). In this context, the Tathāgata-garbha concept is no more than a teaching device, a figurative expression (*vyañjana*), a figure of speech (*paryāya*), a conventional term (*pada*), devoid of the absolute value attributed to such a significant concept as the Ātman, behind which an all-pervasive, real, and powerful ontological substance is believed to exist. And yet, the question of its origination, as well as that of its close association with the concept of the Ātman in the minds of some Buddhist novices is worthy of investigation, to say the least.

We know, for instance, that one of the oldest terms used for the creator of the universe, source of all life, human and celestial, as well as ground of the world by which the continuity of phenomena is maintained, was *Hiraṇya-garbha* (lit., the "Golden Womb") (*Ṛg-veda*, 10. 121. 1). This concept represents the first use of the word *garbha* in a compound with metaphysical (cosmogonic) implications. Significantly, for the purpose of our investigation, this compound was used interchangeably with *Hiraṇyāṇḍa* (lit., the "Golden Egg"), already conveying a sense of ambiguity, or dilemma, of "the chicken and the egg" type.

Gradually, though, such naturalistic principles regarding the origins of the world were superseded by anthropomorphic ones symbolized by names of divine beings—Prajāpati and Brahmā (who himself was born from a golden egg),[14]—and, eventually, by the thoroughly abstract principles of *brahman* and *ātman*, *prāṇa* (neuter, impersonal power) and *śakti* (feminine power), *puruṣa* (spirit) and *prakṛti* (matter). With the exception of the last two, used mainly by the Sāṃkhya school, all those terms were also used interchangeably, at one time or another. The general meaning was that of all-pervasive essence, filling the air, the earth, and heaven (*Ṛg-veda* 1. 115. 1), accounting for the unity of the universe, its vital force (*ātman, prāṇa*), and the cosmic Self (*brahman, paramātman*).[15]

Later, the Upaniṣads and the Āraṇyakas attempting to build a monistic view of the world, expanded the range of speculative considerations to include the realm of subjective reflection, that is to say, of a thinking individuality or personal self (*ātman*). The older concept of *Hiraṇya-garbha* was still referred to (especially in the later Upaniṣads), along with all the other metaphysical entities accumulated side by side, in the course of time. In the *Śvetāśvatara Upaniṣad* 3. 4, we read:

> yo devānāṃ prabhavaś codbhavaś ca viśvādhipo rudro maharṣiḥ/ hiraṇya-garbhaṃ janayāmāsa pūrvaṃ sa no buddhyā subhayā samyunaktu/
>
> He who is the source and origin of the gods, the ruler of all, Rudra, the great seer, who of old gave birth to the Golden Germ (*hiraṇya-garbha*), may He endow us with clear understanding.

This stanza is repeated elsewhere (4. 12) with slight modification (". . . who beheld the Golden Germ when he was born," *hiraṇya-garbhaṃ paśyata jāyamānaṃ*), revealing an ambivalence regarding the order of birth which echoes the Vedic ambiguity concerning the womb and the egg.

Now, it is not altogether unlikely, although difficult to prove, that such multiple levels of meaning may have been carried over into the later Buddhist concept of Tathāgata-garbha. The senses of Womb, Germ (or Embryo), as well as that of cosmic Essence, or Self (acquired as a result of Hiraṇya-garbha's close association with Ātman) are present in both compounds (Hiraṇya-garbha and Tathāgata-garbha) which include the term *garbha*, as we have seen. In the *Maitrī Upaniṣad*, one of the late Upaniṣads, which—according to Radhakrishnan—shows the influence of Buddhist thought, we find the following enumeration, repeated twice (7. 7; see also 6. 8):[16]

> He is the Self which is free from sin, ageless, deathless, sorrowless, free from uncertainty, free from fetters, whose conception is the real, whose desire is the real. He is the supreme lord, he is the ruler of beings, he is the protector of beings. He is the determining bridge.
>
> This Self, verily, is the lord, the beneficent, the existent, the terrible, the lord of creatures, creator of all, the Golden Germ (*hiraṇya-garbha*), truth, life, spirit, the ruler, the unshaken, the pervader, Nārāyaṇa.
>
> He who is in the fire, he who is here in the heart, he who is there in the sun, he is the one. To *you* who are this, endowed with all forms hidden in the real space, be adoration!

If we compare these lines with the description of the Tathāgata-garbha given in the *Laṅkāvatāra-sūtra* II: 77; ll. 13-18 (vide supra), the numerous similarities in imagery and style would not fail to impress us. The flow of ideas between the late Upaniṣadic and early Mahāyāna scriptures should not be very surprising after all, especially if we consider the fact that both were products of the *śramaṇa* culture of the wandering ascetics, who were so fond of exalted flights of speculative imagination.

In his discussion about "The World-Soul," Dasgupta seems skeptical with regard to the direct connection between the monotheistic tendencies of the later *Ṛg-veda* (10. 121. 1) and the Upaniṣadic doctrines, such as those reflected in the *Śvetāśvatara* 3. 4 and 4. 12 (vide supra). He says (*History* v. 1, 52):

> The passages in *Śvetāśvatara* clearly show how from the supreme eminence that he had in R.V. X.121, Hiraṇyagarbha had been brought to the level of one of the created beings.

Concluding from this that the Hiraṇyagarbha doctrine is philosophically "wholly irrelevant" in the Upaniṣads, he comes in sharp disagreement with Paul Deussen, whose estimation is totally the opposite, as seen from the following passage (which Dasgupta quotes):[17]

> . . . The entire objective universe is possible only in so far as it is sustained by a knowing subject. This subject as a sustainer of the objective universe is manifested in all individual objects but is by no means identical with them. For the individual objects pass away but the objective universe continues to exist without them; there exists therefore the eternal knowing subject also (*hiraṇyagarbha*) by whom it is sustained. Space and time are derived from this subject. It is itself accordingly not in space and does not belong to time, and therefore from an empirical point of view it is in general non-existent; it has no empirical but only a metaphysical reality.

Be this as it may, in so far as its relevance to the Upaniṣads is concerned, the fact is that the Garbha concept reverberates, to some degree or another, throughout many major Indian religious texts, both Hindu and Buddhist.

In the *Bhagavad Gītā*, for instance, it is said that Lord Kṛṣṇa (i.e., Viṣṇu) delivers his seed, or germ (*garbha*) in the womb, or matrix (*yoni*, not *garbha*) of the great Brahmā, resulting in the creation of all beings (*Bhagavad Gītā*. 14, 3):

> mama yonir mahadbrahmā tasmin garbhaṃ dadhāmy aham
> In that great Brahmā's womb I deliver my seed.

Likewise, in Aśvaghoṣa's *Buddhacarita* we find cosmological imagery, bringing together the ideas of womb, its gold-like contents (i.e., Embryo of Buddhahood) and the subsequent illuminating impact upon the world:[18]

> prātaḥ payodādiva tigmabhānuḥ samudbhavanso 'pi ca mātṛkukṣeḥ / sphuranmayūkhairvihatāndhakāraiścakāra lokaṃ kanakāvadātam // (Book 1, verse 26)
>
> Like the bright sun bursting from a cloud in the morning, so he, too, when he was born from his mother's womb [here *kukṣa* instead of *garbha*], made the world bright like gold, dispelling darkness.
>
> dīptyā ca dhairyeṇa śriyā rarāja bālo ravirbhūmimiva-avatīrṇaḥ / (1. 31, first line)
>
> Radiating with constancy and inflamed, he shone like a young sun-god descended upon the earth.
>
> jagatyayaṃ mohatamo nihantuṃ jvaliṣyati jñānamayo hi sūryaḥ // (1. 74, second line)
>
> He will shine forth as a sun of knowledge to destroy the darkness of illusion in the world.

Other Buddhist texts also make use of birth imagery in which the word *garbha* appears frequently in association with the name of the Buddha. The somewhat apocryphal *Milinda-pañha* (which Mrs. Caroline Rhys Davids believed to have been composed "by a Brahman of Buddhist collegiate training, called Mānava")[19] compares the creation of the path to salvation (*ārya-mārga*) to a birth process (4. 5, 15).[20] Paul Demiéville's translation of Hiuen-tsang's Chinese version of the *Saṅdhinirmocana-sūtra* reads:[21]

> Within the Fruit of the Buddha there is nothing but true identity (*bhūtatathatā*) and wisdom about true identity (*bhūtatathatābodhi*), without any quality constituted by the coarse *lakṣaṇa*-s such as form and sound.

We cannot but concur with Paul Masson-Oursel's observation that since "the fundamental entity of the Yogācāras, the *bhūta-tathatā* (i.e., the Suchness of Existence), is purposely the 'fruit de Bouddha,' it is of little concern whether the Sanskrit word rendered by the Chinese translator is *garbha*, or *phala*."[22]

Even more poignantly, the *Laṅkāvatāra-sūtra* itself echoes the implications of Hiraṇya-garbha as the source and ground of all beings, which becomes visible by purification, like shining gold among pebbles (*Sagāthakam:* 358; gāthas 750, 751):

> The originally clear Mind is the pure essence (*garbha*) of Buddhahood; for, being granted to [or, the ground of] every being, it is free from limitation and non-limitation.
>
> As the splendid color of gold, and brilliancy of gold among pebbles become visible through purification, so is the essence of personality aggregates [here *garbha* is substituted by its equivalent, *ālaya*, nn.] in a sentient being.

Thus, Deussen's interpretation of the Upaniṣadic Hiraṇya-garbha as the "sustaining subject of the objective universe," "manifested in all individual objects, but by no means identical (or limited) to them," and therefore, having "no empirical but only a metaphysical reality," (vide supra) is fully validated by the corresponding descriptions of the Tathāgata-garbha in the *Laṅkāvatāra-sūtra.* Indeed, the only and crucial difference between the Ātman and the Tathāgata-garbha is that the latter is not taken as an empirical entity, a real individual and/or cosmic substratum, but as a merely metaphysical construct, adopted for convenience and didactic expediency. The *Sūtra* makes this clear when it states (II: 79; ll. 1-13; v. 139):

> Thus indeed, Mahāmati, they (the Tathāgatas) proclaim through the doctrine regarding the Essence-of-Buddhahood the goal of attracting the philosophers (still) persevering in the doctrine of Self-hood, toward the doctrine of the Essence-of-Buddhahood.
>
> In what manner the minds who have fallen into the views of imagining the non-existent Self as real, succumbing in their fallen hearts to the domain of the triple emancipation, may quickly be awakened into the state of supreme Enlightenment?
>
> In this manner, Mahāmati: The Tathāgatas, the Arhats, the fully enlightened ones, produce the doctrine of the Essence-of-Buddhahood. Yet, this is not the same as the heretics' doctrine of Selfhood (*ātmavāda*).
>
> Therefore, Mahāmati, in order to relinquish the philosophers' view, you must strive after the essential (*garbha*) egoless nature (*nairātmya*) of the Tathāgata.
>
> At that moment, the Lord appropriately recited this verse:

> The personal Self, its continuance, the personality aggregates, the causal conditions, the atoms, the Supreme Spirit, the Lord, the Creator—they are merely imagined by the mind (*citta-mātra*).

Clearly, here and in other similar lines, the concept of the Tathāgata-garbha is posited as a transcendental, supramundane ideal with great inspirational value for the religious life of the Buddhist novice, which does not by itslef contradict the basic Mahāyāna ontological postulates regarding Self-lessness (Anātman), Impermanence (Anitya), and Voidness (Śūnyatā).

According to the author of the *Sūtra*, though comparable with the Hindu concept of Ātman (through both historical and philosophical association), the idea of Tathāgata-garbha is not to be adhered to, for, like all other metaphysical constructs, it is devoid of real ontological substance (attributable by the Hindus to the Ātman), being no more than a skillful means (*upāya kauśalya*) devised by the Teacher for the benefit of those who cannot yet envisage the awesome truth of the ego-lessness of all things (*dharma-nairātmya*).

Tathāgata-garbha as Embryo, and the Dynamics of Buddhahood

In his study of the *Vijñaptimātratāsiddhi*, La Vallée Poussin reproduces the following lines from the *Tathāgata-garbha-sūtra* (Nanjio 384, Wassilieff's French translation):[23]

> In all beings is hidden the nature of the Tathāgata: as the precious child is hidden in the entrails of the poor mother, as gold in an impure place . . . etc.

As we have already pointed out, such imagery is common in the *Laṅkāvatāra-sūtra* (e.g., II: 77-78, supra), as well as in other texts (such as the *Gaṇḍavyūha*, the *Śikṣāsamuccaya*, quoted by Poussin, loc. cit.), where it is stated that the Bodhisattva is an embryo of the Buddha (*buddhagarbha*) because he is the "germ of the thought of enlightenment" (*bodhicittakalala*), and a "tender foetus" (*kṛparbuda*) growing toward Buddhahood.[24]

When taken in this dynamic aspect, usually associated with the system of the Five Sense-perceptions (the Vijñānas which are not subject to transmigration), the Tathāgata-garbha compound is best translated as the "Embryo-of-Buddhahood." Such is the case in the following excerpt from the *Laṅkā* VI: 236; ll. 4-8:

> Mahāmati, the system of the five Sense-perceptions is not (subject to) transmigration, neither does it follow as a consequence of pleasure and pain, nor is it the cause conducive to Nirvāṇa. However, Mahāmati, it is the Embryo-of-Buddhahood (*tathāgata-garbha*) which develops along with the cause of pain and pleasure that are experienced (as a result), and it is the Embryo-of-Buddhahood which recedes, (having been) thickened with the fourfold habit-energy [or memories, *vāsanās*].
>
> Still, the immature do not understand this, for (their) thinking is infused with the habit-energy [or impressions, memories] of discrimination, due to the (wrong) views (regarding) momentariness.

In asserting the capacity for development of the Tathāgata-garbha, when taken as 'embryo', the author of the *Laṅkāvatāra-sūtra* clearly distinguishes between one level of meaning ('embryo'), and another ('womb', or 'matrix'). It is quite possible, as we have already suggested, that this distinction came about gradually, in the course of the accretion of Mahāyāna literature.

Gishin Tokiwa, in his article on the "Tathāgata Garbha," attempts to outline a chronology in the development of the concept.[25] According to him, the idea of "Tathāgata's matrix-abode derives from that of Śākyamuni as a bodhisattva, or an Awakened being in quest of Awakening, abiding in the womb of his mother Lady Māyā." This idea is traced back to the line: *bodhisattvo mātuḥ kukṣi-gataḥ*, found in the sixth chapter, "Entering the Matrix" (*Garbha-avakrānti*) of the *Lalitavistara* (Vaidya edition, p. 50 et al.).[26] Thus, "the bodhisattva being in the belly of his mother" can only be in the shape of an embryo, namely the embryo of the Buddha to be.

The *Tathāgata-garbha-sūtra* further developed this idea, when it stated that:[27]

> . . . At that time there was a Buddha named Perpetual-light-Emitter . . . When as a bodhisattva he was in his mother's womb, he emitted light, which shone through . . . //
>
> . . . The Limitless-light bodhisattva once asked the Buddha about this truth of the Embryo-of-Buddhahood (*tathāgata-garbha*).

The next stage in the historical development of the Tathāgata-garbha concept is the *Śrīmālādevī-sūtra*, which, according to Tokiwa, directly succeeds *Lalitavistara* and "should be regarded as the most important of sūtras on the *tathāgata-garbha* view."[28]

Indeed, as we have already pointed out at the beginning of this chapter, all three possible interpretations of the word *garbha* may be distinguished in certain portions of this important text. One such passage, in Alex Wayman's revised translation referred to above, reads:[29]

> Lord this Tathāgatagarbha is the womb of the Illustrious Dharmadhātu, the embryo of the Dharmakāya, the essence of supramundane *dharma*, the essence of the intrinsically pure *dharma*.

Likewise, the *Ratnagotravibhāga*, which contains many expressions from the *Śrīmālādevī-sūtra* in Sanskrit, contains the verse (in Zuirū Nakamura's edition, p. 57, k. 34) which says:[30]

> *garbha-sthānaṃ dhyāna-saukhyam*
>
> Comforting meditation (of the Bodhisattva) abiding in the womb [*garbha*, matrix].

Elsewhere in the *Ratna* other, complementary meanings can be found, as in this passage translated by Takasaki:[31]

> And now, in every living being, there exists the Essence-of-the Tathāgata arisen, in the form of embryo (*garbha-gata*). But these living beings do not know about it.

Such quotes echo similar statements found in the *Laṅkāvatāra-sūtra* (VI: 236, ll. 5-8, quoted above) since—according to Takasaki—the *Laṅkā* predates *Ratnagotravibhāga* by at least half a century.[32]

Other sūtras, later than the *Ratna*, continued to develop the Garbha theory up to the sixth century A.D. One is entitled *Ārya-candrottaradārikā-vyākaraṇa* and is preserved in its Chinese translation of A.D. 591,[33] and the other is the *Mahāyāna-śraddhotpāda-śāstra*, which contains—again according to Takasaki—the most systematic exposition of the Garbha theory, as well as its final development.[34] For the purpose of our investigation, however, suffice it to say that the sense of 'embryo' seems to have emerged initially from the association with the birth of the Bodhisattva from the Lady Māyā's womb. Almost immediately, the texts also expanded the meaning to include the womb itself, which sometime later acquired cosmic dimensions (perhaps in association with the Dharmadhātu idea, or the Upaniṣadic notions of Ātman, of Hiraṇya-garbha). In this later sense, the meaning of *garbha* became the equivalent of "essence," or "essential, pure nature."

The distinctive criterion between womb, or essence, on the one hand, and embryo, on the other, is—to be sure—the static or dynamic quality of each, respectively. Thus, the *Ratna* is replete with statements of the following sort:

> The Tathāgata's matrix-abode is not born, does not get old or die; it does not perish or rise.[35]
>
> The Essence that exists since beginningless time
> Is the foundation of all elements,
> Owing to its existence, all Phenomenal Life (*gati*)
> As well as the acquisition of Nirvāṇa exists.[36]
>
> O Lord, the Matrix of the Tathāgata is the transcendental Matrix; the Matrix, perfectly pure by nature.
>
> The Buddha's Body penetrates everywhere,
> Reality is of undifferentiated nature,
> And the Germ (of the Buddha) exists (in the living beings) (*sarve dehinaḥ = sarvasattvāḥ*)
> Therefore, all living beings (*sarva śarīriṇaḥ*)
> are always possessed of the Matrix of the Buddha. (28)[37]
>
> It is indivisible from the Buddha's Properties,
> Its Germ has been perfected as it is (*tadgotrasya tathāgamaḥ*),
> It is not of false, deceptive nature (*aṃṛṣamoṣadharmitva*)
> And it is quiescent (*ādiprakṛtiśāntatā*) from the very outset. (86)[38]

The *Śrīmālādevī-sūtra*, too, describes the Tathāgata-garbha with similar words:[39]

> But, Lord, the Tathāgatagarbha is not born, does not die, does not pass away to become reborn. The Tathāgatagarbha excludes the realm with the characteristic of the constructed. The Tathāgatagarbha is permanent, steadfast, eternal. Therefore the Tathāgatagarbha is the support, the holder, the base of constructed (Buddha natures) that are non-discrete, not dissociated, and knowing as liberated from the stores (of defilement); and furthermore is the support, the holder, the base of external constructed natures that are discrete, dissociated, and knowing as not liberated.

Surely, this sort of Tathāgata-garbha cannot be the same as the Tathāgata-garbha referred to in the *Laṅkāvatāra-sūtra* as evolving among the individual components of personality, physical and psychological, which are in continuous agitation, subject to birth and dissolution. In such a case, the word *garbha* can only admit the rendition of "germ," or "embryo." Thus, *Laṅkā* VI: 221; ll. 12-19:

> And when a transformation does not take place in the Receptacle-of-impressions, known under the name of the Womb-of-Buddhahood, there is no cessation of the seven evolving Sense-perceptions. Why? Because the evolution is dependent upon this ground (of the five senses), but anything out of the reach of the Sense-perceptions evolves among the bases, the elements, and the personality aggregates, from the sum of one's own individual and general characteristics, out of the perception of egolessness of one's person, for [the benefit of those who are] versed in the discipline of the philosophers, and of all Śrāvaka disciples and of the fully enlightened ones.
>
> The Embryo-of-Buddhahood (*tathāgata-garbha*) becomes quiescent (*nivartate*) due to the understanding of the egolessness of things through the five Knowledge-states, and by returning to the following of the gradual stages (of the Bodhisattva's path), one is able not to be led astray by the views in regard to the paths of the other philosophers [i.e., the heretics].

What this passage clearly states is that, in opposition to the statements quoted from the *Ratna* and the *Śrīmālādevī* (see supra), Tathāgata-garbha (or, at least a certain kind of garbha, which we translated as "embryo") is a constituent part of an individual's psycho-physical make up, and—as a consequence of that—can become subject to growth, agitation, and eventual quiescence. Being closely associated with the system of the Sense-perceptions (Vijñānas), it is only through its purification, or reabsorption (*parāvṛtti*) that the Embryo-of-Buddhahood may emerge in its original state. To this aspect of Tathāgata-garbha we shall turn next.

Tathāgata-garbha as Womb or Matrix of Buddhahood

If the womb of Lady Māyā is the place where the Embryo of Buddhahood, or the Bodhisattva, is first conceived, then it is again a womb-like quality of peace and quietude which is the goal of Buddhist striving in this world of Saṃsāra. Except that this time, the womb (or matrix, *garbha*) is not a clearly perceivable physical reality, but rather a hard-to-obtain, ineffable, metaphysical ideal, which is attained only by practicing assiduously the meditational, trance-like states which are referred to in the *Sūtra* as "the ten Samādhis." Thus, the *Laṅkāvatāra* states (VI: 221-22; ll. 19, 1-8):

Now, by establishing oneself at the Bodhisattva stage of the (eighth) immovable [concentration, *acalāyā*], he [the Bodhisattva disciple] attains the path leading to the bliss of the ten Samādhis. Supported by the Buddhas in Samādhi, with humility towards the observance of one's own contemplation of the law of Enlightenment [or, the truth of the Buddha] which is beyond thought, refraining from (reaching) the limit of reality, (which is) the bliss of Samādhi; by means of the noble course of inner Self-realization, by the paths of (various) disciplines (*yogamārga*), but not by the refuge obtained by the heretics, the novices, and the self-enlightened ones—(thus) one reaches the ten-fold path of the noble family (of Tathāgatas), and the body which is made of will and knowledge, free from passing into (the state of) Samādhi [i.e., into Buddhahood].

For this reason, Mahāmati, let the Womb-of-Buddhahood (*tathāgata-garbha*), which is known as the Receptacle-of-impressions (*ālaya-vijñāna*), be purified [or cleansed] by the Bodhisattvas, the great beings, (who are inspired by this) most excellent goal.

The passage underscores the connection between theTathāgata-garbha and the Ālaya component of the Vijñāna system. One important point needs to be emphasized, however. While the Garbha taken as "embryo" is associated with the seven evolving Vijñānas (i.e., the five Sense-perceptions, the Manas, and the Manovijñāna), the Garbha as "womb" is virtually identical with Ālaya-vijñāna. This is said to be the deepest stratum of consciousness, in itself pure and tranquil, and from which all the other Vijñānas emerge (*Laṅkā* VI: 220-1; ll. 13-16, 1):

Because of the habit-energy of erroneous thinking accumulated variously since the beginningless time, the so-called Receptacle-of-impressions (*ālaya-vijñāna*) is accompanied by the seven Sense-perceptions (which) are produced by the condition due to the habit-energy and ignorance. It is like the waves of the great ocean, forever rolling, (while) the body [i.e., the mass of deep waters, or the Ālaya] continues to be uninterrupted (or undisturbed), free from the fault of impermanence, unperturbed by the doctrine of Selfhood, and thoroughly pure in its essential nature.

From this passage it would seem that the Vijñānas are of two kinds: the evolving, dynamic *pravṛtti-vijñānas*, and the pacific, pure Ālaya-vijñāna. In fact, the *Sūtra* tells us of three kinds of Vijñānas, as follows (*Laṅkā* II: 37; ll. 12-15):

> There are three kinds of consciousness in manifested aspect: the (cause-) produced [or developing] form; the active [or effect-producing] manifested form; and the generic [i.e., fixed by birth, genetic, or family lineage, inherent character of its race, its true] form.

Now, it is this generic, inherited, original form of consciousness, referred to here as *jāti-vijñāna*, and elsewhere as *sva-jāti-lakṣaṇa* (i.e., "having the mark of one's own lineage, or racial, genetic, originally pure form"), which is the equivalent of both Ālaya-vijñāna and Tathāgata-garbha (when taken with the meaning of "womb," or "matrix"). Without further insistence upon the complex intricacies of the theory of the Eight Vijñānas (which will be treated as a separate topic in Ch. 2.3. of this work), let us say that the Ālaya can neither originate, nor disappear, but can only be purified and tranquillized. For to allow its complete cessation would be the theoretical equivalent of Nihilism (Ucchedavāda), one of the two extreme views the Buddha warned against, in no uncertain terms.[40] Thus, the *Laṅkā* II: 38-39; ll. 13-19, 1-2:

> Even so, Mahāmati, if the evolving perceptions were different from their original form, the Repository-of-impressions (*ālaya-vijñāna*), their cause(s) (*hetukāni*) could not be the Repository-of-impressions.
>
> Now, if they were not different (*ananyāni*), the cessation of the evolving perceptions would mean the cessation of the Repository-of-impressions, but there is no cessation of one's own original form [*svajātilakṣaṇa*, the equivalent of the *ālaya-vijñāna*].
>
> Therefore, Mahāmati, what (causes) the Sense-perceptions' (dissolution) is not the cessation of one's own pure, original form (of consciousness), but the cessation of the tainted, active form [of consciousness, i.e., *karma-lakṣaṇa-vijñāna*].
>
> However, had there been any ceasing of one's own original form [or consciousness, *svajātilakṣaṇa*], the cessation of the Repository-of-impressions would have occurred.
>
> Moreover yet, if the dissolution were to take place in the Repository-of-impressions, this doctrine would be in no way different [or distinguishable] from the Nihilism of the heretical philosophers.

To regard Ālaya-vijñāna, on the other hand, as an indissoluble, persistent ontological entity (comparable with the Hindu Ātman) may bring one dangerously close to the other perverted theoretical extreme of Eternalism (Śāśvatavāda). Sensing such a danger, the author of the *Laṅkāvatāra-sūtra* proposes a dialectical way out of this philosophical tightrope, when he states in the following gāthas (II: 46; vv. 102-104) that the seven evanescent Vijñānas are neither the same nor different from the eighth, quasi-permanent, Ālaya, for they are all part of the same, organically interdependent system called the Mind (*citta*):

> They [i.e., the seven evolving *vijñānas* plus the *ālaya*, here referred to as *citta*, the deep, subconscious mind] are neither different, nor non-different, they are considered as the waves and the ocean; thus are the seven Sense-perceptions connected with the mind (*citta*).
>
> As the waves in their multiplicity are stirred upon (the surface of) the ocean, so in the Repository-of-impressions (*ālaya*) is produced a variety of what is known as Consciousness-states (*vijñānas*).
>
> Citta [or Ālaya, the subconscious mind], Manas [or volition, the preconscious mind, as it were], and Vijñāna [the conscious perception] are discriminated in respect to their form (*lakṣaṇa-artha*); (yet in substance) the eight (*vijñānas*) are not to be individualized (as something distinctive), for there is neither that which is qualified [or observable, *lakṣya*], nor that which qualifies [or observing, *lakṣaṇaṃ*].

In other words, we are facing here a categorical denial of the absolute validity (or existence) of both the intrapsychical categories subsumed under the Vijñāna system (which are to be regarded as mere mental constructions, Citta-mātra), and of the enduring personal consciousness (i.e., the illusion of Selfhood, Anātman, or the observing agent, *na ca lakṣaṇaṃ*).[41]

Moreover, the same position is reflected in the similar descriptions of the role of the Tathāgata-garbha in the system of Vijñānas as both the source and the ultimate resting place of the seven evolving Consciousness-states. Here is one such example (*Laṅkā* VI: 222; ll. 9-14):

> Mahāmati, if—as it appears—there were no Womb-of-Buddhahood, known as the Receptacle-of-impressions, there would be, Mahāmati, neither the developing nor the disappearing [of thought forms, the *vijñānas*] in the Receptacle-of-impressions, known as the Matrix-of-Buddhahood (*tathāgata-garbha*).

> But Mahāmati, there is rising and disappearing of the foolish as well as of lofty (thoughts, *vijñānas*). (Knowing this), the Yogis who spend (their time) by wandering in the bliss of Dharma and contemplating their inner noble Self-realization, do not abandon (working) hard and are not frustrated (in their efforts).

Thus, the polemical tone in which this discourse is presented betrays a certain ambiguity (or ambivalence?) regarding the ultimate validity of the Vijñāna system, as well as the specific functions attributed to its various components. This ambiguity, which the author of the *Laṅkāvatāra* attempts to overcome, reflects the fluidity of the Tathāgata-garbha theory, its nature and role within the Vijñāna system, at the time when this text was compiled.

Consider, for instance, the issue of purity, which is strongly emphasized in the *Laṅkāvatāra*, as we have already pointed out in previous descriptions of the Tathāgata-garbha. The Yogācāras apparently held the view that the Ālaya-vijñāna (or Tathāgata-garbha, its synonym in the *Laṅkāvatāra*) is pure in its essential nature, while other Buddhists held the view that it is tainted by adventitious defilements (*kleśas*). This is clearly stated in the following passage (*Laṅkā* VI: 222; ll. 14-19):

> Mahāmati, this domain of the Receptacle-of-impressions, which is the Womb-of-Buddhahood, is primarily pure, and is beyond the (speculative) views of the philosophers, the self-enlightened ones, and of all the disciples; and yet it appears to them (as being) impure, as it is soiled by these external defilements; but not so to the Tathāgatas. (For), again Mahāmati, to the Tathāgatas it is the realm of direct perception, like (seeing) the Āmalaka (myrobalan fruit) in the palm of the hand.

This confusion regarding the purity of the Tathāgata-garbha may very well be due to the various meanings attributed to the word *garbha*. Thus, in the case of "embryo" (*garbha* seen as potentiality for Buddhahood) one can speak of an impure condition, while in the case of "womb," or "essence" (*garbha* taken as fulfillment, or actualized Buddhahood) the impurities have been removed, as a result of the purifying process of meditation.

This point of interpretation is supported by both the *Ratnagotra-vibhāga* (where the Tathāgata-garbha constitutes the central topic, the text itself being based upon a lesser-known scripture, the *Tathāgatagarbha-sūtra*), and the *Śrīmālādevī-sūtra* (which is mentioned by name in the *Laṅkāvatāra*). Further light on this issue is shed by

Wayman in his Introduction to his translation of the *Śrīmālādevī-sūtra*, where he says:[42]

> The term "Thusness" (*tathatā*) is also employed in a qualified way for the Tathāgata-garbha. According to the *Ratnagotra-vibhāga* (E. H. Johnston, ed., *The Ratnogotravibhāga Mahāyānottara-tantraśāstra*, text 1, 26, Patna: 1950), Thusness defiled is the Tathāgatagarbha, and Thusness undefiled is Enlightenment. The *Śrī-Mālā* states, "Lord, 'incomparable rightly completed enlightenment' is an expression for the nirvāṇa-realm. 'Nirvāṇa-realm' is an expression for the Dharmakāya of the Tathāgata." In the *Śri-Mālā* there are two main conditions for the "embryo of the Tathāgata": either covered by defilements, when it is called only "embryo of the Tathāgata"; or free from defilements, when the "embryo of the Tathāgata" is no more the "embryo" (potentiality) but the Tathāgata (= Dharmakāya) (actuality).

Seen in its actuality, or as Dharmakāya, the Tathāgata-garbha is characterized in the *Śrīmālādevī* (and other related texts) by four qualities: permanent (*nitya*), steadfast (*dhruva*), calm (*śiva*), and eternal (*śāśvata*). In a passage from the *Mahābherīhāraka-sūtra* a fifth, Self (*ātman*) is also added:[43]

> Kāśyapa, accordingly at the time one becomes a Tathāgata, a Buddha, he is in nirvāṇa, and is referred to as 'permanent,' 'steadfast,' 'calm,' 'eternal,' and 'self' (*ātman*)."

Furthermore, these terms are explained in yet another scripture, the *Anūnatvāpūrṇatvanirdeśaparivarta*, quoted by Wayman:[44]

> This Dharmakāya, Śāriputra, is permanent, by reason of being the unalterable true nature with boundless natures (dharma). This Dharmakāya, Śāriputra, is steadfast, by reason of being the steadfast refuge at the uttermost limit. This Dharmakāya, Śāriputra, is calm, by reason of being the nondiscursive true nature with nondual natures. This Dharmakāya, Śāriputra, is eternal, by reason of being the unfabricated true nature with indestructible natures.

One more point needs to be made here, namely that the degree of understanding of the Tathāgata-garbha theory varies with advancement on the path to Buddhahood. From the combined reading of the *Śrīmālādevī*, *Ratna*, and *Laṅkāvatāra*, there seem to be at least three, and perhaps four, categories of understanding, according to the class of person.

The first belongs to ordinary people, non-Buddhists, sometimes referred to as heretics (*tīrthyas*), or to the philosophers (ordinarily brāhmins). They are either nihilists (materialists), or eternalists (believers in Ātman, the Hindus).

The second class of beings are the Hīnayāna Buddhists, usually called the two "Noble ones," the Disciples (Śrāvakas) and the Self-Enlightened ones (Pratyekabuddhas). They only see impermanence, suffering, the non-Self, and impurity, but do not reach the Nirvāṇa-realm (Dharmakāya, the Womb of the Tathāgatas) which has permanence, pleasure, Self, and purity.

The third would be the Mahāyānists who take Voidness (Śūnyatā) as the ultimate and do not see the absolute nature of Buddha's Essence (Tathatā) which is not void, but steadfast and pure, as described in the texts.

Finally, there are the Tathāgatas, or Bodhisattvas, the Great Beings who, having eliminated through insight (*prajñā*) the defilements of lust, hatred and delusion, have attained the spiritual power to help others in their own striving along the same path, towards the final goal: cessation of suffering (Nirvāṇa).

Free from imagination concerning the world of Saṃsāra and Nirvāṇa, they regard the Tathāgata-garbha as Thusness (Tathatā), that is beyond all dualities of Self and non-Self, pure and impure, permanence and impermanence. This is how the texts describe them. First, the *Ratnagotravibhāga* (pp. 76-77, alluding to the preceding p. 74) says the following:[45]

> (1) The embryo of the Illustrious Dharmadhātu is not accessible to ordinary persons, who fall into the belief in a real personality; because the embryo of the Illustrious Dharmadhātu is the realm without flux that is the cessation of a real personality.
>
> (2) The embryo of Dharmakāya and the embryo of supra-mundane dharma are not accessible to the Disciples and the Self-Enlightened, who adhere to waywardness; because they contemplate the ideas of impermanence, suffering, nonself, and impurity (of saṃsāra) instead of the permanence, pleasure, self, and purity of the Tathāgatagarbha (= nirvāṇa).
>
> (3) The embryo of the intrinsically pure dharma is not accessible to the Bodhisattvas newly entered in the Great Vehicle, whose thoughts are distracted by voidness; because they seek the

"voidness door of liberation" for destruction of modes-of-beings, and do not understand voidness as the Tathāgatagarbha which is void of defilement and not void of Buddha natures [according to *Śrī-Mālā*'s interpretation].

The fourth class of beings, not mentioned in the *Ratna*, is described in the *Laṅkāvatāra* as the Bodhisattvas, the Great Beings who are not attached to the letter of the texts, but realize through their own inner experience the meaning of the concept of Buddhahood, which is only alluded to in the scriptures. Thus the *Laṅkā* VI: 222-23; ll. 20, 1-13:

> This is what was indicated to me in the canonical text relating to the Queen Śrīmālā and in another (text) which relies upon the Bodhisattvas endowed with subtle, sharp and pure psychological insight:
>
> The Embryo-of-Buddhahood, known as the Receptacle-of-impressions, evolves together with the seven Sense-perceptions. This is expounded for the purpose of making the disciples who are persevering (in their wrong views) see into the egolessness of things, and the realm of the Tathāgata is (also) expounded (here) for the scope of (the spiritual) attainment of the Queen Śrīmālā. This realm does not belong to the speculative system of the (heretical) philosophers, or of the self-enlightened ones and of the disciples.
>
> On the other hand, Mahāmati, the realm of the Tathāgatas, which is the same as the Womb-of-Buddhahood, the range of the Receptacle-of-impressions, belongs only to the Bodhisattvas, the Great Beings, those who like you are endowed with penetrating intellect, with sharp and subtle thought-power, and (whose understanding) is in accordance to the *meaning*, and not to the self-enlightened ones, the disciples, and all other philosophers who are attached to the *letter* of the canonical books.
>
> For this reason, Mahāmati, may you and other Bodhisattvas, Great Beings, practice the yoga of comprehending the Receptacle-of-impressions, the Essence-of-Buddhahood in which (you will find) the dominion of all the Tathāgatas, so that you may not become (constrained) by mere (bookish) learning.

This particular passage expresses in a uniquely condensed form the essential features of the Tathāgata-garbha theory as presented in the *Laṅkāvatāra-sūtra*. Not only do we find all four levels of understanding of the concept referred to above (the four classes of beings on the path of Buddhahood), but we can also discern the three nuances of meaning implicit in this important Mahāyāna construct. For, the meaning of *garbha* in the first paragraph can only be translated as "embryo" (i.e., the dynamic sense, since it evolves together with the "developing sense-perceptions," or *pravṛtti-vijñānas*), that of the second paragraph admits the sense of "womb" (i.e., the static sense, the source of the power of the intellect), and in the third paragraph the reference to the teaching of the Buddha contained in the canonical books (Dharmakāya), suggests the sense of "essence," since it is this essential nature of the Buddhist Dharma which constitutes the goal of Buddhist strivings and not learning per se. In this, all related texts seem to agree.

Thus, the *Uttaratantra*, quoting the *Tathāgatagarbha-sūtra* states: "All sentient beings are endowed with the Essence of the Buddha." The meaning of this statement is explained by Maitreya himself, the presumed founder of the Yogācāra school, with the words:[46]

> The Absolute is (one) undifferentiated (whole).
> And the Germ of (Buddhahood) exists (in every living being),
> Therefore, for ever and anon, all that lives is endowed with the Essence of the Buddha.

And also:

> Just as, being essentially free from (dialectical) thought-construction, the element of space is ubiquitous,
> In the same way the Immaculate Essence which is of Spiritual nature, pervades all that exists.

The *Ratnagotravibhāga* also presents three senses as implicit in the statement regarding all sentient beings (pp. 25-26):[47]

(1) The Tathāgata's Dharmakāya permeates all sentient beings;
(2) The Tathāgata's "Thusness" (*tathatā*) is omnipresent (*avyatibheda*) in them; and

(3) The Tathāgata's species (*gotra*) occurs in them.

Finally, what remains truly unique to the *Laṅkāvatāra* is the radical interpretation of the Tathāgata-garbha as a soteriological device, a didactic construct meant to be discarded, once its symbolic value has been understood. For it is the object, the moon, and not its symbol, the finger-tip pointing to the moon, that needs to be grasped by the mind. This is conveyed in rich poetical imagery by the *Sūtra*, as follows (*Laṅkā* VI: 223-24, vv. 1-4):

> The (essential) nature of the Tathāgatas is indeed united with the seven Consciousness-states (*vijñānas*); Duality arises from attachment, (but) from accurate understanding, it ceases [i.e., the subject/object duality].
>
> The thinking mind, created by thought [or desire, *mati*] since the beginning, is seen like a (reflection in the) mirror, (but) when reality (*bhūta*) is seen as such [or, as it is, *yathā*], there is neither object (*artha*), nor subject [or, the reality-maker, *artha-akāra*].
>
> As the immature observes the finger-tip and not the moon (to which it points), so indeed those who cling to the letter (*akṣara*) do not see my truth (*tattva*).
>
> (For) the mind (*citta*) dances like a dancer, the impulses (*manas*) resemble a clown, the power of will [or, the thinking consciousness, *mano-vijñāna*] along with the five (Sense-perceptions, *pravṛtti-vijñānas*) imagine a world (*dṛśya*) like a stage [i.e., made of mere appearance contrived by the mind, *citta-mātra*].

We can only add that these celebrated lines opened a new and higher level of awareness regarding the power of metaphorical speech, which left deep traces in the minds of succeeding generations of Buddhists. Particularly, the Ch'an and Zen schools of China and Japan found in such verses the inspiration for the creation of a new genre of religious literature, the aphoristic *kōans*, as well as a fresh way of looking at nature through highly symbolic forms of art, such as painting, rock-gardens, and flower arrangement, where every detail has a self-transcending significance.

Conclusion

The Tathāgata-garbha concept is a relatively late arrival into the Buddhist metaphysical pantheon. Most probably, it was brought in by converts from the Hindu educated strata, familiar with Vedic and Upaniṣadic cosmogonic speculations. One such myth of cosmic genesis spoke of a Golden Germ (Womb or Egg), named *hiraṇya-garbha*, from which all things were born. This ancient Vedic image re-emerged in the Buddhist Yogācāra texts, during the first centuries of our era, perhaps as a lay reaction to the hard-to-digest Nihilism of the Mādhyamika philosophers. By contrast, many scholars agree that the Tathāgata-garbha concept admits the possibility of at least two meanings: the containing and the contained. In the preceding sections, we had the opportunity to show that in the *Laṅkāvatāra-sūtra*, and other related texts, the term can appear in three different contexts, with three different meanings, namely as "Essence" of Buddhahood, as "Germ" (or "Embryo"), and as "Matrix" (or "Womb") of all things in the universe.

Now, the term was important in the development of Buddhist philosophy and religion for a number of reasons. First, from a purely *theoretical*, doctrinal point of view, it rekindled the old, yet ongoing 'Self versus non-Self' controversy, by providing the Yogācāras with a new, positive platform of defense against both the Hindu Eternalists and the Buddhist Nihilists. As we will see in the next chapter (ch. 1.2), the Yogācāras embraced the original Middle Way position of the Buddha against all extremes (i.e., the Personalists on one side, and the Abhidharma Nihilists on the other), by saying that the Self neither is, nor is not present among the five personality constituents (Skandhas).

Second, from the *practical* point of view, the Tathāgata-garbha could be used as an intermediary step in the process of meditation, half-way between the familiar Hindu concept of Self (Ātman) and the difficult to grasp Buddhist concept of non-Self (Anātman). The importance of the correct understanding of the non-Self concept in Buddhism cannot be understated. Let us remember that in the Indian religious traditions, Hindu, Buddhist, and Jain, the view of Self was perceived as inextricably bound to the larger view of the world, with the theory of Being and of Becoming. As a direct consequence of this fact, the understanding and the realization of the personal Self was believed to be tied in with, and to bestow upon one the mastery of the power of Being itself, in its cosmic dimensions.

Thus, the religious quest of Self-realization, the paramount goal of all the esoteric traditions of India, acquired a cosmic significance in the mind of the adept. For, by understanding correctly the nature of the Self, one could also gain insight into the nature of the universe itself. The Tathāgata-garbha concept afforded the disciple the opportunity to visualize the Self as the Embryo to be nurtured to fully-grown Buddhahood, the universe as an all-encompassing Matrix-of-Buddhahood, and all things partaking of the same Essence-of-Buddhahood, identified with the universal teaching of Buddhism (or Dharma). The effect of such visualizations would, of course, be the broadening of one's mental horizons, the weakening of one's attachment to a narrowly defined concept of Self, and eventually, the emergence of one's consciousness into the broad, indeed unlimited freedom of non-Self.

Furthermore, from the *ethical* point of view, the Tathāgata-garbha theory reinforced the new altruistic ethos of the Mahāyāna school, for it affirmed the claim to freedom and perfection for all beings, on account of the ever-present Buddha nature in all things, even "in the tiniest speck of dust." In contrast with other religious doctrines of both East and West, which focus more on the negative aspects of the human soul (such as, for example, the Original Sin), the Womb, or the Essence-of-Buddhahood concept, represents a strongly positive affirmation of the fundamental goodness of the world, and of all creatures contained therein.

This essential goodness of the universe, however, should not be regarded as a justification for a complacent and passive attitude towards the world, since it is balanced by the presence at the individual level of the Germ-of-Buddhahood, in ever-present need of nurturing and self-perfection. For, if the Essence-of-Buddhahood symbolizes the passive, static quality of the Dharma teaching, the Embryo represents its active, dynamic potential for growth and development. Thus, one may say that the Tathāgata-garbha signifies both the *source* and the final *aim* of spiritual strivings, according to Yogācāra Buddhism. That explains why so many other important Mahāyāna ideas were also drawn into its sphere of meaning, or sometimes even used as its synonyms (e.g., Dharmadhātu, Dharmakāya, Tathatā, Hetu, etc.).[48]

One such synonym, Ālaya-vijñāna (or the "Repository-of-impressions"), was a characteristic innovation of the Yogācāra school (see chapter 2.3. on the eightfold Vijñāna system, below). Nevertheless, its identification with the passive aspect of the Tathāgata-garbha concept (i.e., the Essence of pure dharmas) is not found in any other Vijñānavāda work prior to the *Laṅkāvatāra*, including those of Vasubandhu, the most prominent systematizer of the school.[49] Later, in China, this innovation was continued by the followers of the Avataṃsaka school as well, who further combined the Garbha theory with the Citta-Mātra (Mind-only) concept, yet another *Laṅkāvatāra* doctrinal hallmark.[50]

Last, but not least, let us also point out the unique insistence of the *Laṅkāvatāra* upon the primarily *didactic* function of the Tathāgata-garbha concept, as an intermediary stepping-stone toward the more difficult understanding of the non-Self doctrine (Anātman). For, to take the Garbha concept literally, that is, to believe in its real, ontological substance, would amount to confusing Tathāgata-garbha with the Hindu Ātman, or Self (the sin of believing in metaphysical Eternalism). According to the text, it should only be regarded as a tool, a teaching device, to be discarded once the goal of understanding of the true doctrine of non-Self has been reached. It is yet another demonstration of the Teacher's skill-in-means, a compassionate concern for the pupils' progress on the arduous path of knowledge and spiritual development.

Let us now shift our focus from the *essence* of Being, to the *temporal* manifestation of Being, the human personality, or the fivefold personality aggregates, in order to better understand the difference between Self and non-Self, according to Yogācāra Buddhism.

1.2. The Five Skandhas: the *Temporal* Manifestation of Being

Introduction

If Tathāgata-garbha symbolizes the *essence*, or the Germ of Buddhahood in Yogācāra Buddhism, the transcendental notion of Being which permeates all animated existence, the Skandhas represent its most conspicuous embodiment on the *temporal* plane of physical reality, the psycho-physical complex known as the human personality. This fivefold group of personality constituents, fused together in a dynamic river of energy, is the Buddhist equivalent of the Hindu-Brahmanical answer to the problem of Self, the concept of Ātman, which triggered a cluster of other issues related to human destiny, karma and transmigration, the nature of the world and of human salvation.

In the *Laṅkāvatāra-sūtra*, too, there are several strands of ideas connected with the group of five personality aggregates, namely: the problem of Selfhood, the issue of the Realized Being, the Tathāgata, the relation between the material and immaterial components of a being, the problem of transmigration, the Selfhood of inanimate objects, the interaction between life and matter, Being and Non-Being, subject and object, and so on. Therefore, a separate treatment of the most relevant ideas, or group of ideas, will be required. In addition, as we shall see, the Skandhas in the *Laṅkāvatāra-sūtra* are constantly compared with, and differentiated from the Hindu Ātman (or Pudgala), whose knowledge is taken for granted by the author of the *Sūtra*.

To better understand the nature of the Ātman-Skandhas controversy, a brief review of the relevant Brahmanic and early Buddhist literature on these important subjects will also be necessary. Thus, the highlighting of the doctrinal landmarks of the Self concepts within the historical background of Indian Buddhism will provide the substance of our first subsection.

The second and third subsections will focus specifically upon the analysis of the Five Skandhas in the *Laṅkāvatāra*, according to their two major divisions into the formative (*rūpa*) and formless (*nāma*) elements, or constituents of human personality. The last three subsections are organically related to the first three, in that they present the continuous elaborations of the Personality theory in the Mahāyāna schools, particularly Yogācāra. Each subsection highlights a particular aspect of the Skandhas theory, in relation to the personal or empirical self (*pudgala, ātman*), the transcendental or trans-empirical Self (the Tathāgata or the Realized Being, the Buddha), and the impersonal, abstract metaphysical principles (such as Being and non-Being, life and matter, subject and object, oneness and bothness, etc.), as distinguishable in our representative text, the *Laṅkāvatāra-sūtra*.

It is the contention of the writer that without an initial, historical review of the doctrinal disputations regarding the Self in the primitive Buddhist scriptures, the later, more complex arguments regarding the doctrine of non-Self (Anātman, and the Five Skandhas) —as found in the *Laṅkāvatāra* and elsewhere—could hardly be understood. Thus, the careful observer will not fail to notice that the argument sustained in the *Sūtra* is, in some meaningful way, connected with the view of the Self presented in the Pāli scriptures, which is considerably different from that of the later Abhidharmists.

Brief Overview of the Ātman Controversy Prior to the *Laṅkāvatāra-sūtra*

Unlike the Upaniṣadic Self (Ātman), which was said to be blissful (*ānanda*), imperishable and indestructible (*avināśī vā are 'yam ātmā an-ucchitti-dharmā, Bṛhadāraṇyaka Upaniṣad* 4. 5. 14), the Buddhists regarded the notion of Self merely as a convenient appelation used in lieu of the psycho-physical pentad (*rūpa* and *nāma-skandhas*), which was believed to be in constant change and transformation toward the ultimate dissolution brought about by death, or Nirvāṇa:

> For there is suffering, but none who suffers;
> Doing exists, although there is no doer;
> Extinction is, but no extinguished person;
> Although there is a path, there is no goer.

Thus spoke Buddhaghosa in *Visuddhi-Magga* 16. 90; and he concluded:[1]

So void of lastingness, and beauty, pleasure, self,
Is the first pair, and void of self the deathless state,
And void of lastingness, of pleasure and of self
Is the path, too; for such is voidness in these four.

These lines summarize a millenium-long tradition of resistance against the temptation to regard the common-sense perception of the unity of human personality as more than an illusion. In a sense, one could say that Buddhism is more orthodox, that is, more faithful to the Vedas, than is the Upaniṣadic tradition. For, the Vedas already contained the germ of a process ontology of sorts, when it asserted that the primal (and also the ultimate) condition of the universe is the amorphous state of "neither Being, nor Not-being" (*Ṛg-veda* 10. 129), appropriately symbolized by the unfathomable ocean, the cosmic egg, the golden embryo "which the waters bore" (*hiraṇya-garbha*), the windless energy (*svadha*), and so on.

The Upaniṣads, on the other hand, developed a static, 'substance' ontology, strongly revolving around the personal entity called *Ātman* or *Puruṣa*, like the universe around the Earth, in the archaic cosmologies. The idea of a primordial state of pure Being-ness is forcefully asserted in the fourth *Brāhmaṇa* of the *Bṛhadāraṇyaka Upaniṣad*, entitled "The Creation of the World from the Self" (1. 4. 1). It is well worth quoting, as it offers a strong contrast to the subsequent Buddhist development of the subject of Self, as we shall see later in this paper.[2]

> In the beginning this (world) was only the Self (*ātman*), in the shape of a person (*puruṣa-vidha*). Looking around he saw nothing else than the Self (*ātman*). He first said: 'I am.' Therefore arose the name of I. Therefore, even to this day when one is addressed he says first: 'This is I' and then speaks whatever other name he may have. Because before (*pūrva*) all this, he burnt (*auṣat*) all evils, therefore he is a person (*puruṣa*). He who knows this, verily, burns up him who wishes to be before him (*pūrvo bubhūṣati*).

Bearing in mind this view of the person as the crux of Upaniṣadic ontological and psychological thinking, which was influential in Buddha's time, we can better grasp the revolutionary dimension of Buddhist philosophy, which became the official worldview by the time of the Aśoka empire, barely two hundred years after the great Teacher's demise.

Official acceptance, however, does not usually have the power to automatically dissolve deep-seated beliefs that have long historical, literary, and folk traditions behind them. So, between the time of Aśoka (240 B.C.?) and that of the Yogācāra school, as reflected in the *Laṅkāvatāra* (4th century A.D.), a long and tortuous history of doctrinal disputes and rivalries followed.[3]

The ensuing controversies have their roots in the very questions that the Teacher left unanswered, such as the ultimate nature of Self, of Buddhahood, of Nirvāṇa, of the world. Thus, the question of the universal accessibility of Buddhahood split the Saṃgha during the first Council, while that pertaining to the nature of *attā* versus the *anatta* reached its peak around the time of the third Council, held under Aśoka's leadership at Pātaliputra (Patna) in the third century B.C. There, many of those who supported the Attā viewpoint (such as a certain very learned, but wicked brāhmaṇa, Vatsa of Kashmir) were not only expelled, but also killed.[4]

Subsequently, the Anatta doctrine came to be regarded as the only orthodox teaching adopted by the Sthaviras, or the Vibhajyavādins (lit., "Those who make distinctions"). The supporting evidence comes from both Aśoka's rock edicts condemning the dissent-causing monks (the Sarvāstivādins and the Pudgalavādins, those who believed in the reality of all dharmas, including the personhood, Pudgala),[5] as well as from various texts, the most important of which being the *Kātha-Vatthu* ("The Points of Controversy," or "Subjects of Discourse," the fifth of the seven books of the *Abhidhamma Piṭaka* of the Pāli canon). This apologetic work was written, according to the "Commentator's Introduction," for the purpose of "giving account of the soul (*attā*) and such points controverted" at the time of the third Aśokan Council, where "to avert all bases of heresy that had arisen," the Elder Tissa Moggali's son separated "by the method which had been delivered by the Master" five hundred orthodox statements from five hundred heterodox ones, thereby "purging religion of its stains."[6]

The book presents the points of view of the two major parties of that time, the Theravādins and the Puggalavādins, in the form of dialogues, interspersed with the author's own commentary.[7] The main thrust of the Theravādin argument went in the direction of forcing the opponent to admit that *puggala* (Sanskrit *pudgala*, i.e., "person"—the term that gradually replaced *attā* in the Abhidharmist literature) cannot be something different, as a "real and ultimate fact," than each of the fifty-seven "real and ultimate" *dhammas* that constitute the totality of our conscious experience, nor can it be the sum of all these taken together, for this would account for a composite (*saṃskṛta*), not ultimate (*asaṃskṛta*) reality.[8]

Apparently, the Personalists were not convinced by this argument, and returned the polemical fire by quoting the Teacher as saying that "there are (souls or) persons working for their own good," which would imply continuity of personality. A counter-quote was then presented by the Theravādins from the *Sutta-Nipāta* (1116), which records the following words of the Buddha to a disciple: "Consider, Mogharāja, that the world is empty of soul (*attā*)." At this point, the commentator inserts his own thoughts, albeit in a somewhat neutral, philosophical tone:[9]

> Hence, by the quotation, it is as easy to deny soul (*puggalo nātthi*) as to affirm it (*puggalo atthi*), or to say: 'that which exists not is all persons' (*nātthi sabbo puggalo*) as to say that 'that which exists is not all persons' (*atthi na sabbo puggalo*).

The meaning of these enigmatic words is clarified in conjunction with the Personalist assertion that although there is a clear line between Being (*atthi*) and non-Being (*nātthi*), not all existent things are persons (i.e., have independent being, or *atthi*):[10]

> Theravādin: Is the person something that is, and conversely?
> Personalist: Nay, that cannot truly be said . . .
>
> Theravādin: Does the person exist, and conversely?
> Personalist: The person exists. Conversely, of the existent, some is person, some is not person.
>
> Theravādin: Does 'person' mean a reality and conversely?
> Personalist: 'Person' is a reality. Conversely, 'reality' means in part person, in part not person.

Far from being gratuitous, the subtleties of this dialogue are directed to a specific target, namely to bridge the apparently contradictory statements of the Teacher into a coherent ontology, agreeable to all factions, so that the split of the Saṃgha could be healed and the Order prosper, unhindered by internal dissension. But, as is often the case, the wish for unity did not materialize beyond the level of polite discussion at best, and later we find a whole chapter of Vasubandhu's *Abhidharmakośa* (9) devoted to the same topic: the refutation of the heretical Ātmavāda doctrine. Indeed, with the passing of time, the polemic on this subject—far from diminishing—became even more complex, especially when other schools of thought opened new lines of inquiry with new terminology.

Thus, the cumbersome issue of continuity of personal identity over a life-span (memory, habits), as well as before and after it (rebirth, transmigration, karma), received a number of hypothetical solutions, none of which proved satisfactory enough to overcome the others and settle the dispute once and for all. The orthodox Abhidharmist position was, in fact, also the most vulnerable. Its roots branched out into certain canonical passages regarded as highly authoritative, although subject to interpretation, such as this from the *Saṃyutta-Nikāya* 3. 127:[11]

> With regard to these five groups (*khandhas*), I do not find any Ego (*attā*), or something "belonging to an Ego" (*attāniya*) . . . I am no longer subject to the thoughts of "I am," or "This I am."

Having taken Buddha's words literally, the Abhidharmists rejected out-of-hand any counter-evidence and as a result, they fell an easy prey to the annihilationist trap. Their contention in regard to the idea of transmigration (*saṅkanti*), in order to be consistent with the Khandhas theory (as per Buddhaghosa, *Visuddhi-Magga* 16), was that "it is the wandering (*saṃsāra*) which wanders," a nonsensical statement, according to Professor E. Conze.[12]

At some point, the Theravādins put forward the theory of a 'life-continuum' (*bhāvaṅga*). which was said to be subconscious to a certain degree.[13] The idea of a "continuous existence of a very subtle consciousness" had already been embraced by the Sautrāntikas, while another important Buddhist school, the Mahāsaṅghikas, argued in favor of a basic (*mūla*) consciousness, the seat of karmic accumulations.[14] Hence, the Yogācāras' metaphysical constructions, such as the Receptacle-of-perceptions (or, the Store-consciousness, Ālaya-vijñāna), the Sphere-of-Dharma(s) (Dharmadhātu), the Body-of-Dharma (Dharmakāya), Thusness (Tathatā), the incorruptible 'pure seeds' (*anāsrava-bījas*, or the *āryadharmas*), and so on.[15]

We have pointed out above that the Puggalavādins' position was that "the person is neither identical, nor different from the Khandhas." In contrast, other Samatiya groups (such as the Sautrāntikas, the Vatsiputriyas, or the Avantakas) supported their belief in the persistence of a personality core (the 'seeds of goodness', which lead one to Nirvāṇa) by invoking Buddha's words as recorded by Vasubandhu in the *Abhidharmakośa*, which says: "I see this extremely subtle seed of salvation like a seam of gold hidden in metal-bearing rock."[16]

The more one tries to comprehend the kaleidoscopic variety of the proposed solutions to the Anatta concept, the more one is inclined to agree with Theodore Stcherbatsky that "the whole of the history of Buddhist philosophy can be described as a series of attempts to penetrate more deeply into this original intuition of the Buddha, what he himself believed to be his great discovery."[17] One of the most poignant, if not the clearest expressions of this intuition is found in the *Dīgha-Nikāya* 1. 31. 1 (repeated also in 32. 4; 34. 1 & ff.):[18]

> Some Brāhmaṇas maintain, in 16 ways, that the soul after death is conscious (*sannim attānam*) . . . some maintain, in 8 ways, that the soul after death is not subject to decay, and inconscious (*asannim attānam*); others maintain, in 7 ways, the theory of annihilation . . .

After having considered all these doctrines, without committing himself to any, the Buddha, elsewhere, denies having preached "the disintegration, destruction, and extirpation of existing creatures," that is Annihilationism (Ucchedavāda) (*Majjhima-Nikāya* 1. 140).

On the other hand, however, he also states that when an Arhat (or a 'truth-finder', a Tathāgata) "is thus delivered, not Indra or Brahmā or Prajāpati, with all their trains of gods, can succeed in tracking down aught on which depends a truth-finder's consciousness (*viññāna*). And why? Because, say I, already, here and now, the truth-finder is untraceable."[19] This idea is also stated in the *Dhammapāda* 2. 1. 57: "With minds by perfect knowledge freed, No track or path the Slayer [i.e., Māra, the god of death] finds."[20]

But still, what is the fate of the individual consciousness in the case of the ignorant, who—according to Buddhist doctrine—will be subject to rebirth in a future existence? The most respected spokesman of the orthodox Abhidharma tradition, Buddhaghosa, gives a rather ambiguous explanation in that regard (*Visuddhi-Magga* 17. 163):[21]

> (When) the body, like a green palm-leaf exposed to the sun, dries up by degrees . . . then consciousness residing in that last refuge, the heart, continues to exist by virtue of *karma*, otherwise called predispositions. This *karma*, however, still retains something of what it depends on, and consists of such former deeds as were weighty . . . ; or else this *karma* creates a reflex of itself, or of the new mode of life now being entered upon, and it is with this as its object that consciousness continues to exist . . . in as much as desire and ignorance have not been abandoned.

In other words, according to Buddhaghosa, it is karma which transmigrates, the deeds independent from the doer who performed them. He says: "Ignorance (through deeds) causes karma, and karma (through transmigration) causes consciousness" (*Visuddhi-Magga* 17. 41).[22] It is worth mentioning, however, as a number of noted authorities have pointed out, the fact that the Buddha himself taught nothing on the doctrine of Rebirth to begin with, since it contradicted his fundamental theory of non-Self ("all things are passing away," *sabbe dhammā anattā*).[23] Jennings, for instance, has indicated that the only word alluding to rebirth found in the famous first sermon, the *Dhammacakkappavatana-sutta* (which is *ponobbavika*, lit., "causing re-existence"), is a later interpolation that fits badly in the context.[24]

Buddhaghosa, however, in an attempt to pull the orthodoxy away from the Annihilationist trap, which would make it succumb to the attacks of its opponents, revived and tailored to his purpose the classical doctrine of the two Nirvāṇas, with and without defilements.[25] Although his solution was as debatable from the Pudgalavādin point of view as any of the Buddha's own utterances on the subject, it had at least the practical advantage of preserving the most-cherished Anatta doctrine, while offering a compromise rooted in the solid ground of tradition. In addition, it also came half-way to the then very influential Śūnyavādin position, which asserted—as Ninian Smart puts it—"that all views about reality are contradictory, while the positive teachings of the Buddha, for example about the 'groups' (as part of his Anatta doctrine), are intended only as a thesis that has to be transcended."[26]

Now, all later doctrinal developments, such as those elaborated by the Mādhyamika, Yogācāra, and even the Vajravāda (Tantric) school of Tibet, share in a common ideological nucleus, the doctrine of universal Voidness (Śūnyatā). This—as Professor Stcherbatsky pointed out—is but the old theory of the insubstantiality of the Self writ large (i.e., expanded to cosmic proportions), with a renewed emphasis upon the teaching of Dependent Origination (Paṭiccasamuppāda).[27] And yet, the exponents of the Śūnyavāda doctrine had to defend themselves constantly against the accusations of Nihilism. "We are Relativists, not Negativists!" wrote Candrakīrti in the sixth century.[28] In that, he followed faithfully the principles laid down by his teacher, Nāgārjuna, in his influential *Mūla-mādhyamika-kārikās*, where he said (ch. 18, v. 6):[29]

> The Buddhas have disclosed the (idea of) *ātman*, and they also taught the (truth of) *anātman;* and yet, neither Self, nor non-Self whatsoever has been taught by the Buddhas.

We shall now see to what extent the position adopted by the author of the *Laṅkāvatāra-sūtra* is consistent with, or differs from the traditional Buddhist teachings regarding the Self, as summarized above.

Rūpa, or the Formative Elements of the Five Skandhas

Beginning with the Pāli utterances, such as the oft-quoted *sabbe dhammā anattā* (*Dhammapāda*, v. 279) and ending with the celebrated simile of the chariot from the extra-canonical writings (*Milinda-pañha* 25. 1), the idea of non-Self (Anatta), became the most distinctly Buddhist concept from the point of view of the outsiders, and probably the most fiercely debated one within the Buddhist community itself. To account for the phenomenal unity of the human personality, or Self, an alternative explanation was needed. Hence, the 'bundle' of personality factors, or constituents: the five Khandhas (Sanskrit, Skandhas). This psycho-physical pentad was not purely descriptive. It also fulfilled a soteriological function, for it helped the novice learn how to dissociate himself from each and every factor which accounts for the misperceptions of one's own continuous existence. Thus, the *Saṃyutta-Nikāya* 3. 45:

> If a monk's *citta* is not attached to the element of form (feeling, perception, activities, consciousness), and is released from the obsessions without basis, then by its release it is steadfast; by its steadfastness it is content; being content it does not become excited; free from excitement it attains *nibbāna* by itself.

Now, the term *khandha* can also be found in the Upaniṣads, albeit only twice (in the *Chāndogya Upaniṣad* 2. 2. 3 and the *Maitrī Upaniṣad* 7. 11), according to C. A. F. Rhys Davids, having the general meaning of 'body' of doctrine, and of 'mass' of smoke, respectively.[30] This word evokes a peculiar blend of static and dynamic qualities, as described in the *Psalms of the Sisters* (v. 69, 43), and of the *Brethren* (1255):[31]

> She taught me the Norm, wherein I learnt
> The factors, organs, bases of this self—
> Impermanent compound.

These "factors" (Khandhas) of personality are usually translated as "aggregates," "elements," "classes," "groups," or "heap" of qualities, or constituents.[32] They are of two kinds: material (*rūpa*) and mental, or immaterial (*nāma, arūpin*). The latter are further subdivided into four categories pertaining to specific activities of the mind, such as: sensation or emotions (*vedanā*), perceptions (*saññā*), volition, predispositions, or impulses (*saṅkhāra*), and cognition or consciousness (*viññāna*).[33]

A comprehensive presentation of the *rūpa* elements is given in the *Māha-Hatthi-Padopama-sūtta* of the *Majjhima-Nikāya*, where Sariputta speaks about the attachment to visible shapes. The realm of visible forms is here explained as being constituted of the four principal elements, that is, water, fire, wind, and earth.[34] Each of these can be either personal or external (to the physical person). Through a detailed analysis of all possible identifications with such elements, or with their adjectival derivatives (that is, fluidity, heat, breath, and solidity, respectively), Sariputta arrives at the conclusion that no self-identification is acceptable with the physical substances, on account of their continuous transformation:

> The right way to regard this as it really is . . . is to say: "This is not mine, this is not I, this is no self of mine . . . (for) . . . No 'I' is here, no 'mine,' no 'I am,'—nothing at all."[35]

Now, the author of the *Laṅkāvatāra* must have been quite familiar with this sort of ratiocination, for a similar presentation of the 'gross' material elements (*mahābhūtas*) and their secondary derivatives (*bhautikas*) is found in the text (*Laṅkā* II: 124; ll. 2-10):

> Now, Mahāmati, which are the secondary elements derived from (*bhautikas*) the gross elements (*mahābhūtas*)? They are said to be the following:
>
> The gross element discriminated as moisture, Mahāmati, issues forth the element of water (*abdhātu*), inner and outer.
>
> The gross element discriminated as fiery energy, Mahāmati, brings about the element of fire (*tejodhātu*), inner and outer.
>
> The gross element discriminated as mobility, Mahāmati, produces the element of wind (*vāyudhātu*), inner and outer.
>
> The gross element discriminated as the divisibility of form, again Mahāmati, gives birth to the element of earth (*pṛthivīdhātu*), together with (the element of) space (*ākāśa*), inner and outer.
>
> (However), it is (only) because of the attachment to the imaginary [or, incorrect, *mithyā*] truths (such as) the multitude

[or bundle] of the five personality aggregates (*skandhas*), that (the notion of) the primary (gross) and secondary (derivative) elements arises.

We have pointed out that the Pāli scriptures rejected the identification between the Skandhas and the individual Self on account of their impermanence. Here is an example of the ancient argument which can be found throughout the Pāli canon with only minor modifications (*Saṃyutta-Nikāya* 4. 54; also in *Vinaya-Piṭaka, Mahā-vagga* 1. 6. 38f; 1. 13f; 1. 21, etc.):

> Our physical form, feeling, perception, impulses, and consciousness are all transitory, and therefore not permanent (and not good). That which is transitory, suffering, and liable to change, is not the eternal soul. So, it must be said of all physical forms whatever past, present, or to be; subjective or objective; far or near; high or low: "This is not mine, this I am not, this is not my eternal soul."

The Yogācāra writer carries this line of argumentation one step further to include the physical elements themselves, in as far as they represent mere imaginary constructs devised by naive minds trying to freeze an unstable reality into artificial categories of thought, by means of naming. For, the names we use become meaningless when we consider the natural fact that what we call "fire" can quickly disappear into thin "air," which may turn into "water," which is dissipated into "earth," which again—as solid matter—may be burnt as coal, or wood, by means of "fire," scattered by the "wind," and so on . . . In addition, according to Buddhism, supernatural elements may also intervene in this cyclical process of causation. Thus, the following explanation of human genesis is given in *Laṅkā* II: 124; ll. 10-16:

> Further, Mahāmati, as to the Sense-consciousness, because it is the cause of attachment to sense-objects at various levels, the Sense-consciousness proceeds to union with another destiny.
>
> O yes, Mahāmati, indeed there is an instrumental cause (on account of) the secondary and primary elements of earth, but (the Sense-consciousness itself) does not belong to the primary elements.
>
> Why so? Because it is this way:
>
> The characteristics of a living thing [*bhāva-liṅga*, state of

> being, concrete state, embodiment] of those that have union with the shape being chosen (acquired) are due to the occurrence of the coitus of the parents, but this does not take place when there is no presence of a subtle body [getting embodied in a concrete state of a living thing, *bhāva-liṅga*].
>
> Therefore, Mahāmati, this [i.e., living thing, *bhāva-liṅga*] is sought after by the heretics in the characteristics of the secondary and primary elements, but not so by me.

This passage attempts to elucidate the mysteries of human birth, and by implication, the mystery of life itself. While the coarse elementary particles, or primary elements (*mahābhūtas*), are evidently present in all animate life, life itself represents the outcome of a complex interplay between the primary and secondary, or derivative factors (*bhautikas*), as well as the immaterial factors, such as the shape of an intermediate state of being known as *gandharva* (Pāli, *gandhabba*), seeking its embodiment.[36] This explanation is consistent with the Buddhist tradition, as first explained in the *Assalāyanasutta* of the *Majjhima-Nikāya:* "We do know, sir, how there is conception. There is here a coitus of the parents,it is the mother's season and the *gandhabba* is present; it is on the conjunction of these three things that there is conception."[37]

Now, having considered the process by which the personality aggregates come into existence, and the important role played by the formative elements (*rūpa, bhūta, bhautika*) in this process, the author goes next to analyzing the more imponderable, formless elements (*nāma*) of the personality compound (i.e., *nāma-rūpa*). We shall pursue our investigation along the same lines.

Nāma, or the Formless Elements of the Five Skandhas

According to Vasubandhu's *Abhidharmakośa*, Chapter 3, 30a, "*nāma* is the aggregates (*skandha*) that are not *rūpa*."[38] As Professor Wayman points out, however, this use of the compound *nāma-rūpa* for the five personality constituents is of later, Upaniṣadic origin, and it is not encountered within the old Vedas, where they are treated separately.[39] That such a twofold division of the Skandhas came only later in Buddhism as well, can be seen from the fact that in the *Laṅkāvatāra* (whose older portions precede Vasubandhu's works) the first aggregate is separated from the other four by means of the expressions *rūpa* (having form) and *arūpin* (without material form), and not by means of the *nāma-rūpa* compound. So we read in *Laṅkā* II: 124-25; ll. 17-18, 1-4:

Furthermore, Mahāmati, I will explain what characterizes the self-nature of the personality aggregates. Now, Mahāmati, what are the five personality constituents? They are: form, sensation, perception, volition, and cognition. Further, Mahāmati, four of these personality constituents have no (material) form (*arūpin*)—sensation, perception, volition and cognition. Form (*rūpa*), Mahāmati, belongs to what is made of the four primary elements, and these elements are different from one another in their characteristics (*vilakṣaṇas*).

Having denied ontological reality to the four primary elements and to their derivatives, the author turns next to the formless aggregates (*arūpin-skandhas*), which—the text points out—are even more elusive for those who seek a firm basis for self-identification. In this respect, the *Laṅkāvatāra-sūtra* is in full agreement with the earlier scriptures, such as the *Sutta-Nipāta* of the *Mahā-vagga*, which says:[40]

anattani attamāniṃ passa lokaṃ sadevakaṃ /
niviṭṭhaṃ nāmarūpasmim idam saccan ti maññati //

The world—both men and gods—seeing the non-Self as Self,
devoted to name-and-formation deems this as 'true.'

This is explained in the *Mahā-vagga* 1. 6. 38 to mean that:[41]

As respects all sensation whatsoever . . . as respects all perception whatsoever . . . as respects all predispositions—past, future, or present, be it subjective or existing outside, gross or subtile, mean or exalted, far or near—the correct view in the light of the highest knowledge is as follows: 'This is not mine; this am I not; this is not my Ego.'

The same position is presented in the *Laṅkāvatāra*, with the added argument that the formless constituents differ from the formative one (*rūpa*), like space from the physical matter which it surrounds, and, just like space, they are not subject to precise computation, lacking reckoning marks. Hence, they are also removed from the dualities of Being and non-Being, sameness and otherness, and so on. As a result, they are nothing more that a product of constructive imagination, like images seen in a dream, or a vision. Thus *Laṅkā* II: 125; ll. 4-15:

> But, Mahāmati, the reckoning of the four formless [aggregates, *arūpin*] is like (the reckoning of) space. For, Mahāmati, as the space cannot be described through reckoning, and it is (only due to our) imagination that space is (perceived) as such, likewise, Mahāmati, the personal aggregates which are beyond (exact) computation, as they have no reckoning marks, are exempt from (the categories of) Being and non-Being, and removed from the four alternatives; (and yet) they are being thought by the immature (as endowed with) the certainty of (precise) computation; not so by the wise.
>
> Again, Mahāmati, by the wise ones (the *skandhas*) are regarded as free from the (duality of) otherness and non-otherness, being like the manifold (or various) constructions and figures, like people and images in a dream (*svapna*), or in a vision (*māyā*).
>
> As they have nothing inherent on which to depend [i.e., for their independent existence], and as they obscure the passage of Noble Wisdom, there is, Mahāmati, what is known as the imagination of the personality aggregates. This is, Mahāmati, what characterizes the self-nature of the (five) personality constituents. And this imagination is to be rejected, and having turned away from it, you should declare the teaching of the truth of solitude [or purity, *vivikta*].

This long passage is concluded with an equally long exhortation concerning the practical implications of this freedom from the belief in and the tyranny of metaphysical constructs (such as Self, non-Self, material or formless Skandhas, etc.). The *Sūtra* says (*Laṅkā* II: 125-26; ll. 15-18, 1-5):

> With the teaching of the truth of solitude, Mahāmati, the views of the heretics are to be kept off among the multitudes of the assemblies of all the Buddhas and—having done so—the teaching of the egolessness of (all) *dharmas* is purified and the entrance upon the stage of the Far-going takes place.
>
> He who (does this) becomes the master of many Samādhis, entering upon the great stage of the Far-reaching. And from realizing the body made of mind, the Samādhi (known as the) Māyā-like is reached. Thoroughly progressing and unrestrained through his (own) psychic faculties and powers, he (the Bodhisattva) becomes like the earth, the supporter of all beings.

> As the great earth, Mahāmati, is the supporter of all (sentient) beings, and exactly so, Mahāmati, is the Bodhisattva, the great being (and) the supporter of all beings.

This exhortation ends on a strongly ethical note which emphasizes not only the reality of the external world, but also the supreme duty of the Realized Being to bestow his hard-won virtues back upon the world.

The Skandhas and the Empirical Self, or Personality

In the *Abhidharmakośa* (4, 71c-d), Vasubandhu warns against taking the *nāma-rūpa* as the object of false views. But the *Laṅkāvatāra-sūtra* was first (since its main ideas must have preceded the actual compilation of the text) to express the theoretical position (distinct from that of the Abhidharmists), namely that the Skandhas were "neither the same, nor different" (*nānyo nānanyaḥ*) from the individual person, or self. The common denominator of all the passages in the *Laṅkāvatāra* relative to the fivefold psycho-physical complex is precisely this denial of both sameness *and* difference between the aggregates and whatever larger entity they were credited to constitute in their totality. For, although the essence of the argument is similar, the terms vary to include not only the personal self (*pudgala, ātman*), but also that of the Tathāgatas (presumably transcendental, or immaterial), as well as such abstract principles as Being and non-Being, life and matter, subject and object, oneness and otherness.

Thus, the already thorny problem regarding the proper relation between the five Skandhas and the self which greatly preoccupied the minds of the early Buddhist philosophers, became even more complex as the scope of the debates grew to include the transcendental notions mentioned above. In addition, the ontic domain covered by the Skandhas in later literature has also been broadened through the introduction of new categories, such as the eighteen *dhātu*s (realms or spheres) and the twelve *āyatana*s (bases or abodes), with which the aggregates became increasingly associated.[42]

In the *Laṅkāvatāra*, ch. III: 146-47; ll. 17, 1, is written the following:

> The personality aggregates, the realms and the bases, by succeeding and combining (with one another), having disappeared, now they are returning . . .

These lines show that by the time the *Laṅkāvatāra* was compiled (c. fourth century A.D.), a certain kind of ontology had developed—one in which *processes,* not entities, predominate, and the separating lines between phenomena, be they internal or external (to the person), is rather diffuse and constantly shifting. Let us now see how the argument is presented from the vantage point of this new ontological perspective.

First, we shall look at the relation between the Skandhas and the Self (the Self being here alternately referred to either by the term *ātman,* or *pudgala*). The most clearly stated passages are found among the gāthas of the last, and somewhat apocryphal chapter, the *Sagāthakam,* where it is said (pp. 358-59, vv. 752-61):

> The Buddha is neither the personality-soul (*pudgala*), nor the personality aggregates (*skandhas*); he is knowledge free from defilement(s). Clearly perceiving (him) to be eternally serene, I take refuge (in him).
>
> The best of speakers points out that the originally clear mind (*citta*), along with the defilements, (such as) pride, etc., are united within the Self (*ātman*).[43]
>
> The originally pure mind is certainly different from that pride, etc.; but since karmic accretions are piled up by those (defilements), the result is that both (*citta* and defilements) are tarnished.
>
> The clear Self has been soiled by primal and adventitious defilements and (therefore) is regarded like a soiled garment which has been washed off.
>
> As the destruction of dust in a garment, or as the gold is free from its impurities, they (the garment and the gold) are not destroyed (completely), but remain as they are (clean, pure); so is the Self (*ātman*) freed from its defilements.
>
> Now, as an exquisite sound is produced in a lute, a conch-shell, and in a kettle-drum, so would an unskilled person seek something of a personal entity (*pudgala*) among the personality aggregates (*skandhas*).
>
> As one tries to find jewels in the earth, in water, and also in the treasure-house, so (do they seek for) the personal entity in the personality constituents.
>
> As the unskilled do not understand the mind, the bundle of mental elements, and their functions connected with the

personality constituents, so (they cannot find) the personal entity (*pudgala*) among the personal aggregates (*skandhas*).

Indeed, as the womb cannot be seen by the woman who feels it, in the very same manner he who lacks wisdom cannot see the Self (*ātman*) among the personality aggregates (*skandhas*).

Like the power of the medicinal herb, or like the fire in the kindling, so those without wisdom do not see the personal entity (*pudgala*) within the personality constituents (*skandhas*).

In so far as the Self is said not to reside among the Skandhas, the *Laṅkāvatāra* argument presented above falls along the orthodox tradition of the Abhidharmists (Anātman). But in so far as the personal Self (*ātman*) is said to be somehow associated with the Skandhas (their sum total minus the adventitious impurities, the *kleśas*, or *doṣas*), the position adopted in the *Laṅkāvatāra* sides with the Pudgalavādin school. To better understand the difference, let us recall a frequently invoked argument against the Absolutist position of the Abhidharmists, which was used from old by this factional school of the Personalists. The argument is laid out in "Burden-Sutra 22" (the *Bharam-sutta* of the *Saṃyutta-Nikāya* 1, repeated in the *Khandha-saṃyutta* and the *Khandha-vagga*), where the Teacher is said to have uttered this:[44]

A burden indeed are the five compound (aggregates, or *khandhas*), and the bearer of the burden is the individual (*puggala*).

The taking of the burden in the world is sorrow (*dukkha*)
The laying down of the burden is bliss (*sukha*).

He who lays down the heavy burden,
And does not grasp at any other,
Having eradicated craving (*tanha*)
Being without longing, he is completely at peace
(*parinibbuta*).

Here, a clear attempt is made to differentiate between the individual, person, or ego (*puggala*), and its various determinants, with which it is usually identified (*khandhas*). The goal of the Buddhist adept, or the 'burden-bearer' (*Aṅguttara-Nikāya* 1. 22 and 9. 259), was to lay down the burden, that is, "to eradicate craving," to detach himself from the five compounds, whose essential mark is transitoriness.

Does this imply that there was, beyond the five ephemeral aggregates, some kind of permanent entity waiting to be liberated from the heavy burden? Not in the least, claimed the orthodox Abhidharmists, for the preceding Khandhas oppress the subsequent ones, and are therefore the burden, the latter being the Bearer of the burden (*Abhidharmakośa*, 9. 257). "Yes and no," replied the Pudgalavādins, arguing that "the Person is neither identical with the Khandhas, nor is he in the Khandhas, nor outside them," and he (the Person) "can be conceived in correlation with the Khandhas which have been appropriated at any given time inwardly" (*Abhidharmakośa*, 9. 233).[45]

That is to say, according to an explanation given by Professor Conze, the Person (Skt.: *pudgala*) does not disappear with the flashing of the various skandha-moments (which is proven by the persistence of memory and habits), nor does he subsist eternally, attributeless and without any connection with the Skandhas (or at least some of them).[46]

To be sure, a categorical denial of the individual entity, or Self, is rather foreign to the spirit of the early discourses of the Master, who—according to the Pāli texts—consistently refused to commit himself to either the Eternalist (Sassatavāda), or the Nihilist (Ucchedavāda) point of view. That this was so is made crystal clear in two celebrated instances, in which the Buddha replies to the question of the existence of the individual entity apart from the five aggregates in two different ways, according to the inquirer's own level of understanding. Thus, a first answer is given to the feeble-minded Vacchagotta through silence. As the Teacher subsequently explains to the puzzled Ānanda, his favorite disciple, the silence was sufficient to refute both of the extreme views that arose in the mind of those limited to the common-sense, dual logic of: the Self either is, or is not (*Saṃyutta-Nikāya* 4. 400f.; 3. 99; *Udana* 67).[47]

A second, and more sophisticated answer is given to the venerable Malukya (*Cūla-Malukya-Ovada-sutta* in the *Majjhima-Nikāya* 1. 427f.),[48] where by making use of the "Four-cornered Negation" (the tetralemma, *catuṣkoṭi* logic),[49] the Buddha—in the suggestive words of Dr. Herman Oldenberg—"closes up all joints and loopholes, by which the true facts of the case might escape being caught in the logical net:"[50]

> What have I said to thee before now, Malukyaputta? Have I said: '. . . I shall teach thee, whether the vital faculty is identical with the body or separate from it? Whether the Perfect One lives on after death or does not live on, or whether the Perfect

One lives on and at the same time does not live on after death, or whether he neither lives on nor does not live on?'

This purposeful evasiveness of the Buddha in regard to the ultimate questions, is further justified by his thoroughly practical, non-speculative approach to the problems of the human condition, aiming not at the continual stimulation and unrest of thought, but rather at its appeasement, its passionlessness, tranquillity, liberation, Nirvāṇa (*Majjhima-Nikāya* 1. 431). When prevailing over the facts of experience, the speculative views—such as the unwarranted insistence upon one of the six wrong outlooks: "I have a Self; I have not a Self; by Self I perceive Self; by Self I perceive non-Self; by non-Self I perceive Self; by non-Self I perceive non-Self,"[51]—are all just as "unprofitable and not fundamental to the higher life," are as irrelevant as questions regarding the archer's social status or the technology employed for the production of arrows are for a man transfixed by a poisoned arrow (see *Majjhima-Nikāya* 1. 429).

"Therefore, Malukyaputta," concludes the Master, "whatsoever has not been revealed by me, let that remain unrevealed, and what has been revealed, let it be revealed" (*Majjhima-Nikāya* 1. 432).

These two different answers lead us to believe, in concordance with most authorities on this subject (Conze, Dutt, Oldenberg, Poussin, Rhys Davids, Robinson, Stcherbatsky, Thomas, Trenckner, Wayman), that initially nothing was taught dogmatically one way or the other, and only later the balance was tipped (by the Abhidharmists) toward the notion of synonymity between the five Skandhas and the Anātman (non-Self).[52] Undoubtedly, the personal preference of the two great commentators, Buddhaghosa (*Visuddhi-Māgga* 14. 218) and Vasubandhu (*Abhidharmakośa*, ch. 9), or rather their misapprehension of the original intent of the Buddha (which was thoroughly undogmatic, as indicated), played a significant role in the subsequent depersonalizing tendency of the Abhidharmists.[53]

Their position is pursued to the limit by the followers of the Śūnyavāda-Mādhyamika school of Mahāyāna. In spite of their persistent denials, the absolutization of the doctrine of Voidness (Śūnyatā) brings them in fact dangerously close to their being viewed by the Yogācāras as Nihilists. This is clearly seen from a careful reading of the *Laṅkāvatāra* discussion of the existence of Self in relation to the five aggregates. Thus, the *Laṅkā* X: 359, vv. 762-771 (*Sagāthakam* chapter):

Trying to find permanency and voidness in all things, the unenlightened cannot see (them); likewise, (they cannot see) the personal entity (*pudgala*) among the aggregates (*skandha*s).

For, truly if there is no personal entity (*ātman*) there are no (Bodhisattva) stages, no psychic abilities, no highest initiation, and no excellent Samādhi.

If a (Buddhist) Nihilist, having come around, would say: "If that (Self) exists, let it be shown (proven)!" He, the wise man, should reply: "Your own discrimination [*svavikalpa*, i.e., between Self and non-Self] made it visible (clear)!"

Those who propound the doctrine of non-Self are to be shunned in the religious rites of the monks, and not to be spoken to, for they are offenders of the Buddhist doctrines, having embraced the dual views of Being and non-Being [existence and non-existence].

The doctrine of the Self shines brilliantly; it is like the rising of the apocalyptic fire [lit., the fire of the end of the world, *yuga-anta-agni*], burning up the forest of Self-lessness, wiping away the faults of the heretics.

Molasses, sugar-cane, sugar, and honey; sour milk, sesame oil, and ghee—each of them is found (to have) its own taste; but one who has not tasted it, cannot conceive it.

Likewise the Self being taken to be fivefold in the accumulation of the personality aggregates, the ignorant cannot see it, but the wise having seen it, are liberated.

By means of illustrations provided by the sciences, etc., the (nature of the) mind is not accurately determined [i.e., it cannot be measured precisely]; whither, from which, and what meaning has the sum (of mental phenomena)?—That cannot (accurately) be determined.

Indeed, things (*dharmas*) have different characteristics, but the mind is one (*cittam ekaṃ*)—this is not (properly) understood among the (speculative) philosophers (who imagine it) as causeless (*ahetu*) and unevolving (*apravṛtti*); (thus) one becomes attached [to the notion of personal Self].

But when the Yogin reflects upon the mind, he does not see the mind in the mind; the perceiving (*paśyaka*) is produced by the perceived [or, what is seen, *dṛśya*]. (For), what is seen (by the mind) (*dṛśya*)—how is (its) rising, and what is (its) cause [i.e., if not the external world which causes the sight]?

If these gāthas are not interpreted as an attack against the rival Mahāyāna school of the Śūnyavāda, they would, indeed, seem very confusing in the light of those immediately preceding, which (as we have seen) forcefully deny the presence of the Self among the Skandhas. In two notes appended to gāthas 764 and 765 of his translation of the *Laṅkāvatāra-sūtra* (Boulder: 1978, pp. 283-84), D. T. Suzuki writes the following:

> The statements so far made here regarding an ego-soul (*ātman* or *pudgala*) as they stand seem to contradict one another, and some really violate the Buddhist doctrine of Non-ātman as far as we know. (p. 283, n. 1)
>
> . . . It is not easy to determine the purport of these verses as they stand all by themselves without any explanatory prose. In fact these verses in the *Sagāthakam* which have no direct connection with the main text, except those that are quite obvious in meaning, are mostly difficult to know precisely what they intend to signify. (p. 284, n. 1)

But the verses aim precisely at dispelling both extreme views, namely: (a) that the Self is the same as the Skandhas (i.e., the Eternalist position forcefully rejected by the Hīnayānists through the doctrine of Anatta (Skt.: Anātman) and presented here in gāthas 752-61), and (b) that the Self cannot be accounted for, since all dharmas are void, including the Skandhas, *sarvabhāveṣu śūnyatāṃ* (i.e., the Nihilist position attributed to the Śūnyavādins and rejected by the Yogācāras). This will be made clear in the next section of this presentation, which deals with the relationship between the Skandhas and the Tathāgata. For now, let us mention only in passing that this neutral position taken by the *Laṅkāvatāra* (between the two extremes) is rather unique in its clarity. For even Asaṅga's own view regarding the Self, which carries the weight of his authority as the founder of the Yogācāra school, seems to have been closer to the Mādhyamika Nihilism than to the middle position expressed in the *Laṅkāvatāra*. To wit, here are the first three verses of Asaṅga's treatise, the *Paramārtha-gāthā*, as translated by A. Wayman in *Buddhist Insight* (Delhi: 1984), 335:

1. svāmī na vidyate kaścin na kartā nāpi vedakaḥ /
   dharmāḥ sarve 'pi niśceṣṭā atha ced vartate kriyā //

   There is no proprietor at all, no doer, no feeler;
   Although all the *dharmas* are inactive, yet possible activity evolves.

2. dvādaśaiva bhavāṅgāni skandhāyatanadhātavaḥ /
vicintya sarvāṇy etāni pudgalo nopalabhyate //

The twelve members of phenomenal life are the aggregates (*skandhas*), sense bases (*āyatanas*), and realms (*dhātus*). Pondering all those, a person (*pudgala*) is not found.

3. śūnyam ādhyātmikaṃ sarvaṃ śūnyaṃ sarvaṃ bahirgataṃ /
na vidyate so 'pi kaścid yo bhāvayati śūnyatāṃ //

Void is all within; void is all without.
Nor exists anyone who contemplates voidness.

In spite of his overt allegiance to the Middle Way expressed in the opening line of his own commentary to the treatise, Asaṅga concludes the work with a de facto denial of the personal entity which transmigrates, or attains Nirvāṇa. Here is the first line of his commentary on the treatise (again quoted from Wayman, p. 341; tr. p. 345):

pudgalanairātmyaṃ paramārthatas tadadhikārāt paramārthaṃ gāthā /

As an adversary to the extremes of affirmation and denial, there are the Verses of Supreme Meaning, [which means: "This and no other," acc. to Wayman] referring to "non-selfhood of a person" (*pudgala-nairātmya*) from the standpoint of supreme meaning.

And now, the concluding verse of the same Treatise (Wayman, 341):

44. pravāhe pudgalākhyā syād dharmasaṃjñā ca lakṣaṇe /
na veha kaścit saṃsartā nirvāty api na kaścana //

The term "person" (*pudgala*) means "continuous stream" and the expression "nature" (*dharma*) means "character." Neither is there any transmigrator here, nor is anything allayed (in *parinirvāṇa*).

In contrast to Asaṅga's outright denial of the existence of a personal entity within the five aggregates (which is contrary to Nāgārjuna's Middle Way, and to Buddha's silence on the subject, but similar to Buddhaghosa's and the Abhidharmists' denial of Self), the author of the *Laṅkāvatāra* consistently refuses to take a firm position on the side of those who reject the reality of Self altogether.

In this he seems more faithful to the original insight of the Teacher, and closer to the Mādhyamika point of view than to that of the Yogācāras, Asaṅga and his brother Vasubandhu. Thus, the following two gāthas (*Sagāthakam:* 357, 358; vv. 746 & 748) seem to contradict one another. In fact, however, they illustrate the Middle Way adopted by the author of the *Sūtra:*

> The Self (*ātman*) is indeed characterized by purity, and is the state of inner Realization; this is the essence (*garbha*) of the Tathāgata which is not the realm of the logicians [or theorizers, *tārkikā*].
>
> The Receptacle-of-impressions (*ālaya*) is described by the heretics (*tīrthyā*) as the desired seat of the Essence-of-Buddhahood (*garbha-saṃsthāna*), which is united with the Self (*ātman*); but these are not the approved teachings (by the Buddha).

As pointed out in the preceding chapter, the Tathāgata-garbha is nothing more than a teaching device, the Ālaya-vijñāna is only a mental construct, and the Ātman neither is, nor is not (present among the Skandhas).

The Skandhas and the Trans-empirical Self, the Tathāgata

Another entity against which the analysis of the Skandhas is applied is that of the Realized Being, the Tathāgata. This term can either mean "He who has thus gone" (*tathā-gata*), or "He who has thus come" (*tathā-āgata*). Presumably, in the first case, the implication is "gone beyond, into Nirvāṇa," while in the second case, it may mean "come hither, into the Buddha's refuge," or "arrived to one's inner Self-realization," which is the sense most frequently given in the *Laṅkāvatāra-sūtra.* Another indication of the meaning is the number of the compound: when used in the singular, it usually indicates the Master, the Buddha, while in the plural form it designates all Enlightened Beings, i.e., the Buddhas of the past and of the future, the innumerable Bodhisattvas, and the Arhats.

Theodore Stcherbatsky gave us an outstanding explanation of the meaning and function of the word 'Tathāgata' in relation to other terms indicating the Absolute in Buddhism (such as 'Dharmadhātu,' 'Dharmatā,' or 'Tathatā'). He writes:[54]

> Tathatā is the Truth, but it is impersonal. In order to reveal itself, it requires a medium. Tathāgata is that medium.

Tathāgata is the epiphany of Reality. He is Reality personalized. Tathāgata is an amphibious being partaking both of the Absolute and phenomena. He is identical with Tathatā, but embodied in a human form. That is why Tathatā is also called Tathāgata-garbha (the womb of Tathāgata).

The most important characteristic of the Tathāgata is that he is untraceable: *tathāgatam ananuvejjoti vadāmi* (*Majjhima-Nikāya*, vol. 1, p. 140, *Pāli Texts Society* ed.), or trackless (*apada*, in *Dhammapāda*, vv. 179, 254), that is, above all dichotomies of thought.

Now, in regard to the personhood of the Tathāgatas in light of the Five Skandhas theory, the text says the following (*Laṅkā* III: 188-89; ll. 16-17, 1-7):

> Likewise, the Tathāgata is neither different (*nānya*), nor non-different (*ananya*) from the aggregates. If he were not different from the personality constituents, he would be impermanent (*anitya syād*), as the personal aggregates are something fabricated [or, composite, constructed, *kṛtatva*];
>
> But (on the other hand) if they were different (*anya*), they would be two distinct entities (*dvaye satyani*); certainly, it [i.e., this dilemma] is like a cow's horns:
>
> In as far as they (the horns) look alike, they are not different; (but) when one seems short and the other long, they are different. This can be said of all things [or, beings, *sarva-bhāvā*]. Indeed, Mahāmati, the right horn of a cow is different from the left horn, and also the left is distinct from the right, since one is shorter or longer than the other and so is with the variety of colors.
>
> Thus, the Tathāgata and the personality aggregates, the realms and the sense-bases, are neither different, nor non-different from one another.

This "neither, nor" approach is strongly reminiscent of the definition of an Enlightened Being given by the Buddha in the *Saṃyutta-Nikāya* 3. 163-64 as an answer to a questioning monk regarding the five aggregates (Skandhas):[55]

> Monk, if he (an adept) is freed by this turning away from material shape, from feeling, perception, the impulses, consciousness, by dispassion in regard to these things, by their

cessation, it is fitting to call him a monk who has attained Nirvāṇa here and now.

Of course, this statement is primarily ethical in its purpose, showing that the delicate balance between 'is' and 'is not' can function on multiple levels of meaning and significance. The cessation (*nirodha*) referred to above, is the cessation of mental pollutants (*kleśas*), which would trigger a state of inner detachment characteristic of the liberated being (the Tathāgata). It does not indicate a physical, or mental annihilation, since the person who is freed from the attachment to the servitude of the Skandhas continues to exist and to function, albeit on a different spiritual level: he both is and is not at the same time. This paradoxical state is explained by Mircea Eliade in the following way:[56]

> . . . He who understood the ontological unreality of the various "composite" universes—physical, vital, psychic, mental, metaphysical, and so on—at the same time entered the transcendental plane of the Absolute, the unconditioned and incomposite, and could attain deliverance.

Now, the personal individuality is retained even in this higher state of being, in which the identification of the self with the Skandhas is relinquished. In this sense, we may refer to the description given in the *Mahā-parinibbana-sutta* of the *Dīgha-Nikāya* 6. 15, which says that the Buddha retained his personal identity while absorbed in the highest transic state of pure consciousness (without sensations or ideas), so that his closest disciples Ānanda and Anuruddha, can follow him (telepathically?) till the last moment of his life. It is of the utmost interest to note, in anticipation of the subsequent controversies about the personal identity and the five Skandhas, such as those outlined in the *Laṅkāvatāra-sūtra*, that at that exact moment, just before the Great Passing Away of the Buddha, a forceful affirmation of individuality is put into the mouth of the highest of the gods, Brahmā Sahaṃpati:[57]

> They all, all beings that have life, shall lay aside their complex form—that aggregation of mental and material qualities, that gives them, or in heaven, or on earth, their fleeting individuality!

Evidently, the implied assumption of these lines is that, ultimately, all sentient beings will dissolve into the undifferentiated, attributeless state of Nirvāṇa, but concomitantly, the reality (albeit ever-changing) of the human personality is positively admitted. And if this were not so, we may be tempted to ask along with Professor C. A. F. Rhys Davids why would a teacher, such as the Buddha, ask his disciples in the last hours of his life to take their selves as lamps and refuges, if he did not believe in their very reality? (see the expressions *attā-dipa* and *attā-saraṇa*, found in *Dīgha-Nikāya* 2. 26 and the *Mahā-parinibbāna-sutta* 155-56).[58] In light of these arguments, it seems more plausible to believe that the Buddha of the primitive texts, as well as the author of the *Laṅkāvatāra*, never denied the empirical reality of the Ātman as the personal Self, but rather the Ātman as a metaphysical principle underlying all reality, eternal, unchanging, and transcendent to the five Skandhas. This abstract principle was taken to mean that indescribable, immaterial 'something' (such as the Theravādins' 'life continuum' (*bhāvaṅga*), or Buddhaghosa's 'wandering' (*saṃsāra*), or karma by itself, etc.) which allows for the transition of individual characteristics from one state of existence to the next, in spite of the avowed belief in the insubstantiality and the evanescence of Self, and of the personality factors (Skandhas).

It seems that the idea of the Tathāgata, too, had an extra-Buddhist origin. For, according to Stcherbatsky, its meaning is best understood when compared to its usage in the non-Buddhist works, such as the *Mahābhārata* (*Śāntiparva*, 181. 12):[59]

> śakuntānam ivākāśe matsyānām iva codake /
> padaṃ yathā na dṛśyate *tathā* jñānavidāṃ *gatiḥ* //
>
> Just as the footprints of birds (flying) in the sky and of fish (swimming) in water cannot be seen, Thus (*tathā*) is the going (*gati*) of those who have realized the Truth. [Stcherbatsky's italics, nn.]

The same idea of untraceability is mirrored in the Buddhist texts, such as the *Dhammapada* 2. 1. 57: "With minds by perfect knowledge freed, No track or path the Slayer (Māra) finds." (also in the *Majjhima-Nikāya* 1. 140, and *Saṃyutta-Nikāya* 1. 109, quoted above). The indeterminacy of the Tathāgata, either by way of the Skandhas, or in terms of its existence after death, only proves our conceptual reasoning to be ineffectual when applied to the higher realm of transcendental ideas. Nāgārjuna expressed this beautifully in the *Mūlamādhyamika-kārikās*, chapter 22, "The Examination of the Tathāgata" (*Tathāgata-parīkṣā*), in relation to both the Skandhas, as well as the Tathāgata's existence after death. First, in respect to the five psycho-physical constituents (ch. 22. 1):

skandhā na nānyaḥ skandhebhyo nāsmin skandhā na teṣu saḥ /
tathāgataḥ skandhavānna katamo 'tra tathāgataḥ //

The Tathāgata is not the *skandhas*, nor is it different from the *skandhas*. Neither is he in the *skandhas*, nor are the *skandhas* in him. Since the Tathāgata cannot possess the *skandhas*, who then is the Tathāgata?

Second, its existence after death (ch. 22. 14):

svabhāvataś ca śūnye 'smiṃś cintā naivopapadyate /
paraṃ nirodhād bhavati buddho na bhavatīti vā //

(As the Tathāgata) in its self-existence is in the nature of the void (*śūnya*), it is not possible to think that the Buddha either exists, or does not exist after liberation [or cessation of life, *nirodha*].

And third, the conclusion regarding the limit of conceptualization (ch. 22. 15-16):

prapañcayanti ye buddhaṃ prapañcātītam avyayam /
te prapañcahatāḥ sarve na paśyanti tathāgatam //

tathāgato yat svabhāvas tat svabhāvam idaṃ jagat /
tathāgato niḥsvabhāvo niḥsvabhāvam idaṃ jagat //

Those who describe the Buddha who is beyond conceptual categories of thought [i.e., transcendent] (and therefore) beyond destruction [indestructible, *avyaya*], are all victims of the conceptualizing mind (*prapañca-hata*), and cannot see the Tathāgata.

Wherefore the Tathāgata is self-existence, therefore the world (*jagat*) is self-existence; (but) when the Tathāgata is non-existence, then the world is non-existence.

The Five Skandhas and the Denial of Metaphysical Dualities

The *Laṅkāvatāra* also warns against misinterpreting the theory regarding the inadequacy of conceptual categories of language (e.g., "the Tathāgata, or Self, is neither the same, nor different from the Skandhas") as a doctrine of Indeterminacy (e.g., "good, bad, and indistinct, neutral, indeterminate," *avyākṛta*, Pāli, *avyākata*).[60] Since the Master remained silent on certain complex metaphysical topics, such as the Self, the existence of Tathāgata after death, and the nature of the universe, certain disciples mistakenly assumed that either the Buddha did not know the answer to these and other similar topics (which would be in opposition to the very nature of an Enlightened Being), or the issues are in themselves untractable, or indeterminable. However, as shown, the Buddha was moved by other considerations when he refused to commit himself to a specific answer, namely that thorny metaphysical questions are not "conducive to liberation, to Nirvāṇa, freedom from suffering, the goals of religious life." This is thoroughly explained in Sutta 63 of the *Majjhima-Nikāya* 1. 431 entitled "Questions Which Tend Not to Edification:"[61]

> I have not elucidated, Malukyaputta, that the world is eternal; I have not elucidated that the world is not eternal; I have not elucidated that the world is finite; I have not elucidated that the world is infinite; I have not elucidated that the soul and the body are identical; I have not elucidated that the soul is one thing and the body another; I have not elucidated that the saint exists after death; I have not elucidated that the saint does not exist after death; I have not elucidated that the saint both exists and does not exist after death; I have not elucidated that the saint neither exists nor does not exist after death. And why, Malukyaputta, have I not elucidated this?
>
> Because, Malukyaputta, this profits not, nor has to do with the fundamentals of religion, nor tends to aversion, absence of passion, cessation, quiescence, the supernatural faculties, supreme wisdom, and Nirvāṇa; therefore have I not elucidated it.

This is the position of the Buddha, according to the oldest available records. The Yogācāras, however, saw these things in a different light. For them the 'indeterminables' were only presented as such by the Teacher in order to spare the immature disciples the unnecessary difficulty of grappling with complex philosophical issues. This would allow them the freedom to focus their energies exclusively toward the realization of the religious goal: Nirvāṇa, or freedom from pain.

For the most advanced, or mature disciples, on the other hand, the metaphysical issues would disappear once they had reached the point of meditation where all distinctions would disappear (i.e., the stage of detachment from the duality of object and subject). These distinctions, in any case, are due only to the mental habit of discrimination (or imagination, *vikalpa*) on account of the nature of the thought-process which can only take place by means of linguistic categories, or conventional symbols of one sort or another. Consequently, the indeterminable categories themselves are also unreal, or as the *Sūtra* puts it most frequently, "They are nothing but (the product of) one's own mind (*svacittamātra*)." Here is the passage which clarifies this particularly difficult point (*Laṅkā* II: 114-15; ll. 12-17, 1-6):

> And also, Mahāmati, these indeterminables [or, inexplicables, *avyākṛta*], are not spoken of by the Tathāgatas for the purpose of discarding the arguments and the views of the (speculative) philosophers. For, Mahāmati, the philosophers are declaring thus: "What life is, that is the body; (or) life is one thing, body is another." In that (consists) the doctrine of indeterminacy (*avyākṛtavāda*). Mahāmati, the (doctrine of) indeterminacy truly belongs to the philosophers who are bewildered by (the idea of a) creator, but in my teaching (this idea) is not found.
>
> Now, in my teaching, Mahāmati, discrimination does not arise when one becomes detached from the (duality of) object [*grāha*, apprehended] and subject [*grāhya*, apprehending]. But how could there be their [i.e., the discriminating philosophers'] setting aside (of the object-subject duality)? For, Mahāmati, they who are attached to the object-subject (duality) do not have a certain understanding of what is but the seeing of one's own mind, and (consequently) among them there is the setting aside (of the indeterminable questions).
>
> Now, Mahāmati, the Tathāgatas, the Arhats, the Fully Enlightened Ones teach the Truth to all beings by means of the four kinds of questions and answers [these are explained in the succeeding gātha 173, p. 116, vide infra, nn.]. As to the set apart [propositions, as inexplicable], Mahāmati, they are pointed out by me on different occasions for those whose senses are not yet fully matured; but for those with mature senses, there is nothing to be set aside [i.e., since the discrimination itself disappears].

The four ways in which any issue can be explained, according to the text, are enumerated in gātha 173, Ch. II, p. 116, which Suzuki says ought to follow the quote given above.[62] It says:

> The four kinds of explanation are: direct statement, inquiry, discernment, and determination; (hence) the refutation of the doctrines of the philosophers.

When these ways of analysis are applied to any object, or issue, the only thing that can be determined with any degree of certainty is their lack of self-nature (*niḥsvabhāva*), or indeterminacy (*anabhilāpya*). this second meaning attributed to the issue of the indeterminables (*avyākṛtāni*) seems to have a more positively ontological value, since it does make a statement about the nature of Reality, while the first sense is intended primarily for the avoidance of whatever may distract the untrained minds from their religious concentration. This is made clear in the concluding verse (gātha 175, II: 116):

> (When) the self-nature of these [dharma-objects] being investigated with intelligence, (it) cannot be pinpointed; therefore, they [i.e., the objects of investigation, the dharmas] are shown (to be) inexpressible and without self-nature.

A more extensive explanation is given in the succeeding Chapter Three, where a distinction is made (by means of a metaphor) between what is meant by "being without self-nature" (*nirātmānaḥ sarvadharmāḥ*), on the one hand, and the empirical observation that "all things have their own individuality" (*svātmanā sarvadharmāḥ*), on the other. The metaphor employed in order to show the observable fact that things do possess individual character, in spite of their lack of 'beingness' (in the ultimate sense), is the irrefutable distinction which one can make between a cow and a horse. Thus, the *Laṅkāvatāra* reads (III: 188; ll. 7-16):

> This is also told by me that all *dharmas* are selfless (*nirātman*); by this is also meant, Mahāmati, that the world (*artha*) is regarded as being without self-nature (*nirātmabhāva*), that the existence lacks what belongs to a self (*nairātmya*), (and also) that all dharmas are to be regarded as having their own individuality (*svātman*) which does not belong to another (*na parātman*), like a cow versus a horse.
>
> For instance, Mahāmati, the being of a cow is not that of a horse-nature (*aśvātmaka*), and the being of a horse is not that of a cow-nature (*gavātmaka*), (for) there is neither Being, nor non-Being, nor is it found that they are without their own individuality (*svalakṣaṇata*), (since) they are such as they are in

> their own self-nature; (therefore), Mahāmati, all *dharmas* are not found (to be) without self-nature!
>
> And so, because of this, the meaning of egolessness is not understood by the immature and common folks (on account of their) discrimination (*vikalpa*). In this manner, the lack of self-nature (*asvabhāvya*), non-birth (*anutpāda*), and the void (*śūnya*) of all *dharmas* are to be exactly known, and not through your imagination (*vikalpa*).

Again, the author manages to steer away from both opposing extremes by admitting, in fact, two different viewpoints on the issue of Selfhood: one immediate, the other ultimate. From the former perspective, things do retain their individuality which allows one to recognize their distinct character (e.g., the cow-nature and the horse-nature). But from the *ultimate* standpoint, their transitoriness, their origination through dependence on causal factors and conditions (Hetu-pratyaya), and their composite nature (Anātman) prove their lack of a definite and stable self-identity, or being (*niḥsvabhāva*). Professor Suzuki correctly sensed the meaning of the text when he made the following comment:[63]

> Therefore, things in one sense are as they are, but in another sense they are not. This is what is meant by Buddhist phenomenalism, but we are not to be carried away by its doctrine of emptiness as was explained before, as Buddhism has after all something to affirm. Its superficially paradoxical way of presenting the truth is often baffling to logicians. The *Laṅkāvatāra* proceeds to say that the ignorant and confused use their own way of discrimination (*vikalpa*) to grasp the theory of non-ego, but as existence is really beyond any system of categories, the Tathāgata's wisdom alone is capable of penetrating into reality. It is, therefore, declared by him that he is not distinct from the Skandhas, nor is he identical with them.

These two verses from the *Sagāthakam* clearly bear out Suzuki's interpretation in this matter (gāthas 19, 20, p. 266):

> Except for imagination, indeed there are neither compounded (things), nor uncompounded (things); the immature hold on (to them) like a barren woman pressing (an imaginary child) in her sleep; what fools [or how silly] they are!

> Let it be known that the personal entity (*pudgala*), the continuity of the personal aggregates (*skandha-saṃtati*) are without self-nature (*naiḥsvābhāvya*) and unborn [or, unproduced, *anutpāda*], (and that) the causal factors, the elements, and the Voidness are both existent and non-existent (*bhāva-abhāva*).

This paradoxical statement stems from the desire to express both the interim (empirical) and the ultimate (or trans-empirical, transcendental) views on the nature of observable entities, or things (dharmas). Later, in the course of the development of Mahāyāna literature, such contradictory statements will be subsumed under the umbrella of the 'two truths' doctrine (the relative truth, *saṃvṛti-satya*, and the absolute truth, *paramārtha-satya*). In effect, this doctrine did nothing more than shift the focus from the ontological domain onto the epistemological realm, while maintaining dualism in the way in which Reality is being presented to the eyes of the observer. Having perceived this difficulty, the author of the *Laṅkāvatāra* blames it on the intrinsic nature of conceptual reasoning, which will never be able to express (due to the limitation of language) the complex structure of Reality, the multifaceted world of being. This conclusion is most eloquently presented in the *Laṅkāvatāra* III: 189; ll. 13-17:

> Mahāmati, that which is neither eternal, nor non-eternal; neither effect, nor cause; neither compounded, nor uncompounded; neither understanding, nor that which is understood; neither characterized (object), nor characterizing (subject); neither personality aggregates, nor different from the personality aggregates; neither that which is expressed [significant], nor its expression [signifying, or name]; nor what is bound up with oneness and otherness, with bothness and non-bothness—this is something removed from all measurement (*pramāṇa*), (and) that which is removed from all measurement cannot be put into words [lit., "amounts to nothing but words"].

Faced with the fundamental inadequacy of language, the philosopher turns mystic, urging his readers to follow the religious path of the Tathāgata, the path of mental concentration, indicated here by the expression 'mind-only' (*citta-mātra*). This is the only path that offers freedom from all contradictory theories, and mental constructs, as enumerated below (*Laṅkā* II: 43; ll. 2-6):

Therefore, Mahāmati, the Bodhisattvas, the Great Beings, who wish to obtain—through emulation—the body of the Tathāgata, must become free from erroneous reasoning and discrimination in regard to arising, abiding, and destruction, to discipline, performance, cause and conditions, mind, sense-bases, realms and personality constituents (*skandhas*), thereby being in compliance with (the truth of) the "Mind-only" [doctrine, or *citta-mātra*].

The truth of the Mind-only doctrine, as will be explained below (ch. 2.1.), is that all metaphysical constructs are mere products of the conceptualizing function of the mind (*citta*), and should be treated as such. The ever-present danger to be guarded against is the common tendency to absolutize one's own mental products or ideas, out of an all-too-human need for mental comfort, and self-confidence, or—sometimes—short-sightedness. In an ever-changing Reality, conceptual language will always be one step behind the stream of events, thereby rendering all statements relative to the time, place, and circumstances under which they were brought into being.

Concluding Remarks on the Notion of Self and its Varieties

The search for Self, in the general sense, and for one's own self, in particular, has been a central issue in the religio-philosophical traditions of both East and West. As the most basic ontological category, or unit of existence, the manifestation of Being *in time*, it has received various definitions, covering an enormous range of possibilities.

At one end of the spectrum, we have the 'skin-encapsulated ego' (to use Alan Watts' expression), Leibniz's individual 'Monad', Fichte's separated 'Ego', Schopenhauer's 'Will', Kant's '*a priori* category', the Jain '*jīva*', and so on. At the other extreme, we have the ever-present reality of Bergson's '*élan vital*', Hegel's '*Geist*', or 'Spirit', Berkeley's all-pervasive 'Thought', Jung's 'Collective Unconscious', the Hindu 'Ātman-Brahman' continuum, and certain Buddhist concepts, if taken at face value (a risky endeavor at best!), such as the Essence/Matrix/Embryo-of-Buddhahood (Tathāgata-garbha discussed above, ch. 1.1.). In between these two extremes of narrow individualism and broad, substantial universalism, we find various versions of 'collective selves', larger than an individual, but not as large as the universe. A few such examples are: totemic tribalism, the Confucian family system, the Hindu caste-system, and strong ethnic, national, party, or even corporate identifications.

What all these 'substantialist' definitions of Self have in common (regardless of breadth) is their fixed, static nature. That is to say, their focus is on the underlying psychological *structure*, rather than on the dynamism of ongoing psychological *processes*. By contrast, Buddhism embraced from its very beginnings (at least in its written, doctrinal form) a dynamic concept of Self, more like a stream of psycho-physical events, than a strictly defined entity, 'psychic substratum,' or metaphysical 'substance.' Its definition was pragmatic and tentative, rather than dogmatic and mandatory. For lack of a better term, they called this Self "non-Self" (Pāli: Anatta, Sanskrit: Anātman).

A great deal of energy was spent during the first centuries of Buddhist history on trying to find a more specific meaning or content to this important, yet ambiguous concept, the non-Self. For, if Buddhism is to be accepted as a path of salvation from suffering, *who* is to be saved (in absence of Self), and *who* is experiencing the suffering? These were not vain metaphysical sophisms, but urgent, practical questions, which begged for an immediate answer.

As we have indicated in the course of this chapter, the problem was not the lack of answers to such questions, but the Buddha's refusal to commit himself to any of them, thus putting an end to the potentially schismatic debate. Between the two extreme camps of Personalists and Nihilists, there was a full array of 'creative euphemists', who attempted to substitute the ancient notion of Self (Ātman) by such vague metaphors as the 'flame' (of life?), the 'burden' of life (and its 'bearer'), the 'life-continuum' (*bhāvaṅga*), the 'wandering' (*saṃsāra*), and even karma itself, which transmigrates by creating a reflex of itself (i.e., "the deeds independent from the doer who performed them," according to Buddhaghosa). Later, two more terms were added to this list, in a final attempt to put an end to this centuries-old controversy, which became a stumbling block, a constant obstacle and threat to the mental peace required for meditation. They were: Suchness (Tathatā) and Voidness (Śūnyatā), the very goals of meditation.

Interestingly, in both Sanskrit and Pāli, one technical word for Yogic meditation is *bhāvanā*, which may be derived from the verbal root *bhū*, "to be," or "to become," the implication being that such a mental process would result in a radical transformation of one's personality, in the ontological sense. But if such a radical change was possible, the Buddhists argued, how could one conceive of a quasi-substantial, permanent, and immutable Self (Ātman)? Surely, they reasoned, the Self must have a dynamic, fluid quality, which is capable of evolution, if one is to accept both individual differentiation and ontological transformation.

The search for Self, as described in the early Upaniṣads, already admitted four different modalities of existence, that of the waking state, the dream state, the state of deep, dreamless sleep, and the "fourth state" (*turīya*), the transcendental, enstatic mental condition of the Yogis. *Neti, neti,* "neither this, nor that,"—said the Upaniṣadic sages about each of these states, when asked which of them represents the manifestation of the real, true Self (*ātman*).

The Buddha, too, adopted this skeptical attitude, but he took the empirical search one step further, and described (in his first sermon) the psycho-physical complex, known as the human personality, along five different strands, or streams of events, bundled together in a dynamic river of energy, accessible to everyone through self-observation. These five strands (or Sanskrit: Skandhas; Pāli: Khandhas) were classified in the Theravādin *Abhidhamma Piṭaka* under three headings: (1) physical body (*rūpa*); (2) sense-perception and reaction to it, that is, sensation of feeling (*vedanā*), perception (*saṃjñā*), volition or impulses (*saṃskāra*); and (3) consciousness (*vijñāna*). These three groups were also called: "form" (*rūpa*), "concomitants" or "conditioning factors of consciousness" (*cetasikā*), and the "state of consciousness proper" (*citta*).

And yet, the question still remained: was the Self identical, the same, or different from the five personality constituents (the Skandhas)? The Buddha's response, as preserved in the Pāli *Nikāyas,* was either a silent smile, or an enigmatic: "Neither . . . the same nor different from the *khandhas.*" Only later, the Abhidharmists came to identify the Skandhas with Non-Self (*anātman*). The position expressed in the *Laṅkāvatāra-sūtra,* however, is consistent with that of the Teacher, as well as with that of the Mādhyamikas, the apostles of the Middle Way. On the other hand, other Yogācāra texts, as for instance those of the two brothers, Asaṅga and Vasubandhu, seem to rely more on Buddhaghosa and the Abhidharmists who categorically denied the existence of a personal entity among the five aggregates. These two different positions among the authorities of the Mahāyāna movement indicate the degree of misapprehension of the original intent of the Buddha, which was thoroughly undogmatic, and uncommitted to either extreme viewpoint, as mentioned above.

Admittedly, if the Buddhists themselves found it so difficult to grasp the significance of the ambiguity involved in the Non-Self concept, how much more difficult would it not be for someone removed from their world, both geographically and culturally?

Perhaps, with the help of a metaphor, we can make the task easier. Imagine a row of five billiard balls set in motion by the strike of a cue. The five balls are the five personality constituents, and the cue is the sense-stimulus coming from the outside. The Self cannot be said to be restricted to the Skandhas, just as the motion (what gets the balls rolling, what makes them come 'alive') cannot be reduced to exclusively internal causal factors. In other words, the Self does not exist as such, that is, in and by itself, independently from the outside world. The very cause of its birth, its sustenance, and its demise, comes from the outside world, on which it is totally dependent, like a foetus on its mother, through constant interaction. Thus, the separating line between the inner and the outer, between the Self and the non-Self, is not only very diffuse, but constantly shifting, as well. Consequently, the Self cannot be defined in a static way, by means of its attributes and its structure; it can only be defined, if at all, by means of describing its *processes*, its particular form of dynamic interaction between the inner and the outer, its intensity and its effects.

This important truth, which was systematically pursued by the Buddhists for the last 2,500 years, has only recently begun to emerge as a new paradigm in Western psychology and biological science. New forms of dynamic, contextual, and transpersonal approaches to the understanding of mental phenomena have multiplied in the last few decades. From psychosomatic medicine, which perceives the mind/body system as an integrated whole, to various forms of Gestalt therapy, which treats the individual as part of a larger unit (i.e., the family and its cultural milieu), and recently, to more holistic approaches to environmental science, humanity as a whole is becoming increasingly aware of its impact upon the biological eco-system, of which it is a part.[64]

An innovative example of this multileveled, systemic approach to the understanding of mentation as a multidimensional phenomenon, has been offered by Francis Hsu's concept of Self as a 'psycho-social homeostasis'.[65] This new paradigm of Self seems to offer a more appropriate model for an emerging world culture, where the old, fixed definitions of Self have become too narrow and constrictive. Hsu's proposal may be considered along with David Hume's intuition of Self as a 'bundle of perceptions', as more systematic and refined versions of the ancient Buddhist understanding of the human personality with its empirical and trans-empirical constituents, as presented above.

Thus, the empirical Self corresponds to the individual, *private* self (which is both expressible and conscious, and unexpressible and unconscious, according to Hsu's model), while the trans-empirical Tathāgata may be regarded as an archaic version of a given socio-cultural *ideal*, the *public* model of the social Self (i.e., a persona which incorporates both the strong attachment to one's immediate socio-cultural symbols, as well as the weaker influences caused by different, foreign and distant worlds, which may be either real, or ideal). These are the two psycho-social components which need to be in a stable (i.e., homeostatic) balance, for the healthy development of the human personality.[66]

By way of an example, let us say that the private, or empirical self is more strongly typified in the West, while in the East it has been traditionally subservient to the public, or social ideal (e.g., religious or caste identification). Of course, along the mental health continuum, this idealized Self could, in any society, occasionally get out of balance to the detriment of the individual's private existence. To wit, one might even say that the price in human suffering which is sometimes paid for personal social success in the modern, highly competitive society, is in some ways comparable to the abandonment of family life for the sake of a higher ideal, by the traditional Indian renunciant, or Yogi.[67]

Finally, when assessing the practical implications of various models of Self, one might consider the obvious advantages of an open, and flexible notion of Self, especially in an era when the dialogue between people and cultures is not only rapidly expanding, but also increasingly necessary. Considering the dramatic changes taking place in the world today, and their sometimes hazardous effects on both people and our natural surroundings, many may feel compelled to look for inspirational value to the ancient traditions, such as the Hindu and Buddhist, where the concept of Self has always been bound to the larger picture of the world, and to complex theories of ongoing change and inner transformation.

1.3. Dharmadhātu: the *Spatial* or Cosmic Dimension of Being

Introductory Remarks

So far, we have presented two of the necessary three pillars, or ontic categories, which provide—according to Husserl-the general outline of any metaphysical system. The first designates the *essential* nature of Being, and we have pointed out that in the *Laṅkāvatāra-sūtra* this is described under the technical term of *Tathāgata-garbha*, or the "Essence-of-Buddhahood," which can be both static and unmanifested, as well as dynamic, active, and manifested. Furthermore, one can say that the second and third ontic categories represent precisely this latter, *manifested* form of Being, in its *temporal* and *spatial* dimensions. In the *Laṅkāvatāra*, the *temporal* dimension of Being is best symbolized by the aggregate of the five personality constituents (Skandhas), which by their very nature are constantly appearing and disappearing from one's field of vision, thus casting serious doubt about the validity of such a theoretical construct as the personal entity, or Self (Ātman, or Pudgala).

In this section, I will investigate the second, *spatial* dimension of Being in its manifested form, which stands for the third ontic category within the metaphysical system presented in the *Laṅkāvatāra-sūtra*. The technical term which best symbolizes this notion of spatiality is *Dharmadhātu*, or the "Realm-of-the-existential-elements."[1] Two things need to be pointed out right at the beginning of this treatment.

First, Dharmadhātu stands in a complementary relationship vis-à-vis the five Skandhas, for, while the Skandhas represent the *personal* aspect of the manifestation of Being, Dharmadhātu (along with its synonyms, Tathatā, Buddhatā, Śūnyatā, etc.) indicates its larger, *cosmic* manifestation. However, one cannot say that the former points to the subjective, and the latter to the objective dimensions of existence, since both partake of both aspects of reality.

The Skandhas have an objective, material aspect (*rūpa*), just as Dharmadhātu has a subjective dimension. This brings us to the second point which needs to be emphasized in relation to Dharmadhātu.

As a technical term, the word includes not only the *physical* universe in its domain of significance, but also any number of ideal, or *mental* universes (*lokas*), which are but symbolic representations of the first, or 'objective' world. The spatial order of these 'perceptual' universes may or may not be taken literally, or—in other words—be given ontological validity, depending upon the text one reads.[2] The *Laṅkāvatāra-sūtra*, for instance, tends to downplay the reality of all ontological concepts, which are treated (as we shall see over and over again) as mere didactic devices for the purpose of attaining one's ultimate goal, which is religious in nature rather than cognitive.

According to Suzuki, the concept Dharmadhātu, as used in the *Laṅkāvatāra*, expresses "the most comprehensive view of the universe, including not only this visible sense-world, but all possibly conceivable ideal worlds."[3] His interpretation, however, reflects only one possible meaning of the term. Another meaning is given by Edgerton (based on a number of early Mahāyāna texts, which he quotes), in conformity with the Pāli expression *dhamma-dhātu*, the 'sphere of religion'.[4]

Naturally, judgement should be made in relation to the context in which the term is used, for the word *dharma* (*dhamma*) had a double meaning in primitive Buddhism as well, namely (1) *dharmas*, as the smallest constituents of existence, physical and mental, and (2) *Dharma*, as the Truth, the Law, or religious teaching proclaimed by the Buddha, as the way of salvation from suffering. Hence, Edgerton's rendition of Dharmadhātu as the "Sphere-of-religion." Sometimes, the two meanings almost coalesce, as in this passage from the *Gaṇḍavyūha* 500.8, where the physical universe is metaphorically alluded to for the purpose of conveying the breadth of Tathāgata's teaching:[5]

> dharmadhātu-gagana-gocarāṇāṃ tathāgata-mahājñāna-sūrya-candramasāṃ/
>
> The sun and the moon of the great knowledge of the Tathāgata have the heaven of the Sphere-of-religion as their scope (*gocara*).

The fusion between the two meanings of the word *dharma* is not in the least accidental, since in the Buddhist view religious law is the same as the fundamental law according to which the entire universe is ruled. This includes the multitude of worlds, divine and human, which are usually grouped under three headings or spheres (*dhātus*): *rūpa, arūpa,* and *kāma* (i.e., the realm of form, the formless realm, and the sensuous realm, respectively). Together, they are referred to (in the *Laṅkāvatāra* and elsewhere) as *traidhātuka, tribhava,* or *trikāya* (the triple world, or the universe in its totality).[6] As Stcherbatsky states, "the moral teaching of a path towards Final Deliverance is not something additional or extraneous to this ontological doctrine, it is most intimately connected with it and, in fact, identical with it."[7]

The relationship between the mental, or moral elements on the one hand, and the physical elements (*dhātus*) is further explained through the correspondences between the eighteen different *gotras,* or *dhātus* (*Abhidharmakośa* 1.20), which include six perceptual faculties (from *cakṣur-dhātu* up to *mano-dhātu*), six objective elements (from *rūpa-dhātu* up to *dharma-dhātu*), and six kinds of consciousness (from the sensuous types, such as the *cakṣur-vijñāna-dhātu,* up to the non-sensuous, or purely mental consciousness, the *mano-vijñāna-dhātu,* achieved either through transic meditation, *samāpatti,* or through rebirth, *utpatti*).[8] Together they make up the *kāma-dhātu.*

When taken separately from the six elements of consciousness, the sense-faculties and the objective elements can also be referred to as the twelve sense-bases (*āyatanas*) which constitute the objective world. In the *Laṅkāvatāra,* the compound *skandha-dhātu-āyatana* is often used to mean the totality of the subjective and objective universe, to which we gain access through experience.[9] It may be noted that this kind of systematic classification is not exclusive to Buddhism, and Stcherbatsky has pointed out that the number of constituent elements (*tattvas*) of the rudimentary body in ancient Sāṃkhya philosophy is likewise eighteen.[10]

As far as the origin of the term *dhātu* is concerned, Stcherbatsky had no doubt that it was a concept borrowed from the medical science of pre-Buddhist times, where it meant "element of the body."[11] The early Buddhists also used the term *dharma-kāya* for the sum total of the qualities (*dharmas*) of the transformed body of the Buddha, which the followers were trying to emulate.[12] Therefore, the combination *dharma-dhātu* may also carry soteriological connotations subsumed under later Yogācāra innovations, such as the Saṃbhoga-kāya ("Body of Bliss"), and the Dharma-kāya ("Body of Law"). Like them, the Dharmadhātu is both transcendent and immanent. As Stcherbatsky put it, "it is transcendent as ultimate Reality, but it is present in everyone as his inmost ground and essence."[13]

Dharmadhātu as Cosmic Law: the Fundamental Structure of the Universe

Having considered these various doctrinal implications of the expression *Dharmadhātu,* let us now see how the text of the *Laṅkāvatāra-sūtra* bears them out. We have already pointed out that the term *dharmadhātu,* taken as the manifestation of Being in its very essence, is sometimes replaced by its synonyms: Tathatā ("Thatness"), Buddhatā ("Buddhahood"), Śūnyatā ("Voidness"). Therefore, when the *Sūtra* explains the meaning of these terms, it implicitly expounds on the nature of the Dharmadhātu as well. Thus, in the third chapter (p. 140, ll. 9-17) the *Laṅkāvatāra* reads:

> And again, Mahāmati said: "May the Blessed One tell me what (makes) the Buddhas and the Blessed Ones (such as they are) and what is, O Lord, the Buddha-nature (*buddhatā*) of the Buddhas?" The Lord answered:
>
> "When the Selflessness of persons and things is understood, Mahāmati, and when the knowledge of the two-fold hindrances [lit., coverings, *āvaraṇa*] is understood, when the two-fold dying [lit., vanishing, falling, *cyuti*] is accomplished, and when the two-fold group of impurities [or defiling passions, *kleśas*] is destroyed, then, Mahāmati, the Buddha-nature of the Blessed Ones, of the Buddhas, comes into existence. It is only from the acquirement of these things, Mahāmati, that the Buddha-nature of the self-enlightened ones and of the disciples is obtained.
>
> Now, on account of this, Mahāmati, I teach the one-pointed concentration (*ekayāna*)."
>
> Thus it is said:
>
> The duality of egolessness, the twofold hindrance, likewise the group of the double defilement(s), (which is) beyond thought (*acintya*), and the transforming consequences of the (two-fold) death—when these are obtained, there is the Tathāgata!

Here again we have a fusion between the soteriological and ontological domains by means of a technical term (*buddhatā*), rich in meaningful connotations. Thus, on the moral and religious plane, it is associated with the gradual path to Buddhahood, the various purifications and meditations (beyond thought, *acintya*) and the two kinds of Nirvāṇic cessations (in this life, after Enlightenment, and after the physical death, the *parinirvāṇa*).

But, on the other hand, the mention of the twofold egolessness (of things and persons) points toward the fundamental *structure* of the universe and the cosmic *law* which governs it, namely the interdependence of entities, animate (*pudgalas*) and inanimate (*dharmas*), or Pratītya-samutpāda. In that, the Buddha-nature (Buddhatā) closely resembles the Thusness (Tathatā) of the universe, with which the Buddha as a cosmic Being is frequently identified as the "Tathāgata."

For, as the apex of the realm of animate existence (both human and divine), the Tathāgata is simultaneously part of the eternally-abiding Reality, the ultimate cosmic substratum in its utmost purity, or essence, referred to alternatively in the *Laṅkāvatāra-sūtra* as Truthfulness (Dharmatā), or Voidness (Śūnyatā), as we shall see. Hence, he teaches through his mere presence, or existence, in the pure Realm-of-Truth (Dharmadhātu), where words are superfluous. This is the meaning of the following passage found in the *Laṅkāvatāra* III: 142-43; ll. 16-17, 1-3:

> And again, Mahāmati said: "This was spoken by the Blessed One: 'From the night of the Enlightenment till the night of the Parinirvāṇa, the Tathāgata has not uttered even a sound, nor will (a word) ever be uttered by the Tathāgata, (for) not speaking—this is Buddha's speaking.'
>
> "According to what sense (given) by the Tathāgata, by the Worthy One, (is the expression) 'Buddha's speech is no speech' (to be taken) with the correct understanding?"

The answer to this question reveals the double significance of the Dharmadhātu concept: As the eternal and essential Reality of the universe, it is identical with the notion of Tathatā (the inherent nature, or Essence, of the world). As supreme realization of the inner Self, it represents the realm, or the sphere where all such Self-realized beings co-exist. Therefore, the discussion in the *Sūtra* regarding the Dharmadhātu constantly vacillates between these two poles of significance. Thus, the *Laṅkāvatāra* III: 143; ll. 3-14:

> The Lord said: "According to the two things, Mahāmati, this statement is made by me. What are the two things?
>
> They are the Reality [or, the inherent nature, essence, *dharmatā*] of the inner Self, and according to the primevally-abiding Reality [or Nature, *paurāṇasthiti-dharmatā*]. According to these two things, Mahāmati, this statement is made by me. Now, in

respect to the Reality of one's inner Self (*svapratyātmadharmatā*), which has been realized by the Tathāgatas and which is also my own realization, that is the realm of one's inner Self-realization which can neither be excelled (*anadhikaṃ*), nor diminished (*anūnam*), and which is removed from discrimination (based upon) words, being freed from dualistic terminology.

"Now, what is the primevally abiding Reality?

"That is, Mahāmati, this ancient road of Reality which is like gold, silver, or pearl (found) in the mine, Mahāmati: whether the Tathāgatas rise or do not rise (in the world), the Dharmadhātu [i.e., the Realm-of-existential-elements, the Realm-of-Truth, or Law] abides forever; as these (Tathāgatas) abide, so does the nature of (all) things (*dharmāṇāṃ dharmatā*); (for) the Reality (Dharma) abides forever; it is the governing order of the Law (which abides), just like the roads of an ancient city, Mahāmati."

In order to better convey the inexorability of the underlying structure of the universe (here referred to as the *dharma-niyāmatā*), the author introduces at this juncture the metaphor of a city whose structure is determined by the ancient layout of its roads, regardless of the various impressions and movements of the people who walk through it. The whole image has a ring of the ancient Vedic concept of *Ṛta* attached to it (see *Ṛg Veda* 10. 124. 5). Here is the *Laṅkāvatāra*'s metaphorical explanation of the objective character of the natural order of Reality (*Laṅkā* III: 143-44; ll. 14-16, 1-13; vv. 7-8):

"This is (for instance), Mahāmati, just like some man who is wandering over a forest and discovering an ancient city, he is stepping on its orderly streets, so he may enter this city; now, having entered it, he is conducting himself in the city (like a citizen) so he may enjoy the pleasure accruing (therefrom).

What do you think, Mahāmati? Were the roads by which he entered the city and also the various (things) in the city generated by this man?" (Mahāmati) said: "No, O Blessed One!" The Lord said: "Just so, Mahāmati, what has been attained by me and other Tathāgatas is like this abiding Reality, the eternally abiding Law, the governing (order) of Nature, the Thusness (*tathatā*), the Beingness (*bhūtatā*), the Truthness (of things, *satyatā*). For this reason, Mahāmati, it was stated by me that from the night of the Tathāgata's Enlightenment till the night of his Parinirvāṇa, not a word was uttered by the Tathāgata in the meantime, nor will a sound ever be uttered." Thus it was said:

"From the night of the Attainment, till the night of the Parinirvāṇa, in the meantime, by me it was not made any proclamation whatsoever.

This is told by me in accordance with the abiding truth of the inner Self; nothing more whatsoever superior in any way (was told, or added) by me, or by other Buddhas."

Several important things are being asserted here. First, there is an affirmation, loud and clear, regarding the cosmic (that is orderly, structured) nature of the external Reality. This is a statement of principle rather than a detailed description which is found elsewhere (in the Abhidharma literature).[14] The second observation is implicit in the first, namely that the world is real (having a perceivable *order*), and its structure is governed by cosmic *laws* which are independent from and above the perceiving subject (including the Buddha and other Tathāgatas, or Enlightened Beings). This point is particularly important with regard to the alleged denial of the external world, which many interpreters of the Yogācāra school believe to be implied in its core concepts (such as the Citta-mātra or Vijñapti-mātra doctrine).[15]

A third point to be made here with reference to the process of Enlightenment is that the realization of one's inner Self is subject to the same law which governs the evolutionary process of the entire universe, the law of Dependent Origination (*pratītya-samutpāda*). Its understanding not only determines the difference between enlightened and non-enlightened beings, but it also provides access into the void realm of nature (*dharmadhātu*), from which the laws (Dharma) are derived.[16] These three points are, in fact, interrelated, as is explained in the Mahāyāna scripture "The Meeting of Father and Son" (*Pitāputrasamāgama-sūtra*), which states: "Therefore, by understanding Dependent Origination, one understands the *dharmadhātu*," and "Lord, the Tathāgata is devoid of characteristics (*lakṣaṇa*), . . . ; is Dharmadhātu, Thusness, True End (*bhūtakoṭi*). All *dharmas* are also *bhūtakoṭi*. Therefore, all *dharmas* are the Tathāgata."[17]

These complex relationships appear to have originated from the earliest discourses of the Buddha, as preserved in the Pāli canon, such as the *Sālistamba-sutta* of the *Majjhima-Nikāya* 1.191, which states that: "Whoever sees Dependent Origination, sees the Dhamma, or the *Vakkali-sutta* of the *Saṃyutta-Nikāya* 2. 120, which teaches that:

"Whoever, Vakkali, sees the Dhamma, sees me; whoever sees me, sees the Dhamma."[18]

Dharmadhātu as Universal Void: the Ground of Being

Having so many aspects, or forms, the Realm-of-Dharma is ultimately devoid of specific characteristics (*lakṣaṇas*). Therefore, in the last analysis, when one reaches the ultimate nature of Reality, the very ground of Being, one can only refer to it as "Voidness" (Śūnyatā), for: "The unreality of both [subject and object], and the reality (subjacent) of this unreality has the characteristic of the Void" (*dvayābhāvo hy abhāvasya bhāvaḥ śūnyasya lakṣaṇam*).[19]

The same idea is presented in the *Laṅkāvatāra-sūtra*, where, as a result of the incremental process characteristic of Buddhist docetics, seven types of Voidness are described in detail. Thus the *Laṅkāvatāra* II: 73 and 74; ll. 12-16, 1-8:

> Tell me, O Lord, about all things which are characterized by the lack of self-nature, non-duality, non-origination and Voidness, by which I and other Bodhisattvas, great beings, may be awakened to the mark of the lack of self-nature, of non-duality, non-origination and Voidness, and thereby become free from the discrimination between Being and non-Being, (so that) we may quickly attain the highest, perfect Enlightenment.
>
> The Blessed One said this: "Voidness, Mahāmati, thus is Voidness: this is a term whose inherent nature is false imagination. Moreover, Mahāmati, through attachment to one's own nature characterized by imagination, there is the talking about the occurrence of (such things as) the lack of self-nature, non-duality, non-Being, non-origination and Voidness."
>
> "Now, briefly, Mahāmati, there are seven kinds of Voidness, namely: (1) The Voidness of characteristic marks; (2) The Voidness of the self-nature of existence; (3) The Voidness of no practice; (4) The Voidness of practice; (5) The Voidness of all things in the sense that they are unpredictable; (6) The great Voidness of the noble Wisdom in its highest sense; and (7) The Voidness of mutuality, which is the seventh."

These seven kinds of Voidness together constitute a powerful statement regarding the relativity of all things when seen in the light of the Dependent Origination theory. A better understanding of the meaning of each proposition may be obtained by juxtaposing the *Laṅkāvatāra*'s enumeration over against the list given by the Mādhyamika text *Śūnyatāsaptati*, attributed to Nāgārjuna.[20]

There the *first* Voidness, of characteristic marks, is expressed as the non-birth (*anutpanna*) of all dharmas which exist only in the conventional sense (lit., according to wish, *vyavahāravaśāt*, i.e., *saṃvṛtitaḥ*), verses 1-6; the *second*, of the Self-nature of existence, is expressed as the Pratītya-samutpanna of all existence (*bhāva*), verses 7-23; the *third* and *fourth*, that is, the Voidness of no-practice (which leads to accumulated karma) and the Voidness of practice (which leads to Nirvāṇa), are expressed as the Śūnya of karma (verses 33-44), and the *anutpāda* of Nirvāṇa (verses 23-32).

The *fifth* Voidness, of all things as unpredictable, is expressed as the indeterminacy (*animitta*) of the marks (*liṅga*) of the four great elements (*mahābhūtas*), which, through their combination, along with the causes and conditions (Hetu-pratyaya), give rise to the realm of form (*rūpakāya*). The five Skandhas themselves have their basis in causes and conditions arising from the realm of form, which is ultimately non-existent (*rūpābhāva*), according to the *Śūnyatāsaptati* (verses 45-57). Hence the Voidness of all things in the sense that they are unpredictable, and—as a consequence of that—the Voidness of the Noble Wisdom (*paramārtha*) together with the Voidness of ignorance (*avidyā*), with which it is correlative, or mutually co-arising, as described in verses 58-73 of the *Śūnyatāsaptati*. This would correspond with the *sixth* great Voidness of the *Laṅkāvatāra*, given above.

The *seventh*, and last, Voidness of mutuality follows logically from the relativity of all dharmas upon their correlatives (father-son, pleasure-pain, Being-Non-Being, freedom-transmigration, wisdom-ignorance, self-existence versus mutuality itself, *svabhāva-anyonyahetutaḥ*) (verses 8-21).

These seven kinds of Voidness can be said to represent in a nutshell the *essence* of Mahāyānistic ontology, as presented in the early scriptures of its two major schools, namely the *Laṅkāvatāra* (for the Yogācāra school) and the *Śūnyatāsaptati* (for the Mādhyamika school). The *Laṅkāvatāra-sūtra* goes one step further than the mere description given in the *Śūnyatāsaptati* by asserting the conventionality of all descriptions or discussions about the nature of Reality (*Dharma-saṃketa*). They include all Buddhist concepts given in the sacred texts, such as Tathatā, Śūnyatā, Bhūtakoṭi, Nirvāṇa, and Dharma-dhātu ("Thatness," "Voidness," "Limit of Reality," Nirvāṇa, and the "Essential Realm," respectively).

The following verses from the last chapter, the *Sagāthakam*, render this most clearly (pp. 289-90, vv. 185 & 190-193):

> It is said that this (word) it is only a convention (*saṃketa*) of Reality (*dharma*), and apart from this convention, there is nothing actually real (*bhūta*) which is born, and nothing which is destroyed.
>
> Existence (*bhāva*) in its conditionality cannot be (described) through (its) unity or diversity; it is only in the general manner of speech that there is birth, cessation and destruction (of things).
>
> Unborn Voidness is one thing, Voidness among the born (things) is another; unborn Voidness is better (for) born (Voidness) is destroyed.
>
> Thusness (*tathatā*), Voidness (*sūnyatā*), the Limit (*koṭī*) (of Reality, *bhūta-*), Nirvāṇa, and the Realm-of-Law (*dharmadhātu*) are like the multiple bodies made of mind (*manomaya-kāya*)—these are taught by me as synonymous (*paryāya*).
>
> Those who discriminate according to the Abhidharma, the Vinaya, and the Sūtras (follow) books and not the (inner) meaning (*artha*); they are not relying upon (the doctrine of) non-Self (*nairātmya*).

Here, the dichotomy between words (or signs) and meaning (or reality) is brought into sharp focus. One may argue that this issue should not concern us here, since it properly falls under the epistemological realm of discourse, to be dealt with in the succeeding sections. However, in the philosophical context of the *Laṅkāvatāra-sūtra* in particular, and of Buddhist doctrine in general, the highest Reality (Paramārtha, "Absolute Truth"; Bhūtakoṭī, "Limit of Reality"; Dharmadhātu, "Essential Realm"; Nirvāṇa, "Extinction of Suffering" etc.) is simultaneously perceived and existentially realized (i.e., united with), precisely at the moment when the symbolic realm of language ceases to operate (from the point of view of the Buddhist observer). This Reality is identified as Voidness on account of the relativity and insubstantiality (in the ultimate sense) of all perceived objects.

True, one may say that such a Reality is utterly subjective, but according to the Yogācāra Buddhist ideas presented here, it can readily be verified by anyone who takes the trouble to thoroughly analyse the way in which objects come into and disappear from existence, and the role of conditional factors, as well as the imaginative nature of our own opinions and constructs about Reality. Consequently, it is only when even the Buddhist *ideas about* the Reality are seen as such, that the true nature of the world reveals itself "as it really is" (Tathatā), that is, devoid of self-existence (Śūnyatā). The *Sūtra* explains this in effective and poetic language (II: 87-88; ll. 8-17, 1-13, vv. 145-48):

> The Lord said: "Mahāmati, words are not the highest Reality (*paramārtha*), nor is it what is expressed by words that highest Truth. Why? For this reason: the highest Reality is an exalted state of bliss (*āryasukha*) which cannot be entered into through verbal statements (about it), for words are not the highest Reality.
>
> Now, Mahāmati, the highest Reality is the state of inner Self-realization by means of the Noble Wisdom and not the realm of intellectual discrimination by means of words; therefore, the (verbal) discrimination does not express the highest Reality. Moreover, Mahāmati, the verbal expression (*vacana*), which quickly rises and quickly disappears, is mutually generated from causes and causal factors, and that, Mahāmati, which is mutually generated from causes and causal factors cannot express the ultimate Reality (*paramārtha*), (since) a verbal sign (*vāglakṣaṇa*), Mahāmati, cannot express the non-existent characteristic mark of Self, or of something other (than Self).
>
> Furthermore, Mahāmati, the verbal discrimination (*vāg-vikalpa*) cannot conceive the supreme Reality (*paramārtha*) on account of the non-existence of the external objects' various sorts of characteristic marks and (also) due to the following of the mere perceptions of one's own mind. In that case, therefore, Mahāmati, you must become free from discrimination through various words. Thus it is said:
>
> 'All existence is indeed without self-nature, and words, too, are without reality; as the immature does not understand the meaning of Voidness, it is nevertheless Voidness which runs through (the universe).'
>
> 'There is no self-nature in all things, and they are but men's words; those which are discriminated, they too, do not exist; even Nirvāṇa is like a dream; nothing is seen as being in transmigration (Saṃsāra), nor is anything ever released into Nirvāṇa.'

'As a king or a wealthy householder alluring his sons with various clay-made animals and having had them play with these toys, then he gives them real wild beasts (to deal with),'

'So I, by making use of various forms of concepts, teach the limit of Reality (Bhūtakoṭī) to my sons, which is actually the knowledge of the inner Self.'"

Here, the author of the *Sūtra* again throws his reader back into the fundamentally religious search for Self-realization, away from the speculative verbal representation of Reality especially in its absolute aspect (Bhūtakoṭī, "Limit of Reality"; Paramārtha, "Absolute Truth"; Dharmadhātu, "Essential Realm" etc.). The words (*vacana*) are not to be taken too seriously, since they are only teaching devices employed by the Master for the sole purpose of helping his disciples realize the truth regarding the reality within (*pratyātmavedyā, pratyātma-gatigocara*). With this, the second pole of significance, around which the concept Dharmadhātu revolves, is explained (vide supra: *Laṅkā* III: 143, *svapratyātma-dharmatā*, the Reality, or Nature of one's inner Self). As the realm belonging to the purified Self, Dharmadhātu can be identified with Tathāgata-garbha and Ālaya-vijñāna.[21] According to Dasgupta's interpretation:[22]

> Enlightenment is the perfection of the mind when it is free from the corruptions of the creative instinctive incipient memory (*smṛti*). It penetrates all and is the unity of all (*dharma-dhātu*). That is to say, it is the universal *dharmakāya* of all Tathāgatas constituting the ultimate foundation of existence.

Noriaki Hakamaya, on the other hand, following Vasubandhu's and Aśvabhāva's commentaries on the *Mahāyāna-saṃgraha*, points out that the doctrine (Dharma, *pariniṣpanna, paramārtha*) flows out from the pure Dharmadhātu (*viśuddha-dharma-dhātu-niṣyanda*), which is synonymous with the Original Purity (*prakṛti-vyavadāna*) and includes everything.[23] Outflow (*niṣyanda*), he explains, "means flowing out of the same essence (*sadṛśaḥ-syandaḥ*), a result that is consistent with that (essence) (*tad-anurūpam-phalam*)."[24] What flows out is the manifestation of inner subjectivity which becomes conscious of *paramārtha* as the non-discriminative wisdom (*nirvikalpa-jñāna*), said to transcend verbal expression (*nirabhilāpya*).[25] Hence, the unity of essence between the two aspects (the 'subjective' Realm-of-Enlightenment, and the 'objective' cosmic realm, or the Realm-of-the Universal-Law) which make up the Dharmadhātu concept. This common essence is best expressed as the universal Void (Śūnyatā), the ground of Being (Bhūtatā).

Commenting on this unique feature of the *Laṅkāvatāra-sūtra*'s presentation of the Dharmadhātu concept, Professor J. Takasaki identifies the meaning of the term *dharmatā*, as found in other Mahāyāna sūtras (such as the *Dharmadharmatā-vibhāga*), with the sphere of those dharmas to be realized (*sākṣātkaraṇīya*) in the ideal state of Nirvāṇa, which are therefore different in essence from those dharmas belonging to the world of Saṃsāra, which are to be abandoned (*prahātavya*).[26] Such a distinction, however, is not found in the *Laṅkāvatāra*, as we have seen. In our text, it seems, the two terms, *Dharmatā* and *Dharmadhātu*, are interchangeably used, as in the compounds: *paurāṇasthiti-dharmatā* (which stands for *dharmadhātu-sthititā*), and *svapratyātma-dharmatā* (which renders the meaning of *pratyātmagatigocara*, which stands for Dharmadhātu itself, when taken as the fulfillment of the Law, the ideal state of Nirvāṇa). (vide supra: *Laṅkā* III: 143).

As far as the concept of Dharmadhātu itself is concerned, Professor Takasaki distinguishes quite rightly between two different meanings admitted by the author of the *Laṅkāvatāra-sūtra*, although his interpretation is somewhat different from my own. He says: "The term *dharmadhātu*, here, may be interpreted as the nature (*dhātu*) of a thing (*dharma*), or the truth concerning things (*dharmāṇāṃ dharmatā*)." And he continues:[27]

> Thus the *dharmadhātu* has two characteristics, the one being the *dharmatā*, i.e., the law of *pratītyasamutpāda*, and the other being *sarvadharmāḥ*, i.e., the whole sphere of *pratītyasamutpanna-dharmāḥ*. Remarkable is the combination of the two aspects of *dharma* in one word, such being not the case with the term *dharmatā*.

This interpretation, while not without basis, is incomplete, for it fails to underline the significance of the law of Dependent Origination as the attainment of Self-realization, which is the essential message of the text. In other words, Dharmatā, the manifestation of Being *in space*, is not merely the law of Interdependent Origination of all things, *pratītya-samutpāda* (as Takasaki is content to indicate), but rather, and more importantly, is the *svapratyātma-dharmatā* (the Law, or Reality of inner Self-realization). Thus, ontology has become soteriology, for, according to the Buddhist view of things, knowledge of the universe can only be complete through, and indeed be fulfilled by, the knowledge of man himself.

Concluding Observations

To conclude, let us say that our division of the Yogācāra ontology into three separate aspects not only makes sense in light of modern philosophical thinking, but is also supported from within the Buddhist Mahāyāna tradition itself. Thus, in the *Madhyāntavibhāga* we find the following theory of the three-fold nature of Being, attributed to the founder of the Yogācāra school himself, the legendary Maitreya:

> svabhāvas trividho 'sac ca nityaṃ cāpy atattvataḥ/
> sad-asat-tattvataś ceti svabhāva-trayam iṣyate//

This can be more conveniently arranged (and translated) thus:[28]

> The nature of being is three-fold: 1. Always non-existing (*asac ca nityaṃ*); 2. Though existing, yet not from the absolute point of view (*sac cāpy atattvataḥ*): 3. From the absolute point of view, existing and yet non-existing (*sad-asat-tattvataḥ ca*). One should investigate (the nature of dharma) in this three-fold nature of being.

Now, all these three aspects of Being can be said to have found a doctrinal expression in the three concepts analysed above. *First*, Tathāgata-garbha (with its three distinct meanings, as Womb, Embryo, and essential supramundane Dharma), it is specifically stated in the *Sūtra*, is only a provisional concept and a teaching device, to be abandoned once the true meaning of Anātman has been obtained. That renders it "always non-existing," in the ontological sense.

The *second* formulation: "Though existing, yet not from the absolute point of view," can accurately apply to the Five Skandhas as the *temporal* manifestation of Being, obviously existing, but only in the relative sense, being thoroughly dependent upon causes and conditions (Hetu-pratyaya).

The *third* and last ontological possibility, "existing and yet non-existing, from the absolute point of view," is well illustrated by our third construct, Dharmadhātu, which may be said to symbolize the manifestation of Being in its *spatial* dimension. Now, Dharmadhātu—as the expression of the absolute, universal Law (Dharma), the source and apex of all Causation (Pratītya-samutpāda), as well as the representation of the ultimate state of Thusness (Tathatā) or Voidness (Śūnyatā)—is indeed ontologically real, for it reflects the essential nature of the cosmos as a whole, and its orderly functioning according to certain patterns.[29]

The Dharmadhātu, however, is said by the Yogācāra philosophers (also from the absolute point of view) to be non-existent, if it is taken to mean the world of phenomenal elements (the totality of dharmas), which—as we have seen—do not *really* exist, except interdependently, in accordance with the Law of Causation (Pratītya-samutpāda). This is the meaning of the Vijñānavāda doctrine, which says that the world does not exist, except as "mere representation" (*vijñapti-mātra*) of one's own mind (*svacitta-mātra*). This does not constitute, however, an outright denial of the world in its relative, immediate sense (as has been, we think, mistakenly inferred), but rather—and quite correctly—it underscores the deceptive nature of our perceptions (*vijñānas*) and judgment (*vikalpa*). Therefore, even the nature of Self-realization (*svapratyātma-dharmatā*) is said to be true only in the relative sense (of existing interdependently), but void of absolute, independent existence. This reasoning will become clear in our next section, dealing with epistemological concepts.

Part Two:

CONCEPTS OF KNOWING

2.0. Buddhist Epistemology, Buddhist Dialectics

Truth, Untruth, Half-truth, "the Truth"

In the most general sense, epistemology is said to be concerned with the nature and scope of knowledge, its presuppositions and basis, and with the distinction between truth and untruth, or more specifically, between true and false statements and propositions. Such distinctions represent the more theoretical side of this particular branch of philosophical endeavor. The practical side, however, is concerned with the elaboration of methods by means of which such distinctions can be made in the daily application of epistemic analysis to concrete issues. But before we look at some of these methods (while keeping our focus on the Buddhist approach to these issues in mind), let us state from the outset that there is yet another important distinction to be made in the theoretical sphere of epistemological inquiry, one that is frequently overlooked, or blurred over by many writers, for one reason or another.

The distinction I am referring to here is that between "truth," in the most commonly accessible, empirical, and formal sense, as applied to individual statements, and "the Truth," taken to represent an ultimate, all-encompassing explanatory Principle, or absolute Reality, heavily laden with all sorts of implications (ontological, ethical, soteriological, and emotional), none of which are readily accessible to validation by ordinary means.[1] This latter notion, unlike the former, does not admit a plural, since it represents the final goal of the epistemic pursuit, as well as the ultimate referent of—in the words of a religious scholar—any "structure of religious apprehension."[2] Therefore, I would propose the use of the term *enlightenment* (as in the title of this book) when analyzing or discussing a system or structure of primarily religious knowledge (such as that of Yogācāra Buddhism, for instance), so that we may distinguish it from other types of epistemological pursuit, such as those which do not admit the existence of an absolute referent or goal (as for instance, the pursuit of aesthetic, scientific, ethical, or political knowledge).

Another thing that needs to be kept in mind when looking at various epistemological approaches, is the local coloring, or the predominant cognitive attitude, out of which every quest for truth emerges, or takes its particular, unique shape. To wit, the very notion that one can clearly and at all times distinguish between truth and error in all matters, as if they were two fundamentally different and always opposing entities, is in itself a specific cultural datum. For, in the Indian context, as well as in other Asian cultures, we find a different cognitive mode from that predominant in the West up to modern times, namely that the search for truth looks more like a continuous process of gradual approximation from a partial to a more complete truth, (a graded series of half-truths, one might say), rather than a sudden leap from the darkness of error into the brightness of the 'pure Truth,' whatever its name happens to be. This is best illustrated by the ancient Jain simile of the elephant and the six blind men, who each try to describe the whole animal from the part he is touching. As Professor Chandradhar Sharma puts it:[3]

> Almost all philosophical, ideological and religious differences and disputes are mainly due to mistaking a partial truth for the whole truth. Our judgments represent different aspects of the many-sided reality and can claim only partial truth. This view makes Jainism catholic, broad-minded and tolerant. It teaches respect for others' points of view.

In Jain epistemology, each point of view (*naya*), in order to be accepted as a valid judgement (*pramāna*), must be qualified by certain conditions (*syāt sat*). Therefore, the term *syāt* (lit., "somehow," "in a certain sense," "relatively speaking," "maybe") is regarded as the symbol of truth (*syātkāraḥ satyalāñchhanaḥ, Āptamīmāṃsā* X. 112).[4] Its function in Jain logic is to remove all contradictions among the different points of view, all equally relative and successive in time.

For instance, a table may exist in its own matter (such as wood), in its own specific form, length, breadth, and height, in a particular space, and at a particular time. It does *not*, however, exist in other matter (such as metal), other form, and in other space and time. So a table is both existent and non-existent when viewed from different points of view, and by specifying those, the apparent contradictin is removed. To reject the use of *syāt*, the specific condition under which a statement is made, is to leap blindly into unwarranted absolutism which is "directly contradicted by experience."[5]

This mode of dialectical reasoning was known as the Syādvāda, the doctrine of Relativity, or Anekāntavāda, the doctrine of Many-sidedness (of reality). It was also referred to as the Sapta-bhaṅgi-naya, or the "septalemma," being in sharp contrast with the Western, Aristotelian, and absolutist two-valued "either, or" type of logic known as the "dilemma." The Jain seven-fold relativism may be summarized as follows:

1. *Syādasti:* Relatively speaking, a thing is real.
2. *Syānnāsti:* Relatively speaking, a thing is unreal.
3. *Syādasti nāsti:* Relatively speaking, a thing is both real and unreal.
4. *Syādavaktavyam:* Relatively speaking, a thing is indescribable.
5. *Syādasti ca avaktavyam:* Relatively speaking, a thing is real and is indescribable.
6. *Syānnāsti ca avaktavyam:* Relatively speaking, a thing is unreal and is indescribable.
7. *Syādasti ca nāsti ca avaktavyam:* Relatively speaking, a thing is real, unreal, and indescribable.

According to C. Sharma, this sevenfold dialectical reasoning was not the invention of the Jainas. The first four steps were borrowed from the Buddhists, and the last three are nothing but combinations of the fourth with the first, the second, and the third alternative, respectively.[6] That seems to be borne out by the earliest mentions of a primitive form of Syādvāda in the Jain canonical text, the *Bhagavatī-sūtra*, quoted by the commentator Mallavādi in his *Naya-cakra*. Here are the two passages quoted by Mallavādi: (a) "Relatively, the soul is knowledge; relatively, the soul is ignorance" (*āyā siya ṇāṇe siya aṇṇāṇe*, Prakṛt); and: (b) "Relatively, the soul exists; relatively, the soul does not exist; relatively, the soul is indescribable" (*siya āyā, siya no āyā, siya avattavvam āyā*, Prakṛt).[7] The first fully developed form of the Jain septalemma appears, according to Sharma, in Kundakunda's *Pañcāstikāya-sāra* and *Pravacana-sāra*.[8]

Since it is not our purpose to elaborate further on Jain epistemology and logic (we will devote more space to their Buddhist equivalent in subsequent sections), let us return to our general considerations regarding epistemic methods.

Now, there are, broadly speaking, three *methods* available for the discovery of truth, or knowledge. These three methods may also be regarded as the three sources, bases, or proofs of the validity of knowledge. They are:

(1) **Sense-perception**, which may be important, but is by no means sufficient, since it may often be misleading (as, for instance, when a rope is mistaken for a snake, on account of darkness, fear, or both);

(2) **Reason**, which may be either inductive, empirical, inferential (i.e., from the particular to the general), or deductive, intuitive (i.e., from the general to the particular); and

(3) **Authority**, which may be either written (i.e., the scriptural tradition, the accumulated knowledge of generations), or oral (i.e., the inspired knowledge of a person, a charismatic individual, a guru, as it were). The Indian religio-philosophical tradition recognized the foregoing by admitting (1) perception (*pratyakṣa*); (2) inference (*anumāna*); and (3) testimony (*śabda*), as the fundamental bases of knowledge. Ninian Smart explains their application in the following words:[9]

> The first two of these were generally considered adequate sources of knowledge of the empirical world, given that the problem was conceived in terms of arriving at new facts, so that memory could be excluded (except in so far as it was built into the process of constructive perception). The chief importance of testimony was as a source of transcendent truth through revelation. For this reason, it was not, in this sense, recognized by the unorthodox schools [i.e., Buddhism and Jainism].

Another important distinction between the orthodox (i.e., those who accepted the validity of Vedic revelation) and the unorthodox (those who did not), was the search for the limits of knowledge, or of the human power of reasoning. In the case of Jainism, this may be seen in the example of the Syādvāda doctrine described above, while in the case of Buddhism, it was implied in such notions as the "Limit of the Reality of experience" (*bhūtakoṭi*), and especially in the widely used fourfold negative formula, the tetralemma (*catuṣkoṭi*).[10]

Of these two, the latter deserves special attention, for it represents the key to the understanding of Buddhist logic and epistemological method. The Buddhist tetralemma is truly the primal building block of the Buddhist mode of reasoning, with application not only in the epistemic domain, but in the ontic and ethical domains, as well, as we shall see. Used by the Buddha himself, as attested in the Pāli *Nikāyas*, it later became the cornerstone of that magnificent philosophical edifice built by Nāgārjuna and his followers. Through his skillful and extensive use of the tetralemma as the most powerful dialectical tool of his logical arsenal, this most brilliant Buddhist philosopher drew from his rivals accusations of nihilism and irrationality, along with their envious borrowing of the very same rhetorical technique they had criticized, in order to mount their counterattack. We shall now look more closely at the development, usage, and historical significance of the tetralemma formula in Buddhist logical discourse.

The Tetralemma Logic: a Thousand Years of Buddhist Dialectics

From the Upaniṣādic times onward, a new class of religious philosopher challenged the Brahmanical establishment in the very heart of their view of the world, that is, their cherished belief in the immutability of the universal order, best symbolized by their ancient ritual formulae, and more recently by the philosophical equation: Ātman = Brahman. This new class of non-Vedic freethinkers, known as the Śramaṇas, trusted nothing outside their own reason and experience. Thus they arrived at a radically new view of the world which they believed to be an incessant flux of events, in constant agitation and change.

Now, since their direct experience of this changing world was mediated only by reason, logic acquired great significance in their attempt to grasp and describe it, and thus gradually replaced the empty Brahmanical ritual and dogmatic formalism. Having developed a dynamic worldview, (what we called earlier a "process ontology") the unorthodox thinkers of Buddhism, Jainism, and of other schools of thought, needed to approach it with an equally dynamic, fluid, non-static, indeed dialectical logical method. This method was found in an ancient Indian normative structure which, although it may well have pre-dated Buddhism, it achieved undisputable prominence in the Buddhist scriptures (especially those of the Mādhyamika school), as the principle of the four-cornered negation, the tetralemma (*catuṣkoṭi*), and in turn may have influenced Jain logic in the form of the sevenfold alternative discussed above, the septalemma (Syādvāda).

Furthermore, over centuries of philosophical debate between various schools of thought, the Hindu philosophers reasserted their preeminence over their Buddhist and Jain rivals, precisely by incorporating their (the Buddhists' and the Jains') logical innovations into their own thought, which later blossomed into the great philosopher Śaṅkara's synthesis: the school of non-dual (Advaita) Vedānta.[11]

Now, the Buddhist application of the tetralemma culminated with the writings of Nāgārjuna, the founder and most illustrious philosopher of the Mādhyamika school. Particularly in the *Mūla-mādhyamika-kārikās* and the *Vigrahavyāvartanī*, this exhaustive logical formula was applied ruthlessly to every verbal statement pertaining to the nature of existence, and in such a thorough manner that if any ontological substratum is left in the aftermath of Nāgārjuna's sweeping analysis, it can only be of a relative, that is relational nature, as process not substance, and ultimately devoid of any speculative construction generated by the observer.

Here is the schematic expression of the tetralemma logic:

(1) x	is
(2) -x	is not
(3) x * -x	both (is and is not)
(4) -x * -(-x)	neither (is nor is not)

Note how thoroughgoing this type of logic is: it not only includes the two basic opposite alternatives of the classical either/or dilemma, but it also operates with a combination of the two, either conjunctively or disjunctively (both affirmation and negation, or neither affirmation nor negation). In addition, one has also the option of denying all four alternatives, in which case another, transcendental dimension will be created, which stands in opposition to all four, taken either individually or together. This fourfold negation is a metaphysical category, which the Buddhists are very fond of using in discussing ultimate matters, and which they call Voidness (Śūnyatā), while we may refer to it as the Zero (= Śūnya) category, as we proceed.

Of course, this is only one of the possible interpretations of the Buddhist tetralemma; several others have been proposed (by Chakravarti, Jayatilleke, Matilal, Nakamura, Raju, Robinson, Staal, Wayman, and others), which will be discussed below. For the moment, however, we shall content ourselves with its exposition as a perfectly viable, although not yet completely understood, modality of metaphysical inquiry, which in spite of its discomfort, so to speak, due to its seeming irrationality, has proven remarkably fruitful in the course of Buddhist (and not only Buddhist, as indicated previously) spiritual history.[12] For, Nāgārjuna was not only the greatest Buddhist dialectician and the father of the Mādhyamika school (the tetralemma being the very kernel of its dialectic), but also the grandfather of Ch'an and the great-grandfather of Zen, with their vast cultural implications over many centuries up to modern times, in both East and West.

Yet, it is interesting to note that the tetralemma was not a Buddhist discovery (as already hinted above), and not even an exclusive monopoly of the Indian philosophical tradition, as is commonly believed. It is true, however, that the Indians have the first written record of it in the refutations of Gautama (the founder of the school of Nyāyā) against the Vitandavādins, or "critics without a position of their own," whose main remembered representative was Sañjaya.[13]

Sañjaya, who lived and taught before the time of the Buddha (sixth century B.C.) is said to have given negative answers to all such questions as: "Is it good? Is it not good? Is it both good and not good? Is it neither good, nor not good?" The Buddhists at first refused to enter into any controversy with such thoroughly destructive criticism, which they called "eel-wriggling" philosophy, with no position of its own. Sometimes, Sañjaya, according to Buddhist records, would not even deny a proposition, and would refuse to answer "Yes" or "No" to a question. Of course, he was not alone in his position. The Jains, too, as pointed out above, were fond of this particular mode of prevarication or straddling.

The Early Use of the Tetralemma in the Pāli Canon

Before turning to Nāgārjuna's use of the dialectical method, let us trace its roots back to its earliest formulations found in the Pāli scriptures of the Theravāda canon (the *Tripiṭaka*). For our purpose, we will select from the rich metaphysical texture of these scriptures only three salient concepts, or doctrines: the Middle Way (*madhyamā-pratipad*), the Non-Self (*anātman*), and Dependent Origination (*pratītya-samutpāda*). In discussing each of these crucial concepts, the Buddha is compelled to use the method of dialectical reasoning, for none of these three is amenable to clear-cut disposition one way or the other, once and for all. Thus, arguments in the Pāli canon may take the form of a dual logic in which both terms are denied, of the tetralemma, or even of a sixfold combination of both. We shall illustrate each such instance, leaving the largest amount of examples pertaining to the aplication of the tetralemma for the last.

First, the *dilemma* is frequently employed in asserting the proper ethical conduct of the Buddhist novice, which was the middle way between the two prevalent, but equally undesirable extremes of asceticism and sensualism. The Buddha says:[14]

> These two extremes, mendicant brothers, are not to be approached by him who has withdrawn (from the world) . . . . . . Avoiding both these extremes, the middle road (*majjhimā paṭipadā*) . . . bringing insight, knowledge, leads to tranquillity, to highest knowledge, to full enlightenment, to peace (*nibbānāya*). (*Vinaya-Piṭaka, Mahā-vāgga*, I.6, vv. 10-29)

The proper beliefs ("right views," *samyag dṛṣṭi*) about the nature of the world are also introduced by means of the double negation:[15]

> But for one who in the light of the highest knowledge, O Kaccāna, considers how the world arises, belief in the non-being of the world passes away . . . and . . . belief in the being of the world passes away.
>
> (*Saṃyutta-Nikāya* 22.90).

In the same way the doctrines about the intrinsic nature of things are rejected:[16]

> That things have being, O Kaccāna, constitutes one extreme of the doctrine; that things have no being is the other extreme. These extremes, have been avoided by the Tathāgata and it is a middle doctrine he teaches.
>
> (*Saṃyutta-Nikāya* 22.90).

About human nature one can find a similar statement:[17]

> If, O priest, the dogma obtain that the soul and the body are identical, then there is no religious life; or if the dogma obtain that the soul is one thing and the body another, then also there is no religious life. Both these extremes have been avoided by the Tathāgata, and it is a middle doctrine he teaches: 'On existence depends birth . . .'
>
> (*Saṃyutta-Nikāya* 12.35).

It should be noted, also, that the Buddha recommends in a consistent manner the doctrine of Dependent Origination (*Pratītya-samutpāda*) as the middle way between Eternalism (Sassatavāda) and Nihilism (Ucchedavāda), by means of the same verbal technique (i.e., the negation of both antithetical extremes).

Now, here is one example where the Buddha uses a combination of double negation and fourfold negation (*catuṣkoṭi*) to convey an idea about human existence related to the one exemplified above:

> Gotama denies that: . . . Life and the body are identical, Life and the body are distinct; the Tathāgata passes to another existence after death here, . . . does not pass to another existence after death here, (that) both does and does not pass to another existence after his death here, (and that Tathāgata) neither passes nor does not pass to another existence after his death here.
>
> (*Majjhima-Nikāya* 72, *Aggi-Vacchagotta-Sutta* 1.484).

And the practical reason for such wholesale negation is given by the Gotama himself in the lines immediately following:[18]

> To hold that the world is eternal, or to hold that it is not, or to agree to any other of the propositions you adduce, Vaccha, is the thicket of theorizing, the wilderness of theorizing, the bondage . . . the tangle and the shackles of theorizing, attended by ill, distress, perturbation and fever; it conduces not to aversion, passionlessness, tranquillity, peace, illumination and Nirvāṇa. This is the danger I discern in these views, which makes me scout them all. (Ibid., 'Of Fuel' 1.486).[19]

In the *Cula-Sihanada-sutta* of the *Majjhima-Nikāya* 11.65-67, the Buddha speaks about the four attachments to be avoided by the monks: the attachments to sensuous pleasure, to speculative ideas (which are two: Eternalism and Nihilism), to works, and to soul-theories. They are all caused by ignorance, and dissipated through knowledge.[20] It is interesting to note that the Buddha uses here the plural (soul-theories), that is, he does not single out any particular concept of Self, or non-Self for that matter. It appears from this context that his intent was to deny the validity of the current theories of Self and not to affirm or commit himself to any particular view in that matter.

Elsewhere (*Panca Ttaya-sutta* C2.228, 233-36), by using the logic of the tetralemma, the Buddha refutes each and every one of the five possible interpretations of the Self theory, as supported by various groups of ascetics of his time.[21] The principle of the four-cornered negation is also applied in regards to the views of the Self and of the world as eternal and endless, to the views concerning the continuity and the limits of consciousness, to its pleasantness, and even to the concept of Nirvāṇa being in the "here and now." The advice given to his disciples is to "leave all views about past and future . . . behind," for "the Truth-finder's perfect way of utter peace . . . knows no grasping" [of speculative views], and thus he wins "full Enlightenment . . . and his Deliverance." (*Majjhima-Nikāya*, C2.237).[22]

On a number of occasions, the Buddha avoided unwelcome inquiry into speculative matters, either by keeping silent (vide: *Saṃyutta-Nikāya* 4.400f.; confer 3.99; and *Udana* 67),[23] or by using the four-cornered negation in order, as Dr. Oldenberg put it, to "close up all joints and loopholes, by which the true facts of the case might escape being caught in the logical net."[24]

This purposeful evasiveness of the Great Teacher in regard to the ultimate questions, is further justified by his thoroughly practical, non-speculative approach to the problems of human existence, aiming not at the continual stimulation and unrest of thought, but rather at its appeasement in Nirvāṇic bliss. When they prevail over the facts of experience, speculative views, ideas, theories, concepts, and dogmas, are all just as "unprofitable and not fundamental to the higher life" as it would be for a man transfixed by a poisoned arrow to ask questions about the archer's social status or the technology employed in the production of arrows.[25] One such example of clinging stubbornly (*tṛṣṇa*) and unprofitably to dogmatic views, is that given in the *Majjhima-Nikāya* 1.429-31 in relation to the six wrong outlooks pertaining to the Self:[26]

> (1) I have a Self; (2) I have not a Self; (3) By Self I perceive Self; (4) By Self I perceive non-Self; (5) By non-Self I perceive Self; and (6) By non-Self I perceive non-Self.

The above illustrations will suffice, I believe, to underline the continuity in epistemological method between the early Hīnayāna Buddhism of the Pāli canon, and the later Mahāyāna texts in general, and in particular, to prove the case of Nāgārjuna's indebtedness to the logical structures used by the Buddha himself (as recorded in the *Nikāyas*). In addition, the above quotations also reveal the direct relation between the open-ended tetralemma logic, and its variations, on the one hand, and the dynamic ontological postulates on which the entire Buddhist tradition was based: the doctrine of the Middle Way (between extremes), the non-Self (flexibly conceived) and their immediate corollary, causality through Dependent Origination. Next, we shall turn to Nāgārjuna's work itself.

Rationality and Irrationality in Nāgārjuna's Relativistic Logic

In a recent book on Nāgārjuna, Professor David J. Kalupahana makes the following piercing observations:[27]

> Some writers on Buddhism, intoxicated by this conception of the evolution of thought, have shown reluctance to recognize the sophistication with which philosophical ideas were presented by the Buddha 2,500 years ago. Having miserably failed to perceive the philosophical ingenuity of the Buddha as reflected in the Nikāyas and the Āgamas, as well as the subsequent degeneration of that system in the later commentarial tradition, followed by a revival of the earlier system by philosophers like Moggaliputta-tissa and Nāgārjuna, these writers are insisting upon a gradual sophistication in Buddhist thought comparable to what one can find in the Western philosophical tradition.

True as this may be, there are other misconceptions in regard to Buddhist thought (such as the accusations of irrationality, and of blatant ignorance of the basic rules of logic), which are even more startling (as they are unfair and inaccurate) when they come from such great scholars of Buddhism as Louis de La Vallée Poussin. Speaking of the tetralemma, which he calls "a four-branched dilemma" of Buddhist dialectic, he fails to grasp its crucial significance in Buddhist epistemology, as a versatile, multi-valued logical tool:[28]

> Indians do not make clear distinction between facts and ideas, between ideas and words; they have never clearly recognized the principle of contradiction. Buddhist dialectic has a four-branched dilemma: Nirvāṇa is existence or non-existence, or both existence and non-existence, or neither existence nor non-existence. We are helpless.

If the first misconception pointed out by Kalupahana was dealt with in the preceding section on the continuity between early and later Buddhist logical thought, the second, that is Poussin's (and others') accusation of irrationality will be looked at—in the succeeding pages—from two points of view: (a) the purely formal, theoretical principles of classical Aristotelian logic, and (b) the practical, functional role it played within the larger context of the Buddhist culture, centered on meditation.

First, let us take a look at the Buddhist multi-valued logic from the point of view of the Greek, and Western, philosophical tradition. Professor McClure says that the famous Greek sceptic Pyrrho, who accompanied Alexander the Great in his Indian campaign, was influenced in his extreme scepticism by the sceptics of India.[29] The fact is that the four-cornered negation, in one form or another, has appeared in Greek philosophy by the time of Alexander's campaigns (fourth century B.C.), and Aristotle, who was Pyrrho's contemporary, does indeed make use of it in some of his late writings. To wit, in the fourth book of his *Metaphysics*, where he speaks about some logical contradictions inherent in certain supposedly apodictical statements, such as: "Everything is true" (or false, or being, or not-being), or—as Heraclitus and Anaxagoras attempted to resolve it—"Everything is and is not" (or mixed up, "neither good, nor not good," respectively).[30]

Even more intriguing is the fact that, just as Nāgārjuna arrives at his metaphysical ultimate, Śūnyatā (Voidness), by means of the four-cornered negation, so does Aristotle discover his concept of the "Unmoved Mover" by denying the four possible alternatives, namely that: (1) Everything is at rest; (2) Everything is in motion; (3) Everything is sometimes at rest and sometimes in motion; and that (4) Nothing is always one or the other. "For," concludes the Philosopher, "there is something that is always moving the things that are moved, and the first mover is itself unmoved."[31]

Now, on the other hand, if the Greeks did have some familiarity with the logic of the fourfold denial, and, as we have shown, attempted to use it whenever they wanted to avoid the paradoxical dead-ends of the either/or dual logic (which they favored), the Mādhyamikas by the same token did not, as they have been accused, ignore the three traditional "Laws of Thought," so dear to the proponents of the dual logical system. According to Richard H. Robinson, these laws are invoked constantly throughout Nāgārjuna's *Kārikās*.[32] Thus, the "principle of non-contradiction" is stated in general form in two places:[33]

> Existent and inexistent in a unity is not true to fact. (7.30)
>
> . . . Since they are mutually contradictory; where are there both real and unreal in the same place? (8.7)

The second "law of the excluded middle" is also mentioned explicitly, or implicitly, in a number of places:

> A goer does not go, and a non-goer does not go; what third one other other than goer and non-goer goes? (2.8)
>
> A goer does not stand still, and a non-goer does not stand still; what third one other than goer and non-goer stands still? (2.15)

> That existent would be either permanent or impermanent. (21.14)

The third "law of identity" (on which the classical three-footed syllogism is based) is nowhere explicitly stated in the *Kārikas*, but it is clearly implied in certain statements regarding the nature of causation:

> Otherness does not occur in an other and does not occur in a non-other; and when otherness does not occur, there is neither an other nor an identity. (14.7)
>
> An "A" that comes into being dependent on "B" is not identical with "B" and not other than "B". (18.10)
>
> If there were oneness of effect and cause, there would be oneness of producer and product. If there were difference of effect and cause, the cause would be the same as a non-cause. (20.20)

Clearly, the greatest Buddhist philosopher was not ignorant of the most basic rules of logical reasoning. His dialectic did not automatically exclude the common sense dichotomies of thought, but he incorporated them explicitly or not, in a complementary manner, within a larger, more flexible and exhaustive logical framework.[34] We shall now turn to the argument of functionality, in connection with the practical role played by the tetralemma in the context of Buddhist meditation. This, too, will help dispel the myth of the irrationality of the *catuṣkoṭi* logic.[35]

Professor Alex Wayman in his article "Who understands the four alternatives of the Buddhist texts?", following Tsoṅ-kha-pa's separation of the causation and the existence aspects of the tetralemma (each denied), quite rightly points out the main reason for the prevalent misunderstanding of this problem, namely, the failure to perceive the practical, meditative function of the *catuṣkoṭi* as a mental technique with various specific applications.[36]

By removing it from its original meaningful context of Buddhist religious practice, and studying it *in abstracto* (using the artificial language of a symbolic system, for instance), in an attempt to find its universal, almost mathematical value, one runs the risk of falling into the very trap that modern logic set out to avoid: the growing gap between words, signs, symbols, and the content (i.e., the Reality) that they purport to express. In an extreme case, one may even fail to see the forest from the trees, as Jayatilleke does, and utter the strange statement that Nāgārjuna himself did not understand what he was talking about when applying "the logic of the four alternatives," for, presumably, he did not know the magic of the formal symbolic system.[37]

Let us see for ourselves whether Nāgārjuna understood *catuṣkoṭi* (tetralemma) logic or not, that is, whether his use of it was in any way consistent with the way in which the Buddha himself used it in his discourses (the Pāli *Nikāyas*) (see supra). Again, for practical purposes, I shall restrict my inquiry to the same essential concepts in relation to which the four-fold denial most frequently appears (in both Theravāda and Mahāyāna scriptures), namely: the Middle Way, Non-Self, and Dependent Origination.

The Middle Way (*madhyamā pratipad*) represents the very essence of the Mādhyamika school in that it avoids all dogmatic dichotomies in all realms: the ethical, the metaphysical, and the epistemological. Indeed, as Jacques May writes: "all Buddhists should be called Mādhyamaka or Mādhyamika," for the middle course in all things was the fundamental attitude of their Master.[38] This view is repeatedly confirmed in the writings of Nāgārjuna:

> In the Discourse with Kātyāyana both "is" and "is not" are denied by the Lord (who) makes manifest "being" and "non-being." (15.7)

> "Is" is the notion of the Eternalism; "is not" is the view of Annihilationism; therefore, the clear-sighted should not adhere to "being" and "non-being." (15.10)

The above passage refers to the Buddha's exposition on the right views (*sammādiṭṭhi*) in the *Saṃyutta-Nikāya* (*Pāli Texts Society* 2, p. 17),[39] which shows beyond all doubt Nāgārjuna's familiarity with, and reliance upon, the early scriptures. Having denied both opposite views regarding existence, it follows, implicitly, that they will not stand scrutiny either conjunctively or disjunctively (which is what the third and the fourth alternatives of the tetralemma are about).[40] Thus, the result will always be voidness (Śūnyatā), or the denial of independent status to all extreme views, each having been proved in the last analysis dependent upon the other for its mere existence. In other words, one may say that all "existential elements" (*dharma*s) are ultimately de-void (rather than "empty") of self (or self-existence, *svabhāva*); they can only come into being, exist, and vanish interdependently, or "relatively." In the chapter entitled "An Analysis of the Noble Truths" (*āryasatya*), Nāgārjuna explains:

> That which is Dependent Origination we call "Voidness." This is an appellative convenience for the Middle Way. (24.18)

> Since no independently originated element of existence (dharma) can be found, no non-Void element of existence can be found. (24.19)

We come across the same idea in the *Vigrahavyāvartanī*, where it is stated that the Teacher is That "Who expounds Voidness, Dependent Origination, and the Middle Path, with one and the same meaning."[41]

Now, in respect to the individual self (*ātman*), the argument follows the same pattern:[42]

> "Self" is taught, "non-Self" is also taught, "no Self nor non-Self at all" is also taught by the Buddhas. (18.6)
>
> Everything is true, or not true, both true and not true, neither true nor not true—this is the instruction of the Buddhas. (18.8)
>
> If something arises interdependently, it is not *that*, nor, moreover, is it *other;* therefore, it is neither continuity nor interruption. (18.10)
>
> If the Self were the aggregates (*skandhas*), it would be subject to arising and disappearance; if the Self were other than the aggregates, it would be without the characteristics of the aggregates. (18.1)
>
> Consequently, the Self (*ātman*) cannot be either identical or different from the dependency (on the *skandhas*); the Self does not exist apart from this dependency, nor is it certain that it does not exist. (27.8)

The similarity of this with the Buddha's own Middle Way position between these two extreme views regarding the self, is obvious. (vide supra). True enough, as Stcherbatsky observed, "the question of identity between the self and the body is usually formulated as a dilemma, whereas the antinomies regarding the post-Nirvāṇic Self (e.g., the Tathāgata) are formulated in the familiar Indian method of quadrilemma."[43] The combination between the two gave rise to the "14 insoluble points," or *avyākṛtavastūni*, on which the Buddha remained silent, as enumerated by Candrakīrti, Nāgārjuna's foremost disciple.[44] However, to arrive at his own conclusion that none of the views about the self can be definitely substantiated, Nāgārjuna does make use of the tetralemma, in both negative and affirmative ways. (vide 18.8 above). But, since each of the four alternatives stands opposite to the other three, they cannot all be true *at the same time.* Taken *in toto,* the result is devoid of independent status, or validity, being annulled by the other three. Therefore, Nāgārjuna concludes that the character of the true, absolute, unconditioned Reality (*tattvasya lakṣaṇa*), is indeterminate, that is, can never be expressed through verbal construction (*prapañcair aprapañcita*):

> Non-conditionally related to any entity, quiescent, indeterminate through verbal expression, free from discrimination, undifferentiated—this is the character of true Reality (*tattva*). (18.9)

> Non-identity, non-differentiation, non-interruption, and non-eternity—these are the immortal teachings of the Buddhas, the guides of this world. (18.11)

Now, this conclusion gives rise to some interesting observations. "Indeterminate . . . undifferentiated" means "that which is neither this way, nor the other, neither positive, nor negative." Thus, it may equally refer to both words and numbers. Suppose we want to substitute numbers for words in the tetralemma formula. We can use either a single number, or any arithmetical combination of numbers. For example, take the following series of real numbers:

$$\infty\ (-)\ \ldots\ 987654321 \quad 0 \quad 123456789\ \ldots\ (+)\ \infty$$

If we choose a random combination of, say, two numbers: 3 and 7, and apply the tetralemma formula, the first two alternatives will be: (1) $x = (+3+7)$ and (2) $-x = (-3-7)$. Now, if we combine them conjunctively or disjunctively, as the last two alternatives require, and then effectuate the algebraic operations, the result in both cases will be zero:

$$(3)\ (+3+7) + (-3-7) = (+10) + (-10) = 0 \text{ and}$$
$$(4)\ -(+3+7) - (-3-7) = (-10) - (-10) = 0$$

Since zero, while still a number in the series, is neither positive nor negative, it may be said to be indeterminate, in terms of plus and minus, as well as numeric quantity. (It goes without saying that it cannot be both positive and negative, since it is neither). Yes, a Nyāyā or Buddhist Realist would say, zero is indeed indeterminate, but it does not follow that all four alternatives can be reduced to zero, since the first two, when taken separately, do have a reality of their own, that is, are different from zero, so that all four alternatives cannot be so readily equated and denied *in toto.*

This is true, would answer the Mādhyamika Buddhist, only relatively speaking, for, ultimately, every number (or combination thereof) exists by virtue of its relation to the other(s), and all point to, and derive meaning from, the beginning of the series (the first unit). Therefore, when the Realist ascribes absolute Reality (or existence) to a number, he misses the essential point, namely that every number is nothing but a sign, or a landmark indicating the relative distance (in number of units) from the only absolutely "real" number (i.e., which stands on its own, without reference to another): *zero,* the beginning of the series. In this way, all the four alternatives *can* be reduced to zero, in the ultimate, absolute sense.

Now, in the early Sanskrit texts, zero has been called "*śūnya.*" According to Stcherbatsky, the word was borrowed by the early Buddhists to denote the concept of limit with regard to the relativity of the empirical world (*bhūtakoṭi*).[45] However, the exact meaning of *śūnya* became later confused with one of its synonyms (mathematically speaking), the word *ambara,* whose secondary meanings were "sky," or "empty space," and which was represented not by a point, but by an empty circle. Thus, says P. T. Raju in his article "The Principle of Four-cornered Negation,"[46]

> . . . in spite of repeated protests by Nāgārjuna and his followers, even his own contemporaries took the word *śūnya* in its secondary meaning (i.e., nothingness, emptiness, absence of a content, as opposed to its indeterminacy), and accused Nāgārjuna of being a nihilist, a negativist, and so forth.

Through subsequent translations of the term (probably influenced by the Hegelian view of oriental dialectics), this confusion survives even today, so that the renditions "empty" (i.e., lacking in content) and "void" (i.e., devoid of either positive, or negative content, or qualification, indeterminate) are loosely interchangeable. True, the distinction is a very subtle one, but it is essential for the proper understanding of this important Buddhist concept, *śūnya* (=void of self-existence, *svabhāva*). By substituting numbers, instead of words, the original meaning of the Void (*śūnya*), of co-origination through dependence of all verbal notions, that is of the fundamental relativity of all concepts and philosophical entities (being *devoid* of independent status), comes to the fore. This, in our view, is the functional role played by the tetralemma logic in Buddhist epistemology.

Another, equally valid interpretation, but from a different

standpoint, has been offered by Professor Alex Wayman, in agreement with Candrakīrti's commentary on *Mūlamādhyamika-kārikas* 18.8 quoted above.[47] Just as in algebra one goes from the simple to the more elaborated problems, so can the tetralemma be presented as a gradual teaching device, as a "ranking in a disjunctive system," as Wayman puts it. Without reproducing the evidence he adduces from both Candrakīrti and from Asaṅga's *Mahāyāna-Sūtrālaṃkāra* (to be found in his article), let us just say that each of the four alternatives is to be seen as one step on the path of omniscience about the true nature of Reality (*tattva*).

Interestingly, Robinson arrives at a similar conclusion, following largely the same authoritative commentary of Candrakīrti, the *Prasannapadā*, namely that the tetralemma was used as a therapeutic device for the Buddhist practitioners still attached to one particular view or another. Unlike Wayman, however, he forcibly introduces Hegelian dialectics, seeing negation where there is in fact integration and transcendence. He writes:[48]

> This is a dialectical progression, each lemma negating and cancelling its predecessor, and the whole argument moving forward to the negation of the fourth lemma, which is supposed to dispose of all 'views'.

Robinson also fails to see the connection between the fusion of opposite polarities and the Void, for he says:[49]

> It is doubtful whether "positive" and "negative" have anything to do with the meaning of "emptiness," except as signalling emotional acceptance or rejection.

Such myopia seems to be hopelessly rooted in a persistence in looking for the meaning of "emptiness" in the absolute sense, where there is rather a lack (i.e., a "void") of something, namely of self-existence. Therefore, his considerations on 'emptiness' will lead him nowhere, and his last statement on this topic:[50]

> The 'emptiness' class has 'designations' as members, and some designations are cogent; thus the emptiness class is not null, but is co-extensive with the universal class.

is, so to speak, the polar opposite of what Nāgārjuna himself says on the subject:

> Voidness was proclaimed by the Conquerors (i.e., the Buddhas) as the remedy (*niḥsaraṇa*) to all views; but those were declared incurable (*asādhya*) for whom there is a view of Voidness. (13.8)

Consequently, the viewpoints, or various philosophical systems (when the views are developed into elaborate constructions about the absolute, ultimate nature of Reality), may also be seen as interdependent variables, arising through mutual interaction, at different degrees of opposition toward each other and at a variable distance from a central gravity point (*śūnya*), which is the point of mutual annullment. Graphically, they might be pictured as a scattered plot, or tri-dimensionally, as a sphere containing various free-floating points of reference.

This functional interpretation seems to be almost unanimously supported by those researchers who applied the tetralemma to causality or Dependent Origination: A. Wayman,[51] T. R. V. Murti,[52] K. Venkata Ramanan,[53] and David J. Kalupahana.[54] Kamalaśīla's commentary quoted by Professor Wayman, explains the four alternatives in terms of the Sāṃkhya position, the Jain and certain Buddhist doctrinal views, the Nyāyā-Vaiśeṣika philosophy, and of the Lokāyata materialist and Sañjaya sceptical positions, respectively. This seems to be yet another possible interpretation, which may be borne out, at least implicitly, by the last verses of the last chapter of the *Kārikās:*

> If both the finite and the infinite could be demonstrated, then, likewise, neither the finite nor the infinite can be proven. (27.28)
>
> Moreover, since all entities display the nature of Voidness, where, by whom, and in what manner could such views on continuity, etc., ever be sustained? (27.29)
>
> I honor Gautama (the Buddha), who out of compassion has taught the true doctrine for the destruction of all views. (27.30)

Nāgārjuna's position was confirmed by his pupil Āryadeva, in his short poetical treatise "The Dialectic which Refutes Errors, Establishing Logical Reasons," in which he states:[55]

> These errors such as Permanence, Nihilism, Non-existence, Existence, and other extremes, are held to by people who fall under the power of bad views fallacious as dreams.

Thus, the tetralemma (*catuṣkoṭi*) became a "meditative exercise" (part of the *vipassanā* meditation), serving a double function, as, Professor Wayman observes, namely (a) to classify and reject all philosophical positions as equally pernicious to the pacification of the mind, and (b) "to establish the absolute by negating the notional activity of the mind" (*asaṃjñā-skandha*).[56] As a result, the principle of Causality (*pratītya-samutpāda*), that is, the principle of Relativity itself, came to replace for the Mahāyāna Buddhists the immutable absolutes promulgated under different names by various religio-philosophical systems of that time (e.g., Ātman-Brahman, Puruṣa-Prakṛti, etc.). But, since according to Nāgārjuna (vide *Mūlamādhyamika-kārikās* 24.18; 25.19-24), the ultimate Reality is *śūnya*, or the four-fold negation, the essential nature of everything (*sarvadharma, sarva-bhāva*) is *śūnya*, or the four-fold negation.

At this point, one should note, the border line between the epistemic domain (i.e., *catuṣkoṭi* as a logical tool, a principle or gnoseological method in the hands of Sañjaya, and of the Buddha and his early disciples) and the ontic domain (i.e., *catuṣkoṭi* as the expression of the absolute Reality itself, first tentatively by Nāgārjuna and later more definitely by his followers), seems to be fading away. One begins to wonder where one ends and the other begins, as if the subject, the *knower*, is becoming immersed in the object, the *known*, of his contemplation. Perhaps, this was indeed the very purpose of using the tetralemma, namely to bring about a suspension of the restless activity of the mind by annulling the opposing points of view and fixing one's attention on the zero category, the Void (*śūnya*).[57] But this sort of Enlightenment is "adoxic," rather than "paradoxic," for, in the light of the doctrine of the two truths (the conventional, *saṃvṛti-satya*, and the ultimate, or absolute, *paramārtha-satya*), *śūnya* itself will have to be abandoned, like a raft after crossing a river. This is explained by Nāgārjuna in the chapter on the noble truths (*āryasatya*), where he addresses his "dim-witted" opponents thus:

> Resting upon two truths is the Dharma-teaching of the Buddhas: the relative (worldly) truth and the absolute (ultimate, supreme) Truth. (24.8)
>
> Those who do not discern the distinction (between) these two truths, do not discern the profound nature of the Buddhas' teaching. (24.9)
>
> Without resorting to pragmatic truth (*vyavahāra*), the ultimate it not revealed; without approaching the ultimate (Truth), Nirvāṇa cannot be attained. (24.10)

Language, that is, worldly truth, is useful only in so far as it brings one closer to Reality, the 'other shore' of Nirvāṇa, but once there, it becomes a nuisance. For, in Robert F. Olson's words, "All thought is about thought, all talk is about talk—'reality,' the world as it is, is free from fabrication (*avyaktavya*), quiet (*śānta*), and beyond words (*avacana*)."[58] Therefore, even *śūnya*, the Void itself, in as far as it is a mere mental construct, a verbal indicator, will lose its usefulness at some point:

> Consequently, in all cases, the dependency and the dependent are void; then how could a void Tathāgata be known by means of a void? (22.10)

> Neither "void" nor "non-void" may be ascertained, nor both, nor either; they are spoken of only for the sake of expedient teaching (*prajñapti*). (22.11)

This purpose was missed by many, and Jacques May is only one of them when he asserts that "the Mādhyamika thought primarily refers to metaphysics or ontology, and secondarily to epistemology."[59] The truth of the matter, as we have seen, is that precisely the opposite was the case, and May himself is forced to admit that "it nowhere states a positive doctrine of being," and that "nothing in the empirical reality reaches full being," since "emptiness (*śūnyatā*) is not an entity."[60] He seems closer to the truth, however, when he states the following:[61]

> Emptiness is the true ontological status of the universe and its constituents, with the restriction that such a status is not really to be caught anywhere, and is just a projection from the mundane truth toward the real truth . . . Emptiness, in my opinion [and here he closely follows Stcherbatsky, nn.[62]], is a relativity in which the aspect of ontological unsubstantiality is stressed extremely strongly, so strongly that the Mādhyamikas have constanty to deny being nihilists . . . (For) . . . A dream, a mirage, have a very tenuous existence; but they exist somehow; they are there somehow; they are not nothing. Emptiness is not nothingness. The Mādhyamika is a 'quasi-nihilism,' but not a nihilism.

In such ways does Nāgārjuna's approach to knowledge still puzzle the philosophers of older and more recent times, when they fail to consider the fourfold negation as a practical, albeit *sui-generis* epistemological tool, serving primarily a didactic purpose as a meditative exercise, the function of which being to free the mind for the unmediated experience of Reality.

Epistemology in the Laṅkāvatāra-sūtra: A Radical Critique of Language, Logic, and Knowledge

Now in the *Laṅkāvatāra-sūtra*, which is generally considered part of the early phase of Yogācāra thought, a shift occurs from the purely argumentative logic of the Mādhyamikas to a more thorough investigation of the cognitive mental processes by which knowledge is acquired, stored, and retrieved. The emphasis upon the importance of meditative practice, and of the immediacy of experience will become increasingly obvious. Hence, the two names of this school: the Yogācāra (lit., "the practice of Yoga"), and the Vijñānavāda (lit., "the doctrine of Consciousness"). In this sense, one can speak of continuity of concern, but only insofar as one is willing to accept the interpretation of the tetralemma logic as a didactic tool for the purpose of directing one's energies away from philosophical speculations toward meditative practice, as indicated above.

The major difference, however, is the replacement of the Voidness concept by a number of psycho-ontological categories, such as the "Repository-of-impressions" (Ālaya-vijñāna), or the "Essence-of-Buddhahood" (Tathāgata-garbha), which gave rise to bitter accusations of substantialism. Interestingly enough, such imputations fall at the opposite end of the spectrum from those hurled against the Mādhyamikas, namely those of Nihilism, as we have seen. The accusations of Eternalism were due to the close resemblance between the "Essence (or embryo/womb)-of-Buddhahood," pregnant with all possibilities and throbbing with karmic seeds of all states of consciousness (Vijñānas), on the one hand, and the Hindu concept of Ātman, or Self, on the other.

To defend themselves, the Yogācāra metaphysicians had to appeal once more to the time-proven epistemological device: the denial of both extreme viewpoints (the Middle Way) and of any combination thereof (the tetralemma logic). Thus, the distinction between the Hindu substantial Self and the Buddhist Essence-of-the-Enlightened-Being is put in the following terms (*Laṅkāvatāra-sūtra* II: 79; ll.5-11):[63]

> The Lord replied: "Not at all, Mahāmati, my 'Essence-of-Buddhahood' is not equal to the Ātman doctrine taught by the philosophers. For what the Tathāgatas teach, Mahāmati, is

the doctrine of Essential-Nature-of-Buddhahood having the meaning of being devoid of will-effort, ineffable, unborn, Nirvāṇa, Reality-limit, voidness."

"The Tathāgatas, the Arhats, the Fully Enlightened ones, teach the doctrine pointing to the Essence-of-Buddhahood for the purpose of making the immature cast aside all trace of fear due to (the teaching of) Selflessness, and (for the purpose of realizing) the state of non-imagination and non-discrimination."

Elsewhere, the same problem is put in more general terms, and solved by means of three alternatives (trilemma), all denied (*Laṅkāvatāra-sūtra* II: 80; ll. 13-15):

> How, again, Mahāmati, does the Bodhisattva the Great Being get rid of the views (regarding) birth, abiding, and disappearance? By this is meant that all entities are to be regarded as the forms born in a dream or a delusion, since they are not brought into being either through themselves, through other, or both.

A more complete explanation regarding the ambiguities of language, and hence the limits of knowledge, is given at the end of the fifth chapter, "On the Deduction of Permanency and Impermanency of Tathāgatahood" (*Laṅkāvatāra-sūtra* V: 217; ll. 3-5, 14-16; and, 218; ll. 1-2, 5-8):

> The Lord said: "Mahāmati, the Tathāgata [i.e., the Buddha, the Enlightened Being] is neither permanent nor impermanent. Why? For this reason, namely because of the wrong attachment to either. (. . .) Again, Mahāmati, the Tathāgata is *not permanent;* hence, the attachment (to the Tathāgata) is useless, like gathering up space. That is to say, Mahāmati, space is neither permanent nor impermanent, on account of the exclusion of (both) permanence and impermanence, and it is only due to the false (views of) Oneness and Otherness, of Bothness and non-Bothness that it is spoken of (as such)."
>
> "However, Mahāmati, there is another condition by which the Tathāgata may be said to be *permanent.* Why? For this reason: because of the permanence about the knowledge regarding the mastery of clear understanding, the Tathāgata *is* permanent. For, Mahāmati, the knowledge of the mastery of clear understanding is indeed permanent, belonging to the Fully Enlightened Ones, the Arhats, the Tathāgatas."

The seeming contradiction, described above, is explained away in relation to the cognitive context (religious versus empirical). The metaphor of space (*ākāśa*) reinforces the empirical side, that of the Tathāgata, the religious, or the transcendental side. This represents an echo of the idea of the two truths, the conventional (*saṃvṛti-satya*) and the ultimate, absolute (*paramārtha-satya*), found in Nāgārjuna's *Mūlamādhyamika-kārikās* 24.8-10 (vide supra). In one form or another, this epistemological distinction runs like a red thread throughout the *Laṅkāvatāra*, as will be shown in the succeeding sections of this book. For the moment, let us read the end of the fifth chapter on the Tathāgata, where two types of cognitive processes are explained: one based upon opposite alternatives (*vikalpa buddhi*), the other transcending all contradictions, derived from the intuitive understanding obtained during the solitude of meditation (*vivikta buddhi*). Thus, the *Laṅkāvatāra* V: 219; ll. 1-9 vv. 1-3;

> The holding of the immature onto [the duality of] permanence and impermanence, Mahāmati, comes from the abiding in the mode of cognition based upon disjunctive alternatives (*vikalpa-buddhi*), and not from the abiding in the understanding based on the views derived from solitary [meditation, *vivikta-buddhi*].
>
> Therefore, it is said:
> "By abandoning the (ideas of) permanence and impermanence, (and yet) by mastering (both) permanence and impermanence, those who always see the Buddhas (as their goal), will not become subject to the power of philosophical viewpoints [or doctrines, *dṛṣṭi*].
>
> "When (both) permanence and impermanence are adhered to, the preparation (for Buddhahood) (is achieved) through complete knowledge. Through the (very) imperfection of knowledge based on dichotomous (thinking), (both) permanence and impermanence are warded off.
>
> "Whenever an affirmation is made, all becomes ambiguous. (But when) it is understood that there is nothing but one's own mind [i.e., making a one-sided assertion], disputes are not engaged in."

An interesting illustration of such a non-dual mode of thinking, taken from the realm of modern physics, is given by Bertrand Russell, who was not only a scientist, but also one of the most important analytic philosophers of our time. In his book *Human*

Knowledge, Its Scope and Limits, he writes:[64]

> Take, for example, the question of waves versus particles. Until recently it was thought that this was a substantial question: light must consist either of waves or of little packets called photons. It was regarded as unquestionable that matter consisted of particles. But at last it was found that the equations were the same if both matter and light consisted of particles, or if both consisted of waves. Not only were the equations the same, but all the verifiable consequences were the same. Either hypothesis, therefore, is equally legitimate, and neither can be regarded as having a superior claim to truth. The reason is that the physical world can have the same structure, and the same relation to experience, on the one hypothesis as on the other.

For the ancient Indian philosophers, the transcendence of the dual categories of thought was best achieved through the use of the four propositions, the tetralemma logic (*catuṣkoṭi*), which were all answered in the negative by the Buddhists. Here is yet another such instance found in the *Laṅkāvatāra,* where a materialist (Lokāyata) philosopher of the brāhmin caste questions the Buddhist teacher on a number of metaphysical issues. Thus, *Laṅkāvatāra-sūtra:* 176; ll. 16-20 and 177; ll. 1-5:

> Again, Mahāmati, the Lokāyata brāhmin spoke to me thus: "O Gautama, is all Oneness? Is all Otherness? Is all Bothness? Is all non-Bothness? Is it all subject to causality, since it is seen as arising from manifold causes?"—This, brāhman, is the tenth school of Materialism.
>
> "Again, O Gautama, is all unexplainable, is all explainable? Is there a Self, is there no-Self? Is this world real, is this world unreal? Is there another world, is there no other world, and is another world existent or non-existent? Is there liberation (*mokṣa*), is there no liberation? Is it all temporary, is it all non-temporary? Are space, cessation (of pain) without preparation and Nirvāṇa [i.e., cessation of pain through meditation] created or uncreated, O Gautama? Is there an intermediate existence, is there no intermediate existence?"

The answer to these questions, as given in the *Laṅkāvatāra-sūtra,* perpetuates a continuing stream of meaningful Buddhist ambiguity. It began with the Buddha's own meaningful silence in answer to the ultimate questions recorded in the Pāli scriptures, was rejuvenated through the masterful use of the tetralemma dialectic in the works of the Mādhyamika philosophers, and it was to achieve its ultimate expression in the metaphysical riddles (the *Kōan*) of the Ch'an and the Japanese Zen traditions. Thus, *Laṅkāvatāra-sūtra* III: 177; ll. 15-16:

> Nirvāṇa [i.e., the extinction of suffering through *gradual* training of purification], space, Nirodha [i.e., the *sudden* cessation of pain, the third unconditioned entity, *asaṃskṛta dharma*, of Buddhism], they (only exist) on account of their categorization [or designation by name]; (their) reality is indeed unobtainable. Therefore, the questioning [about their nature] is done away with [is superfluous, futile].

The issue of Nirvāṇa, being of central importance to Buddhist practice, requires perhaps further comment. It is interesting to note that its solution in the *Laṅkāvatāra-sūtra* is very similar to that given by Nāgārjuna in his chief work *The Verses of the Middle Way*, including the denial of all alternative statements, and the mention of the Void (*śūnya*) as the only key to correct understanding. Here are what have become over the centuries, perhaps, the most celebrated verses in Mahāyāna Buddhism (*Mūlamādhyamika-kārikā* 25.19-20, and 22-23):

> There is no distinguishing whatsoever of Saṃsāra [the world of empirical existence] from Nirvāṇa; there is no distinguishing whatsoever of Nirvāṇa from Saṃsāra.
>
> The extent (*koṭi*) of Nirvāṇa is the extent of Saṃsāra; there is not even the tiniest interval between them.
>
> All existential elements being void (of self-existence), what is infinite and what is finite, what is both finite and infinite, and what is neither finite nor infinite?
>
> What, indeed, is "that," what "another," what permanence, impermanence, both permanence and impermanence, or even neither (permanence nor impermanence), then?

And now, here is how the compiler(s) of the *Laṅkāvatāra-sūtra* formulated this extremely delicate issue (*Laṅkāvatāra-sūtra* II: 76-7; ll.7-17, 1-2; vv. 137-38):

> "Again, Mahāmati, what is meant by 'non-duality'? It means

that black and white, long and short, light and shade, are relative terms, Mahāmati, and not independent [from each other]. Thus, as Nirvāṇa and Saṃsāra are, Mahāmati, all things are non-dual; there is no Nirvāṇa, Mahāmati, (except) where is Saṃsāra; and there is no Saṃsāra, (except) where is Nirvāṇa, due to the existence of the state of manifold [or, indeterminate, mutual, *vilakṣaṇa-hetu*] causation. This is what is meant by 'All things—[including] the Parinirvāṇa and Saṃsāra—are non-dual.'

Consequently, Mahāmati, yoga practice should be directed towards the aim concerning the absence of self-existence, non-duality, no-birth, and Voidness."

At that moment, quite appropriately, the Lord recited this couple of verses:

"I always preach Voidness, which is free from (both) Eternalism and Nihilism; Saṃsāra is like a dream, or an illusion, but the karma does not disappear.

Space, and likewise Nirvāṇa [i.e., the gradual extinction of pain], Nirodha [i.e., the sudden cessation], and even the duality [i.e., of Parinirvāṇa and Saṃsāra, see above]—(these) the immature imagine as *not* being produced by causation, and *not* as being free from (both) being and non-being."

The striking similarity of both content and expression between the two sources cited can only indicate that the authors of both texts, the *Mūlamādhyamika-kārikās* and the *Laṅkāvatāra-sūtra*, drew from a common pool of ideas circulating freely in central and southern India, between the first and the third centuries, as suggested in our historical introduction. While both texts show evidence of concern with the traps and limitations of language and conceptual thinking (in dualistic terms), the *Laṅkāvatāra* points to a practical, existential solution, to which all analytical discussions are to be subjected, as means to an end.[65] The religious goal, that is, the practice of Yoga, is always foremost in this writer's mind. This is clearly stated throughout the *Sūtra*. Here is just one salient example, from *Laṅkāvatāra* III: 172; ll. 10-14:

That is to say that there is a noble transcendental state of inner attainment, which is beyond the conscious volition (*mano-vijñāna*), the pre-conscious will-power (*manas*), and the (empirical) mind (*citta*), which does not fall into the dualism of Oneness

> and Otherness, of Bothness and not-Bothness, which has nothing to do with illustrating, theorizing, philosophizing and logic, and which (has never been understood) by any bad logicians [or sophists, *kutārkikā*], (such as) the Self-enlightened Buddhas, the novices [i.e., the Hīnayānists], and the [non-Buddhist] philosophers, who have fallen into the dualistic extremes of Being and non-Being. This I call "the final attainment" (or Self-realization, *siddhānta*).

Now, the entire epistemological reasoning of the *Laṅkāvatāra-sūtra* is geared toward this ultimate goal, the achievement of Self-realization, or Self-actualization, referred to by various terms (Siddhānta, Āryajñāna, Prayātmagocara, Tathatā, etc).[66] All theoretical constructs elaborated in the *Sūtra* are treated as nothing more than mere stepping stones toward, or rungs on the ladder of Self-realization. Whether purely epistemic concepts, such as the five cognitive categories (Dharmas), the three modes of cognition (Svabhāvas), the eight states of consciousness (Vijñānas), or a combination of both epistemology and psychology, or even cosmology (as in the case of the Mind-only doctrine and of the theory of Causation, respectively), the purpose of the writer is to liberate the reader's mind from the fetters of language, logic, and even conceptual thinking itself. For, according to the *Laṅkāvatāra-sūtra*, the *summum bonum* of knowledge is the complete abandonment, or detachment from all views, since they are all tainted by dualistic discrimination (*vikalpa*) and contextual limitations.

This is explained in the same way as the analysis of light phenomena given by Bertrand Russell, in his lines quoted above: one cannot *definitively* say that light is made of either waves or particles. Either hypothesis is equally legitimate, while neither is sufficient to *completely* explain light phenomena as observed by scientists at one time or another. It all depends on the specific circumstances, or conditions under which the observations are undertaken.

Since language is inherently deficient in describing something from all points of view at once, knowledge, too, being dependent upon language for its expression, will always be limited in its potential for representing Reality in all its awesome complexity. Therefore, the *Sūtra* says, it will have to be abandoned in favor of *direct* experience. This is the only "Right-knowledge" (Samyag-jñāna), or "Noble-knowledge" (Āryajñāna). It is transcendent in the sense that it is intuitional, beyond dual categories of logical reasoning (*nirvikalpa*), and beyond concrete imagery (*nirābhāsa*).

Dual categories of discrimination (i.e., Being and Non-being, high and low, Saṃsāra and Nirvāṇa, true and false, right and wrong, etc.) are used in tetralemma dialectics solely for the purpose of demonstrating their limitations in explaining the world of experience, but they are gradually dispensed with as the novice reaches higher levels of understanding. Thus, knowledge is used to transcend itself. Consequently, Buddhist Gnosis may be said to be both paradoxic and adoxic, at the same time. Having abolished itself, *gnosis* opens the door to *praxis*. Hence, the name of the school of Yogācāra: the "practice of Yoga."

Conclusions and Preview of Part Two

In appraising Buddhist epistemological methodology, we have chosen the fourfold negation formula of the tetralemma logic (*catuṣkoṭi*) as the key and foremost paradigm for its understanding. The use of the term "dialectics" in relation to this formula has now become almost universal (e.g., de Jong, Murti, Robinson, Streng, Staal, *et. al.*), following the earlier Westernizing parallels (of such scholars as de La Vallée Poussin, Shayer, Stcherbatsky, and others).[67]

Perhaps it would be interesting to note at this point that before the introduction of multi-valued logical systems in our time, there were only four types of dialectical reasoning with concrete application within a fully-fledged religio-philosophical system, or worldview. They were:

(1) The **dilemma**, the "either/or" classical Aristotelian logic, which became the paradigm of Western thought for over two thousand years;

(2) The **trilemma**, made famous through the Hegelian triad: "thesis," "antithesis," and "synthesis"; a true revolution in Western thought, with broad implications at all levels;

(3) The **tetralemma**, or the fourfold negational logic, known as the *catuṣkoṭi* in Buddhist logic, our main subject here, and,

(4) The **septalemma**, or Syādvāda (Anekāntavāda), the sevenfold relativistic logic, used by the Jains but probably inherited from an earlier tradition of the sceptical schools, possibly via Buddhism, mentioned briefly at the beginning of this chapter.

Proceeding from an analysis of the Buddhist model, the tetralemma, and of various antinomical statements on which early and late Buddhist doctrines were founded, an attempt is made here to indicate that this particular form of Buddhist logic deserves more attention than it has hitherto received, and a proper place in the broader history of dialectical reasoning.[68] To achieve this purpose, we have pursued the following four pertinent lines of discussion:

(1) The four-cornered negation, or *catuṣkoṭi*, as such was not invented by Nāgārjuna, but was rather extensively used by the Buddha himself, and even before him, in a different context, by Sañjaya, a contemporary sceptical philosopher (sixth century B.C.). As a mode of resolving contradictions, the negative dialectic was also used by Jain and Vedāntic logicians, as well. It most likely stems, as Mircea Eliade put it, "From a venerable and pan-Indian tradition of paradoxical coincidences of being and non-being, eternity and temporal flux, beatitude and suffering."[69]

(2) The denial of four contradictory statements, as an epistemological method, was also known and used in ancient Greece, first by sceptics (Zeno), then by Socrates, Plato, and Aristotle.[70] We cannot but agree, however, with Professor Murti (and others) that the credit for its *first systematic* use, if not its discovery, should be given to the founder of Buddhism, chronologically speaking.[71]

(3) Nāgārjuna, in his turn, knew and respected the three laws of the double-valued logic (applicable to the domain of purely empirical knowledge), and emphasized them in his debates by using the formula: "Then, it necessarily/logically follows that . . ." (*punar prasajyate*) (*Mūlamādhyamika-kārikās* 20.9, 18). However, this did not stop him from side-stepping their requirements when a different level of reality, for which common-sense language was not devised, or even appropriate, had to be expressed.[72]

(4) As a versatile epistemological tool, the tetralemma is best understood in its context: as a dialectical, logical method (especially in Nāgārjuna's *Kārikās*), as a cognitive system (especially in the *Laṅkāvatāra-sūtra*), or, as an aid to meditation, a teaching device, a soteriological technique for the purpose of freeing the mind from the oppressive fetters of all dogmatic viewpoints and attitudes. Its concrete application as such will be the subject of the second part of this study.

Thus, the first section (ch. 2.1.) introduces the Citta-mātra, or Mind-only doctrine. This is perhaps the most misunderstood of all Yogācāra concepts. Without going into detail at this stage, suffice it to say that it has been taken by many as an ontological statement about the external world, along the lines of Absolute Idealism. When the relevant passages of the *Laṅkāvatāra-sūtra* are looked at with great attention, it will become clear that this concept does admit a number of interpretations, but the outright denial of ontological reality to the external world is not one of them. However, the concept may definitely be taken *prima facie* as an affirmation of the reality of the *Mind itself*. Nobody, I am positively certain, will take issue with that.

Therefore, one may say that it represents an instantiation of the first affirmative limb of the tetralemma: "Mind is." The entire conceptual structure of meaning revolving around the Citta-mātra doctrine, is an elaboration of these two words, explaining *what* "Mind" (*citta*) is.

The second section (ch. 2.2.) focuses on the five Dharmas (epistemic categories) and the attainment of the Āryajñāna (the noble, transcendental level of wisdom) through its three cognitive aspects, Svabhāvas. However analytical these cognitive modes are, it will become clear that their ultimate goal, following their appropriate understanding and application, is to lead the practitioner to a level of absolute transcendence of analytical reasoning (Vijñāna). This form of absolute cognition is variously referred to in the *Sūtra* as "Noble-knowledge" (Āryajñāna), "Right-knowledge" (Samyagjñāna), "Insight" (Prajñā), "The Realm of Inner Attainment" (Pratyātmagatigocara), or simply abstract "Wisdom" or "Gnosis" (Jñāna), in order to differentiate it from the concrete empirical cognition, based upon verbal categories and discrimination between them (Vijñāna).

Again, this may appear as a different formulation of the now familiar theory of the two levels of truth, the conventional and the absolute, or ultimate. This distinction can be found under various terms in the *Laṅkāvatāra* almost at every turn of the page, as we shall see. For the moment, let us say that the absolute level of Wisdom is obtained while in a meditative trance, and is therefore devoid of content (i.e., imagery, thoughts, ideas, categories, etc.). Being pure intuitional religious feeling, akin to aesthetic contemplation, one may very well call it, from the empirical point of view, a state of *No-mind* (*acintya*, or "imagelessness," *nirābhāsa*) and hence, the opposite of any positive affirmation of mind, as in the case of Mind-only.

Now, the third section (ch. 2.3.) deals with a complex combination of *both* Mind *and* No-mind, in that it includes both *abstract* (i.e., devoid of ideational content) and *concrete* (i.e., empirical) levels of knowledge, that is, Jñāna versus Vijñāna, as well as other similar dichotomies, all integrated into a complex psycho-ontological system, known as the eight Vijñānas, or States of consciousness and subconsciousness. The importance of this elaborate system cannot be stressed enough, for it not only represents a giant leap forward in the empirical study of cognitive processes (at a time when the West was still under the spell of the classical Greek theory of the four humours), but it also comes surprisingly close in its systematic approach and terminology to the modern dynamic, psychoanalytical approaches to the workings of the mind (*mutatis mutandis*, of course).

This archaic, yet not unsophisticated Buddhist psychology, as presented in the *Laṅkāvatāra-sūtra*, includes several layers, both conscious and subconscious, with occasional transgressions of such fixed boundaries (e.g., semi-consciousness, or trans-consciousness). On the conscious level we have five modes of apprehending reality, relating to the five sensory organs: the eyes, ears, nose, tongue, and skin. Putting them all together in a meaningful way, is the thinking consciousness, which also functions as the conscious volition referred to in the *Sūtra* as the "Manovijñāna."

To mediate between the conscious and the subconscious layers, there is yet another conative faculty, the pre-conscious, or semi-conscious volition, the "Manas." It is the seat of psychic energy, of impulsive drives, of desires, of personal dispositions and talents. Finally, a third level, the deepest stratum of the Ālaya-vijñāna, the "Repository-of-impressions," is described. It appears to be closer to the Jungian "Collective Unconscious" than to the Freudian individual subconscious, due to its trancendental, or trans-conscious function of identification with the "Essence-of-Buddhahood" (the Tathāgata-garbha), which is unique to the *Laṅkāvatāra-sūtra*, according to many scholars.[73]

The fourth and final chapter (2.4.) analyzes complex issues related to the Buddhist theories of Causation, devoting special attention to the shift from the early linear and psychological determinism (i.e., from desire and ignorance to birth, sickness, and death), to the Mahāyānist understanding of Causation as a complex interplay, or interaction, between multiple causes and conditions (Hetu-pratyaya). The key concepts of Inter-dependent Origination (Pratītya-samutpāda) and of the Middle Way (Madhyamā-pratipad) between two extremes (such as Being and Non-being) may also be regarded as more complex elaborations upon the fourth logical alternative of the tetralemma, that is, "neither this, nor that." For, to the understanding of the Yogācāra Buddhist, as preserved in the *Laṅkāvatāra-sūtra*, one cannot speak of a Mind clearly distinct and substantially different from the object of knowledge (i.e., the external Reality), nor can one really express "No-mind" by means of conceptual discourse, since Āryajñāna is spontaneous, intuitive insight, the mind of Enlightenment, which is free from any attachments (to any rules of logical reasoning), and "it neither enters nor goes out, like the moon in the water." (*Laṅkāvatāra-sūtra* III: 158; l. 1). Here is a quintessential example of the Buddhist Law of Causation, as expressed in the *Laṅkāvatāra*, where we find that *both* views of birth and no-birth, of Being and non-Being of any dharma (existential elements, including, of course, the Mind, *citta*), are rejected. This is because no one-sided view would suffice to explain the process of production (and dissolution) of things, but only a systemic view of an entire complex of causal factors. Thus, the *Laṅkāvatāra* III: 202-203; ll. 13-15, 1:

> Nothing is born, there is no being, nor non-being; nowhere is being-and-non-being (produced);
> Except indeed (where there is) a system [of causal factors]—this indeed evolves and devolves. (103)
>
> And it is (only) on account of the severance of the system of causal factors, that the (idea of) birth has even any meaning (at all). (104)

Like all other metaphysical constructs, or epistemological methods, this system of Causation should also ultimately be regarded, according to the *Sūtra*, as nothing more than an expedient, a teaching device toward the higher religious goal of detachment from all views, as discussed above. In this practical sense, all four epistemological constructs outlined here complement one another in fulfilling the same function, namely to liberate the mind from dogmatic, one-sided absolutist views, as do the four alternatives of the tetralemma, their schematic model or paradigm.

2.1. The Epistemological Reduction of the Citta-mātra (*Mind-only*) Doctrine

Preliminary Considerations

If in the development of Buddhist thought one can say that the Mādhyamika school represented a critique of phenomenal existence promulgated from the vantage point of epistemology and logic, the Yogācāra-Vijñānavāda school, on the other hand, was a critique based on psychology (or, more precisely, on Buddhist "ontological psychology," according to some scholars).[1] In this respect, it constituted a return to the early emphasis on meditational practice, although its theoretical foundation shifted rather drastically away from the early nominalistic dualism of the Theravāda school.

The alternate name for the Yogācāra school, "Citta-mātra," which is most commonly translated as "Mind-only" (more about the rendition of this term later), clearly suggests the idealistic departure from the quasi-realism, or even empiricism, characteristic of the Pāli scriptures. Taking flight into the realm of constructive imagination, however, did not diminish the Yogācāras' enthusiasm for Yogic practice (hence the very name of their school), but it did create problems for later historians of Buddhism who attempted to circumscribe the meaning of this crucial term, as we shall see.

To be sure, Yogācāra is concerned first and foremost with the nature of the mind (*citta*), its structure, its functions and development. This is due precisely to the fact that it constitutes the vehicle through which one can achieve Enlightenment, the ultimate state of mind in Buddhist soteriology. Yet, this state affords paradoxically, the transcendence of mind itself, just as the 'raft' is discarded—to use early Buddhist parlance—once the 'other shore' of Nirvāṇa is attained. Therefore, *Citta-mātra* (lit., "mind only," "wholly mind," "nothing but the mind") seems to refer to this meditational context of Buddhist practice dealing with various visualizations and other mental processes for the purpose of spiritual transformation.

There is, in addition, a second meaning of the term pertaining to a certain philosophical interpretation of the nature of Reality, as consisting of Mind-only, where the word 'mind' (*citta*) may not necessarily be used in the restricted sense mentioned above. To further complicate the problem, these two meanings seem to replace one another, according to the Yogācāra texts in which the compound word *citta-mātra* appears. The different renditions of this crucial expression given by a number of Buddhologists (both Eastern and Western) who took an interest in this matter (Suzuki, Ueda, Wayman, Kalupahana), as "mind," "thought," "consciousness," "transmigrating entity," "ultimate Reality," etc.—according to the changing context (meditational or philosophical)—add to the misunderstandings surrounding this issue. Given the importance of the term, which in the words of one recent author "has come to represent for most scholars the very hallmark of the (Yogācāra) school,"[2] further light on this issue is needed.

First of all, how did the Yogācāras arrive at this concept of Thought, or Mind, being the absolute, true Reality? In an article entitled "The Absolute in Buddhist Thought," J. W. de Jong points out that many scholars, such as La Vallée Poussin,[3] Schayer,[4] Frauwallner,[5] and the Japanese scholars Kimura, Akanuma, Nishi, and Sakamoto,[6] have drawn attention to a passage in the *Aṅguttara-Nikāya* (volume 1, p. 10) and in Vasumitra's *Treatise on the Buddhist Schools* (confer A. Bareau, *Journal Asiatique*, 1954, p. 244), which says: "Luminous is that thought, but it is defiled by adventitious defilements" (*pabhassaram idaṃ cittaṃ taṃ ca kho āgantukehi upakkilesehi upakkiliṭṭham*). This passage of the *Aṅguttara Nikāya* clearly refers to meditational practice, which affords the mystic the opportunity to purify his mind from the defilements (*kleśas*) caused by the passions (*rāgas*) and the erroneous views (*asamyagdṛṣṭi*).[7] However, just as the Mādhyamikas magnified the originally psychological idea of non-Self (Anātman) into the cosmological notion of the universal Void (Śūnyatā), so did the Yogācāras transfer onto the absolute plane this purely ethical concept of a pure mind realized in the course of meditation. Referring to this process, de Jong writes:[8]

> In a certain sense one can say that the Yogācāras with their theory of Mind-only have done nothing else than develop the idea of the purification of mind which plays such an important role in early Buddhism as is testified by the well-known verse: "To abstain from all evil, to do good, and to purify one's mind, that is the teaching of the Buddhas" (*sabbapāpassa akaraṇaṃ kusalassa upasampadā sacittapariyodapanam etaṃ buddhāna sāsanam,*

Dhammapada 183; *Udanavarga* 28, 1; *Digha Nikāya* 2.49; *Mahāvastu* 3.420).

In addition, this process of expansion of meaning from the ethical into the ontological realm became associated with certain ideas of an "invisible, infinite consciousness radiating in all directions," already present in the oldest texts (e.g., *viññaṇam anidassanam anantam sabbato pabham, Dīgha-Nikāya* 1.223; *Majjhima-Nikāya* 1.329).[9] Hence, the gradual process of identification between *citta* (mind, thought), or *vijñapti* (imagination, representation), and the world at large (*tribhava, traidhātuka*), which became completely dissociated from the meditational context only in the later Yogācāra texts.[10]

In the *Laṅkāvatāra-sūtra*, however, an intermediate stage in this process of disassociation can be discovered, for, reading through this early Yogācāra scripture, one cannot help being puzzled by the multiplicity of meanings attached to the term *citta-mātra*, which not only run the gamut from the experiential (psychological) to the speculative (metaphysical) domains, but are often incongruent to such an extent that it becomes impossible to maintain one consistent rendition, or meaning, throughout the text. Yet, there is no doubt, that the Citta-mātra concept is paramount in the development of the complex metaphysical edifice advanced in this text.

Suzuki, for instance, in his *Studies* states that Citta-mātra (which he calls "the warp and weft of the sūtra . . . the chief subject of the text") is "the transcendental mind, or Mind itself, or Mind-only" (p. 281). Yet, elsewhere, he regards *citta* as "corresponding to the Subconscious" (p. 249). Furthermore, in the context of this sūtra, according to Suzuki, "everything hinges on this one point (*citta-mātra*), the salvation of the world, not to say anything of the individual" (p. 244). In other wrods, one can say that Citta-mātra—as used in the *Laṅkāvatāra-sūtra*—can be three things, depending on the context, namely:

(1) The **empirical mind**, that is, the mental elements, the sum total of the *cetasikās*, the conscious activity of the mind, or the ontological entity known as the ordinary self;

(2) The **transformed Mind**, the purified or transcendental Self, referred to in the *Sūtra* as the Ālaya-vijñāna, the undefiled Tathāgatagarbha (when taken as essence), and understood to designate the Unconscious in its original state; and

(3) The **universal Mind**, that is, the mind projected upon the world at large (*tribhava, traidhātuka*), when perceived to be the substitution, or explanation for the triple world. It might, therefore, be called the trans-conscious, or even the pan-conscious Mind, when

it is thus interpreted (albeit erroneously, in our opinion) by scholars from within and without the Buddhist tradition, as we shall see below.

Our contention, however, is that the term *citta*, when taken in the cosmological context, should be regarded rather as the semantic equivalent of the Tathāgata-garbha (the "universal Womb," or "Matrix" of Buddhahood, the "Essence of all dharmas").[11] This is, of course, a metaphysical notion, having more to do with the religious aspirations and mind-set of the fourth-century Buddhist practitioner, than with physical reality as we conceive it today in Western secular culture. This minute, yet crucial, detail escapes many interpreters of Yogācāra Buddhism, from both East and West, when they take key statements, such as *lokacittamātraṃ*, or *cittamātraṃ traidhātukaṃ* (or *tribhavaṃ*) to mean: "The (triple) world is made of mind (only)," or "The world is nothing but the mind." For, "the world," as understood by the Buddhists, was altogether different in meaning than our meaning of the word; *traidhātuka* (the "triple world") included the physical realm (*rūpa-dhātu*), the ideal realm (*arūpa-dhātu*), and the realm of desire (*kāma-dhātu*), or the form, the formless, and the mental, phantasy realms, respectively. A Western approximation of such notions may be found only in the Jungian concept of the Collective Unconscious, full of mythical and magic images, or archetypes. We shall now look at each interpretation of the Citta-mātra concept, with its various contextual meanings, as they come forth in the *Laṅkāvatāra-sūtra*.

Citta as the Empirical Mind

In his *Studies* (p. 248), Suzuki points out two ways in which the term *citta* is used in the *Laṅkāvatāra:* one general, the other more specific. The first, he says, represents the "sum of all mental activities" (i.e., "both the mind proper and its various functions"); the second, more specific sense, is described in contrast to this "principle of unification by which all the activities are understood as issuing from one center," as the individual faculties, the specialized functions, when taken apart from this center. They are (from the deepest layer upward): Citta, Manas, Manovijñāna, and the five Sense-perceptions, the Vijñānas of the eyes, ears, nose, tongue, and body.

Now, if we follow Suzuki's interpretation, we should also be careful to distinguish between what he calls the "specific" use of the term *citta* and the use of *citta* in the *Laṅkāvatāra-sūtra* with the meaning of "empirical mind." The latter includes all the specific activities of the mind as enumerated above, *except* the first and the deepest, Citta, which is to be identified with the Ālaya-vijñāna (the Repository-of-impressions), as we shall see. Of course, the generic usage refers to the totality of all mental functions, without distinction, as indicated in gātha 459 from the *Sagāthakam:* 322-23:

> The (empirical) mind, that is, the mental discrimination and representation, the activity of volition (*manas*) and indeed the Sense-perception; the Receptacle (-of-impressions, *ālaya*) and the triple world [with its apparent] movement—these are all synonyms of the Mind.

The Ālaya and the triple world are *not* the empirical mind, since the former possesses trans-personal, trans-empirical connotations, while the latter is a metaphysical, rather than a functional, descriptive concept regarding the mind, strictly speaking.

From the remaining seven empirical functions, the five Sense-vijñānas are self-explanatory and will be further discussed in the subsequent chapter on the Vijñāna system (2.3.). Manas and Manovijñāna, however, represent an interesting problem. They seem to be the most difficult to interpret and to translate at times, partly because they are not as extensively treated as other mental functions in the *Sūtra,* and partly because they are so difficult to distinguish from one another.[12]

In our view, they both refer to the volitional or conative function of the mind, the active source of psychic energy, or drive, of all mental activity. But, while *Manovijñāna* stands for *conscious* volition, *Manas* symbolizes the deeper, *pre-conscious* willpower, the spontaneous impulsivity of both biological instincts and individual predispositions, inclinations, or talents. It has, of course, a very important role to play in the cognitive drive, as well. However, we are disinclined to subscribe to Suzuki's view (*Studies,* p. 248) that the Manovijñāna is completely separated from the Manas, and that it can be translated as "the intellect." They are both part of the same, organically integrated system, called "Mind" (*citta*) in its generic sense, and they are fueled by the same energy of volition. The difference is only of depth, intensity, and direction, not of function. For, one cannot say that the Manovijñāna represents the energy of the intellect, while the Manas that of the affect, or emotions. Both conscious and pre-conscious conation can be charged emotionally, or have a predominantly intellectual coloring.

From the intellectual, cognitive angle, two terms are mentioned most frequently in relation to the Manovijñāna. One is *vikalpa,* "discrimination," the other is *vijñapti,* "mental representation," or "imagination." The former is usually associated with the dualistic categories, characteristic of the empirical mode of reasoning; the latter refers to the whimsical ability of the mind, its propensity toward imagination and fabrication, which interfere with direct experience of Reality. This ability is indicated most saliently when the term is used in its compounded form: *Vijñapti-mātra* ("Representation-only"). In such cases, the term is interchangeable, at least in the *Laṅkāvatāra-sūtra,* with the compound *Citta-mātra* ("Mind-only").[13]

It is interesting to note at this point that it was precisely in the difference of usage of the two terms *Citta-mātra* and *Vijñapti-mātra* that Suzuki found the main distinction between the *Laṅkāvatāra-sūtra* and the writings of the two luminaries of the Yogācāra school: the brothers Asaṅga and Vasubandhu. According to him, while the term *Vijñapti-mātra* (as used in Vasubandhu's *Triṃśikā* and *Vijñaptimātratā-siddhi-Bhāṣā,* and in Asaṅga's *Mahāyāna-Sūtrālaṃkāra-Śāstra*) designates our inability to circumscribe Reality by means of contrived names and representations (on account of the limitations of language), the term *Citta-mātra,* as used preeminently in the *Laṅkāvatāra,* comes to mean that the world itself is "made of Mind," and only through the realization of this ultimate Truth, one can attain liberation (*Studies,* p. 281).

Our contention, however, is that this is not so, for as far as the *Citta-mātra* is concerned, its meaning *is* consistent with its synonym *Vijñapti-mātra* as used by Asaṅga and Vasubandhu in the above-quoted works. The succeeding sections of this chapter will amply substantiate this point, and hopefully will convince the reader of the validity of our position vis-à-vis this very crucial aspect in the understanding of the Yogācāra school overall.

To come to grips with this thorny issue, let us first trace the etymology of the compound *citta-mātra* itself. In the introduction to his translation of the *Sūtra,* Suzuki derives the word *citta,* as used in the *Laṅkāvatāra,* not from the root *cit,* "to think, to fix the mind upon,"[14] but to the root *ci,* "to pile up, to arrange in order."[15] To justify this rather curious derivation, he gives the following explanatory statement, which I will quote here in its entirety, to prevent any possible misunderstanding:[16]

> The Citta is thus a storehouse where the seeds of all thoughts and deeds are accumulated and stored up. The Citta, however, has a double sense, general and specific. When it is used in the *general sense* it means "mind", "mentation", "ideas", including the activities of Manas and Manovijñāna, and also

> of the Vijñānas; while *specifically*, it is a synonym of Ālaya-vijñāna in its relative aspects, and distinguishable from all the rest of the mental faculties. When, however, it is used in the form of Cittamātra, *Mind-only*, it acquires still another connotation. We can say that Citta appears here in its highest possible sense, for it is then neither simply mentation nor intellection, nor perception as a function of consciousness. It is identifiable with the Ālaya in its absolute aspect.

Clearly, while *citta* is here identified with *ālaya* (the Repository-of-impressions, or of memories, the Subconscious, as it were), in its more general sense it can also be understood as "mind," "ideas," or "mentation." In such a case, why should one not interpret *citta* along the lines of the participial forms of the root *cit*, rather than *ci*, particularly since the past participle of the latter, *cita* ("heaped," "piled up," "collected"), never appears in the original Nanjio edition used by the translator, as far as I have been able to ascertain?[17] Attempting to disentangle the various overlapping meanings of the technical terms used in the *Laṅkā*, Suzuki mades this statement:

> The following equations hold true: the transcendental Citta = Ālayavijñāna = Tathāgata-garbha. Ālaya is a psychological term belonging to the Vijñāna system; Tathāgata-garbha has a religious connotation; and Citta has been in use since the early days of Buddhism as denoting a certain function of the mind.[18]

Now, the author does not make clear what specific function he is referring to. Could it be that this function was that of collecting, piling up (impressions, memories, mental impurities, and so on)? Or merely that of observing, aiming, reflecting, imagining, thinking, perhaps during the practice of meditation? Suzuki does not seem to bridge the gap between the two types of cognition, leaving us somewhat in the dark on this issue, but Alex Wayman in a review article of A. K. Chatterjee's book *The Yogācāra Idealism*, gives us a clue when he states that certain cognate words derived from the same root *cit*, such as *cetanā* ("volition") in early Buddhism and *citta-saṃtanā*, or *citta-saṃtati* (both: "stream of thoughts") in later Buddhism, were used to designate *karma* (action), or what transmigrates. According to Wayman, one can conjecture the following:

> Thus, the words *karma* and *citta* are doctrinally equivalent to indicate the transmigrating entity. If a "stream of thoughts" can bring about a set of external circumstances compensatory

and retributive of past acts, we have at once the idealistic picture of a subjective element of a conscious or subconscious nature projecting the "world." (i.e., *Citta-mātra*, "Mind-only").[19]

Put in the perspective of doctrinal equivalence between *citta* and *karma*, the former could readily admit both the implications of thinking and of piling up, for both mental functions are required in activating one's karma, one referring to the present, the other to the past (mental) activities, as it were. Such an assumption would leave open the possibility of interpreting both Ālaya-vijñāna ("the Repository-of-impressions") and Tathāgata-garbha ("the Womb-of-Buddhahood") along the psychological lines suggested by Wayman above, which also tally with Suzuki's views (see footnote previously cited) on this topic. That is to say that if *citta* represents the "stream of thoughts" determining one's karma (or transmigrating entity), then its doctrinal equivalents *Ālaya-vijñāna* and *Tathāgata-garbha* are its conscious (or presently active consciousness) and sub-conscious (or generative) aspects, respectively.

Let us also bear in mind that the word *mātra* is commonly used at the end of a *bahuvrīhi* compound with the meaning of: "amounting (only) to," "nothing but," "entirely," "only," "just," "being no more than," "simply or merely," "the full or simple measure of anything," "the whole or totality," "the one thing and no more nor less than anything,"—according to Monier-Williams.[20] Consequently, the expression *Citta-mātra* could most readily be rendered by "Mere/ Only Thought," or "Simply Thinking," which would suggest *prima facie* the activity of the empirical mind.

Now, the elements and manifestations of mental activity were well-known and carefully recorded—with minor variations—by all Buddhist schools, old and new. An entire Buddhist psychological taxonomy was developed over many centuries in which the word *citta* and its derivatives appear to have been used with surprising consistency. We find, for instance, 51 mental properties or concomitants (*cetasikā*) mentioned in Vasubandhu's *Vijñaptimātratā-siddhi*,[21] as against 52 accepted by the Sarvāstivādins,[22] and 46 recorded by the Theravāda Abhidharmists.[23] These were classified by Vasubandhu under six subcategories, which can be easily reduced to three essential ones, as follows: (1) positive qualities, including 5 universal, 5 determinate, and 3 meritorious *cetasikā;* (2) negative qualities, which comprise the 6 major and the 20 minor defilements (purely mental *kleśas*); and (3) 4 indeterminate *cetasikā*.[24] Moreover, in his *Abhidharmakośa-kārikā* and *Bhāṣya*, other cognate terms are used, such as *citta*—for pure mentation—and *caitta-dharmas*—for its accompanying mental phenomena, one of which is called *cetanā* ("volition").[25] The antiquity of these technical terms is proven by their usage in the *Abhidhamma Piṭaka*, in the fourth century B.C. Its first book, *Dhamma-Sangaṇi*, translated by Caroline Rhys Davids as "Compendium of States, or Phenomena," reads (v. 1022):

> Which are the states that have limited objects of thought?
>
> Those emotional, perceptual and synthetic states, as well as those of intellect applied to sense-impressions (*citta-cetasikā dhammā*), which arise in connexion with limited matters.

and in v. 1187:

> Which are the states that are of the intellect (*citta*)?
>
> Cognition applied to sense-impressions; the element of ideation and the element of ideational cognition.[26]

It is clear that the term *citta* and its derivatives designates cognitive functions of a sensory and empirical nature, "which arise in connection with limited matters" processed by the mind.

Now, let us turn to the text of the *Laṅkāvatāra-sūtra* in order to see if this early use of the term is preserved. Here is one explicit statement denoting the involvement of the mind with empirical reality (*Laṅkāvatāra* II: 130; gātha 182):

> The mind is bound up with the objective world; knowledge operates in logic, while in the excellent state of imagelessness, (transcendental) insight does proceed.

Similar passages are found throughout the *sūtra*. One more will suffice to convince us of the contrast between transcendental insight, or Wisdom, Gnosis, and the common, empirical cognition, here referred to as the "bundle of thoughts and mentals" (*citta-caitta-kalāpa*). To wit, *Laṅkā* III: 200; ll. 5-8:

> Therefore, Mahāmati, by Nirvāṇa is meant the looking at the state of reality as it really is [i.e., in accordance with facts]; (and) after the turning back of the entire bundle of thoughts and mentals, there is the attainment of the Noble Wisdom (by means of) the self-realization of the Tathāgata—this I call it Nirvāṇa."

Undoubtedly, the purpose of the *Sūtra*, as of the whole of Buddhist doctrine and practice, was not merely to understand the workings of the mind in its common state of random activity, but rather to overcome its confusion, to transcend its randomness, in an almost superhuman effort of calm re-integration into the essential Reality which preceded the agitation of constructive imagination (*vikalpa*). To this ideal, non-empirical state we shall turn next.

Citta as the Transcendental Mind

The correlation of *Citta-mātra* with the nature of Reality is to be seen within the meditational context regarding the habit of discrimination (*vikalpa*) and in the pursuit of the Middle Way between opposing views (Madhyamā pratipad). We read (in the *Laṅkāvatāra* X: 311; gātha 358):

> When, by the understanding of Mind-only external entities are disregarded, there is cessation of discoursive thought and there is the middle among the paths.

While the Yoga practitioner withdraws the senses from outside objects during his meditation and concentration exercises, the act of withdrawal in itself implies the external reality from which the adept tries hard to detach himself. That this process is of a purely mental nature is clearly suggested by the early Yogācāra writers, such as Vasubandhu, for instance:[27]

> But when (the objective world which is) the basis of conditioning as well as the wisdom (which does the conditioning) are both eliminated,
> The state of Mind-only is realized,
> Since the six sense-organs and their objects are no longer present. (*Triṃśika* 28)

The author of the *Laṅkāvatāra* seems to be in complete agreement (X: 276; gātha 93):

> When the Mind operates it has the manifestation of all forms; when there is no mind in this situation, there are no forms. The mind has been deluded since beginningless past. Then the Yogin by his (transcendental) insight sees the world shorn of its appearances (*abhāsa*).

Now, these appearances are nothing but the thought-forms (here called *vijñānas* of various kinds), which emerge out of the still surface of the unperturbed Mind (here referred to as the Ālaya, the Repository-of-mental-impressions), just like the waves out of the ocean. This is one of the most suggestive and persistent metaphors employed in the *Sūtra* (II: 46; gāthas 99-100):

> Just as the waves on the ocean, stirred by the wind, are dancing and rolling without interruption,
>
> In the same manner the Repository-ocean, constantly stirred up by the wind of the object, is dancing and rolling by the thoughts (*citta*), with the Sense-perceptions (*vijñānas*) as the waves.

The relation between the pure, tranquil Mind (Citta, Ālaya) and the agitated, empirical mind (*citta-manovijñāna*) is explained in similar terms (*Laṅkāvatāra* II: 46; gāthas 102, 105):

> They are neither different, nor non-different, they are considered as the waves of the ocean—
> Thus are the seven (kinds of) thought-forms (*vijñānas*) connected with the Mind (*citta*).
>
> And just as there is no distinction between the waves of the ocean, so in the Mind the development of the states of consciousness (*vijñānas*) is not found [i.e., distinctly, apart from the Mind, *citta*].

On the other hand, the *Laṅkāvatāra* clearly states that the elements included in the psychic system *citta-manovijñāna* fulfill different mental functions in relation to the external world, and it is through them that the karmic pollutants attach themselves onto the person (*Laṅkāvatāra* II: 46; gātha 106):

> Karma is accumulated by the (empirical) mind (*citta*) and is analyzed by the intellect (*manas*); through the (conative) consciousness (*mano-vijñāna*) one investigates (it), while the visible (world, *dṛśya*) is discriminated by the five [i.e., *vijñānas* = Sense-consciousness].

However, this process occurs on the empirical level only, for on a deeper level, the mind (Ālaya) is not only tranquil, but pure, as well (*Laṅkā* II: 47; gātha 111):

> The ocean should be contemplated as dancing with the appearance of waves; then, how is it that the unfolding of the Repository-of-impressions is not understood by the intellect in the same manner?

In his "concluding remarks" to the chapter on the Citta-mātra theory, Suzuki explains the system of the multiple Vijñānas in the following manner (see *Studies*, p. 277):

> It is evident that the mind regarded here as the unitive principle of experience is not our empirical mind, and, naturally, it is variously designated by the author of the *Laṅkāvatāra* as it is observed from various points of reference.

From a list of eleven such "unitive principles of experience"—which he selects as equivalents of the Mind-only doctrine when interpreted as the ultimate psychological experience of Reality—I shall give, for the purpose of edification, only two:

(1) *Pratyātmādhigama-viśeṣa-lakṣaṇa,* that is, "an excellent state of consciousness attained inwardly by oneself;" and,

(2) *Tathāgata-svapratyātma-āryajñāna-adhigama,* or, "the realization by the Tathāgata of Supreme Wisdom in his own inmost consciousness."[28]

This inner, yet transcendental Wisdom, or Gnosis (Jñāna), as we will have the opportunity to investigate in greater length in the course of the next chapter (2.2), is ultimately explained by alluding to the unifying experience of deep meditation, beyond empirical cognition, the state of No-mind, characterized by the lack of verbal, or visual support (*nirvikalpa, nirābhāsa*), and by the feeling of joy (*pramuditā*). To wit, *Sagāthakam:* 335; gātha 569:

> In the (state of) imagelessness there is not duality, or five Knowledge-states, and not even [any kind of] Reality, (such as described in) the (concepts of) False-knowledge (*parikalpita*), or in the Relative-knowledge (*paratantra*), nor (in the teachings of) the Supreme [Brahman, or the Absolute-knowledge, *pariniṣpanna*].

The mind itself is repeatedly stated to be pure and imageless (*nirābhāsa*), that is free from the manifold illusions due to intellectual discriminations (*Laṅkāvatāra* IV: 215; gātha 1):

> The abodes and the stages of Buddhahood (are established) in the Mind-only (*citta-mātra*), (which is) imageless [lit., free from imagining]—this was told, is told, and will be told by the Buddhas.

Undoubtedy, the author had the meditational context in mind, for the next gātha states *Laṅkāvatāra* IV: 215; gātha 2):

> The (first) seven stages are still (of the) mind; but here the eighth is imageless; the two stages [i.e., the ninth and the tenth] have (still) something to rest themselves on; the (highest) stage that is left belongs to me [i.e., the Buddha-stage].

Now, this highest mental state which is imageless, is the stage of mental awakening (the Buddha = the Awakened One), of the return to a primal state of pure consciousness, which the *Sūtra* alternately calls Ālaya-vijñāna, or Tathāgata-garbha, or—on occasion —Citta-mātra (when taken to mean the transcendental Mind, rather than the empirical mind). That its realization implies a revulsion to, a reversal of, or opposition to (*parāvṛtti*) the common state of consciousness, related to the sensory input (i.e., the activity of the seven evolving *vijñānas*) is seen from this, and other similar statements (*Laṅkāvatāra* VI: 221; ll. 12-13):

> When a reversal [lit., turning back, *parāvṛtti*] has not taken place in the Repository-of-consciousness, known under the name of "The Womb-of-Buddhahood," there is no cessation of the seven fluctuating States of sensory-analytic consciousness (*vijñānas*).

Most commonly, in the Mahāyāna literature, the term *tathāgata-garbha* has an ontological significance, and its identification in the *Laṅkāvatāra-sūtra* with *ālaya-vijñāna* (a primarily psychological term, the equivalent of *citta* taken in its transcendental aspect), establishes in fact a fundamental tripartite equation between the ontological, psychological, and epistemological levels of discourse.

Such a breakdown of rational categories in interpreting Reality is readily accepted in Buddhist thought, which recognized courageously how conventional, indeed inaccurate, and ultimately futile are even the most refined attempts to encapsulate Reality within a limited (and limiting) symbolic system, be it philosophical, religious, or otherwise. For, the *Sūtra* boldly asserts, the only forms that can be studied, analytically, as well as intuitively, are those created by the mind. Thus, in regard to analytical ratiocination, the *Sūtra* says the following (*Laṅkāvatāra* II: 54; gāthas 125-128):

> The (external) world [lit., what is seen] is not found [or known to us]; yet, from the visible (world) in different ways [or, the manifold] the mind is set in motion [or, proceeds].
>
> The body, the possession [or enjoyment] of senses and of material habitat are declared (to be) for men (no more than) a Store-house of impressions.
>
> Long and short, etc., are produced connected with one another [or, mutually bound up];
> Existence is proven to be partly non-existence, (while)
> Non-existence is demonstrated to be partly existence.
>
> Analyzed [lit., broken down] into the minute particle, there is, indeed, no form to be distinguished.
> Mind only (*citta-mātra*) is (found to be) enduring, which is not well known by those having erroneous views.

Moreover, even the intuitive forms created by the mind for the purpose of explaining the spiritual practice of the Yogī, are to be seen as ultimately unreal, outside the experience itself. Therefore, the *Laṅkāvatāra* states (II: 121; gāthas 176, 178):

> The meditations, and the immeasurables [four virtues of infinite greatness: *maitrī, karuṇā, muditā* and *upekṣā*], the formless (states), the concentrations and the complete cessation of (intellectual) ideation—(all of this) is not found when Mind alone is (experienced).
>
> The meditator, the meditation, and (what is) meditated (upon), the abandoning (of thought), the seeing of the truth—(these are) no more than inventions of the imagination [or, constructive thought, *kalpanā*]. He who awakens to this (truth), that one is liberated [from delusion and suffering].

The *Sūtra* is replete with such statements, but those given above will suffice for our purpose, namely to show that the expression *Citta-mātra* is sometimes used to point to a transcendental state of mind, which—although not beyond the reach of the Buddhist practitioner—is completely devoid of all mental processes, no matter how abstract in content. Most probably, such an extremely negative assessment of mental potential, to be hold as the ideal of the supreme achievement, was not taken literally (the *Sūtra* itself stands as proof of that!), but metaphorically, as a spiritual exercise. By forcing the practitioner to give up even his most cherished attachments to religious concepts and dogmas, the teacher pushes the adept into the realm of pure experience, where the fleeting insubstantiality of all mental constructs regarding the world, the Self, and the meditational process itself, can be felt. For, to paraphrase the author of the *Laṅkāvatāra-sūtra,* it is simply "thinking about" these notions which permeates the mind, and not their "objective" essence. That "essence," which is beyond intellectual "grasping", can only be "felt" with one's whole being. The *Sūtra* makes precisely this point when it says (*Sagāthakam:* 335; gātha 568):

> Truly, as a sword can neither cut nor touch its own blade; just as a finger cannot touch its own tip, so is the Mind (*citta*) in respect to seeing itself.

Indeed, no matter how hard we try, the mind cannot see itself; it can only reflect itself in the distorted mirror of its own external projections (i.e., the mental fabrications about the world outside), or transcend itself by stopping (at least temporarily) its persistent rambling about, thus allowing the much-needed moment of silence for the Essence of Being to be 'heard'.

Citta-mātra as Explanation for the Triple World (Tribhava)

Another important meaning of the Citta-mātra construct is the alleged (by Suzuki, Chatterjee, and others) denial of the external world (*tribhava, traidhātuka*).[29] The Hindus have, since the time of the Upaniṣads and even before, emphasized that the world's appearance is like a dream (*svapna*), or a net of illusion (*māyā, moha*),[30] while the Buddhists themselves have exhibited at times the tendency to disregard the validity of sensory input, at least with respect to the world's non-substantiality (*anātman*) and impermanence (*anitya*). Later Buddhism pushed this tendency even further by expanding the primarily psychological meaning of the term *anātman* (Non-Self) into the cosmological realm, which in turn gave rise to such metaphysical constructs as Śūnyatā, Samatā, Tathatā (Voidness, Sameness, and Suchness, respectively). It is well known that the Buddha himself repeatedly warned—as recorded in the *Nikāyas*—against the extreme views of Eternalism (*Sassatadiṭṭhi*) and Annihilationism (*Ucchedadiṭṭhi*),[31] but it is less known perhaps that the early Mahāyāna writers were accused by their Hīnayāna opponents of committing both ideological sins: the Yogācāras through the absolutization of thought, or Mind (Vijñapti-mātra, or Citta-mātra), and the Mādhyamikas through the absolutization of the universal Void (Śūnyatā).

However, their statements were originally meant to clear the way for their mystical experience, which is by definition ineffable, beyond words and concepts (*svapratyātmagatigocaraṃ vāgvikalparahitam*). This misunderstanding continues to the present day, although the *Laṅkāvatāra-sūtra* (a text often quoted by both the Mādhyamikas and the Yogācāras) clearly rejects the absolute validity of all statements about Reality (*avacanaṃ buddhavacanam*).[32] A. K. Chatterjee, for instance, in his *Yogācāra Idealism* (Varanasi: 1962), p. 37, says that:

> *Laṅkāvatāra-Sūtra* alone distinctly contains idealistic teachings. It teaches the sole reality of consciousness and denies the reality of the external world.

David J. Kalupahana holds identical views when he writes in his *Buddhist Philosophy, A Historical Analysis* (Honolulu: 1982), p. 143:

> While denying that the external object has any reality, the Yogācārins differed from the Mādhyamikas in maintaining that the mind or consciousness is real . . . (and) . . . an absolute form of Idealism is found in the *Sandhinirmocana-sūtra* and the *Laṅkāvatāra-sūtra,* as well as in the works of Asaṅga and Maitreyanātha . . .

Edward Conze, it seems, takes a somewhat different position on this issue of denial (which is crucial to the understanding of Yogācāra thought), when he states the following in his book on *Buddhist Thought in India* (London: 1973), p. 252:

> The bare statement denying the existence of external objects belongs to a fairly low and preliminary stage of realization, and though it may loom large in the philosophical discussions with rival schools, it is no more than a stepping stone to better things. The real point of asserting the unreality of an object *qua* object is to further the withdrawal from all external objective supports (*ālambana*), both through the increasing introversion of transic meditation and through the advance on the higher stages of a Bodhisattva's career when, as we saw (pp. 236-7), no longer tied to an object he acts out of the free spontaneity of his inner being.

The insight he presents may not be without value, but in the absence of documented evidence to support his leap of faith into the Yogācāra soteriology, he is forced to withdraw to a milder position, by saying (p. 253):

> Unfortunately, the Buddhist theory of transic experiences is one of the least explored parts of Buddhism, and much of it we simply do not understand.

Stcherbatsky, on the other hand, is convinced that the denial of the (external) world was a general feature of the entire Mahāyāna movement, and a major one at that, for—according to him—it constituted the essential distinction between its Idealism and the early Realism of the Hīnayāna school. Here are his exact words, as expressed in the first volume of his monumental *Buddhist Logic* (New York: 1962), p. 525:

> Roughly speaking a real external world is assumed in Hīnayāna, denied in Mahāyāna and partly reassumed in the logical school.
>
> As a matter of fact it is denied in all the schools of the Mahāyāna. But the school founded by Maitreya-Asaṅga in opposition to the extreme relativism of the Mādhyamikas is distinguished by assuming a Pure Idea (*citta-mātraṃ = vijñapti-mātraṃ*) not differentiated into subject and object as a final Absolute, and reducing all other ideas to illusions (*parikalpita*).

It is interesting to note the fact that, even if we would try to pass over Stcherbatsky's reading of the Citta-mātra concept (heavily biased with obvious Platonic and Kantian overtones), we cannot ignore certain contradictory statements, which—if taken at face value—will refute the above-quoted lines regarding the rejection of the external object. One such statement is found at page 527 of the same opus. It says that:

> The theory of a store of the germs of all ideas (*ālaya-vijñāna*) is intended as a substitute for the external world. [sic!]

A similar view is held by T. R. V. Murti, who, in *The Central Philosophy of Buddhism* (London: 1980), p. 107, gives us the following comparative appraisal of the positions of the two major Mahāyāna schools:

With his bias in favour of *vijñāna* as the sole reality, the Yogācāra critcises the Mādhyamika for denying the reality of *vijñāna*. His most effective argument against the Mādhyamika is that everything may be dialectically analysed away as illusory; but the illusion itself implies the ground on which the illusory construction can take place. Accepting the *Śūnyatā* of the *Prajñāpāramitās* and even protesting that they interpret it correctly, they modify the *Śūnyatā* of the Mādhyamika; they give substance to the *śūnya* by identifying it with Pure Consciousness (*vijñaptimātratā*) that is devoid of duality (*dvaya-śūnyatā*). They consider themselves the true Mādhyamika—adopting the middle course between the extremes of Nihilism and Realism. A whole treatise —*The Madhyānta Vibhāga*—is devoted to an elucidation of the Vijñānavāda position in contradistinction to that of others. The Yogācāra-Vijñānavāda school is the third and last comprehensive synthesis of Buddhist doctrines. It could certainly incorporate the Vaibhāṣika 'dharmas' taking them as *citta* and *caitta* (mental states); the Yogācāra even increased the number to a hundred.

Professor Murti's interpretation of the contending schools' positions in regard to the reality of the perceptive subject (or Vijñāna) and/or that of the external world (or object) can be tabulated thus:

	Subject		**Object**	
SCHOOL	**REAL**	**NOT-REAL**	**REAL**	**NOT-REAL**
Lokāyata Materialists	—	X	X	—
Hīnayāna Abhidharmists	X	—	X	—
Mahāyāna Mādhyamikas	—	X	—	X
Mahāyāna Yogācāras	X	—	—	X

Murti also distinguishes two different positions within the Yogācāra school itself: one Idealistic expressed in the *Laṅkāvatāra* and the *Sandhinirmocana Sūtras*, and the other purely Monistic, of the Mādhyamika type (i.e., "teaching the non-substantiality and Relativity of all elements of existence, without any limitations whatever," ibid., p. 108), "summarized in the *Abhisamayālaṃkāra*, brought to a further development in the *Jñāna-āloka-alaṃkāra*, the *Śrī-mālā-devī-siṅhanāda* and similar Sūtras and fully expounded in the *Uttara-tantra*." (ibid.) Asaṅga's writings belong to both.

Other scholars, however, arrived at different conclusions on this difficult issue, some by studying later translations and commentaries in Tibetan and Chinese (Wayman, Hattori, Ueda), and others (Schmithausen, Willis, Tokiwa) by taking a fresh look at the earlier texts of the school, which were either insufficiently studied, or mistranslated. Yoshifumi Ueda, for instance, unlike Murti, *et. al.*, attributes the idealistic trend to the later Yogācāra authors Dharmapāla and Hsuang-tsang. In his article "Two main Streams of Thought in Yogācāra Philosophy" (*Philosophy East and West*, vol. 17, No. 1-4, Jan.-Oct. 1967, pp. 155ff), he (Ueda) says that the earlier doctors of the school, Maitreya, Asaṅga, Vasubandhu, and Sthiramati, did not deny objective existence to external reality and, quite the opposite, they developed a "theory of reality" (Ibid., p. 165). This theory, according to him, was derived from the essential incompatibility between two concepts, namely Vijñaptimātratā (interpreted as Consciousness-only identified with the object "as it really is," *yathābhūtārtha*), on the one hand, and Vikalpa (interpreted as "conceptualized, objectified thinking," unrelated to Reality "as it really is"), on the other. His interpretation is based on the following rendition of Sthiramati's commentary (*Bhāṣya*) on Vasubandhu's *Triṃśika*, verse 28, which states (Ibid., pp. 163-64):

> There is not only (no object) to be grasped (and there is no grasping consciousness either), but also there arises the supermundane, non-conceptualizing wisdom (*nirvikalpa jñāna*) in which subject and object (*ālambhya-ālambhaka*) are identical with each other without nullifying and extinguishing their distinction (*sama-sama*). The seeds of the attachment to (the two) [i.e., the object] to be grasped and the grasping (consciousness) have been broken down and the mind is established in the state of being aware of everything as well as of itself as they really are (*yathā-bhūtārtha*). (This is called) the mind has abode in the consciousness only (*vijñaptimātratā*).

Clearly, the text underlies the importance of an increased awareness of Reality and not a denial of its existence.

Similarly, in the early writings of the school, such as the Maitreya chapter of the *Saṅdhinirmocana-sūtra*, taken over by Asaṅga in his *Mahāyāna-saṃgraha* along with Vasubandhu's comment, there is, at most, silence about the external world, rather than a denial of it.[33] By way of evidence in support of this view, Alex Wayman, for instance, presents the following passages from the *Mahāyāna-Sūtrālaṃkāra*, Chapter 14, verses 24-25 (Sylvain Lévi, ed.), and from Sthiramati's commentary on the same, "Bodhipakṣa," chapter, verse 66 (*Pāli Texts Translations*, Vol. 109, p. 61-1-3):[34]

> So as to expand the light of *dharma*, he begins striving in earnest. And having expanded the light of *dharma*, he stands fast in Mind-only (*citta-mātra*). Then, he discerns the appearance of all objects in the mind (*citta*). At that time there are cast off his shifting objects of perception.
>
> The halting of thought on such a single area of thought as "Mind-only (*citta-mātra*) is the three worlds; they are nothing but the mind," constitutes calming (of the mind, *śamatha*).

Sthiramati's understanding of the words of the *Sūtra* is reinforced, according to Wayman, by the authority of Tsoṅ-kha-pa, the celebrated founder of the Gelugpa sect of Tibetan Buddhism, who, commenting on the *Saṅdhinirmocana-sūtra*, says: "In that sūtra it is clearly stated that the denial of an external is in the phase of calming (the mind)."[35] Whatever negation of the world is found in the writings of the early phase of the (Yogācāra) school, concludes Wayman, is to be qualified in light of the special case of the Samādhi situation, as described above.[36]

In a review article entitled "The Yogācāra Idealism,"[37] he further expresses his dismay regarding such pervasive misunderstanding of the basic philosophical position of this school on the part of both Indian and Western writers:

> In short, Voidness or the pure *dharmadhātu* (realm of natures), is the material cause of the world, while the "imagination of unreality" is the formal cause. In respect to content, this system is realistic; in respect to form, it is idealistic. For example, the shape of a pot stems from the mind of the potter, but not the clay. The latter comes from nature (*dharma*) and abides whether a potter arises or not.

Taking into consideration the variety of opinions held on the subject of Citta-mātra, there arises the question as to the origins of the concept. The most widely held belief among scholars, both Eastern and Western, is that it first appeared in the *Daśabhūmika-sūtra* (as the sixth stage Bodhisattva praxis). In Rahder's edition (p. 49) there is the following:

> citta-mātraṃ idaṃ yad idaṃ traidhātukam
>
> There is nothing but mind—this very triple world!

Explaining the significance of this line, Schmithausen, in an article entitled "On the Problem of the Relation of Spiritual Practice and Philosophical Theory in Buddhism," writes (p. 247):[38]

> . . . The thesis of universal idealism originated from the *generalization* of a situation observed in the case of objects visualized in meditative concentration, i.e., in the context of *spiritual practice.*

To document this idea (which incidentally agrees with Wayman's interpretation, as presented above), he adduces evidence from an old Mahāyāna sūtra entitled *Pratyutpannabuddhasaṃmukha-avasthita-samādhi-sūtra*, or *Bhadrapālasūtra*, first translated into Chinese by Lokakṣema as early as C.E. 179, over a hundred years before the *Daśabhūmikasūtra*, and probably just as many years before the first compilation of the *Laṅkāvatāra* was made.[39] What this sūtra essentially says (as the title indicates) is that both pure (i.e., of Buddhas) and impure (i.e., of corpses and skeletons, *aśubhāvanā*) visualizations which are seen by the meditating Yogin (or Bodhisattva) are but projections of his own mind (*cittam eva*, lit. "just mind").

Having acknowledged this discovery, the yogin should extend the ideality, or unsubstantiality of the meditation-images to all phenomena, presumably for the purpose of breaking the attachment to the world: "This whole world consisting of the three spheres is nothing but mind (*citta-mātram idaṃ-yad idaṃ-traidhātukam*). And why? Because (I see in the case of meditation that) it appears just as I imagine."[40]

It is noteworthy that the primacy of mentation can be traced even further back to the famous first verse of the Pāli *Dhammapāda*, which emphatically states that "dharmas are mind-controlled; mind is pre-eminent among them; they are mind-made" (*manomayā*).[41] J. Brough in the *Gandhari Dharmapāda* (London: 1962), p. 243, interprets the expression *mano-javā* to mean that (the dharmas) "have the speed of mind," in the sense that they are momentary.[42] Such factual observations prompted Conze to make the following remarks with regard to the direct link between the later Yogācāra Idealism and the early Theravāda idealistic tendencies:[43]

> Before he became a Yogācārin, Asaṅga had been a Mahīśāsaka, and for some time Mahīśāsakas and Theravādins were one and the same sect.
>
> . . . (Thus) the Yogācārins developed the latent idealism of Buddhism into a full-fledged idealism, according to which Mind or Thought alone is real, and everything else is "mere representation." This doctrine plays a big part in the *Laṅkāvatāra*.

Now, it is quite possible that some of the late Yogācāra philosophers became so preoccupied with speculative metaphysical activity that they lost touch with the meditational experience as described in the older treatises—such as those mentioned above—and developed a new, more elaborate and contrived psychology, based on the literal interpretation of the Citta-mātra concept. That the danger of literal interpretation, or reification of the older ideas was real, we can see from the questions raised by Mahāmati in the *Laṅkāvatāra* itself, with regard to the literality of certain metaphoric images, such as the number of Buddhas equated to the sands of the Ganges (VI: 229), or the finger pointing to the moon, which is taken by some as the moon itself (see *Laṅkāvatāra* III: 223-24; gātha 3):

> As the immature sees the finger-tip and not the moon,
> So indeed those (who are addicted to the letter do not understand the essence [or truth, truly] of my (teaching).

Moreover, later commentators—such as Tsoṅ-kha-pa—referred to the *Laṅkāvatāra* as a sūtra of "provisional" or "indirect" meaning (*neyārtha*), from which the "final" or "ultimate" meaning (*nītārtha*) should be inferred through interpretation. He even gives a quote from the *Laṅkāvatāra-sūtra* to prove his point (II: 49, gātha 123):[44]

> In the way that a physician offers a medicine to one patient and a medicine to another patient, in that way the Buddhas teach "Mind-only" for the sentient beings.

Such "provisional" interpretation of the "indirect" meaning of the term *citta-mātra* has been offered in more recent times by the Japanese scholar Gishin Tokiwa in his article "'Svacittamātra'—The Basic Standpoint of the *Laṅkāvatāra Sūtra*" (*Journal of Indian and Buddhist Studies*, vol. 26, no. 1, Dec. 1977, p. 478), where he writes:

> The term *'sva-citta-mātra'*, which literally means 'nothing but one's own mind', . . . it signifies the Self that is free from the ego and the object of the ego, the Self without any form even of the mind.

Tokiwa further points out that:

> Here it must be noted that by *'citta-mātra'*, the *Laṅka* never asserts the ultimate existence of *citta;* rather, the term indicates the true mode of being which is free from being and non-being, that is, that which is free from the very mind that manifests itself as being and non-being.

And he brings the following verse to document his findings (*Laṅkāvatāra Sūtra* III: 153; gātha 30):

> Of neither being nor non-being (do I speak), but of Mind-only, which has nothing to do with existence or non-existence, and which is thus free from intellection.

Yet, rather than taking this statement as a reaffirmation of the Middle Way seen in the light of the doctrine of Dependent Origination (Pratītya-samutpāda), as applied to the ideal mental equipose derived from the attainment of *Prajñā-pāramitā* (the perfection of insight), Tokiwa prefers to interpret it, curiously enough, as an appeal for the overcoming of the ambivalence of both history and Self (*sva-*). He sees the "ultimacy of the 'sva' or Self, 'citta' or Mind, as the principle of delusion" to be "overcome immediately here and now." (*Laṅkāvatāra-sūtra*, 477) Thus, he says the following:

> By adding 'sva' to 'citta-mātra', the *Laṅka* does not alter this point—that is, that the delusive manifestation is not final and that the true mode of being which is said to be 'citta-mātra' is free even from the subjectivity of 'citta'—; it goes on to elucidate that this manifestation-no-manifestation is a matter of the fundamental subject of history itself, rather than being anything objective or external to that subject.

In other words, what Tokiwa is really saying, if I understand him correctly, is that the Mind (*citta*), subjective as it is, is prone to "delusive manifestation," while history (i.e., the mind objectified in the world) is "final" and "free from subjectivity," the "true mode of being." He also seems to equate Mind (*citta*) with the Self (*sva*), and since the latter is not real in Buddhism (Anātman), so—concludes Tokiwa—neither is the mind. Hence, history (i.e., world) is real, Mind (i.e., Self) is unreal. This is the exact opposite of Suzuki's interpretation of the Citta-mātra concept in the *Laṅkāvatāra-sūtra*.

In Suzuki's view, the Mind alone is real, while the world (*loka, traidhātuka, tribhava*) is unreal. Having written more extensively than any other writer on this subject, he has contributed more than anyone to the general misunderstanding of Yogācāra thought as pure subjectivism, or as he himself put it—"a form of pure idealism" (*Studies*, p. 244). Here is his assessment of the central thesis of this school:

> All that we habitually consider having an objective value, such as our own body (*deha*), property (*bhoga*), and the land (*pratishṭāna*) where we have our abodes, are no more than our own mind projected and recognised as externally extending and real.

In order to substantiate this thesis, Suzuki collects a series of quotes which, when removed from the general philosophical context of the *Sūtra*, do indeed seem puzzling, to say the least, or—in Suzuki's own words—"shrouded in obscurity." Here are the quotes, taken from various places in the *Sūtra*, along with Suzuki's English renditions in parentheses (see *Studies*, pp. 243-44). We shall take them one by one and consider the validity of Suzuki's interpretation. They are:

(1) *Cittamātraṃ lokam*. ("The world is nothing but Mind," II: 73, v. 136). The full gātha is as follows:

> When those who are born of the heart of the Buddha [lit., the Victorious One] will see the world as Mind only, then they will obtain the body of transformation (which is) free from performing rituals, (being) endowed with the powers, the psychic abilities and the self-control.

Clearly, the verse is alluding to the meditative experience, during which the contact with the outside world is entirely abandoned (including that obtained through religious observances, *kriyā-saṃskāra*), for the purpose of acquiring the transformation of the body (*nirmāṇa-kāya*) and the psychic qualities associated with it. Such an interpretation is perfectly acceptable, if we take it to be a case of the double accusative, the second having a locative or spatial sense.

(2) *Cittabāhyādarśanam*. ("Nothing is to be seen outside the Mind"). Again, the respective lines (10-13, p. 42), out of which the above

compound is extracted, deal unmistakenly with the successive stages of meditation culminating with the experience of Samādhi (or the absorption of the mind within itself, that is, away from the sensory world). Here goes the *Sūtra* (II: 42):

> Those who follow the foundation of signlessness *by not seeing* outside the mind (*citta*); who contemplate in the given order by following the objects of Samādhi in the sequence of the stages, and are convinced that the three worlds are one's own mind, attain the highest illusory Samādhi.

It would be misleading and unwarranted, given the meditational context of these lines, as well as the syntax of the first compound (of which *citta-bāhya-adarśana* is but a fragment), to assert that the subject of the passage is the denial of the external world (*a-darśana* = "not-seeing," "not-looking," rather than "nothing is to be seen").

(3) *Svacittamātraṃ traidhātukam.* ("The triple world is Mind itself"). p. 42, line 12 (see above); p. 80, line 7; p. 112, lines 6-7; p. 123, line 17; p. 213, lines 11-12; and so on.

First, the passage on page 80 occurs in reply to Mahāmati's question pertaining to the "clear understanding of the (meditational) discipline" (*yoga-abhisamaya*, p. 79, line 15), and not with regard to the nature of the external world. True, the Buddha in his reply (pp. 79-80, especially line 1, p. 80) divides the answer into four things (to be mindful of)—*caturbhiḥ dharmaiḥ*. The first of these can be translated as an exhortation to the "kind of clear examination of what is seen (or perceived) in one's own mind" (*svacitta-dṛśya-vibhāvanatayā*), which is after all the essence of yogic meditation. Suzuki translates this line as: "To have a clear understanding as to what is seen of Mind itself" (Suzuki's translation of the *Laṅkā*, p. 70), but he himself admits in a footnote (Ibid., note 2) that "this is rather a clumsy translation of *svacitta-dṛśya*." To follow his line of reasoning, let us reproduce here the entire argumentation given in the note:

> *Dṛśya* is "what is seen," that is, this visible world, or this external, objective world, which according to the *Laṅkāvatāra* is a manifestation of Mind itself (sic!) When this truth is realised, the objective world loses its reality as such, and we no more cling to it as if it were a final irreducible fact which stands oppressively against the mind. The Buddhist idea of interpreting existence idealistically is more religious than logical, for Buddhists want to elevate the value of spirit absolutely above matter, so that the latter will be amenable to all the commands to be given by the former.

Unfortunately, it is not clear whether the author is referring to the Yogin's aspiration to detach himself from the "oppressiveness" of the material world, or to the "unreality" of the latter, taken as a philosophical characterization of its nature.

With regard to another thing that the Yogin should consider (from among the four), the *Sūtra* further says that one should "look into (the truth) that the external reality (is) non-reality" (*bāhya-bhāva-abhāva-upalakṣaṇatayā*) (p. 80, line 1), which is an obvious allusion to the doctrine of Dependent Origination (Pratītya-samutpāda) and an echo of the Śūnyatā concept as presented in the *Prajñāpāramitā* literature, and embraced by all Mahāyāna schools following it. Suzuki, however, translates it rather loosely as "to look into (the truth) that no external world obtains" (Ibid.), which again proves his biased reading of the *Sūtra*, in as far as the denial of the world is concerned.

Now, bearing in mind the above considerations, let us return to the clarification given by the Buddha to the first point of the meditational process, namely the examination of one's mind. The Buddha asks and then answers his own question thus (*Laṅkā* II: 80; ll. 5-10):

> Then, how, Mahāmati, does a not-so-clever (*akuśala*) Bodhisattva-Mahāsattva come to a clear understanding of what is seen in one's own mind? To wit, he inquires into that (by thinking) thus: 'This is only one's own mind, (which) in the triple world is devoid of Self and what belongs to the Self, (and which) is influenced (only) by the adherence of the habit energy accumulated since the beginningless time through faulty reasoning, (itself being) motionless, being striven after it is not attained, being renounced it is not got rid of [vide: F. Edgerton's *BHS Dictionary*, Delhi: 1977, p. 102]; on the other hand, it is known (that) the multiplicity of forms and actions, (which) are tied together as the triple world, is to be chosen according to circumstances corresponding with the discrimination between ideas, such as body, sensory enjoyment, and habitat.'

Since the adherence of habit-energy (*vāsanā*), as well as the long string of qualifying compounds of which it is but a part, can only refer to *svacitta-mātra*, ("one's own mind only") it appears that from the syntactic point of view, it is *citta* ("mind") which constitutes the subject of this statement and not *traidhātuka*, ("the three realms of existence") which plays a subordinate function as object in relation to the mind. Moreover, if we were to take *traidhātuka* as the subject, as Suzuki does, we would have to face the seeming contradiction between its lack of Self-hood (*ātmā-rahita*) as an aggregate of inter-related elements, on the one hand, and its equation with *citta*, ("mind") whose existence is clearly stated throughout the *Sūtra* (as a single dharma entity), on the other hand. This is also borne out by such statements as: "The absence of external entities" (*bāhya-bhāva-abhāva*, p. 80, line 1), or: "The *citta* itself is motionless (*nirīha*)," "Being striven after it is not attained, being renounced it is not got rid of (*ayūha-niryūha-vigata*, p. 80, line 7)." Consequently, a sign of equality or identity between the *world* and the *mind* could hardly be conceived, in the terms set forth by the *Laṅkāvatāra*. The following passage reinforces this conclusion (*Laṅkā* II: 123-24; ll. 15-17, 1-2):

> When thus is recognized that there is nothing but imagination (and that)—really (*nāma*)—the external reality is (in fact) non-reality, one is awakened into the seeing of (the fact that there is) nothing but one's own mind, and that this seeing of one's own mind is (itself) nothing but imagination.
>
> That is to say, (if) one recognizes that the triple world has nothing to do with primary and secondary elements, it is devoid of Self and what belongs to it, it is removed from little or perfect knowledge (or philosophical systems), such as the four (logical) alternatives [i.e., is, is not, both, and neither], and (thereby) obtaining one's condition of individuality, of not coming back into existence [lit., of no re-birth], of abiding in that place where reality remains in its original identity.

Suzuki himself mentions in his *Studies*, p. 295, that *anutpāda* (lit., "no-production") is the equivalent of Nirvāṇa, which is "no-birth" (*anutpādo nirvāṇam*). Therefore, the conclusion of this passage clearly underscores its soteriological thrust. That is to say that all thinking about Reality can only tell us about the nature of our own constructive imagination (*vikalpamātra*) and little if anything about the world itself, which can only be experienced directly—as it really is (*yathābhūta*)—by abandoning all pre-conceived philosophical constructs. The *Sūtra* says (II: 112; ll. 6-7):

> Then, Mahāmati, the seeing of the condition of reality as it really is, that is to say of all elements (of existence), is (to come to) the realization that there is nothing to be seen (externally) but (the reflection of) one's own mind.

Another example mentioned by Suzuki appears to set forth a parallel between the external events and the mental phenomena, such as the stages of Bodhisattva's (*bhūmis*). However, the context indicates that both external and internal events are equally spurious due to their mutual conditioning (*Laṅkā* IV: 213; ll. 10-13):

> But, Mahāmati, there is nothing going forward, nor anything retreating elsewhere. This (world) is merely what is seen by one's own mind, to wit, the stages (of the Bodhisattva) that develop successively, as do (all) various doings in the triple world.

This and other similar assertions may lead one to believe that the *Laṅkā* embraces a form of thoroughgoing radical Monism. However, nowhere have we found so far that such monistic tendency is firmly established on the ground of mental, or spiritual exclusivity, which would provide the incontrovertible proof for Suzuki's (and others') contention that the philosophy of the Yogācāras is a form of pure Idealism. For, all these statements do nothing more than reiterate (from various epistemological angles) the basic Mahāyāna position that all mental constructions, no matter how elaborate, are under final analysis, woefully inadequate in their attempt to convey the essence of Reality as such, or even to circumscribe its boundaries. They remain what they are: skillful metaphysical artifacts, nothing more than mind-games, "representations-only" (Vijñaptimātra).

(4) *Cittaṃhi traidhātuka-yoniḥ.* ("Mind produces the triple world," p. 268, gātha 36). The gātha from which this statement is extracted, far from literally asserting that the physical world as such is produced by some omnipotent mind, points out quite simply that as the mind is prone to error, delusion, and distortion (*bhrānta*), so are its productions (or projections?), such as our constructs about reality, or views of the world (*Sagāthakam:* 269, gātha 36):

> This mind, indeed, is the origin of the triple world [i.e., as we know it], for, (when) the mind is deluded, this and that (world) is seen. One does not discriminate this world (which is) non-existent, (but) having recognized the (relative) course of the world, one sees it as such [i.e., non-existent independently, *asatta*].

(5) *Tribhavacittamātram.* ("The triple existence is nothing but Mind," p. 208, line 13). The context of this line is (ll. 12-13):

> However, Mahāmati, I am neither for permanency, nor for impermanency. Why is that? For this reason: it is taught that the triple world is (contrived by the) mind only; the external Reality is not admitted . . .

Ad prima facie, this statement seems to be a strong one in the direction of a denial of the external, objective world. However, the continuation of the text presents us with the identical argument given under number 3 above (p. 80, ll. 5-10).

That is to say that all apparent multiplicity of elements that arise and vanish under our eyes, are due only to our mental activity of discrimination. They are not truly real, in the ultimate sense that is. But, on the other hand, that does not mean that the world *itself* is non-existent, either. What it does mean is that their fleeting existence is conditioned interdependently, and on account of their relative impermanence, they appear almost as a veil of illusion, something like an impressionist or pointillist painting. Therefore, the *Sūtra* clearly states, it would be meaningless and inaccurate to assert either the existence, or the non-existence of the world (*Laṅkā* III: 208; ll. 16-17):

> . . . By recognizing that duality is the process of constructive thought, by casting off the view regarding the existence and non-existence of the external (world, *bāhya*), (one is enlightened) because of realizing that it is merely one's own mind (which is seen in it) . . .

(6) *Cittaṃ hi sarvam.* ("All is Mind," *Sagāthakam,* gātha 134). Taken out of context, this gātha, too, is somewhat misleading. Here is the verse in its entirety:

> All is truly (made of) mind; this is found everywhere and in everybody. It is by the immature ones that multiplicity is perceived, for, there are no individual marks (where) Mind-only is.

The key to the correct meaning of these lines is the word *sarva* ("all"). It can be substituted by *vicitra* ("plurality"), or *lakṣaṇa* ("individual characteristics"). However, if we pay attention to the long-standing commentarial tradition, such as that of the Sarvāstivādin Abhidharmists, we will come to the conclusion that *sarva* is commonly taken as a reference to the plurality of dharmas, the elements of existence, as well as their mental correspondents, known as *cetasikā.*

No doubt, the statement is of epistemic nature, as indicated by the use of the verb *gṛhyate* ("is perceived"). The sense here, as elsewhere, is that all discrimination is entirely due to mental functioning, and its spurious nature becomes evident only in the higher state of self-absorption, when the mind turn back upon itself (*parāvṛtti*).

According to Suzuki himself (*Studies*, Glossary, p. 412), another name for the *Laṅkāvatāra* is *Cittamanomanovijñānapañcadharmasvabhāva-lakṣaṇadharmaparyāya* (*Laṅkā* II: 43; ll.14-15), which may be rendered thus: "The synonym(s) of the *dharma*-set amounting to Mind, the world of particulars perceived by the intellect, the five Knowledge-states, the individual characteristics of one's own existence," and so on. They, *sarvadharmas*, are also said to lack self-substance, or individual existence (*dharmanairātmya*) (*Laṅka* II: 69; ll. 11-13):

> When a Bodhisattva-Mahāsattva recognizes that all dharmas are free from the (three) Cognitive-modes, the five Knowledge-states, the intellectual Consciousness and the empirical mind, he is said to be skilled in the Selflessness of things (*dharmas*).

This *Laṅkā* verse is a late development upon the old *Dhammapāda* line 279, which says that "all things (or everything) are non-Self" (*sabbe dhammā anattā*), including the uncompounded Nirvāṇa, according to I. B. Horner.[45] Indeed, that is precisely what the two preceding gāthas 132, 133 (to that given as example of world denial by Suzuki) are saying:

> (There are) no stages (of Bodhisattvahood), no (noble) truths, no (Buddha-) fields, and no (bodies of) transformation; the Buddhas, the Pratyekabuddhas, and also the Śrāvakas are imaginary [i.e., products of imagination].
>
> The (individual) person (or soul, entity), (its) continuity (or permanence), the (five) personality aggregates, the Causation, the atoms, the Supreme Spirit, the Lord, the Creator—(they are) ascertained in the Mind only [i.e., they exist only in the mind].

Since the gātha cited by Suzuki follows immediately this lengthy enumeration, I have been forced to conclude (in close agreement with the commentarial tradition and the *Laṅkā* itself) that *cittaṃ hi sarvaṃ* refers to the dharmas (that is, all Buddhist metaphysical categories included in the three worlds, *traidhātuka, tribhava*).

(7) *Sarvarūpāvabhāsaṃ hi yadā cittaṃ pravartate.* ("When Mind evolves, all forms are manifested," *Sagāthakam*, gātha 93). The reading of the *Sūtra* is as follows (*Laṅkā* X: 276):

When the mind operates it has the manifestation of all forms; when there is no mind in this situation, there are no forms. The mind (*citta*) has been deluded (*bhrānta*) since beginningless past. Therefore, the Yogin, on account of his (transcendental) insight, sees the world shorn of its appearances.

What the text really says is that the appearance (*avabhāsa*), or delusion (*bhrānta*) in regard to the world (*jagat*) is created by the mind (*citta*) and not the world itself. The forms (*rūpaṇi*) are precisely these artificial creations of the mind, which are subsequently superimposed upon Reality, and not Reality itself. The text is clear in this respect: "no mind—no forms" (*nātra cittaṃ na rūpaṇi*). What is denied here, is the persistent, but deceptive activity of the mind in the process of interpreting Reality through intellectual categories. There is, however, a crucial, albeit subtle, difference between the denial of validity to our mental perceptions and constructs in regard to what *appears* to be real, and the denial of Reality *as such*, in its facticity.

Suzuki (and others who allowed themselves to be misled in this way) seems to have overlooked this crucial difference when he perceived to be *Laṅkāvatāra*'s main thesis the statement that "The world is nothing but one's own mind" (*svacittadṛśyamātram*).[46] Yet, as an afterthought, Suzuki also states that "the strongest of all the proofs that can be advanced for the statement that the world is Mind itself (*tribhavasvacittamātram*), is that of intuitive knowledge (*pratyakṣa*)."[47] Unfortunately, he is forced to admit at this point that, by definition, this kind of knowledge (i.e., the *āryajñāna* of the Tathāgata), or absolute truth (*paramārtha satya*), "is not dependent upon anything logically reasoned," for "it is derived from its immediacy and not from its intellectual precision."[48]

On the other hand, if we turn our attention back to the text, we find that the compiler of the *Sūtra* constantly urges his readers to discover Reality "in accordance with facts," i.e., in its facticity (*yathābhūtaṃ*). Here are a few examples of his attitude (*Laṅkā* X: 353 vv. 708, 709):

The Mind is to be regarded as a reflected image conceived in the primordial past; it is the appearance of Reality [or, 'the thing,' *arthākāraṃ asti*], but not the Reality itself (or, 'not the thing in itself,' *na cārtho 'sti*); (therefore) one should perceive it distinctly, in accordance with facts (*yathābhūtam*).

Just as an image perceived in a mirror is devoid of both oneness and otherness; so the nature of (mental) production is to be regarded—as not altogether non-existent (*na ca tannāsti*).

The contriving ability of the mind along with its propensity to project its contrivances upon the external world, are the causes of all our delusions. This is repeatedly emphasized in the *Sūtra.* To wit (*Laṅkā* III: 154; gāthas 32, 33):

> Multiplicity (of mental images) is produced from the habit-energy of discrimination; it is born of mind, but it is called among the people as (something) external (to the mind)—this I declare to be nothing but mind (*citta-mātra*).
>
> There is nothing to be found outside in the visible (world); it is indeed the mind (itself) which sees the multiplicity (of dharmas). Body, sensory enjoyment, and habitat—these I call nothing but (distinctions made by) the mind [i.e., mere mental notions].

Such passages are found throughout the *Laṅkāvatāra* and, when properly interpreted, a consistent pattern of thought will not fail to reveal itself to the reader, namely that all distinctions are due to our mode of thinking and perceiving, rather than to their objective existence, as such.[49] To wit, *Sagāthakam:* 374, gātha 872:

> Bound up in a continuous chain (all things seem) momentarily separated (and) they are perceived as such due to (the functioning of) one's own mind; (for, while) they do appear to have forms and characteristics (which) hang firmly together, they are (in fact) the products of the eye-consciousness (*cakṣu-vijñāna*) and of the intellectual volition [or thinking consciousness, *mano-vijñāna*].

Having sifted through many similar passages, one will be compelled to admit that the context in which the Citta-mātra concept is cast is invariable of epistemological nature. That is, it is not about the external world *as such* (as Suzuki and others have thought), but rather about the way in which we come *to know it.* The following verses once again illustrate this point (*Laṅkā* III: 153 vv. 25, 29):

> When the compounded things (*saṃskṛta*) are regarded as free from (the duality of) support and supporting, there is positively Mind-only [i.e., merely thought]; (therefore), I teach (the doctrine of) Mind-only.
>
> (What is) removed from all (philosophical) views, free from imagined and imagining, of no attainment and of no generation —(these) I call Mind-norm.

It is interesting to note that in this last gātha 29, the word used is *mātrā* (fem. = "measure, norm") and not the commonly used adverbial form *mātra* ("only, merely"). Although closely related to each other, the former term admits an additional enrichment to the meaning of the expression Citta-mātra, which in such case could be translated as the doctrine of "right, or correct thinking (or mind)."[50] This is best understood within the context of the Mahāyānist middle way, as illustrated in the succeeding gāthas 30 and 31, of the same chapter III, pp. 153 and 154, respectively:

> Of neither Being, nor non-Being (do I speak), but of Mind-only, which has nothing to do with existence or non-existence [or, Reality or non-Reality], and which is thus free from intellection.

Still, what is meant by "Mind-only?" Here are some clear answers. First, *Laṅkā* III: 154 gātha 31:

> Suchness, the pre-eminence of Voidness, Nirvāṇa, the realm of truth, the various bodies made of mind [or, various forms of the Will-body]—these I call Mind-only [or, existing in the mind, mere thoughts].

Such absolute superlatives are frequently said to follow the middle course between extremes of both assertion and denial. To wit, *Sagāthakam:* 335; gātha 565:

> But Suchness and Mind-only belong to the rules for the given things of the wise [lit., the worthy ones, *āryas*]; (for) neither those who deny, nor those who affirm are skilled in my rules.

Now, at the end of our investigation of the Citta-mātra concept, we are forced to conclude that neither the denial of the external Reality, nor the affirmation regarding its essential nature were intended by the early Yogācāras. By allowing himself to slip into one of these two extremes (namely the denial), which were so carefully avoided throughout the text by its author, Suzuki—the commentator—betrayed Suzuki—the translator—when he made the following statement (*Studies*, p. 286):

> It will be interesting to see how this Acittatā (no-mindness) view of the religious experience in the *Prajñāpāramitā* turns into the Cittamātra (mind-only) theory, so called, of the *Laṅkāvatāra.* Both start from the untenability or unknowability

> (*anupalabhyamānatva*) of ultimate reality which is beyond dualism of being and non-being, of birth and death; and while the one ends in a form of negativism, the other comes to an affirmation, saying that there is nothing but Mind, that the mind alone is the last word one can say about the world.

This may be true of the *Prajñā-pāramitā* literature, but in the light of the documentation set forth above, it does not do justice to the true intention of the *Laṅkā*'s compiler(s), which, far from representing a mere affirmation or denial of the world as such, was truly about the factitiousness of speculative metaphysics, on the one hand, and the ultimacy of meditative experience, on the other.

Concluding Words and the Connection Between *Laṅkāvatāra* and Zen

The Citta-mātra concept represents the pinnacle of the Yogācāra philosophy. Unfortunately, its precise meaning has been lost or misunderstood with the passage of time, partly because of the semantic richness of the concept itself, relative to the context, and partly due to the cultural and temporal distance that separates the classical Indian world from the mental frame of reference of the twentieth-century scholar (Buddhist or non-Buddhist).

We too often forget that human language is largely metaphorical and that "the essence of metaphor is understanding and experiencing one thing in terms of another."[51] In fact, unless we communicate in precise, mathematical symbols, language itself is nothing *but* a string of metaphors. The problem with this is that, while human experience tends to constantly change, the metaphors of language tend to solidify, to lose their poetic vitality, and eventually lose their touch with reality, as perceived and vitally experienced at any given time. Periodical "cleansing" the language of "dead" metaphors becomes, therefore, a necessity. But this is not easily done. It is the task of the creative minds of the time—the bard, the poet, the artist, the philosopher, and most recently, the socio-cultural critic—to re-create the language, to carve in gripping expressions the new metaphors which more aptly encapsulate the novel ways of experiencing the world. It is no mere coincidence that along with revolutionary changes in the social, economic, and technological spheres, our century has seen the emergence of parallel and equally revolutionary new ways of interpreting the world, artistically and philosophically.

In philosophy, for instance, a true Copernican revolution has taken place in the first decades of our century, with the growing influence of logical and linguistic analysis over the more traditional, intuitive approaches and methods of inquiry.

Similarly, at the end of the one thousand-year long history of Buddhist and non-Buddhist Indian religio-philosophical quest, a new and radical critique of the long-standing assumptions, symbols, and paradigms, found its way into such influential texts as the *Laṅkāvatāra-sūtra*. This critique not only questioned the ultimate validity of the most prevalent cultural metaphors of the time, but it also addressed the more fundamental issues, such as the ability of language and of conceptual reasoning in general to even fathom, let alone reflect, the ultimate nature of Reality, in its awesome depth and complexity. We found a name for such radical critique of language and of meaning, we called it "semiotics," the study of signs, of symbols, and of their relation to words and to the Reality they purport to express. The Yogācāras, too, gave it a name: they called it the doctrine of "Mind-only" (Citta-mātra), or of "Imagination-only" (Vijñapti-mātra).

The criticism of the old, speculative approaches to solving metaphysical problems by means of this "Mind-only" doctrine brought about an increased level of awareness in two very important areas of concern: (1) the limitations of *reason* and, implicitly, of language, its main tool of operation; and (2) the inescapable role of *subjectivity* in the cognitive processes.

The first problem area was addressed (most eloquently by Nāgārjuna and his followers of the Mādhyamika school) through the skillful manipulation of the fourfold negation logic, known as the tetralemma dialectics (see previous chapter 2.0.).

Continuing its thoroughgoing application, along with an expanded version of the causal theory of Interdependent Origination of all things, and of the well-tested principle of the Middle Way between philosophical extremes, the Yogācāras also pointed out the untenability of metaphysical constructs on the basis of pure reason alone. In addition, they claimed, the metaphorical nature of language itself renders it inadequate in the realm of absolute verities, the realm of religious pursuit par excellence.

But it was in the second area of concern, regarding the crucial role of the *subjective* factors in cognition, that the "Mind-only" doctrine developed by the Yogācāras made its substantial contribution to Buddhist epistemology. The full extent of this contribution, however, can only be appreciated if and when the Citta-mātra concept is correctly interpreted. The main thesis of this book is that the "Mind-only," or "Nothing but the Mind" formula, should be regarded as a disparaging comment applicable to all absolutistic claims of explaining the ultimate Reality through conceptual language, and not as a definitive affirmation of a one-sided and dogmatic monistic idealism à la Bishop Berkeley, as Suzuki and others erroneously believed. To adopt their view that Citta-mātra means that *the world* is "nothing but mind," or that it "is made of mind only," would be tantamount to Buddhist heresy (if there is such a thing), since it would run counter to the principle of the Middle Way, against all one-sided extremes and reductionistic statements, and it would also confuse a linguistic metaphor (that is, a figure of speech, which is supposed to approximate only, not describe, Reality) with Reality itself.

In the *Laṅkāvatāra-sūtra*, we are told that all knowledge about the world is perceived through the 'tunnel-vision', or 'tainted glass' of our past experience, prejudices, and memories (*vāsanā-vījas*, or "memory-seeds," planted in our subconscious, Ālaya-vijñāna, from the beginning of time). Therefore, all knowledge is more about our own mind than about the world, objectively speaking. The importance of subjective bias in the accumulation of knowledge has recently begun to emerge as a legitimate topic of discussion, even in our own "scientific" world, as anyone participating in it can attest. How much broader a role subjectivity can play in a traditional world, which is deprived of objective means of checking the validity of philosophical statements about the ultimate nature of reality, aside from individual intuition and personal inclinations and biases? It is the indelible merit of the Yogācāra philosophers that they not only brought this healthy skepticism out into the open (this has been done from the time of the Buddha!), but they also set it on a firm logical and doctrinal basis, as their mainstay amidst the teeming jungle of claims and counterclaims that was the intellectual landscape of the time. The "Mind-only" theory of the Yogācāras proved to have staying power and growing influence over the centuries—in India and beyond, in more ways than one—as we shall see.

Now, two different solutions, or paths of pursuit (one theoretical, the other practical) were followed in direct response to the two areas of concern mentioned above: the limitations of reason and language, and the role of subjectivity in the pursuit of knowledge. The *theoretical* path led to further pursuit of the logical implications of the dialectics of Nāgārjuna and the Yogācāras, away from speculative metaphysics. This gave rise to the latter school of the Yogācāra logicians (such as Diṅnāga, Dharmakīrti and Śāntarakṣita). Its thoroughgoing criticism made a powerful impact upon the intellectual climate of India for centuries to come, and certainly stimulated the revival of Hindu philosophy through the eighth-century philosophical genius Śaṅkara, the founder of Advaita Vedānta (still the dominant philosophical school in modern Indian culture).

The *practical* solution, on the other hand, was to turn almost completely away from all logical and metaphysical activity (these having been proven to be of little use in reaching the ultimate, religious goal of spiritual liberation, as shown above), and to focus one's energies exclusively on meditation. True, the "Mind-only" concept itself had its roots in the experience of Yogic meditation (hence also the name of the school: "Yogā-cāra," or the "practice of Yoga"). It was only later that philosophical elaborations began to flourish around it, and it became a formula to symbolize reflective criticism against all obstinate attachments to empty words, to reified, objectified concepts, and speculations, removed from the immediacy of personal experience. For, it was the purpose of Yogic meditation, or deep thinking (Sanskrit, *dhyāna;* Chinese, *ch'an-na* or *ch'an;* Japanese, *zen*), to empty the mind of all phenomenal appearances and of cumbersome notions and metaphors.

Particularly hard to dislodge was the deep-rooted attachment to the conviction of a personal ego, or permanent substance, or Self. But this very notion of "Self" was an intrinsic mental obstacle to transformation. For, if one clings to a permanent Self, how can one even conceive of radically altering it, and thereby re-experiencing life and reality from a fresh angle? It was only by meditating on the relativity principle of "Mind-only," or "Voidness," that is, the lack of independent existence of all things (*niḥsvabhāva*), that the illusion of a permanent Self could be discarded and freedom could be achieved. This Relativity principle, indeed, became the cornerstone of Buddhist philosophy, following this Indian phase.

From the day-to-day, empirical self, to the enlightened, trans-empirical Self of the Buddha, nothing was to be regarded as sacred, absolute, and permanently valid. "Vast emptiness—nothing sacred," the first Buddhist missionary to China, Bodhidharma, is said to have replied to the Chinese emperor's question regarding the supreme and sacred truth of his religion. In Japan, the twenty-first case of the classic Zen collection of *kōans* (mystical riddles meant to be meditated upon as aids toward Enlightenment), known as the *Mumonkan*, records the answer of a Zen master to the question, "What is the Buddha?" as "A dried shit-stick!" For the ultimate Reality includes, indeed *must* include, all existential entities, regardless of human conventions, artificial discriminations, and temporal value judgments.

Thus, the *Laṅkāvatāra* set off a new way of looking at the world, both critically, through the negative logic of the tetralemma (leading to non-attachment to conceptual language), and liberating, through meditation (on the untenability of all absolutistic dogmas). The notion of "Mind-only," therefore, should be regarded as an important step forward in the process of evaluating and interpreting the enormous mass of speculative literature growing incessantly on the fertile Indian soil for hundreds of years before and after the Buddha. By reversing the order of priorities from the secondary, "handed-down" type of knowledge to the primacy of personal experience, the Yogācāra Buddhists did in fact put an end to the Abhidharmists' metaphysics, while simultaneously opening the doors for expansion outside of the Indian cultural context. "Mind-only" was a notion assimilable by people with a more practical outlook on life.

Thus, the South Indian brāhmin who became a Yogācāra convert, Bodhidharma, went forth to China to become the first patriarch of the Ch'an school of sudden Enlightenment, also known as the *Laṅkāvatāra* school of Zen. This school, first established in North China, later spread into Korea and Japan (see the Introduction, ch. 0.1.). A direct descendent of this lineage, Dōgen, the 13th-century master of Zazen (or sitting meditation practiced by the Sōtō school of Zen) and, according to one author, the "most original thinker that Japan has so far produced," was the greatest figure of all Japanese Buddhism who left an indelible mark upon Japanese culture, a culture which owes a great deal to Zen principles and practice.[52]

Indeed, from purely aesthetic pursuits (poetry, calligraphy, painting, gardening, and flower arrangement) to activities of social significance (the tea ceremony and the martial arts), all the arts, or "ways" (Japanese: *dō*), that shaped the medieval culture of Japan were fostered in Zen monasteries, where the transfiguration of life was, indeed, *a way* of life. Without claiming that all these noble activities were entirely rooted in the Buddhist tradition of meditation, we can nevertheless say they all have one important thing in common: the total absorption, or concentration of mind, which *is* the main thesis of the *Laṅkāvatāra-sūtra,* as indicated above (i.e., the doctrine of "Mind-only"). At least one such activity, the training of the ruling class of medieval Japan, the *samurai,* was based upon the transcendence of the ultimate duality—that of life and death—by focusing on the mental spontaneity of the uninhibited, enlightened consciousness, without the slightest trace of fear left upon the "pure mirror of the mind."[53]

In a transcendental, metaphorical, and mystical world where the opposites coincide, this enlightened awareness, this "pure mirror of the mind," was said to be "No-mind." From the *Prajñā-pāramitā* texts to the teachings of Zen, passing through Nāgārjuna's *Kārikās* and the *Laṅkāvatāra-sūtra*, an entire literature developed around the "Doctrine of *No-mind*."[54] If "enlightened seeing is non-seeing" (i.e., in the empirical sense), and "knowing is non-knowing" (i.e., insight, wisdom, rather than empirical facts), then, surely, "Mind is No-mind." Of course, as Suzuki correctly pointed out, this doctrine is to be understood in the metaphysical, not the psychological sense, in the metaphorical, not the literal meaning.[55] It merely represents a linguistic attempt to come to grips with impermanence, the only constant in the universe. Thus, the Chinese *Sūtra of the Sixth Patriarch* reads:[56]

> . . . In this teaching of mine, from ancient time to the present, all have set up no-thought as the main doctrine, non-form as the substance, and non-abiding as the basis. Non-form is to be separated from form, even when associated with form. No-thought is not to think, even when involved in thought. No-abiding is the original nature of man.

Consequently, when interpreted correctly, that is, as the outcome of the meditational experience, the "Mind-only" doctrine is the same as the doctrine of "No-mind." That is to say that under the conditions of perfect concentration (of "Mind-only"), thinking itself disappears ("No-mind"). It is pure awareness, Nature contemplating Nature. This is the essence of the "Consciousness-only" school (Vijñāna-vāda), another name attributed to the Yogācāra school. As shown, the name points to the *practice* of Yoga, and not to the *theory*, or theories about the world that the Yogācāras did or did not believe in. For, according to a Chinese text from the T'ang period, attributed to Bodhidharma and quoted by Suzuki himself, it was said that:[57]

> If you wish to seek the Buddha, you ought to see into your own Nature; for this Nature is the Buddha himself. . . . This Nature is the Mind, and the Mind is the Buddha, and the Buddha is the Way, and the Way is Zen.

Thus, in light of the above, we may safely conclude that it was the "Mind-only" practice of meditation (*dhyāna* = Zen, the Way) that provided the cross-cultural bridge between India and China, and later entered Japan to help shape its national character as we know it today.

In the next chapter, we shall look at the doctrine of "No-mind" as described in the *Laṅkāvatāra* under the term *ārya-jñāna*, which may be translated as "Noble Wisdom," "higher insight," or simply

"Gnosis," or religious/spiritual knowledge. Contrasting it with the merely empirical mind (*citta*) provides a perfect illustration of the second, negative limb of the tetralemma logic: (a) Mind *is,* versus (b) Mind *is not* (or "No-mind").

2.2. From Mind to *No-mind*: the Transcendental Leap beyond Empirical Cognition

Introduction

Even though the "*Laṅkāvatāra* school" founded by Bodhidharma in Northern China is believed to have been based upon an older doctrine of sudden Enlightenment, we did not find clear evidence of such teachings in the text itself. What we did find was an elaborate system of Epistemic Categories and Modes of Cognition mapping out a gradual process of cognition, from the ordinary, that is, empirical accumulation of "superficial" knowledge, to the transcendental insight into the essence of Reality, which in Buddhist terminology is called "Suchness," or "Thatness" (*tathatā*).

While we have used in this chapter such terms as "absolute," "perfect," or "right" mode of knowing, as distinct from "relative," "imaginary," or "false" knowledge, they are not to be understood as designations for some absolutistic dogmas of any sort. For, if we understand the thrust of the *Laṅkāvatāra*, the only ideology espoused in the sūtra is the disdain of any ideology, lest it imply a blind belief in one paramount conceptual frame, fixed idea, or point of view. The terms, according to the text, are only utilitarian devices, temporal tools to assist the student to better understand his experience as he progresses toward the higher states of cognition. Once having arrived at the peak of his journey, all conceptual "crutches" will be abandoned, just as a raft is discarded after crossing a river, having served its purpose.

This purpose, according to the *Laṅkāvatāra*, is the attainment of higher Wisdom, or insight (Āryajñāna), which may happen suddenly; that is, unexpectedly and spontaneously, but only after thorough mastery of the five Epistemic Categories (*dharmas*), and of the three Modes of Cognition (*svabhāvas*). This process may be compared to the creative trance of the artist, which can only occur after complete mastery of the technique. The musician's (or painter's) virtuosity comes across in a dazzling manner, without any apparent effort, yet the preparatory work is there all right, even though it is invisible to the audience and perhaps forgotten even by the artist himself. Likewise, for the religious virtuouso, the conceptual framework, the meditative exercises, are forgotten or discarded as soon as liberation, or spiritual freedom, is attained. This liberation is the state of self-realization that may be referred to as the state of "No-mind," which is the flip-side of the empirical "Mind" that operates with the concepts, ideas, and analysis the everyday mind needs to function in the world of empirical experience.

Therefore, if the preceding chapter, chapter 2.1., was a study of the Buddhist notions of "Mind" (*citta*) and its functions, then, in light of the above, the present chapter is a study of the paradoxical (but not necessarily antithetical) notion of "No-mind" (*acintya*). The term "No-mind" is not so far-fetched if we consider that the main topic of this chapter, the attainment of Gnosis, or higher religious Wisdom (Āryajñāna), is described in negative terms, as devoid of both conceptual (*nirvikalpa*) and visual (*nirābhāsa*) content. And, with a further stretch of imagination, *both* "Mind" *and* "No-mind" (i.e., the third, conjunctive alternative of the tetralemma logic) may be applied to the system of the eight States of consciousness (Vijñānas), the topic of our next chapter.[1]

The Five Dharmas or Epistemic Categories

In his *Studies* (pp. 154-55), Suzuki points out four different meanings for the word *dharma*, as used by the Buddhists. First, he says, the commonest and most important sense given to it in Buddhism is "truth," "law," "religion."[2] Second, the word is quite frequently used in the sense of "existence," "being," "object," or "thing."[3] Third, consistently with the Hindu use of the term, it can acquire either an ethical (e.g., "virtue," "righteousness," "norm"), or an intellectual, cognitive sense (such as "truth," "standard," "category"). Finally, a fourth usage is sometimes added to include all of these at once, in a general, comprehensive way, as for instance, when used in contradistinction with its ontological or ethical opposite—*adharma* ("lawlessness," "unrighteousness").

In the *Laṅkāvatāra-sūtra*, the *dharma-adharma* polarity is referred to in the first chapter, in order to underline the supermundane quality of the Noble Wisdom (Āryajñāna), transcending all particularized aspects of existence (*Laṅkā* I:17; ll. 11-13):

> It is on account of discrimination of the immature that there exists the differentiation of *dharma* and *adharma*; Noble Wisdom, however, is not to be attained by seeing (things this way).

When used positively, in the cognitive sense, the word *dharma* can indicate both "what is to be known" (i.e., the Reality, or truth) and "the means, the method, the process of knowing." The *Sūtra* gives five categories under which this gnoseological process takes place (the *pañcadharmas*). They are enumerated according to Suzuki's translation, as follows (see below for alternate renditions): (1) Name (*nāma*), (2) Appearance (*nimitta*), (3) Discrimination (*vikalpa*), (4) Right Knowledge (*samyagjñāna*), and (5) Suchness (*tathatā*) (*Laṅkā* VI: 224f.; 228). By following step by step these categories of transcendental Gnosis, the yogī aims at ultimately eliminating the contradictory perceptions of reality, thereby entering the Tathāgata's condition of inner Joy. Thus, the *Laṅkā* VI: 224-25; ll. 15-17, 1-2:

> When the Name, Sense-perception, Discrimination, Right Knowledge, and Suchness (are comprehended) by the yogis, (who are) facing (both) the worldly existence (and) the abode of bliss (characteristic of) the happy mental condition (of him who) has seen the Dharma, they (the yogis) are kept away from (the opposing) views of being and non-being, eternity and annihilation, (and therefore) they are entering the noble path of Tathāgata's inner realization.

The five *dharmas* are explained in the following manner: (1) *Nāma* —designates that particular propensity of the mind to substitute a name, a sign, or a symbol of an object for the object itself. The *Sūtra* states (*Laṅkā* VI: 225; ll. 6-7):

> O Mahāmati, by devoting themselves to names, conventional appellations and signs, the immature follow (their own) minds.

The paragraph devoted to the elucidation of the first *dharma* is the longest and it would be interesting to see why. The argument developed is a dominant one throughout the *Sūtra*. In fact, it echoes the central motif expressed in the Citta-mātra concept. It runs along the following lines:

Since names are only conventional marks superimposed upon reality, a foolish attachment to what is but a sign would implicitly result in unreal mental constructions (such as "me" and "mine"). As these begin to take hold of the mind (just as the silkworm is swathed in its cocoon), passion, hatred and delusion are engendered (*rāgadveṣamohajan*), which in turn lead to misguided action (*karmābhisaṃskurvanti*) (*Laṅkā* VI: 225). In this way, behavior is wrongly determined by passions caused by faulty cognition. A vicious circle is set up, or (to use Buddhist terminology) the ignorant becomes adrift in the ocean of transmigration and suffering, in the wheel of birth and death (*gati*), just like a water-drawing wheel (*ghaṭīyantra*) cannot help but turn around its own axle all the time. Without realizing that all (metaphysical) things (Īśvara, time, atoms, supreme Being) rise from spurious constructions of the Mind-itself (lit., "one's own mind," *svacitta*), the ignorant gets caught in his own net of false discrimination with which he tries to grasp the world. Thus, the image of Reality, which he builds in his own mind, becomes, in fact, his own (specious) reality, just like the veil of Māyā, a mirage, or a lunar reflection in the water. He is unable to let go of such erroneous views as the idea of Self-substance (*svabhāva*), of notions of "me and mine," of object and subject, of birth, persistence, and death.

Now, in order to break through the net of self-delusion, the *Sūtra* outlines its fivefold epistemological process. *Nāma*, or Naming, as discussed above, constitutes the *first* necessary step of this process —the step toward becoming aware of the deceptive mental proclivity to erect a conceptual screen between the inner and the outer realities.

The *second* step in this process of cognition (*nimitta*) is translated by Suzuki, as well as by others, as "Appearance."[4] "Sense-perception" would, perhaps, be more appropriate, for it agrees with both the dictionary meaning of "instrumental cause,"[5] as well as with the text itself, which states (*Laṅkā* VI: 225-26; ll. 18, 1-2):

> Again, Mahāmati, the sense-perception (*nimitta*) is that which impresses (the mind) as visual perception (*cakṣur-vijñāna*), and thus the form is recognized; (and so with) the recognition of mental phenomena, of touch, taste, smell, and sound, there is the (arising of) the mental perception (*mano-vijñāna*), of tactile, tasting, olfactory, and auditive perceptions as such—this is what I call the "Sense-perception" (*nimitta*).

This is all that is said about *nimitta* in the *Laṅkāvatāra*. There is no appraisal of, or extensive criticism in regard to, the cognitive value of the sensory perception, except in relation to the first six (sensory-) Vijñānas (Manas and Ālayavijñānas being excluded from the sphere of *nimitta*).[6] At a later point, however, the *Sūtra* does seem to suggest the primacy of the Sense-perception over ideation (*saṃjñā*), and the Naming faculty (*nāma*) (*Laṅkā:* VI: 228; ll. 7-9):

> Out of this Sense-perception (*nimitta*) mental constructs [lit., ideation, *samjñā*] are produced (such as) jar, about which it can be said "this is such and no other;"—this is (called) "Naming" (*nāma*).

Both *nāma* and *nimitta* are said to be "unascertained," or "unascertainable," "unobtainable," "unperceivable" (*anupalabdhita*), on account of their mutuality or relative dependence upon one another (*Laṅkā* VI: 228; ll. 10-12):

> These Names and Sense-perceptions are after all unascertainable, (for) when the intellect is dissolved (on account of) mutuality [i.e., their Dependent Origination], (what is) perceived and contrived (by it) is also taken away; this is (called) the "Suchness" of all things.

Suzuki, in the "Introduction" to his *Studies* (p. 27), gives a comparative translation of the "Five Dharmas" chapter extracted from the original Sanskrit and the three subsequent Chinese versions (Sung, Wei, and T'ang). For the purpose of elucidating the meaning of the above passage, here is what seems to be the clearest rendition (from the T'ang edition):

> That Name, that Appearance (—they are all) ultimately non-existent: they are only due to the Discrimination by a perturbed mind of (things) mutually (related). When one thus surveys the world until the disappearance of intelligence takes place, one has what is known as Suchness.

Now, the *third* cognitive step, *vikalpa*, Discrimination, closely resembles the first (*nāma*); it purports to distinguish between different objects and qualities by naming them. The text itself is not of much help here, but the issue may become less obscure when analyzed from the perspective of the three types of knowledge (*svabhāvas*). For the moment, suffice it to say that *vikalpa* refers to "real" objects or phenomena, of which one takes cognizance through the senses, while *nāma* applies to purely mental constructions, products of imagination, or of dream-like activity. The text states the following (*Laṅkā* VI: 226; ll. 3-5):

> Furthermore, Mahāmati, Discrimination is that by which Naming is caused to be declared (as such), (and) thus the Sense-perception is made clear; if one says that this is such

> and no other, (as for instance) this is an elephant, a horse, a wheel, a pedestrian, a woman, a man, and so on, an idea so discriminated is set forth.

In other words, Discrimination, or Judgment (*vikalpa*) represents a cognitive operation by means of which the world of the immediate, sensory experience is further compartmentalized into distinct entities, of either general or particular sort. But, true knowledge cannot be obtained by relying solely on analytical means. Therefore, two more categories are further added. One fulfills the necessary function of synthesis, the other (keeping in touch with the century-old Buddhist religious tradition) aims at transcending not only the process of thought (be it synthetic or analytic), but the ontic distinctions as well (i.e., the state of Suchness, between Being and non-Being).[7]

Fourth is the synthesizing function, here called *samyagjñāna*, or "Right-knowledge," which aims at putting things within the larger perspective of their mutual conditioning. It focuses upon the interrelatedness, rather than on the separatedness of things. Through it, the distinctions between objects are de-emphasized, while their common qualities (impermanence, dependent conditioning, capacity of transformation from one form into another) are revealed (*Laṅkā* VI: 226; ll. 5-8):

> Furthermore, Mahāmati, by Right-knowledge (is meant this): when Names and Sense-perception (are seen as) unseizable because of (their) mutual adherence, there is no more rising of the Vijñānas, (for) there is neither utter destruction, nor endless existence; (and when) there is no falling back to the stage of the Śrāvaka- and Pratyeka-Buddhas, and of all the (other) philosophers [i.e., Brāhmin heretics], it is said that there is Right-knowledge (*samyagjñāna*).

The key word for the understanding of *samyagjñāna* is *anupalabdhi* ("unseizable," "ungraspable," "unobtainable"). With the cessation of Naming, Sense-perception, and Discrimination, their reflection in consciousness begins to subside, and the way to Right-knowledge is cleared up. This is the beginning of grasping the Reality in its totality, according to Buddhist epistemology. The two essential functions of the intellect (*buddhi*), that of analyzing the minute components of experience (*dharmas*) and that of synthesizing them into meaningful patterns, are both to be transcended, in the Buddhist view, on account of their ultimate futility due to their lack of absolute, independent existence (*svabhāva*). They are both misleading in as far as the nature of Reality is concerned, the former because it is conducive to a static, Eternalist vision of the world, the latter because it may obscure, when pushed to its extreme limits, the validity (relative as it is) of our perception, thereby entrapping us in the quicksands of Annihilationism and utter Subjectivism. According to the text quoted above, such was the view of some of the older Buddhist schools (whose proponents are here called the Śrāvaka and Pratyeka-Buddhas), while the other philosophers (the *tīrthakas*) advocated Eternalism of one sort or another. Rejecting such extreme views, the mind, we are told, becomes subdued (*apravṛttirvijñāna*), and the clear perception of Reality, now seen as it really is (*tathatā*), becomes possible (*Laṅkā* VI: 226; ll. 8-10):

> Furthermore, Mahāmati, by means of Right-knowledge, the Bodhisattva, the great being, does not construct the Name as Reality, nor does he turn the Sense-perception into non-Reality.

To be sure, from the contents of the above-quoted passages, *samyagjñāna* designates a mode of knowing, rather than a specific sort of knowledge. It is a type of cognitive attitude that is being recommended here, namely an epistemic negation of all one-sided approaches toward apprehending Reality. It seems obvious that the anonymous author of the *Sūtra* urged his Buddhist reader to appraise Reality in a detached manner, without preconceived notions characteristic of the older schools, Buddhist and non-Buddhist alike. Such an open-minded attitude would singularly allow the observer to perceive the world in its pure quality of Being, "as it really is" (*bhūtatā*). This is also consistent with the meaning of the *fifth*, and last, of the five *dharmas* ("Knowledge-states"), as described under the name of Suchness (*tathatā*) (*Laṅkā* VI: 226; ll. 10-14):

> When confusing, opposing, dualistic views are abandoned, and when the Vijñānas cease to arise on account of Names and Sense-perception, this is what I call Suchness (*tathatā*); and also, Mahāmati, when established in Suchness, a Bodhisattva, Great Being, is reaching toward a state devoid of delusionary appearance and (thereby) he attains the Bodhisattva stage of Joy.

According to this passage, a clear succession of mental processes of perceptual and cognitive nature (i.e., Sense-perception, Naming faculty, the ability to categorize opposing points of view and to transcend them, etc.) would ultimately lead to an affective state of Joy (*pratimuditā*).

We know that from the second century onward a cluster of religious ideas, the core of the Mahāyāna theory of salvation, began to develop. One essential part of this theory was the doctrine of the "ten stages," marking the progress of the Bodhisattva. It first appeared in the Mahāsāṅghika text *Mahāvastu*, but, according to Wayman, it may be traced further back to the so-called "five paths" theory (*pañcamārga*), developed by the Abhidharmists of the Sarvāstivāda school and transmitted through the *Prajñā-pāramitā* literature.[8] No doubt it must have been quite popular before and after the writing of the *Laṅkāvatāra*, for a number of treatises mention it and one even focuses on the "ten stages" as the main topic, namely the *Daśabhūmika-sūtra*. In this classical and most famous presentation of the doctrine of the Bodhisattva stages, the stage of Joy is mentioned as the *first* of the ten *bhūmis*. The other nine are enumerated as follows: 2) Immaculate; 3) Illuminating; 4) Blazing; 5) Unconquerable; 6) Facing; 7) Far-reaching; 8) Motionless; 9) Perfect Wisdom; and 10) Cloud of Doctrine.

What I am driving at here is the interesting fact that in the *Laṅkāvatāra* we find a unique doctrinal elaboration in the form of the five Dharmas theory, which is quite distinct from the *pañcamārga* of the earlier Sarvāstivādins, and also richer in psychological complexity and meaning. Moreover, the text seems to point to the preparatory function of the five Dharmas for the entrance upon the path of Bodhisattvahood, thereby linking the two metaphysical doctrines into one continuous "map of Enlightenment," as it were. Thus, the text states (*Laṅkā* VI: 226; ll. 15-16):

> Having obtained the Bodhisattva stage of Joy, he [i.e., the aspirant to Buddhahood] is freed from all evil (*apāya*) ways of the philosophers and is set upon the path of the super-mundane Truth.

The connection with the stages of Bodhisattvahood is made even more clear in the following lines, in which the last of the ten *bhūmis* (i.e., *dharmameghā*, the "Cloud of Doctrine") is directly mentioned (*Laṅkā* VI: 226-27; ll. 17-18, 1):

> . . . attaining the state (*lakṣaṇa*) of the noble path of Truth (in regard to) the self-realization, he is ardently desirous of turning away from the speculative views [of the philosophers], and, by moving in succession through the stages of Bodhisattvahood, he finally reaches the stage (called) "The Cloud of Doctrine."

It appears from these lines that the author of the *Sūtra* would equate the quest for self-realization with becoming a Bodhisattva. That means, according to the Mahāyāna tradition, that he who has attained such high spiritual station would turn back toward the world below and teach the Dharma to those still suffering, at various stations of the saṃsāric existence. That is precisely the meaning conveyed by the following exhortatory lines (*Laṅkā* VI: 227; ll. 4-5):

> Well entrenched in the eight-fold (noble) path of the Law, he [i.e., the realized Bodhisattva] is determined to teach the Law to all beings, in accordance with their diverse inclinations.

Interestingly enough, the last sentence of this section reverts to the notion of Suchness, thereby establishing a characteristic homology between the cognitive discourse and psychological state, between epistemological theory and ontological status. That is to say that the appropriation of the five Dharmas theory *regarding* the process of knowing, would cause a radical transformation of the process of knowing *itself*, by transforming the very mind of the knower, by changing his fundamental condition of Being. Thus the *Laṅkā* VI: 227; ll. 5-7:

> As the Bodhisattvas, the Great Beings, reach the entrance into Suchness (*tathatā*), O Mahāmati, they attain the natural state [or, temperament, mental condition, *kāya*] which is devoid of mental representation(s) (*manovijñapti-rahitam*).

The use of the word *kāya* in this salvific context needs some clarification. Here this term is employed somewhat ambiguously. While the term is traditionally used with the sense of the individual physical "body" or corporeal "mass," in the Yogācāra literature it can also be encountered as a symbolical, metaphysical term, as for instance, when used in reference to the Three-body doctrine (the Tri-kāya doctrine).[9] It is clear, however, that no such meaning is intended in the above lines, for the subject is the Bodhisattva and not a Buddha, real or symbolic, residing in the heavens above. On the other hand, the words do seem to indicate a mental, or spiritual context, rather than a strictly physical one. True, there remains the possibility of a "body made of mind" (*manomanakāya*), as explained by Suzuki thus:[10]

> He is then no more a Bodhisattva endowed with the coarse physical corporeality like ourselves, but an immortal god

or Buddha endowed with a will-made body (*manomanakāya*), to which the *Laṅkāvatāra* makes frequent allusions.

Again, it seems quite obvious that this passage does not constitute one of many such "frequent allusions" to a Buddha's mythological body being "made of mind." We are, therefore, left with one last possible interpretation, one of a certain psychological nature given the fact that the statement fits neatly within the context of Bodhisattva's career of mental awakening, or development. The rendition of *kāya* as "natural temperament" is also borne out by Indian lexicographers, as well, according to Monier-Williams.[11] However, we are still faced with the question regarding the specific *nature* of this "natural state," or "temperament which is devoid of mental representation(s)" (*kāyam manovijñapti-rahitam*).

Unfortunately, the Western psychological categories, be they psychoanalytical or purely cognitive, can be of little help here, for they do not recognize the possibility of a "state of awareness devoid of mental representation," which is the goal of Buddhist practice. On the other hand, such a state is, to be sure, closely related to the highest meditational states described in the Hindu yoga treatises, such as the fixation of the psychological flux (*ekāgratā*), or the immobility of thought (*samādhi*). Whether this is a "protohistorical, archaic form of mystical experience, . . . a living fossil, a modality of archaic spirituality that has survived nowhere else," or a "form of absolute concentration in order to attain enstasis," as Professor Eliade writes,[12] is of little consequence for our purpose at hand, which is to elucidate the meaning of the text of the *Laṅkāvatāra* by using its own, Buddhist categories, rather than by imposing a subjectively constructed hermeneutics, the brain-child of our own, twentieth-century intellectual experience. For, such a hermeneutics, useful as it may be for the study of the history of culture in general, would tell us little about the fourth-century Buddhist's monk's frame of spiritual perception, which is what we are attempting to reconstruct here.

Consequently, the only way of giving a satisfactory answer to the question regarding the meaning of the statement "the natural temperament which is devoid of mental representation," is to revert back to the text. Thus, in the second chapter, the text states (*Laṅkā* II: 42; ll. 4-7):

> . . . The body, the enjoyment (of property or food), and the material habitat (are) the same as the Receptacle-of-impressions (*ālaya-vijñāna*), (that is) above the dualism (or dichotomy) of

subject [lit., thinker] and object [lit., the realm of sense-perception and of thought, conception]: (and) the state of image-lessness [lit., non-light or non-reflection, non-appearance], subsequent to the awakening of Mind-itself, (is) not affected by such mental changes as the arising, abiding (and) destruction [of mental events, *ābhāsa, vibhāva*].

In descriptions such as this, we recognize the common theme of striving toward a state of consciousness of the purest kind, namely the *ālaya-vijñāna*, usually translated as the "Store-consciousness," but here rendered as the "Repository-of-impressions," for reasons given in the next chapter (Ch. 2.3.), on the system of Vijñānas. In this state, we are told, the constant agitation, due to processes of perception, thinking, and feeling, is somehow transcended and even abolished. An achievement of this kind would then allow one the most clear insight into the nature of reality, "the entrance into Suchness (*tathatā*)." Moreover, when we are told that the external reality (here symbolized by the expression *deha-bhoga-pratiṣṭā*) is the same as the deepest layer of consciousness (Ālaya-vijñāna), this abolishment applies not only to the succession of subjective mental events as such, but also to the distinction between internal and external Reality, as well. For, if the inner changes are nothing but the reflection of, and the response to the constant events of the outside world, then ultimately the highest mental state, "the awakening of Mind-itself," would reconnect itself with the very source of one's thoughts, perceptions, feelings, and so on, which, of course, is nothing but this external, cosmic Reality (*grāhya-grāha*, lit., "that which is grasped, or perceived," and the ideational form that it takes in the mind). The *Laṅkā* confirms this view in the lines immediately following the passage under investigation (*Laṅkā* II: 42; ll. 7-8):

> . . . The Bodhisattvas, the Great Beings, O Mahāmati, will come to realize that Nirvāṇa and Saṃsāra are found (to be) the same (*samatā*).

True enough, this statement only echoes the celebrated equation promulgated some two centuries earlier by the Acārya Nāgārjuna, the foremost exponent of the Mādhyamika school (in his *Mūla-mādhyamika-kārikā* 25: 19, 20). Later, his followers Candrakīrti and Śāntideva (c. 7 C.E.), disputed fiercely the Vijñānavādin contention alleging that consciousness can exist of itself, as for instance in dreams and illusions.[13] It is clear, however, in the light of the above passages, that such a dispute could not have arisen during the time when the *Laṅkā* was written, when the state of pure consciousness (*ālaya*) was perceived to emerge through a gradual process of withdrawal from sensory interaction with the external world, mediated by the seven "revolving" (*pravṛtti-*)Vijñānas, culminating with the attainment of the state of Mind-only (*citta-mātra*). It was only during the subsequent development of the school, that the monistic tendency, already present in germinal form, inevitably tilted the balance toward the idealistic side, but, even that being so, the degree of absolutism of the Yogācāra idealism is still being disputed. (See infra: ch. 2.4., 'Concluding Observations'.)

One can safely state, however, that quite early in the development of Mahāyāna philosophical thought, the monism-pluralism dichotomy was reasoned away on epistemological grounds. In the *Laṅkā*, for instance, the juxtaposition of relative knowledge, or truth, against absolute knowledge can take many forms and is frequently encountered regardless of the topic being discussed. Here is another example, in which the dilemma is expressed in terms of ethical attachment to the unity, or the multiplicity of the world (*Laṅkā* III: 157; ll. 14-15):

> Moreover, Mahāmati, the common [i.e., relative, *vijñāna*] knowledge (is) attached to the multiplicity of objects, but the real [i.e., true, absolute, *jñāna*] knowledge is free from attachment(s) (*asaṅga-lakṣaṇa*).

All the above statements contain a devaluation of the Hīnayāna nominalistic emphasis on the plurality of dharmas, fragments of existence, and a move toward the thoroughgoing idealism of the later Vijñānavāda scriptures. *Jñāna* as transcendental knowledge, that is to say, knowledge which goes beyond or penetrates through the veil of phenomenal manifestations, is synonymous with Prajñā, or the Āryajñāna, according to Suzuki.[14] One could also add that the terms *samyagjñāna* and *tathatā* (discussed above), also refer to this type of knowledge, albeit in a different philosophical context.[15]

The Three Svabhāvas or Modes of Cognition

Another instance in which the two forms of knowing reality are compared is found in the portion of the *Laṅkāvatāra-sūtra* immediately following the discussion of the five *dharmas*, where the theory of the three *svabhāvas* (as Modes of Cognition) is presented. Here, yet another epistemic category is introduced, apparently in order to cover the arbitrary, and even deluding, faculty of the mind, which may develop in the process of Naming (*nāma*) and Sense-perception (*nimitta*), the first two of the five dharmas. The passage reads (*Laṅkā* VI: 227; ll. 9-12):

> The Blessed One said: "In regard to this (question), O Mahāmati, the three self-natures (*svabhāvas*), the twofold egolessness [i.e., of beings and of things], and the eight (kinds of) consciousness, are all included [in the five *dharmas*]; there [i.e., in the context of the five *dharmas*], the Name(s) (*nāma*) and the Sense-perception(s) (*nimitta*) are known as False-knowledge (*parikalpita*)."

We have preferred here the rendition "False-knowledge" to Suzuki's "False-imagination," since the ability to imagine is itself a "paraphrase of Reality," so to speak, and therefore the true-false criterion cannot apply to imagination per se. To use it would amount to saying that "poets are liars," a statement which would miss the sense of poetics altogether. At most, the term could be given an alternative rendition as "Willful contrivance," which again can be said to be at least unwieldy, if not tautological. A closer rendering, perhaps, would be the psychoanalytic term of "Wish-fulfillment phantasy," but it has, unfortunately, too many extra-Buddhist, Freudian connotations, which may further detract the reader from the epistemological nature of the discourse. To make the matter clearer, by means of an example, let us follow Suzuki in saying that *parikalpita* is "the fabrication of one's own imagination or mind,"[16] which occurs when a man reacts with fear to his own misapprehension of a rope for a snake. However, upon closer examination, the man takes the rope for what it is, a piece of reality, gives it a name and thinks nothing more of it. This, the *Sūtra* calls "Relative-knowledge," (*paratantra*, lit., "Dependence-on-another") (*Laṅkā* VI: 227; ll. 12-15):

> Furthermore, Mahāmati, that which is derived from connecting with those [Names and Sense-perceptions], (that is to say) the calling of mental elements (and) the discrimination (between them) (being) produced in simultaneous occurrence, like the appearance of the sun and its rays, that very discrimination, Mahāmati, supporting the (idea of) self-nature on account of perceived marks, (is) the condition which is called "Relative-knowledge" (*paratantra*).

Now, from the above lines, it would appear that the term *paratantra* is close, if not synonymous with *vikalpa,* or Discriminative knowledge. While the sphere may, indeed, be the same, the emphasis of meaning is different. For, *paratantra* designates that kind of knowledge which is dependent upon the objects of senses, as well as the discrimination between various perceptions by means of concepts, imagination, and naming. Therefore, its rendition as "Relative-knowledge" is not to be taken in the sense of the well-known doctrine of Dependent Origination (Pratītya-samutpāda), but rather in the sense of relational, mediated knowledge, derived from the senses, on which it depends for its production. It also represents the opposite of the Absolute, True, Real, or Perfect-knowledge (*parinișpanna*), of which the *Sūtra* says the following (*Laṅkā* VI: 227; ll. 15-17):

> Right-knowledge and Suchness, O Mahāmati, (are) of indestructible nature (and therefore), they are known as "Absolute [or Perfect-] knowledge."

If we want to continue the analogy with the rope and the snake, when seen from the standpoint of this third *svabhāva* (Cognitive Mode), the rope loses its purely external and objective nature and becomes part of the observing subject, part of the inner world of thoughts and feelings. Says Suzuki:[17]

> From the absolutist's point of view which is assumed by the *Laṅkāvatāra,* the rope is a reflection of our own mind, it has no objectivity apart from the latter, it is in this respect non-existent. But the mind out of which the whole world evolves is the object of the Parinishpanna, Perfectly-attained-knowledge.

This amounts to saying that the world would exist through our perception only, which is subjective idealism taken to its most radical extreme. The *Laṅkā,* however, seldom presents us with such categorical statements, and when it does, it is mainly in the apocryphal section called the *Sagāthakam* (or, "The One with Verses") (*Laṅkā* X: 293; gātha 218):

> What is seen (is) my own mind, an external world [lit., external object of the senses, *artha*] is not experienced [or perceived, *dṛśyate*]; so, let the error [or false opinions, *bhrānti*] come out into the open and let one be reminded even more of suchness (*tathatā*).

What this *gātha* really is saying is that the world is experienced only indirectly, via the senses and the mind, and not that "an objective world exists not," as Suzuki translates it. Our view, which represents the main contention of this study, is also confirmed by previous Mahāyāna texts dealing with this subject, such as for instance, the *Bodhicittavivaraṇa* ("The Exposition of *bodhicitta*"), attributed by Lindtner to Nāgārjuna. To wit, the following verse 27 is quoted (in Lindtner's rendition):[18]

> cittamātram idaṃ sarvam iti yā deśanā muneḥ/
> uttrāsaparihārārthaṃ bālānāṃ sā na tattvataḥ//

> The Anchorite's (*muni*) doctrine that 'The entire (world) is mere mind' is (in fact) intended to remove the fear of fools. It is not a (doctrine) concerning Reality (*na tattvata*).

It is only by keeping this perspective in mind that one can interpret the meaning of the more obcure statements found in the *Sūtra*, where the line between denial and acceptance of the external Reality seems very thin, indeed. One such radical statement is acknowledged by Suzuki himself as having a meaning "difficult to gather . . ." and that "this verse section has no organic relation with the main text."[19] Here is the verse, as found in the *Laṅkā* X: 294; gātha 222:

> In the seeing of the Buddhas, of Arhatship, of Buddhahood and of Pratyekabuddhahood (is) the invisible seed that grows into enlightenment [i.e., the Tathāgata-garbha]; but certainly, it is in a dream that that is accomplished.

Indeed, the verse is ambiguous as to what the word "dream" refers to: the state of delusion prior to Enlightenment, or the external Reality in which the Enlightenment occurs? Is it our confusion and ignorance (*bhrānti*, as in gātha 218 quoted above), or is it that the only Reality is that of Nirvāṇa, in which all the Buddhas thrive? Does it pertain to the realm of Being, or to the gnoseological domain? In order to properly address these difficult questions, we will have to look more deeply into the nature of Enlightenment, as described in the *Laṅkāvatāra* under the term *āryajñāna* (Absolute knowledge, Transcendental Wisdom, or Gnosis, highest religious Truth).

The Attainment of Āryajñāna: Transcendental Wisdom, or Gnosis

First, we will find many passages which refer to the highest state of cognition only indirectly, in metaphorical terms, for instance, as a dream (*svapna*), as above, or a vision (*māyā*). Here is one such example (*Laṅkā* X: 287-88, gāthas 173-74):

> Like an appearance, a shadow, an illusion, a mirage, (seen) through (a state of) dream still, like a rotating fire-brand, or the Gandharva's [castle-in-the-sky], or an echo—they [i.e., the primary elements of existence, *prakṛta, svabhāva,* see verse 172 supra] all become visible in the same manner.
>
> Non-duality, Suchness, Voidness, Ultimate Reality and Essence, and Non-discrimination—all these I teach as the symbols [or marks, *lakṣaṇa*] of Perfect-knowledge.

Fortunately, however, there are other passages which are much more specific than this quoted above. Some answer directly the questions pertaining to the *nature* of the highest form of cognition, others describe the *means* by which it can be obtained. And finally, there are also quite a few passages which pose disturbing questions as to the ultimate *validity* of any and all such distinctions between various levels of cognitions and/or Epistemic Categories, as discussed elsewhere in the text.

Let us first look at illustrations of each type of statement, and then we shall attempt an overall hermeneutical assessment of this very thorny subject. To begin, here is a rather lengthy excerpt from the second chapter, which relates the notion of Noble Wisdom (Āryajñāna) to the other cognitive structures (the five Dharmas and the three Svabhāvas, Categories and Modes of Cognition), discussed in our two preceding sections. According to the text, they are to be regarded as prerequisites, or stepping stones, towards the highest state of transcendental, spiritual knowledge, or Gnosis. Thus, the *Laṅkā* II: 67-68; ll. 15-17 & 1-7; gātha 134:

> Now, Mahāmati, what is the condition [or mode, *svabhāva*] of Absolute-knowledge (*pariniṣpanna*)? To wit, it is the abandonment of discriminating notions about Reality, (such as) Name(s) and Appearance(s); it is the realm of inner Noble Wisdom (*āryajñāna*); it is the arriving at the noble knowledge of Suchness (*tathatā-āryajñāna*). This, Mahāmati, is the condition of Absolute-knowledge, which is the core of the Essence-of-Buddhahood.

> Appropriately, at that moment, the Blessed One uttered this verse:
>
> 'Appearance, Name, and Discrimination (correspond to) the two Modes of Cognition [i.e., False imagination, *parikalpita* and Relative-knowledge, *paratantra*]; Right-knowledge and Suchness (correspond to) the Absolute-knolwedge (or Perfect Gnosis, *parinișpanna*].'
>
> This, Mahāmati, is called the investigation into the characteristics of the (three) Modes and the five Categories (of knowledge), (as found) in the sacred works which contain the domain of inner Perfect knowledge; in this, you and other Bodhisattvas, are to discipline yourselves.

Elsewhere, this fundamental distinction between empirical reasoning (based upon discrimination between separate categories) and transcendental Gnosis (which is all-inclusive, intuitive, perceptive of the essence, rather than of the external attributes of things) is further elaborated upon (*Laṅkā* II: 130-133; vv. 182, 187, 196, 202):

> The mind (*citta*) is tied to the objective world (*vișaya*); knowledge evolves from reasoning, but in the superior state of imagelessness, verily insight (Gnosis, *prajñā*) there comes forth.
>
> (There is) conventional and absolute (truth), there is no ground for a third; the False-imagination (Mode of knowledge) belongs to the conventional: (when) that is cut asunder (vanishes), there is the realm of the wise ones.
>
> If truth is the five Dharmas and the three Svabhāvas, then truly when the Yogī clearly perceives this, he does not transgress (violate) Suchness (*tathatā*).
>
> (. . .) When one is freed from the dualistic discrimination, right there, indeed, is the Absolute-knowledge (*nișpanna*).

If one had to choose one word only in order to best describe the essential nature of the Absolute-knowledge, that word would have to be "imagelessness" (*nirābhāsa*). For, it is during the highest state of mental concentration (*samādhi*), obtained through meditation, that the mind is freed from the activity of intellectual discrimination (*nirvikalpa*), and returns (*parāvṛtti*) back to a primal state of pure consciousness, devoid of any sensory input and imagination related to sensory activity. This state is alternately referred to in the *Sūtra* as the Repository-of-impressions (Ālaya-vijñāna), the Essence-of-Buddhahood (Tathāgata-garbha), or, on occasion, the Mind-only (Citta-mātra, as Transcendental Mind, opposed to the empirical mind, vide supra, ch. 2.1.). Thus, *Laṅkā* IV: 215; gāthas 1 and 2:

> The abodes and the stages of Buddhahood (are established) in the Mind-only, (which is) imageless [lit., free from imagining, *nirābhāsa*]—this was told, is told, and will be told by the Buddhas.
>
> The (first) seven stages are still (of the) mind; but here, the eighth is imageless (*nirābhāsa*); the two stages [i.e., the ninth and the tenth] have (still) something to rest themselves on; the (highest) stage that is left belongs to me [i.e., the Buddha-stage].

Now, it is at this highest state of transcendental knowledge (that is, the Buddha-stage, the stage of the Tathāgata) that the process of cognition becomes a vehicle for salvation (i.e., Gnosis), for Self-realization, for change of ontological status: from a disciple into a Buddha. That is why the writer speaks of seven kinds, or seven aspects of the absolute Truth (*paramārtha*), which roughly correspond to the more advanced stages of the Bodhisattva's career (*bhūmis*). As the disciple advances on the path of knowledge, he is also moving closer to that radical step of ontological transformation, the spiritual goal of Buddhahood, the perfection of Being. To wit: *Laṅkā* II: 39; ll. 13-16:

> Furthermore, Mahāmati, the absolute (Truth) is seven-fold: that is to say, the realm of thought, the realm of wisdom, the realm of insight, the realm of dualistic views, the realm beyond dualistic views, the realm beyond the begotten (Bodhisattva) stages, (and) the realm of Self-realization of the Tathāgata.

In as far as *the means* of bringing this ontological transformation about are concerned, the *Sūtra* seems to indicate the possibility of not one, but *three* complementary avenues, all equally important for the attainment of Āryajñāna (highest Wisdom). The first has to do with the mastery of all theoretical knowledge contained in the *sacred texts* of both Buddhist and non-Buddhist philosophers; the second avenue is the *power of grace* available to all adepts by virtue of the Buddhas' own original vows to save all sentient beings (according to the Mahāyāna tradition); and, finally, the third road to salvation is provided by the arduous *practice of meditation*, the "vision" (*māyā*) obtained through concentration which brings forth the

Samādhi-kāya (lit., the "Body-of-concentration"). Thus, *Laṅkā* II: 49-50; ll. 15-17 and 4-12:

> What are, Mahāmati, the three kinds of Noble Wisdom, of which he [the Bodhisattva-Mahāsattva] will partake later?
>
> They are:
>
> (1) the state characterized by *imagelessness;*
>
> (2) the state characterized by *grace* bestowed by all Buddhas;
>
> (3) the state characterized by the *practice* of the inner Gnosis . . .
>
> . . . Now again, Mahāmati,
>
> (1) the state characterized by the attribute of *imagelessness* evolves from the familiarity with all (things known to) the [non-Buddhist] philosophers, the Pratyekabuddhas, and the Śrāvakas [the Hīnayāna disciples];
>
> (2) Again, Mahāmati, as to the state characterized by the power of *grace,* this grace proceeds from the Buddhas' own original vows [i.e., to save the entire world];
>
> (3) Again, Mahāmati, as to the state characterized by the *practice* of the inner Gnosis, which is intent upon (the study of) the essence of all things, it rises from the attainment of the Buddha-stage, from the obtaining of the Samādhi-body [of transic concentration], which is like a vision [or a dream, *māya*].
>
> Of such kind, Mahāmati, is the triad characteristic of the wise ones; furnished with this noble characteristic triad, the wise ones achieve their own inner realm of Self-realization (*sva-pratyātma-āryajñāna-gatigocara*).
>
> It is for this reason, Mahāmati, that you should be cultivating the threefold discipline characteristic of the Noble Wisdom [or Gnosis, *āryajñāna*].

So, the *Laṅkā* tells us that there are three complementary means to reach the ultimate goal of Self-realization, which is referred to in cognitive terms as the "Noble Wisdom," or Gnosis (Āryajñāna). At closer look, however, one discovers only *two active* paths towards the final goal (*siddhānta*): (a) a **theoretical** one (i.e., the study of the holy scriptures), and (b) a **practical** one (i.e., the path of meditation, of yogic trance, which is like a dream, or a vision, *māyā*, according to the text). The third path to Enlightenment, the power of grace conferred by the Buddhas, does not involve an active effort, since it is accessible to everyone equally, by virtue of the Buddhas' own original vows, according to the Mahāyāna tradition. The following passage takes the issue one step further by stressing the point that these two different paths are intended for two types of audiences found at different levels of spiritual development: the path of discourses is for the ignorant (*bāla*, the novice), the path of Self-realization is for the Yogī who moves beyond reasoning based on discrimination. It is in this context that one can justifiably speak of the mind of Enlightenment as *No-mind* (*nirābhāsa*, imagelessness, or *parāvṛtti*, reversal), for it is radically different from, even opposed to the common mode of (empirical) reasoning, based upon discursive thought and logical categories of discrimination (*vikalpa*). Thus, *Laṅkā* III: 172; ll. 4-18:

> The Blessed One said this to him: "Mahāmati, there are two manners of teaching the truth attained by the Tathāgatas, the Arhats, the Fully-enlightened Ones, of the past, present, and future. That is to say, (1) the teaching by discourses, and (2) the teaching by the establishment of the final goal [i.e., the Self-realization, *siddhānta*].
>
> Now, the teaching by discourses is this, Mahāmati: various collections, treatises and texts are taught to sentient beings in accordance with their mental inclinations.
>
> Furthermore, Mahāmati, what then is the teaching by Self-realization by which the Yogis obtain the reversal of discrimination of what is seen as one's own mind?
>
> That is to say that there is a noble (transcendental) state of inner attainment, which is beyond the empirical mind (*citta*), the preconscious impulsivity (*manas*), and the conscious volition (*mano-vijñāna*), which does not fall into the dualism of Oneness and Otherness, of Bothness and non-Bothness, which has nothing to do with illustrating, theorizing, philosophizing and logic, and which (has never been understood) by any bad logicians [or sophists, *kutārkika*], (such as) the Self-enlightened Buddhas, the novices [i.e., the Hīnayānists], and the philosophers [i.e., the non-Buddhists], who have fallen into the dualistic extremes of Being and non-Being. This I call the 'final attainment' (*siddhānta*).
>
> This, Mahāmati, is the characteristic of the doctrine regarding the teaching of Self-perfection wherein you, and other Bodhisattvas and Great Beings, should practice the discipline of yoga." Thereupon it is said:

> "I have two ways of teaching: the discoursing and the Self-realization. It is for the ignorant that I discourse; the final goal (of Self-realization, *siddhānta*, belongs) to the yogis."

What is interesting about this particular quotation is the definition of the transcendental state of Gnosis (Āryajñāna) from the point of view of the tetralemma (*catuṣkoṭi*), the four-fold Buddhist dialectical formula, which has been extensively discussed in our introductory section on Buddhist epistemology (see ch. 2.0.). The inner realization, it is said, transcends all four alternatives of "Oneness and Otherness, of Bothness and not-Bothness" (ll. 10-11), therefore it is devoid of content (*nirvikalpa*), conceptually speaking, and it is imageless (*nirābhāsa*). It represents a radical break (*parāvṛtti*) from all other forms of cognition, since it is beyond imagination (*parikalpita*) and conceptualization (*paratantra-svabhāva*). Indeed, it is, one might say, the flip-side of the ordinary mind, the *No-mind*. It is a form of mentation that opens access to Reality, such as it is, in the ultimate sense, at once mysterious, slippery, and unamenable to clear-cut conceptualization. The only vaguely appropriate terms for it, according to Buddhist metaphysics, are Suchness (*tathatā*) and Existence (*bhūtatā*). Not even the terms referring to Absolute or Perfect knowledge (*pariniṣpanna*) or Ultimate truth (*paramārtha*) can be applied, since they, too, are artificial constructs or concepts woefully short of accurately describing the ever-changing, so-called "Reality."

Thus, the author(s) of the *Laṅkāvatāra* were perfectly conscious that their language, and language in general, can only be metaphorical vis-a-vis the "Reality" it attempts to express, and even more so, when this "Reality" is of the highest, spiritual, sort. This acute awareness regarding the limitations of language is clearly stated in many ways, throughout the *Sūtra*. Here are only a couple of such formulations. First, *Laṅkā* VI: 229; ll. 15-18:

> The Blessed One said: "Mahāmati, certainly, that word ought not to be taken in the literal sense. The Buddha(s) of the three divisions of time is/are not measurable by the measurement of the sands of the river Gaṅgā."

This is a statement regarding the relative ontological status of the innumerable Buddhas of the past, present, and future. Next to it, we shall juxtapose yet another word of caution, this time in regard to the artificial (that is, conventional) nature of the threefold epistemic system, the three *svabhāvas* (Modes of Cognition) previously under discussion. Thus, here is *Laṅkā* II: 132; *gāthas* 198, 199; ll. 8-11:

> However, if one is truthfully discerning with intelligence, (one finds that) there is neither Relative-knowledge, nor False-knowledge; nor is there anything (called) Absolute-knowledge; (then) how (could there be) any state [or Mode of Cognition, *bhāva*] to be distinguished by intelligence?
>
> Reality (*bhāva*) is known (to be) free from (the dualism of) Being and non-Being—(this is) the Perfect knowledge; but, (if Reality) is devoid of (the dualism of) Being and non-Being, just how (could there be) two Modes of Cognition [i.e., relative and absolute]?

Now, consider the necessity of bringing into harmony the *tools* of inquiry (i.e., the five Epistemic Categories and the three Cognitive States) with the *object* of inquiry (i.e., the non-dual Reality); these were legitimate, yet no less disturbing questions, for the fourth-century Buddhist philosopher. The difficulty of finding a satisfactory answer to such questions seems to lie at the roots of our deeply imbedded habits of reasoning, structured by polar opposites and veiled in the conventional symbolism of language. This critique of the process of cognition and the propagation of knowledge represents the leitmotif reverberating throughout the *Sūtra*, as we have already pointed out in the course of the previous chapter (2.1.), on the subject of the "Mind-only" (Citta-mātra) doctrine.

From a contemporary perspective, we might also add that the obstacles to the process of cognition, on the one hand, and to verbal communication, on the other, are compounded in view of the fact that we have to contend not only with an ever-changing Reality, but also with the ever-shifting *meaning* of the words themselves. Considering this fact, the amazing thing is that we can still manage to communicate meaningful ideas to one another, although it would be difficult to say whether in our media-saturated society the chasm between ideas and Reality itself is narrowing, or growing progressively wider. What we can say for sure (echoing the media guru Marshall McLuhan's famous words) is that in our world "the *media* has become the message," and therefore, the message is now more about our own minds than about the "Reality" it is supposed to reflect, objectively and impartially. And this, of course, demonstrates how surprisingly relevant (and perhaps even more so!) the fourth-century Buddhist critique of language and communication can be, even for a modern Western society.

Concluding Remarks

Having reviewed the five Epistemic Categories (*dharmas*) and the three Modes of Cognition (*svabhāvas*), we have arrived at the highest epistemic state, the transcendental intuition, the *Eureka*-state, the desired goal, the Āryajñāna, the Gnosis, a state which by definition represents a Revolution (*parāvṛtti*) in the cognitive process of a peculiar sort. Its peculiarity resides in the fact that it may simultaneously be regarded as a radical shift of ontological status of the person who experiences it, that is, a leap from an *ordinary* human being to an *extraordinary* enlightened being, a Buddha. Consequently, one may say that, at this point, the line between the epistemic and the ontic domains seems to be dissipating, since it is no longer clear where one ends and the other begins. Perhaps the best way to put it is that the (gradual) accumulation of knowledge leads to (sudden) ontological change, that is, to a qualitative leap in the condition of the Being itself. For, the "peak" experience here discussed under the appellation of *āryajñāna*, or higher Wisdom (Gnosis), while primarily a cognitive one, is in essence a process of religious transformation, a "conversion," a "turning over," a "revulsion" (*pravṛtti, vyāvṛtti*), in brief, a shift from one plane of being onto another, from one mode of existence to another.

Now, regarding the way in which this transformation takes place, whether gradually or suddenly (a crucial topic of debate among Buddhists of different sectarian persuasions), the *Laṅkāvatāra* itself is rather ambiguous, allowing both possible interpretations.[20] As we have seen above, the text speaks of *three* paths to Enlightenment: (1) a *theoretical* path, which evolves from the familiarity with the holy texts (Buddhist as well as non-Buddhist); (2) a *practical* path, of yogic meditation and insight into the essence of all things, which leads to the attainment of the body of concentration characteristic of the Buddha-stage; and (3) the path of *grace*, conveyed upon the faithful multitudes, lacking the time and inclination to follow the other two, but still able to benefit from the power of Buddha's original vows to save the entire world, according to the Mahāyāna tradition (see supra: *Laṅkā* II: 49-50; ll. 15-17, 4-12).

At a closer look, however, only two paths emerge as real options for someone intent upon Buddhist Enlightenment, since the third path of grace does not require active involvement and effort. The *Sūtra* itself dismisses it when it states that there are only two manners of teaching the truth (of Enlightenment): (a) the teaching by discourses (collections, treatises, texts), and (b) the teaching through Self-realization, which belongs to the yogis, is totally intuitive and beyond dual categories of discrimination (see supra: *Laṅkā* III: 172; ll. 4-18).

No doubt, some early Ch'an Buddhists have taken the heavy emphasis on direct experience of yogic practice of meditation, found in the *Laṅkāvatāra* and other Yogācāra texts, to mean that *this* is the golden path (reserved for the spiritual elite, who are truly determined to attain the final goal of Enlightenment). The *Sūtra* says that: "It is for the ignorant that I discourse; the final goal (of Self-realization belongs) to the yogis" (*Laṅkā* III: 172; l. 18). Hence, also, the name of Yogācāra for this school of thought in Indian Buddhism.

Furthermore, Suzuki in his *Studies* (pp. 106-107) points out certain passages in the *Laṅkāvatāra* (II: 104-105) which underscore the fact that, while there are words without corresponding objects (such as the hare's horns, the tortoise's hair, a barren woman's child, etc.), there can be communication without words (such as by gestures, by movement of the eyes, by laughing, by yawning, by clearing of the throat, or by trembling, and so on).

Now, the Ch'an (or Zen) masters of China and Japan found justification (or perhaps inspiration?) in such passages for their belief in the instantaneous transmission of the supreme truth of Enlightenment "apart from written signs and words." According to this tradition, the oldest of such passages is to be found in the Pāli discourses, where the Buddha was said to have held out a flower one day to his congregation, without uttering one word, and only one notable disciple, Mahākāśyapa, grasped the significance of his wordless communication, thereby suddenly attaining illumination, which put a bright smile on his face. The following Zen quatrain (*kōan* no. 6 from the *Mumonkan*) celebrates this episode:[21]

> The Great Serpent comes, turns the flower
> And shows it.
> Kāśyapa distorts his countenance.
> Men and heaven remain dark.

True enough, the yogic state does go beyond words, beyond speech, analysis, and theorizing. But in order to attain this state, one has to enculturate oneself, that is, to become familiar with a certain spiritual tradition. This tradition is mostly verbally transmitted, either through written texts, or through oral patriarchal lineage, or both. Therefore, the so-called sudden flash of Enlightenment cannot be said to take place in a cultural vacuum, that is, without prior preparation. It requires a sustained effort of accumulation of knowledge to the point of suddenly reaching a new vision, as if from a higher ground. Whether this revelation is said to occur spontaneously, or is triggered by some fortuitous intervention from the outside (such as a meaningful happening, a gesture or utterance of the Teacher), it is still the culmination of a long process.

In his *Studies* (p. 207, note 1), Suzuki explains this psychological process in the following way:

> The process needed by the Buddha for the cleansing (of the mind) is sometimes gradual and sometimes abrupt. But the notion of revulsion or up-turning (*parāvṛtti*) leads us to imagine the process to be abrupt rather than gradual, while in our actual experience of life what the psychologist calls conversion takes place in either way, gradual or abrupt . . .
>
> . . . The unconscious process that preceded it may have been gradual, but as far as his conscious mind is concerned, the revulsion has taken place instantaneously. This however is a mooted question in the psychology of religion.

His explanation follows closely the text of the *Laṅkāvatāra*, chapter II: 55-56, where the mythical Buddha addresses a question regarding the nature of mental purification, namely whether it is instaneous or gradual. His reply is ambivalent and riddled with metaphorical language. Yes, the Master says, the mind is gradually, not instaneously, purified (*viśudhyati na yugapat*), just as the ripening of the *āmra* fruit, the growing of grass, shrubs, herbs, and trees, the making of pots, the mastery of the arts of comedy, dancing, singing, music, lute-playing, and writing, are all accomplished gradually and not instantaneously.

But the Tathāgata, if he so desires, the Master goes on saying (*Laṅkā* II: 56; ll. 2-3), can lead all beings instantaneously into the state of imagelessness and non-discrimination (*yugapat tathāgataḥ sarvasattvānāṃ viśodhayati nirvikalpāṃ nirābhāsagocarām*). Such an event is compared with the instantaneous and indiscriminate reflection of various forms and images in a mirror, or with the equal illumination of all forms by the light radiating from the sun or the moon. "In the same way," the Master concludes, "the noble truth of Self-realization spontaneously shines out when the false (dualistic) views of existence and non-existence are extinguished" (*evam eva mahāmate pratyātmāryagatidharmalakṣaṇaṃ bhāvābhāvakudṛṣṭivinivartanatayā yugapat virājate*). (*Laṅkā* II: 56; ll. 11-13)

We can glean from these quotations that *all three* paths to liberation mentioned above are conceivable: the illuminating grace of the Tathāgata generously bathing all beings in its pure light, the arduous path of intellectual conquest; and, based upon it, the spontaneous flash of silent illumination. The Chinese Buddhists seemed to have tended to separate one strand from the other, possibly due to their pragmatic frame of mind, rather than the more mystical outlook of their Indian forebearers.[22] Thus, there emerged devotional (Pure Land), scholarly (T'ien-t'ai and Hua-yen) and silent meditation (Ch'an or Zen) schools, respectively. But, at least according to the *Laṅkāvatāra*, the three paths were originally regarded as complementary, not mutually exclusive:

> It is for this reason, Mahāmati, that you should be cultivating the threefold discipline characteristic of the Noble Wisdom (*āryajñāna*). (*Laṅkāvatāra-sūtra* II: 50; l. 12)

Now, as far as the precise nature of the experience of Enlightenment itself is concerned, short of learning from direct, personal experience, there are also three ways of finding out *about* it: (1) from the accounts of those who experienced it in the past, or the present; (2)from the explanations given by scholarly authorities from *within* the Buddhist tradition (such as Suzuki); and (3) from the interpretations found in the writings of non-Buddhist scholars, whose psychological training and insight may (or may not) qualify them to elaborate on such delicate matters. From the point of view of the *history of religion*, however, which does not fall in either of the above three categories, it would be not only difficult, but also presumptuous on our part to pass judgment on the essential nature of Buddhist Enlightenment, especially when so much has already been written, with and without direct knowledge of it.[23] True, as Suzuki points out in his *Studies* (pp. 162-63):

> . . . We must keep one thing always before our minds, . . . which is, that Buddhist thought is always the outcome of Buddhist life; that its logic, or psychology, or metaphysics cannot be understood adequately unless we realize that facts of Buddhist experience are at its basis and, therefore, that pure logic is not the key to the understanding of Buddhist philosophy.

Indeed, we should be aware that applying precise philosophical categories and analysis to a religious text (especially one whose primary aim is to provide the philosophical means for the transcendence of thought altogether for the sake of direct, unmediated, and total experience), is tantamount to trying to measure the degree of aesthetic satisfaction, upon the reading of a poem, by using the criteria of scientific truth, or, for that matter, applying mathematical formulae in order to capture the meaning of a symphony, or the scent of a flower.

Therefore, we may be inclined to agree with Suzuki that in the last analysis, "pure logic" may not be the key to the understanding of Buddhist philosophy (and we might add, of any religious philosophy). But by the same token, neither would "pure experience" open the doors of understanding of a rational philosophical treatise. For, in the realm of utter subjectivity which characterizes the essential core of any experience (particularly a religious one), universally acceptable categories of reason are utterly forgotten, and alas, it is here that the work of the scholar comes to an end, and, perhaps, that of the guru begins.

And yet, by using phenomenological-psychological bracketing, the scholar should at least aspire to penetrate that rational dimension of the mind without which the text itself could not have been written, and then try to extrapolate from the written word what type of human experience generated the thought behind it.

This experience might seem foreign to our understanding at first, but by combining informed reasoning with a quality of *empathy* derived from the universality of human condition, we would certainly be able to relate not only rationally, but also intuitively, to those universally valid human problems, such as freedom from suffering, creation and destruction, birth and death, Self and non-Self, presence and transcendence, appearance and essence, and so on. By studying its mode of structuring such issues, we will discover the way of articulating the highest values of a culture, their historical conditioning and transformation in time. *That* is what makes the work of the historian of religion so intriguing and fascinating, and not whether or not he can possess a "magical key" to the understanding of the Buddhist religious experience and philosophy.

2.3. The Conjunctive System of the Eight Vijñānas: the Integration of *Both Mind and No-mind* States of Consciousness

Introductory Remarks

The cognitive system of the eight Vijñānas occupies a position of major significance in the epistemology of the *Laṅkāvatāra-sūtra.* In fact, it is essential to the understanding of the Yogācāra school in general, which is sometimes also called Vijñānavāda, and its adepts-Vijñānavādins. There are several levels of meaning attached to the term, again depending on the context. According to Suzuki (*Studies*, p. 175, note 1), "when *vijñāna* is used in its most comprehensive sense, it is equivalent to 'mind' as distinguished from unthinking matter, *rūpa.* In its specific, technical sense, it is the perceiving and discriminating activity of mind."

These two broad distinctions are described at length by Edgerton in his *Buddhist Hybrid Sanskrit Dictionary* (Delhi: 1977), pp. 285-86, where five different meanings are given, based on the Buddhist Sanskrit literature. There are:

(1) The first rendering is "practical, applied knowledge," as opposed to the "abstract, theoretical knowledge," or *jñāna.* It corresponds to Suzuki's translation as "transcendental" (i.e., absolute) and (merely) "relative" knowledge (*Studies*, p. 272). This opposition is found in the *Laṅkā* 156.11f., but also in other Mahāyāna texts (e.g., *Mahāvyutpatti* 1548 and *Bodhisattvabhūmi*, pp. 257.16f.), as we shall see.

The next four categories summed up by Edgerton can all be rendered as "consciousness," although, he says quite appropriately, "no single word or brief phrase can, of course, really suffice." They are given in the following order:

(2) Two kinds of knowledge, the Perceiving (*khyāti-vijñāna*) and the Object-discriminating (*vastuprativikalpa-vijñāna*), as per *Laṅkā* 37.14f.; in regard to functions, the corresponding consciousness

is eight-fold (*aṣṭa-lakṣaṇa*), as given in *Laṅkā* 235.7f., and explained by Suzuki in *Studies*, 189, namely: the five sense-*vijñānas*, the *manas*, the *mano-vijñāna* and the *ālaya-vijñāna;*

(3) The sixth of the six elements of existence (*dhātus*), i.e., earth (*pṛthivī*), water (*ap*), fire (*tejas*), air or wind (*vāyu*), space or ether (*ākāśa*), and—of course—consciousness (*vijñāna*);

(4) The fifth of the five personality aggregates (*upādāna*-Skandha): *rūpa, vedanā, saṃjñā, saṃskāra, vijñāna;* and lastly,

(5) The third link in the *pratītya-samutpāda* (Dependent Origination), after *avidyā* and *saṃskāra* (nescience and impulse).

For the purpose of this study, we will limit our inquiry to the first two of these five categories given by Edgerton, namely (1) *vijñāna* as practical, empirical knowledge, and (2) *vijñāna* as perceiving and discriminating faculty of the mind. Both meanings are given extensive treatment in the *Sūtra.*

Now, the word itself is readily explained in Monier-Williams' *Sanskrit-English Dictionary* (Oxford: 1964), pp. 961 and 949, to mean "the act of distinguishing or discerning, knowledge, understanding" (from the root *jñā* = "to know," "to perceive," and the separative verbal prefix *vi* = "apart," "asunder," "away," "without;" originally *dvi* = "in two parts," this prefix is used to express division, distinction, distribution, arrangement, order, opposition, or deliberation). As such, *vi-jñāna* is associated with various cognitive functions related to perceiving, as well as sorting out the sensory data, or input.

In a larger sense, explains Suzuki (*Studies*, p. 176), "it is not mere cognition or understanding, it is a sort of principle of conscious life as distinguished from the body, and it is also the power or faculty of discrimination." Hence, the multiplicity of meanings attached to the term, which in the course of time have piled up over one another, like the aerial roots of the banyan tree, which are so closely intertwined that it is almost impossible to distinguish them independently. The general schemata of this extremely complex psychological system is outlined by Suzuki in the following lines from the same work (p. 174-75):

> According to the *Laṅkāvatāra*, the mind, inclusive of Citta, Manas, and the other six Vijñānas, is in its original nature (*svabhāva*) quiet, pure, and above the dualism of subject and object. But here appears the principle of particularisation known as "Vishaya," which comes from the root *vish* meaning "to act," "to work"; and with the rise of this wind of action, the waves are agitated over the tranquil surface of the mind. It is now differentiated or evolves (*vṛtti*) into eight Vijñānas "Ālaya,

Manas, Manovijñāna, and the five senses"; and simultaneously with this evolution the whole universe comes into existence with its multitudinous forms and with its endless entanglements.

The entire system is a dynamic one, and the term *vṛtti* indicates that the *vijñānas* undergo constant transformation. It is for this reason that the first classification given by the *Sūtra* has to do with the manner in which they arise, abide, and disappear from the horizon of our mental awareness. The frequently used term *pravṛtti-vijñānas* (which includes all but the eighth, unperturbed Ālaya-vijñāna), points to the fact that they arise in response to the agitation caused by the incessant sensory stimulation, directly or indirectly. The *Laṅkā* states (II: 37; ll. 8-12):

> There are two manners, Mahāmati, in which the arising, the abiding and the cessation of Sense-perceptions (*vijñānas*) takes place; and (this) is not understood by the philosophers. To wit: the cessation (*nirodha*) of the continuous activity (*prabandha*) and the cessation of the manifested (or external) form (or aspect) (*lakṣaṇa*) [i.e., of the *vijñānas*]; the arising (*utpāda*) of the *vijñānas* (is also) of two kinds: the arising of (their) continuous aspect and the arising of (their) external aspect; the abiding (*sthiti*) is also (distinguished) in two ways: the abiding of (their) continuous activity and the abiding of (their) external form [or aspect, *lakṣaṇa*].

As to the difference (psychological or epistemological) between *prabandha* and *lakṣaṇa* (continuous presence and manifested form), the *Sūtra* remains rather laconic; we can only speculate along Suzuki's interpretation, which seems to indicate that "all the Vijñānas grow either active or dormant, according to the case" (*Studies*, 183). In other words, while the habit-energy, or the memory of imprints (*vāsanā*) left behind by the activity of thinking and of (the five-fold) sensory-perception is stored up in the Repository-of-impressions called Ālaya-vijñāna, some of them become manifested, or active, thereby making the other imprints seem latent, yet they are ready at any time to take their place on the conscious level of awareness as soon as the changing conditions require or allow such an event to take place.

It should be noted here that *lakṣaṇa* may also, although not necessarily, imply the symbolic activity of the mind, such as naming and categorizing the flow of impressions and thereby organizing them in meaningful patterns, as opposed to the *prabandha* (which, according to Edgerton's, *Buddhist Hybrid Sanskrit Dictionary*, p. 382, is sometimes substituted by the term *pravṛtti-vijñāna*, denoting agitation or movement), representing the incessant flow of unfiltered impressions that wash up on the shore of consciousness. These two interpretations are not mutually exclusive, however, and, in fact, they may very well be complementary, since one refers to the mental faculty which deals with the memory of past impressions and the other indicates the process of receiving new sensory data at the present moment.

Now, in its turn, the external or manifested form of consciousness (*lakṣaṇa-vijñāna*) is said to be of three kinds: that which evolves in the present as a result of past causes, or events (*pravṛtti-lakṣaṇa-vijñāna*); that which is active in the present and will result in future effects (*karma-lakṣaṇa-vijñāna*); and finally, that which remains in its original, generic, and untainted form of its birth, being unaffected by the past and having no negative effects upon the future (*jāti-lakṣaṇa-vijñāna*). The entire system may be regarded as a sort of intuitive genetic theory, which would include inherited, acquired, and unaffected genetic traits, as it were. Here is the description given in the *Sūtra* (II: 37; ll. 12-15):

> There are three kinds of consciousness in manifested aspect: the (cause-) produced [or developing] form; the active [or effect-producing] manifested form; and the generic [i.e., fixed by birth, or family lineage, the genuine character of its race, its true] form.

Such is the general theory of consciousness within which the Vijñāna system is presented in the *Laṅkāvatāra*. We shall now turn to the more specific meanings in which the term *vijñāna* is being used.

Jñāna and Vijñāna: Abstract Intuition versus Concrete Knowledge

In contrast to *jñāna*, or transcendental knowledge, the term *vijñāna* designates the ordinary, empirical knowledge, obtained as a result of constant interaction with the external world of material forms; it is always wanting, on account of its fragmentary nature, and it is illusory, due to the discrimination between dualities (such as Being and non-Being, particularity and generality, Saṃsāra and Nirvāṇa, this and that, etc.). The term *jñāna*, on the other hand, is a much more encompassing term; it includes the dualistic worldly knowledge, that is, the sphere of *vijñāna*, but it goes beyond it, through the use of intuition, for the purpose of grasping both the unity and the egolessness of the world. By obtaining *jñāna*, the text asserts, not only the mind, but the Being itself undergoes a radical transformation. The accumulated karma is burnt out, and the realm of knowledge is fused with the realm of Being. We read in the third chapter (III: 156, ll. 14-15; 157, ll. 8-13):

> There are, Mahāmati, three kinds of knowledge (*jñāna*): Worldly, Super-worldly, and Transcendental. Now, the Worldly knowledge (*laukika jñāna*) belongs to the foolish (commoners), the immature, and to all the philosophers (who are) in the condition of persisting (to hold on to the dualistic) views of Being and Non-Being.
>
> The Super-worldly knowledge (*lokottara jñāna*) belongs to all the Śrāvaka- and Pratyeka-buddhas (who are) in the condition of perseverance in the (discarded) notions of individuality and generality.
>
> The Transcendental knowledge (*lokottaratama jñāna*) belongs to the Buddhas and Bodhisattvas (and) is free from the (dualistic) views of Being and non-Being, (for) it evolves from seeing into (the state of) non-arising and non-destruction, from examining those things which are not (mere) appearances [or imaginary products], (and) from (finally) achieving egolessness (which characterizes) the stage of Tathāgatahood [or Buddhahood].

The difference between the two levels of knowledge, transcendental and empirical, is spelled out in the following manner (III: 157; ll. 1-7):

> Now, perceptual knowledge [or discriminative, empirical *vijñāna*] is subject to birth and destruction, (while) intuitive knowledge [or transcendental *jñāna*] is not subject to birth and destruction.
>
> Furthermore, Mahāmati, the ordinary knowledge (*vijñāna*) falls into (the dualism of) appearance and non-appearance, of Being and non-Being, by reason of the multiplicity of individual characteristics, (but) the intuitive knowledge (*jñāna*) is characterized by the transcendence of (the duality of) appearance and non-appearance.
>
> Moreoever, Mahāmati, the empirical knowledge is characterized by accumulation, (while) the intuitive knowledge is characterized by diminution [or concentration].

> Now, there are three kinds of intuitive [or abstract] knowledge (*jñāna*): that which determines individuality and generality, that which ascertains birth and decay, and that which distinguishes no birth and no decay.

In the last sentence, the word *jñāna* is apparently used in its larger sense of "knowledge" in general, rather than in its more specific, technical sense of intuitive Wisdom, or Gnosis. Otherwise, how would one reconcile this statement with what has been said heretofore, concerning the transcendence of all dualities, the characteristic mark of the intuitive knowledge (*jñāna*)? Like many other terms found in the *Laṅkā*, this too acquires novel connotations that do not displace, but rather enrich the older, less specific, or less specialized meaning.

Other differences between *jñāna* and *vijñāna* are described in terms of attachment to, or freedom from the sensory world (III: 157-58; ll. 14-17, 1):

> Further, Mahāmati, the intuitive knowledge (*jñāna*) is characterized by being free from attachment, but the perceptual knowledge (*vijñāna*) is characterized by being tied to the manifoldness of the sensory world.
>
> Moreoever, Mahāmati, the empirical knowledge (*vijñāna*) is characterized by union, birth and endurance, (which is) the triple attachment, (while) the transcendental knowledge (*jñāna*) is characterized by its own self-nature, free from attachments.
>
> Furthermore, Mahāmati, the intuitive knowledge (*jñāna*) is characterized by non-resulting (from any rule); it is the inner realm of Self-realization by Noble Wisdom, it neither enters nor goes out, like the moon in the water.

Other Mahāyāna scriptures, such as the *Bodhisattva-bhūmi* and the *Mahāvyutpatti*, concord with the *Laṅkāvatāra* in emphasizing the ineffable, spontaneous nature of the intuitive knowledge, in opposition to the gradual, accumulative character of the perceptual type of knowledge (*vijñāna*). Thus, the following passage found in the *Bodhisattva-bhūmi* 257.16f. reads:[1]

> When the Bodhisattva achieves intuitive knowledge (*jñāna*), he acquires the insight into the essential (goodness), which is not the same as the discrimination (*vijñāna*) between external objects, thoughts, and hear-say; (for) whatsoever is inquired

> after by means of transcendental insight (*jñāna*) obtained through meditation, that cannot possibly be known by simple perception, thought, or hearing. Thus having heard the truths of the Tathāgata's sayings, and also having understood their most profound (meaning), he [i.e., the Bodhisattva] does not contradict (them).

The *Mahāvyutpatti-sūtra* similarly exhorts its readers (1548):[2]

> jñāna-pratisaraṇena bhavitavyaṃ, na vijñāna-pratisaraṇena.
>
> One must come to rest in the absolute (*jñāna*), not in the relative [empirical, perceptual] knowledge (*vijñāna*).

And yet, at least according to the *Laṅkāvatāra*, one can only reach *jñāna* by gradually evolving from the aboriginal state of ignorance (*ajñāna*), through the accumulation of *vijñāna*- type of knowledge. The following passage will give us a hint of this complex process of cognition (*Laṅkā* II:68; ll. 11-13):[3]

> The knowledge [based on sense-perception, *vijñāna*] is derived from ignorance (*ajñāna*), *karma* [i.e., effects of past deeds] and desire (*tṛṣṇā*) and is developing be becoming attached to apprehending objects through the sense-organs, such as the eye, etc., (while) the multiplicity (*vikalpita*) is made known on account of discrimination in one's own mind; (hence) the division seen in one's mind (between) body (*deha*) and mind [or Ālaya-vijñāna, the Repository-of-impressions].

To sum up the statements presented up to this point, let us say that knowledge (as distinctive from ignorance, *ajñāna*) can be either dualistic and accumulative (*vijñāna*) or non-dualistic and acquired through concentration (i.e., Gnosis, *jñāna*, or insight, *prajñā*). The former may be further subdivided into False-knowledge (or False-imagination, *parikalpita*) and Relative-knowledge (or Sensory-derived knowledge, *paratantra*).[4] One is "worldly" knowledge (*laukika jñāna*), belonging to the commoners, the immature, and the (non-Buddhist) philosophers, the other is "super-worldly" knowledge (*lokottara jñāna*) and belongs to the disciples (Śrāvakas) and the self-centered Hīnayānists (Pratyeka-buddhas), who still persist in viewing the world in dual terms: individuality and generality, Being and non-Being, Saṃsāra and Nirvāṇa, above and below, etc.

Now, in opposition to those above, there exist Buddhas and Bodhisattvas who attain the utterly transcendental (*lokottaratama jñāna*), absolute knowledge (*parinişpanna*), which, according to the Mahāyāna teachings, is beyond all notions of duality and is obtained through concentration. But ultimately, and the *Laṅkā* is emphatic on this point, all these different paths to knowledge (i.e., the Ayāna of the non-Buddhists, the Śrāvakayāna, the Pratyekabuddhayāna, and the Mahāyāna or the Buddhayāna) are one and the same (i.e., Ekayāna); they are only distinguished for didactic purposes, for the sake of suitability to people who are at different levels of spiritual development. The *Sūtra* explains (*Laṅkā* II: 65; ll. 11-14; vv. 131-32):[5]

> On account of the difference [in spiritual development] between the immature, the ignorant, and the wise ones, I speak of the Triple-vehicle, the One-vehicle, and of No-vehicle,
>
> as the entrance leading to the absolute Truth (*paramārtha*), which is devoid of duality and/of consciousness; where no appearance can stand [i.e., in the transcendent state of *jñāna*], how could (there be) the establishment of the three vehicles?

For the sake of clarity, however, before moving on, here is a tabulated synopsis of the cognitive system developed in the *Laṅkāvatāra-sūtra:*

Mind (empirical cognition)		**No-Mind** (trans-empirical cognition)
Dualistic knowledge—VIJÑĀNA (derived through accumulation)		Non-dual Gnosis—JÑĀNA (attained by concentration)
Nāma *Nimitta*	*Vikalpa*	*Samyag/Ārya-jñāna* *Tathatā*
False-knowledge (Imagination-based) *Parikalpita svabhāva*	Relative-knowledge (Sensory-derived) *Paratantra svabhāva*	Absolute-knowledge/Gnosis (Intuitive Wisdom) *Parinişpanna svabhāva*
Worldly knowledge *Laukika jñāna*	Super-worldly knowledge *Lokottara jñāna*	Transcendental knowledge *Lokottaratama jñāna*
Belongs to:	Belongs to:	Belongs to:
the commoners, the immature, the Brāhmins, the non-Buddhist philosophers (Tīrthikas)	the Śrāvakas (disciples) the Pratyekabuddhas (the self-centered followers of the Hīnayāna schools)	the Bodhisattvas the Fully-enlightened Buddhas (animated by compassion, *karuṇā* and insight, *prajñā*, the Mahāyāna followers)

Obviously, this schematic overview of the epistemic chart presented in the *Sūtra* is far from complete and even further from debate and adjustment; it is, however, helpful for the student of Buddhist epistemology in finding a way out of a thick forest of technical terms and intertwining cognitive structures. For a more detailed analysis of these structures, let us turn now to the functions of *vijñāna* as Perceptual and Discriminative type of knowledge.

Khyāti- and Vastuprativikalpa-vijñāna: the Perceptual and the Object-discriminating Knowledge

From the point of view of empirical cognition, the *Laṅkā* asserts the possibility of two types of *vijñānas*: one which perceives the object (*khyāti-vijñāna*), and the other which discriminates what has been perceived by comparing it with the already acquired knowledge, stored in one's memory (*vastuprativikalpa-vijñāna*, or the Object-discriminating *vijñāna*).[6] This distinction is tied up with our interpretation of *prabandha* as perception of the incessant flow of external stimuli, and of *lakṣaṇa* as categorizing, or individualizing faculty of the mind, as described above. They are both sustained by and connected with the habit-energy (*vāsanā*) accumulated from time immemorial, on account of faulty reasoning and imagination (*vikalpa*). Thus, the *Laṅkā* (II: 37-38; ll. 15-19, 1-2):

> O, Mahāmati, consciousness, which is said to be of eight kinds, can briefly be distinguished as two-fold: consciousness of perception, and object-discriminating consciousness; (and) like the attachment of form(s) on a mirror, Mahāmati, so will the perceiving consciousness (*khyāti-vijñāna*) perceive (the object); and between the two, that is, the perceiving and the object-discriminating consciousness, Mahāmati, there is not a bit of difference, (for) they are mutually conditioned [lit., caused, or determined].
>
> Then, Mahāmati, the perceiving consciousness (functions) by reason of the evolution of the unfathomable memory (or mysterious habit-energy, *acintya-vāsanā*), (while) the object-discriminating consciousness (*vastuprativikalpa-vijñāna*) (functions), O Mahāmati, by reason of discrimination of an objective world, and on account of the habit-energy [or memories, *vāsanā*] expanding diffusely (*prapañca*) since beginningless time.

The final goal of meditational practice, however, is to revert this process of incessant accumulation of sensory impressions and mental delusions, back to the original state of pure consciousness (*jāti-lakṣaṇa-vijñāna*, or *ālaya-vijñāna*).[7] Before investigating how this process is achieved, let us briefly outline the morphology of the Yogācāra psychological system, known as the bundle of the eight *vijñānas* (*aṣṭavijñāna-kāya*).

As such, the term *vijñāna* is to be rendered as "consciousness," or "perception" (of various kinds, according to the specific sense-organ to which it is attached), rather than "knowledge." Again, it is the context that refers us to the appropriate meaning, as we shall see. The following are the eight *vijñānas*, as presented in the *Laṅkāvatāra:* (1) the eye-consciousness (*cakṣur-vijñāna*), (2) the ear-consciousness (*śrotra-vijñāna*), (3) the nose-consciousness (*ghrāṇa-vijñāna*), (4) the tongue-consciousness (*jihvā-vijñāna*), (5) the body-consciousness (*kāya-vijñāna*), (6) the thinking-consciousness, or conscious volition (*mano-vijñāna*), (7) the pre-conscious volition, or impulses (*manas*), and (8) the deeper-most part of the mind, the Repository-of-impressions, or the subconscious mentation (*ālaya-vijñāna*).[8]

Now, the most difficult ones to interpret are the last two Vijñānas: Manas and Ālaya, of which Suzuki (in his *Studies*, pp. 195-96) says the following:

> According to my way of interpreting the *Laṅkāvatāra*, which may not be correct, the Ālaya is a sort of universal consciousness, and Manas individual empirical consciousness. In the Ālaya everything is stored, good and bad, in a state of quiescence and potentiality, but no discrimination, which latter, however, appears with the initiation of Manas. Manas is the active source of all the mental activities we ordinarily experience in this world of particulars.

In relation to the other six Vijñānas, Manas is described by Suzuki thus (Ibid., pp. 196-97):

> While Manas is conceptually separable from the other six Vijñānas, it is practically involved in them . . . (for) the six Vijñānas cannot function in harmony with one another unless Manas comes between them and the Ālaya. Manas is the connecting link. The position occupied by Manas in the system of Vijñānas is thus peculiarly complicated and is apt to get confused sometimes with the Ālaya and sometimes with Manovijñāna . . . which is a sort of door-keeper between Manas and the five Vijñānas.

The *Sūtra* itself does dot make these relationships very clear, indeed, beyond the assertion that the deeper Vijñānas (i.e., Manas and Ālaya) support the others, while these in turn function as active instigators, or energy drives, as it were, to keep the entire system in constant movement and transformation.[9] To wit (II: 127; gātha 180):

> With it [i.e., the *manovijñāna*, the conscious will-power] as cause and support, the pre-conscious volition (or impulses, *manas*) relies upon it [lit., flows together with it] for its power of going; likewise the perception (*vijñāna*) causes the mind [*citta*, taken to mean the entire mental system] to function and is supported by it [lit., is fixed upon it].

Being so closely tied together, the Ālaya, Manas and Manovijñāna are often discussed together in the *Laṅkā*, where the compound *cittamanomanovijñāna* is frequently found. The best explanation of the nature of this relationship is given by the *Sūtra* itself (*Laṅkā* II: 46; gāthas 102-104):

> They are neither different, nor non-different, they are considered (to be) like the waves and the ocean; thus are the seven (forms of) consciousness [or perceptions, *vijñānas*] connected with the mind.
>
> As the waves in their multiplicity are stirred on the ocean, so in the Repository-of-impressions is produced the variety of what is known as thought-forms [or perceptions, *vijñānas*].
>
> Citta, Manas, and Vijñānas [i.e., the subconscious, the preconscious, and the conscious parts of the mind, as it were] are discriminated in regard to (their) form; (but in substance), the eight are not to be individualized (against one another), for there is neither something observable [i.e., as separate entities], nor something distinctive (to set them apart) [or, there is neither that which is qualified, *lakṣya*, nor that which qualifies, *lakṣaṇam*].

Occasionally, however, the *Sūtra* does distinguish between Vijñānas based on certain attributes, as for instance in this gātha, taken from the somewhat incongruous tenth chapter, the *Sagāthakam* (X: 278; gātha 103):

> The (deep, subconscious) mind (*citta*) is always inactive, the (pre-conscious) conation (*manas*) only moves in two ways [i.e., mediating between the conscious and the subconscious mind], (while) the (conscious) volition (*manovijñāna*) is actively functioning, (and) because of that, it is either good or bad.

Within the cognitive system of the eight Vijñānas there is also a hierarchy based on the degree of delusion (*moha*) resulted from the involvement with the polluting matter. Thus, the Ālaya is said to be free from the system (i.e., from the limitations of the physical body, *kāya*), the Manas (impulses, drives, propensities) longs for a way out, according to its destiny, while the (other) Vijñānas are still attached to the external world, on account of their intrinsic qualities (that is to say that, as Sense-perceptions they are prone to delusion and error). Thus, the *Laṅkā* explains (*Sagāthakam:* 293; gātha 217):

> The Repository-of-impressions drops off the body; the Pre-conscious Impulse seeks a way out; the Sense-perception, having seen (only) the appearance of a sense-object, it can (easily) be deceived.

We have already pointed out that, in light of the teachings of the *Laṅkāvatāra-sūtra*, the faulty reasoning (*doṣa*) is perpetuated by the Sense-perceptions by means of the habit-energy of memory (*vāsanā*). There are altogether, says the *Sūtra*, four sources of error, namely: existence (*bhāva*), desire (*kāma*), material form (*rūpa*), and theorizing views (*dṛṣṭi*). The *Sūtra* further says this (*Sagāthakam:* 293; gātha 216):

> The mind [*citta*, here taken to mean the *ālaya*] is thoroughly pure by its own nature (*svabhāva*), but the (power of) Instinct (*manas*) is making it unclean; and the Volition, together with the (six) Sense-perceptions (*vijñānas*), are continually casting out memories [or, habit-energy, *vāsanā*].

Thus, we are told, the relationship between Vijñānas and the material world (*rūpa*) is particularly close, giving rise to adventitious defilements (*kleśas*) and, consequently, to the production of karma. Therefore, karma cannot be destroyed as long as the world is still perceived in dual terms, which in itself (as *vikalpa*, discrimination) further binds the formerly pure consciousness to matter. Hence, a revulsion, reversal (*vyavṛtti*), or turning around (*parāvṛtti*, lit., re-volution) is needed (*Sagāthakam:* 330; gāthas 521, 523):

> If karma would be destroyed through a reversal (*vyavṛtti*) in the perception of (material) form(s), permanence and impermanence are no longer met with, and transmigration (*saṃsāra*) is no longer known (ceases to be).
>
> Matter (*rūpa*) and (its corresponding) consciousness (*vijñāna*) disappear [lit., fall into pieces] in the state of *ālaya* (the Repository-of-perceptions), but when [or, as long as] the forms and (their) perceptions are tied together, karma does not disappear.

Now, the distinctions between the eight Vijñānas arise only as a result of the interaction between mind and matter, consciousness and (material) form, inner and outer worlds, subject and object, etc. When the attention is turned from the outside back toward the inside, the flow of consciousness is channeled back to its original source, which is the Ālaya-vijñāna (also known as the Tathāgata-garbha, the mind referred to in the Citta-mātra concept). Thus, it becomes tranquil, being reabsorbed in its own depth, as it were, like the ocean without a ripple, when the wind (of sensory agitation and of impulses) ceases to blow. For, the *Sūtra* explains, the difference between the waves and the ocean is only apparent, the particles of water which make the substance of both, are absolutely identical (*Laṅkā* II: 46; gāthas 105, 106):

> As there is no distinction between the ocean and its waves, so in the mind [*citta*, the equivalent of *ālaya*] there is no evolution of (various) perceptions.
>
> Karma is accumulated [lit., piled up] by the (subconscious) mind (*citta*), reflected upon by the (power of) Impulses (*manas*), and understood by the (power of) Consciousness (*mano-vijñāna*); (but) the visible (world, *dṛśya*) is discriminated by the five [Sense-perceptions, Vijñānas].

This faculty of discrimination between various objects based upon their Sense-impressions (Vijñānas) is *vikalpa*. In fact, says the Japanese Yogācāra commentator Yoshifumi Ueda, "in Yogācāra philosophy the terms *vijñāna* and *vikalpa* are synonymous."[10] To support his assertion, he quotes the 17th verse from Vasubandhu's *Triṃśikā*, which says:

> This *vijñāna-parināma* [i.e., perceptual evolution] is *vikalpa* [i.e., discrimination]. Anything which is discriminated or con-

> ceptualized by the *vikalpa* does not really exist. Therefore the whole world [which is discriminated and conceptualized by it] is Consciousness-only (*vijñaptimātratā*).

This verse refers in obvious manner to the world as it appears to our mind, mediated and distorted by discrimination and conceptualization. In the *Laṅkāvatāra*, as we have seen, this process is contrasted with the mind of the yogī who has achieved *prajñā*, or *nirvikalpa jñāna* (non-discriminating, directly intuitive Wisdom), thereby "knowing" the external object or Reality (*vastu*) "as it really is" (*yathābhūtārtha*).

La Vallée Poussin, also, quotes the *Yogaśāstra* 3, which basically expresses the same idea, namely that: "Le Vijñāna discerne (*vijānāti*) le caractère général de la chose (*vastu*)."[11] However, according to the *Laṅkāvatāra*, the distinctions effectuated by the Vijñānas, useful as they may be for the purpose of instructing the immature disciples (*bāliśān*, p. 47, v. 113), are like images seen in a mirror (*darpaṇa*), in a dream (*supina*), or an illusion (*māyā dṛśyate*). Thus, *Laṅkā* II: 47-48; gāthas 113-115, 121:

> When the sun rises, (it shines) equally on people high and low; so you who are the light of the world (should) proclaim [or teach] the truth (*tattva*) to the immature.
>
> Even if someone is seeking refuge in the Law of Truth (*Dharma*), the truth [itself, *tattva*] is not preached [i.e., cannot be taught, expressed in words]; (for) although that truth is preached, its essence (*tattva*) is not found in the mind [i.e., as a special thing called "truth"].
>
> Just as the waves appear simultaneously with the ocean, like (images) on a mirror, or in a dream, so is the mind (reflected) instantaneously in its own sense-fields.
>
> I teach to the sons of the Victorious One: this teaching is not (meant) for the immature. (For) what is seen as a multitude (of things) is a net of illusion [or a vision, *māyā*] which does not (really) exist.

These verses are best interpreted in light of the theory of "Mind-only," which underscores the importance of subjective factors in cognition. No matter what object we direct our attention on, its perception will always be tainted by our biases, past experience, and thought processes. One can even say that we see ourselves, that is our minds, no matter where we look. This epistemological paradox, represents the ultimate limitation of cognition, and perhaps even of Being (*bhūtakoṭi*), in the Cartesian sense (*cogito ergo sum*).[12]

The difficulty of transcending one's thought patterns and mental conditioning is also readily acknowledged as the main obstacle to progress by those familiar with either the process of psychotherapy, or with the dialogue between cultures (most notably in international affairs), or both. Therefore, it is fair to say that the solution to this fundamental epistemological problem (which preoccupied the Buddhist philosophers long before Kant wrote his *Critique of Pure Reason*) may hold the key not only to individual inner peace and harmony (the goal of Buddhist soteriology), but also to the ever elusive goal of collective peace and understanding between people with different histories and cultures.

The Inner Revolution (Parāvṛtti): the Return to the Tranquil State of Pure Consciousness (Ālaya-vijñāna)

According to the Buddhist tradition, as presented in the *Laṅkāvatāra*, in order to escape the all-pervasive net of illusion (*māyā*), caused mainly by the paradox of self-reflecting cognition, one will have to experience an inner transmutation, or revolution (lit., "reversal," *parāvṛtti*, or "return," *vyāvṛtti*). This is truly a self-transcending act since as long as there is the slightest breeze on the surface of the ocean of perceptions, as long as the Vijñāna system continues to function impelled by the conditioned memories (*vāsanās*) and by the habit-energy of discrimination (*vikalpa*), it will take continuous effort of will and the achievement of self-transcending Gnosis, or insight (*jñāna, prajñā*) into the nature of Reality (such as it is [*tathatā*], undistorted by our self-reflecting notions), in order to stop the continuous mechanical reeling of the system.[13]

Now, this cessation (*nirodha*) is described as taking place on two distinct levels: first, there is the cessation of the active, manifested form of consciousness (*lakṣaṇa-vijñāna*); and then, there is the cessation of the continuous aspect (*prabandha-vijñāna*), as follows (*Laṅkā* II: 38; ll. 3-8):

> Now then, Mahāmati, the cessation of all the Sense-perceptions, that is to say, of the Repository-of-impressions' (*ālaya-vijñānasya*) variously accumulated memories [or manifold habit-energies], produced on account of discrimination of unreality [or delusion] —this indeed, Mahāmati, is the cessation of the manifested aspect [of consciousness, *lakṣaṇa-nirodha*].

> Again, Mahāmati, the cessation of the continuity aspect [of consciousness, *prabandha-nirodha*] develops from this: to wit, Mahāmati, when (both) that by which is supported and that on which it depends [cease to function].
>
> Now, the support means the habit-energy [or memory, *vāsanā*] accumulated by erroneous thinking since beginningless time, and that on which it depends means the discursive thoughts (in regard to) sense-objects (*viṣaya*), for the Sense-perceptions, (are in fact) the world of one's own mind [i.e., due to the unreliability of the sensory mediation, n.n.].

As far as the *Laṅkāvatāra* is concerned, the accrued perceptions (*vijñānas*) do disappear (for the Yogī who follows the prescribed practices), but not so the Repository-of-impressions (Ālaya-vijñāna). This is explained by means of a number of metaphors, such as the waves and the ocean, the lump of clay and the particles making up its substance, the ornaments and the gold of which they are made, and so on (e.g., *Laṅkā* II: 38, ll. 8-13). They are said to be neither the same, nor different (lit., "neither different nor non-different," *na cānyo nānanyaḥ*), the disappearance of one does not imply the destruction of the other (*vide Sagāthakam:* 354; gātha 722):

> Mind, Volition, and the six other Sense-perceptions are by their own nature united and devoid of Oneness and Otherness —this is set out to mean Ālaya-vijñāna [i.e., the Repository-of-perceptions].

To assume the opposite view, would mean to fall into the deadly trap of Annihilationism. To wit, *Laṅkā* II: 38-39; ll. 13-19, 1-2:

> Even so, Mahāmati, if the developing [or cause-produced] perceptions were different from their original form, the Repository-of-impressions, the Repository-of-impressions cannot be (considered as) their cause (*hetuka*).
>
> Now, if they were *not* different (*ananya*), the cessation of the evolving perceptions could mean the cessation of the Repository-of-impressions, but there is no cessation of one's own original [or generic] form [i.e., *svajāti-lakṣaṇa*, which is the equivalent of the *ālaya-vijñāna*, as described above, n.n.].
>
> Therefore, Mahāmati, what (causes) the Sense-perceptions' (dissolution) is not the cessation of one's own pure, generic

> form [of consciousness], but the cessation of the effect-producing [i.e., tainted] form [of consciousness, i.e., the *karma-lakṣaṇa-vijñāna*].
>
> However, had there been any ceasing of the generic form [of perceptive consciousness, i.e., *svajāti-lakṣaṇa-vijñāna*], the cessation of the Repository-of-impressions would have occurred. Moreover yet, if the ceasing of/in the Repository-of-impressions (is admitted), this doctrine would be in no way distinguished from the Annihilationism of the philosophers.

The *Sūtra* presents us here with a multi-layered structure of consciousness, not unlike certain modern psycho-dynamic theories of the mind. What seems to be different from the modern models is not so much the *vertical* morphology, or division of mental activity into a deep, stable Reservoir-of-impressions (i.e., the Ālaya-vijñāna, identified with the subconscious *jāti-lakṣaṇa-vijñāna*, the genetic pool, as it were) and a more agitated surface, gathering and organizing data from both without and within (i.e., the other Vijñānas representing the conscious and the preconscious levels of activity), as the extension on the *horizontal* plane, as it were (both into the past, the *pravṛtti-lakṣaṇa-vijñāna*, and into the future, the *karma-lakṣaṇa-vijñāna*) of these mental phenomena generically called Vijñānas, thereby establishing an almost infinite causal chain of events, criss-crossing both space and time. Mutually conditioned, these mental events have but a fleeting existence, like the sensory impressions upon which they feed, so to speak. The Repository-of-impressions, or the Storehouse-of-consciousness (as is sometimes called), on the other hand, is said to have a more permanent, or at least relatively stable, existence in relation to the other seven Vijñānas, for, it is at this level that the latter finally would come to rest and lose their (temporary) distinction, or identity.

Interestingly, in the Asaṅga-Vasubandhu works, the Ālaya-vijñāna is not posited as a universal underlying entity, but rather as a stratum present selectively in certain individuals depending on their level of spiritual perfection. Furthermore, a cessation of the Store-consciousness is accepted, which is in sharp contrast with the above-quoted statements from the *Laṅkāvatāra*. For instance, for those who achieve the sixth stage "without thought," of the Nirvāṇa-realm without residual basis, as described in Asaṅga's *Yogācārabhūmi*, there is even a complete cessation of the Repository-of-consciousness.[14]

Alex Wayman has translated certain fragments from this

essential Yogācāra text that are of relevance to this point. Thus, according to Asaṅga, it is possible to have *ālaya-vijñāna* without *pravṛtti-vijñāna*, and vice versa. Four cases are given:

1. Possessing *ālayavijñāna* and *not* possessing evolving perception: persons in states numbers 1-15 in "Establishment of states."
2. Possessing evolving perception and *not* possessing *ālayavijñāna:* Arhats, Pratyekabuddhas, irreversible Bodhisattvas, and Tathāgatas, when in stages "with thought."
3. Possessing *both*: persons other than those (mentioned above), when in stages "with thought."
4. Possessing *neither:* Arhats, Pratyekabuddhas, irreversible Bodhisattvas, and Tathāgatas, when in cessation-equipose, or in Nirvāṇa-realm without residual basis.

As presented, the persons mentioned in numbers 2 and 4 above, lack the *ālaya-vijñāna,* and yet (as in case number 2) they can still have evolving perceptions, when in stages "with thought."

Such metaphysical complexities (if we admit the law of gradual accretion of speculative ideas visible throughout the history of Indian Buddhism) seem to indicate that the theories set forth in the *Laṅkā* are based upon more "primitive" versions of the Yogācāra system. Thus, by the time this *Sūtra* was compiled, at least two divergent views regarding the nature of the Ālaya-vijñāna were already in existence, and the text echoes the debate between them. For instance, in discussing the momentariness (*kṣaṇika*) of all Vijñānas, the author is careful to qualify the statement by introducing the possibility of a second Ālaya-vijñāna, connected with the state free from impurities (*anāsrava,* lit., "non-outflows"), which is not momentary (*Laṅkā* II: 235-36; ll. 12-17, 1).[15]

> . . . And having evolved, they [i.e., Vijñānas] vanquish; but, out of the lack of understanding that what is seen is one's own mind, yet another (Vijñāna system) arises, following the cessation of the first; (and again) the Cognitive-will (Manovijñāna) is developed in connection with the system of five Sense-perceptions (Vijñānas), apprehending distinctions between forms and figures.
>
> Not remaining still even for a moment—this I call momentariness (*kṣaṇika*). Further, Mahāmati, momentariness (is also) the Repository-of-impressions, known as the Matrix-of-

> Buddhahood, (which is) momentary (when taken) together with the habit-energy of the evolving Sense-perceptions; but, (when taken) together with the habit-energy of the non-outflows (*anāsrava-vāsanā*), it is not momentary.

This sort of ambiguity gave rise to certain amount of confusion and misunderstanding. The author of the *Sūtra*, however, persistently steers the discussion away from speculative metaphysics back into the realm of empirical cognition, by emphasizing the pure conventionality of all theorizing activity about such mental constructs as Nihilism, Eternalism, Ālaya-vijñāna, Nirvāṇa, and so on. Here are a few significant excerpts which illustrate this point. First, *Laṅkā* VII: 242; ll. 15-17, 243; ll. 1-2:

> Once more, Mahāmati, on account of the cessation of the system of the six Sense-perceptions, the fools and the immature take recourse to the doctrine of Nihilism, and on account of (their) non-understanding of the Repository-of-impressions, they have the doctrine of Eternalism . . . Liberation is obtained (when) precisely this discrimination of one's own thought (*sva-mati*) ceases (to develop).

Since faulty reasoning gathers momentum on account of the habit-energy (*vāsanā*), its cessation would trigger the abandonment of all devious thinking (*Laṅkā* VII: 243; ll. 2-3):

> Due to the abandonment of the four-fold habit-energy [or memory, *vāsanā*], there is the abandonment of all faults (*sarvadoṣa*).

Furthermore, the succeeding gāthas explain the meaning of this fourfold habit-energy, along with the faulty views ensuing therefrom (*Laṅkā* VII: 243, gāthas 4 and 5):

> Existence (*bhāva*), desire (*kāma*), material form (*rūpa*) and theorizing (*dṛṣṭi*)—of them is indeed the fourfold habit-energy (made up); from them is the rising of the Cognitive will and in them do the Repository-of-impressions and the (Power-of-) impulses reside.
>
> Nihilism and the idea of impermanency rise because of the Cognitive will, the visual perception, etc.; and Eternalism rises

> from (thinking that) Nirvāṇa, thought and theorizing are without beginning.

Finally, the explanation for this somewhat paradoxical situation lies partly in the ineffable nature of the spiritual truth derived from a *sui-generis* inner experience (which is by its very nature beyond the commonly perceived duality of Subject and Object), and partly in the various levels of understanding of those to whom the truth is being taught. The ancient Buddhist metaphor of the doctor and his medicine, which is applied differently according to the nature of the illness and the physical condition of the patient, is appropriately used here to explain this difficult doctrinal issue (*Laṅkā* II: 48-49, gāthas 119-20, 122-23):

> For the purpose of (attracting all) beings, the picture is painted [lit., arranged, fashioned] with various colors; the preaching (may be) erring, for the truth [or its essence] is beyond words (*akṣara-varjita*).
>
> Having found a dwelling in the Law of Truth, I instruct (its) essence to (my) devotees: the truth is a personal experience [or, is attained by an inner perception, *pratyātma-gatika*], free from (the duality of) that which is distinguished [i.e., the object, *kalpya*] and that by which one distinguishes [i.e., the senses, or the subjective awareness, *kalpa*].
>
> And yet, the instruction itself is variously taught, thus subject to alteration; (for) the teaching is no teaching whatsoever, if it is not (taught differently) according to each case.
>
> In the way that a physician offers a medicine to one patient and a medicine to another patient, in that way the Buddhas teach "Mind-only" for the sentient beings.

Thus, the system of the eight Vijñānas is presented in the *Laṅkāvatāra* with multiple meanings, the purpose of which is, ultimately, not so much to introduce yet another dogmatic theory about the mind and its functions, but rather to exhort the Buddhist practitioner to pursue his own personal growth, regardless of his (or her) present level of spiritual development and intellectual understanding. For, all distinctions among different cognitive systems and concepts are nothing but mental fabrications, mere steps on the ladder of self-realization, didactic tools to be left behind once their usefulness has been exhausted.

They are not to be taken literally, at their face value, and clung unto as if they were some eternal verities, immutable notions written in stone once and for all. If that were the case, one would fall into the metaphysical trap of Eternalism, a sure hindrance towards the ultimate goal of spiritual freedom and as dangerous as that of attachment to the changing (hence illusive) appearances of the phenomenal world (*māyā*). Therefore, given so many pitfalls, there can be no telling who will be the first to reach this ultimate goal, judging by the starting levels of development. Having become cognizant of various theories and techniques, the ever-alert disciple is wary not to become enslaved by any since no theory or technique can be useful in all places and at all times.[16]

This is clearly stated throughout the *Sūtra* in passages such as the following (*Laṅkā* III: 155-56; ll. 13-17 and 1-2):

> Furthermore, Mahāmati, (when) one is attached to the literal meaning of words, aiming for the (three) Cognitive Modes, the Mind (-only), the five (Epistemic Categories), (as explained in) the Triple-vehicle and the One-vehicle [i.e., Mahāyāna, see above], aiming at the original states of happiness, which are neither created nor destroyed, one becomes prone to falling upon the opposite views of affirmation and negation, prone to being attached to dependence (itself) [i.e., the chain of Dependent Co-production, *pratītya-samutpāda*]. (For), deceptive is the observing of the manifoldness of illusion (*māyā*): statements are erroneously (made), discriminations are (also) deceptively (made).
>
> It is thus, Mahāmati, that the manifoldness of illusion is erroneously being perceived, and erroneously being discriminated (as such) by the ignorant, but not so by the wise ones.

The last two verses of this section suggest the possibility of a metaphysical *unity* which transcends both the *multiplicity* of the phenomenal world, as well as the *dualism* in which the cognitive systems operate (*Laṅkā* III: 156; ll. 7-10, gāthas 36-37):

> The reality of all thoughts [or, conceptions, mental formations, *bhāvana*] is discriminated as such by the ignorant; if it were so as they are seen, all would be seeing the Truth [or, the real state, the Reality, *tattva*].
>
> Given the unreality (*abhāva*) of all things, (is follows that) there is neither defilement nor purity; they (things) are not as they are seen, nor are they otherwise.

Admittedly, there is a certain ambiguity in these verses, but when one reads them against the background of Buddhist ontology (having as its premise a dynamic, ever-evolving universe and the impermanence of all things contained in it), the ambiguity will begin to make sense. Indeed, things are not as they seem (i.e., solid, continuous, permanent), nor are they otherwise (i.e., completely insubstantial, lacking any identity and existence as such). The former would constitute the sin of Eternalism, the latter that of Nihilism. Consequently, nothing can be said *definitely* about something, for the constant change prevailing in the universe affects its conditioned nature even as we speak.

Conclusion

It has been said that not only the *Laṅkāvatāra* thought, but the entire Yogācāra-Vijñānavāda system is based on a theory of perception, and therefore it is more psychological than ontological or even epistemological.[17] But, as P. T. Raju correctly pointed out,[18] unlike certain Western philosophical theories based on perception (such as Berkeley's, Locke's, or Hume's), the method of the Vijñānavādin is the practical goal of spiritual freedom that inspires the Buddhist to analyze, classify, and interpret the multiple states of perception and consciousness that one has to go through in order to reach this final goal of liberation. Knowledge for its own sake is a foreign notion to the mind of the fourth-century Buddhist monk.

And yet, the results of his persistent forays into the dynamic workings of the mind are no less than impressive, in their accuracy of observation, and their logical organization into a coherent, functional system. To recap, there are, according to the *Laṅkāvatāra* theory, *three* different ways of interpreting the cognitive experience:

First, there is the process of *acquiring* the data, which can be systematized under the five Epistemic Categories (*dharmas*), and the three Modes of Cognition (*svabhāvas*), as described in the previous chapter (ch. 2.2.). They may be further subdivided into two types of cognitive activity: empirical ("Mind") and trans-empirical, or intuitive, transcendental cognition ("No-mind"), which we have described as non-dual Gnosis, attained by concentration and not through accumulation of sensory data (see supra: synoptic overview).

Then, we have a complete system of perceptive consciousness, or mental functions, whose purpose is *to process* the data provided through the senses, to direct it, organize it in a coherent pattern, and, finally, store it for future retrieval and usage. This is the eightfold system of Vijñānas (*aṣṭa-lakṣaṇa-vijñāna*), the topic of the present chapter. It, too, deals with two types of knowledge: empirical versus intuitive, concrete versus abstract, perceptual versus object-discriminating (based upon the previously stored knowledge). These dualities may also be expressed in terms of "Mind" versus "No-mind," since the former is empirical, accumulative, while the latter refers to the intuitive, spontaneous insight, which may be called transcendental to the moment and conditions under which it occurs.

For instance, from among the eight States-of-consciousness, only one can be said to be transcendental, or trans-empirical, the deepest Repository-of-perceptions (Ālaya-vijñāna). As a "storehouse" of impressions, the equivalent of the Western notion of the unconscious, it is the source of those instant flashes of recognition, or of intuitive insights, which occur spontaneously only when certain conditions are met. Its *modus operandi* bypasses all mechanical rules and logical restrictions, under which the other seven Vijñānas operate. Its functioning may be compared to the circuitry of artistic inspiration involved in the sudden creation of a masterpiece after a long, arduous period of preparation. By contrast, the five Sense-Vijñānas and the two conative Vijñānas (one conscious, Manovijñāna, the other pre-conscious, or impulsive volition, Manas) are all subject to predictable rules and relatively easy observation.

Finally, after acquiring and processing (or storing) the information from the outside world, there is a third type of consciousness-event, which in the West is only rarely alluded to in psychological treatises: the inner transmutation, the reversal, the revolution, or the return back into the tranquil depths of the Ocean-of-consciousness, from the constant agitation of the Sense-perceptions that takes place on its surface. It was precisely this *Laṅkāvatāra* idea of inner turning (*parāvṛtti*) at the root of consciousness which provided the doctrinal basis for the Zen school of sudden Enlightenment.

This Reversal (*vyāvṛtti*, or *pravṛtti*), according to the text, is actually a cessation (*nirodha*) of the activity of the Sense-Vijñānas, similar to Patañjali's "Sense-withdrawal" (*pratyāhāra, Yoga-sūtra* 2.54).[19] However, it is important to note that it does not imply a complete and final dissolution of all Vijñānas, only a temporary suspension of their frenzied activities. Therefore, Freud was mistaken to associate Buddhism with the negative death instinct (*thanatos*) and *nirvāṇa* with death itself in his *Beyond the Pleasure Principle.*[20]

Indeed, one can speak of a harmonious *integration* between the eight layers of consciousness, with constant alternation of different levels of functioning. For, if the "No-mind," or transcendental level of consciousness, is to be identified with Yogic enstasis, Zen *satori*, or Christian rapture, then, surely, the empirical state of consciousness of nothing more than "Mind" only, does not completely vanish, just as the waves cannot be forever removed from the surface of the ocean. It only takes a light breeze to revive them, for they are inseparable from the ocean itself. Hence, the psychology of the eight Vijñānas system provides a perfect illustration of the third, conjunctive case of the tetralemma logic (i.e., the Mind *both is, and is not*!).

The significance of the Yogācāras' psychological system should be judged, in final analysis, against other, similar systems developed in the West (1,500 years later!), such as the psychoanalytical model. Its focus is on the human potential of the healthy mind, whereas most of Western psychology is geared toward the needs of the sick and the maladjusted, therefore, the scope of Buddhist psychology is broader than that of most psychotherapeutical models practiced in the West. Of course, without rigorous verification and testing, one cannot make a final judgment on its applicability in a different cultural context other than that of its Asian origins. It is interesting to note, however, that the gap between the two approaches is rapidly decreasing. New therapies spring up in the West almost daily that claim to incorporate insights and techniques borrowed from Hindu, Buddhist, Taoist, and other traditional cultures.

In this emerging global psychological culture, the map of consciousness developed by the Yogācāra school of Buddhism and its direct heir, the practice of Zen meditation, may very well play an increasingly significant role. Already, there are dozens of studies, and perhaps hundreds of study-groups, across North America and Western Europe, that search for useful Buddhist ideas to help alleviate modern man's alienation from himself, from his fellow humans, and from his natural environment.[21] Some of these ideas, such as the loosening of the grip of absolutistic beliefs and of excessive attachment to one-sided viewpoints (resulting in ego-centrism, and anthropo-centrism), may considerably diminish the potential for destructive tension and conflicts, both on the individual and planetary levels. Who can foretell the enormous possibilities that might then be open to man to fully experience the joy of life in the way that only freedom from conflict and want and complete harmony with nature can offer?

2.4. The Disjunctive Theory of Causation: Things are *Neither this, Nor that,* for They Are All Subject to Causes and Conditions (Hetu-pratyaya)

Introduction

One of the most important contributions of Buddhism to religious philosophy is the doctrine of Causation. Its centrality to Buddhist thought can only be appreciated when seen within the broader perspective of the Buddhist view of change and impermanence (Anitya). In the *Laṅkāvatāra,* the early, simplistic twelve-fold formula referring exclusively to the unfolding of human existence, although occasionally alluded to, is being replaced by a complex theory which includes two levels of discourse, namely: (a) the causal *principle,* or nexus (*hetu*), and (b) the causal *factors,* or conditions (*pratyaya*).

In this section, I will pursue various aspects of this theory as presented in the *Sūtra,* paying constant attention to the principle of historical and doctrinal continuity within the larger Buddhist (and occasionally non-Buddhist) context. Several subdivisions of the material found in the text, as well as one *excursus* into the relevant Mādhyamika (Nāgārjuna) literature, will bring into sharper focus the specific doctrinal contributions made by this Yogācāra text to the development of Buddhist philosophy and practice. The titles of these sub-sections reflecting these doctrinal ideas, are: The expansion of the relevance of Causation: from the psychological to the cosmic sphere; Causation as a theoretical (epistemological) basis for a monistic view of the universe; Causation seen as a mere teaching device; *Excursus:* Causation in the thought of Nāgārjuna, and, finally, The soteriological value of Causation. The importance of these ideas cannot be underestimated, for, in Buddhism, salvation depends more on *what* you know, rather than *who* you know, as is the case with other, more devotional religions.

The Expansion of the Relevance of Causation: from the Psychological to the Cosmic-philosophical Principle

The various and increasingly complex formulations of the so-called Chain of Causation (as outlined and commented upon by E. J. Thomas and others),[1] reflect a progressive metaphysical sophistication in Buddhist thought, from the early, purely psychological explanation of the origin of pain, old age, and death (included in the previously mentioned formula of Dependent Origination, as found in the *Dīgha-Nikāya* 1. 83; 2. 30, 55; *Majjhima-Nikāya* 1. 249; *Saṃyutta-Nikāya* 2. 7, 144), to the Sarvāstivādin and Vijñānavādin Abhidharmic forms of multiple correlation and causal conditioning (as summarized by David J. Kalupahana in his book on causality).[2]

It was only in the later, Mahāyāna scriptures that the "primitive" Theravādins' emphasis on psychological causality began to expand toward a larger philosophical or cosmological view of universal causal links between phenomena, such as Being and non-Being, spirit and matter, social, moral, and spiritual existence, and so on. Interestingly enough, Jayatilleke's opposition to Thomas's and Keith's belief that in Buddhism causation was never applied as a "universal philosophical principle" is based upon a certain passage in the *Laṅkāvatāra* (Nanjio, p. 444?) which parallels the *Vinaya* 1.41. As given by Jayatilleke, the passage reads as follows:

> *Pāli:* ye dhammā hetuppabhavā tesaṃ hetuṃ Tathāgato āha, tesañ ca yo nirodho evaṃvādī Mahāsamaṇo. (*Vin.* 1.41)
>
> *Buddhist Sanskrit:* ye dharmā hetuprabhavā hetuṃ teṣām Tathāgato vadat, tesān ca yo nirodha evaṃvādī Mahāśramaṇaḥ. (*Laṅkāvatāra*, p. 444 ?)
>
> The Tathāgata has told the cause of those elements of existence which arise from causes, and also of their cessation—thus spoke the Great Ascetic.

Now, aside from the fact that the reference to the *Laṅkā* is either a misprint or mistaken (the Nanjio edition has only 376 pages altogether, including the *Sagāthakam* chapter), the passage does not explicitly refer to physical causation.[3] Rather, it seems more likely that—in spite of the plural form of *dharmāḥ*—it represents a reiteration in a different form of the well-known statement of the Buddha (*Majjhima-Nikāya* 1. 191):

> yo paṭiccasamuppādaṃ passati so dhammaṃ passati,
> yo dhammaṃ passati so paṭiccasanuppādaṃ passati.

> He who sees Dependent Origination (of things) sees the teaching [about suffering, etc.]; and he who sees the truth [of pain, etc.], sees the Dependent Origination.

Since it is not our intention to review the ideas of Causality in the Pāli canon here, suffice it to say that the most generic formulation to be found there is the following relation:

(1) 'whenever A is present, B is present' (*imasmiṃ sati idaṃ hoti*, Udāna 2; *Majjhima-Nikāya* 1.264), and (2) 'whenever A is absent, B is absent' (*imasmiṃ asati idaṃ na hoti*, Udāna 2; *Majjhima-Nikāya* 1.264). But such a schematic formula is open enough to explain both physical and psychological relations (albeit not too complex). And to say that "this is a scientific view of causation as opposed to the practical common-sense view," as Jayatilleke does, is overstating the case, to say the least.[4]

However, at the time when the *Laṅkāvatāra-sūtra* was compiled (3rd-4th centuries A.D.), a philosophically more expanded or, one might say, cosmic view of Causation had come into the foreground (as we shall see), while the psychological aspect had been reduced in significance to the point of representing a mere particular case within the grand and intricate picture of cosmic causality, which included both Being and non-Being. Moreover, not only is the classic twelve-link Chain-of-Causation not even mentioned as such,[5] (or, at best, is alluded to as a mere convention), but at times the very idea of Causal relation, or Origination, is treated as an illusion to be abandoned like all other philosophical views or mental constructs. This position is a far cry from the ancient simplistic view of "This arises, that arises," and the strong impact of the *Prajñāpāramitā* literature upon the *Laṅkāvatāra* (and other major Mahāyāna works) cannot be underestimated, in as far as this change of perspective is concerned.

Turning now to the text itself, we will find that the *Laṅkāvatāra* allows extensive treatment of certain new categories, or new ways of looking at the causal relations, the most prominent being the division into *external* (objective) and *internal* (subjective, psychological) factors of dependent origination of objects, the gradual and simultaneous rising of causes (both denied), and, finally, the six kinds of causes (six types of causation) according to different circumstances. We shall now look at all these categories, in the above-given succession.

Thus, the following dialogue between the zealous disciple Mahāmati and his revered teacher is described in the second chapter (*Laṅkā* II: 82-83; ll. 9-18, 1-2):

"Teach me, O Lord, the character of the cause and conditions of all things, by which comprehension of the character of the cause and conditions, I and other great beings Bodhisattvas may no longer imagine the gradual and instantaneous production of any contemplation and be freed from the mental construction about the views regarding existence and non-existence."

The Lord replied: "Mahāmati, there are two kinds of modalities of Causation of all things (which occurs) through Dependent Origination (*pratītya-samutpāda*), namely: the external and the internal [or inner type].

Now, Mahāmati, the external (agents of) Dependent Origination (are): a lump of clay, a stick, a wheel, thread, water, a worker and his labor, the combination of which produces a jar. And as with the jar, Mahāmati, which is made of a lump of clay, or as a (piece of) cloth which is made of thread, or a straw mat (made with) fragrant grass, or a sprout growing out of a seed, or as fresh butter is produced from sour milk by a man churning it with his own labor, so it is, Mahāmati, with the external type of Dependent Origination which appears in continuous succession."

This explanation of external causality may be regarded as the first step toward a cosmo-physical view of causal relations, as an embryonic form of a generalized theory of Causation. The aim of such theory, once emancipated from the narrow bounds of the early psychological exclusivism which revolved around the origins of pain (*dukkha*), would be to explain the nature of the interaction between various phenomena in the universe at large and their connection with our own inner world of perception, feeling and action, including the idea of Causality itself. The text further states (*Laṅkā* II: 83; ll. 3-7):

Now, first in regards to the inner (factors of) Dependent Origination, namely nescience, craving, and action—such primary things, Mahāmati, account for our idea of Dependent Origination. Born of these, Mahāmati, are what is known as the personality aggregates, the elements and the bases—these (also) account for the idea of Dependent Origination. Though imagined by the immature, they are without discrimination.

Although the causal perspective seems to have expanded to

include the universe as a whole, the ultimate goal for the Yogācāra Buddhist is not pure knowledge of cosmic mechanics, but rather the appeasement of the mind. It is in relation to this goal that one can speak of a unifying thread which links the Yogācāra school to the "primitive" form of Buddhism. Thus, the *Laṅkā* reads (III: 203, gāthas 110-111):

> When even the entire world is regarded as concatenation, as nothing but concatenation, then the mind is tranquilized [lit., unified, integrated, set aright].
>
> Nescience, desire, deed, etc.—these are the inner concatenation (*saṃkalā*); a ladle, clay, a vessel, a wheel, etc., or seeds, the elements (of existence), etc.—these are the outer [or external] concatenation.

Having perceived the intimate connection between the internal chain of events and the events taking place outside the mind (the external concatenation), the Yogācāra philosopher proceeds to lay out the epistemological foundation for a monistic view of the universe. To this process we shall turn next.

Causation as a Possible Theoretical Basis for a Monistic View of the World

In admitting the possibility of two different types of Causation, internal and external, the author of the *Sūtra* seems to shift the perception of duality from the ontic domain (Being versus non-Being) into the realm of knowing (subject versus object, inner and outer, mind versus matter). Moreover, the foregoing leaves open the question pertaining to the essential difference between the author's epistemological duality regarding causation, on the one hand, and the philosophers' extreme views concerning the ultimate validity of the notions of Being and non-Being, on the other (i.e., the division between Eternalists and Annihilationists). In answering this question, one needs to consider the fundamental fact that in the *Laṅkāvatāra-sūtra* these views are repeatedly rejected as erroneous, as are all dogmatic views of one sort or another.

To be sure, the idea of concatenation, whether internal or external, implies in fact a denial of pure birth or destruction of things. Instead, as we shall see, the concept of "no-birth" (*anutpāda*) is extensively explained and repeatedly stressed. The following lines illustrate the author's position in regard to causation against the extreme brahmanical views (*Laṅkā* III: 197-98; ll. 9-19, 1-4):

> There is nothing distinguishable [or special] within the teaching of no-birth and non-annihilation of existence. Why is that? For this reason: the causes of all philosophers, O Lord, are also unborn and undestructed, and you too, O Blessed One, not after your careful consideration, (declare) space, cessation and the realm of Nirvāṇa (to be) indestructible and unproduced. Furthermore; O Blessed One, the philosophers also explain that the world rises from effecting causal factors. Surely, the Blessed One, also considers the world as rising from (such) causal factors (as): ignorance, desire, deed, discrimination.
>
> Thus, the conditions (*pratyayā*) having risen in accordance (with the Law of Causation), the difference is merely of efficient cause (*kāraṇa*). So is (the case) with the external causal factors [or conditions]: (both) you and they [i.e., the philosophers] (admit that) they rise amongst external objects. Therefore, there is no distinction between the doctrine of the Blessed One and that of the philosophers. (With them there are) nine substances [which are regarded as] unborn and indestructible: the atom, the primordial Germ [or Supreme Principle], Īśvara, the creator, etc., (p. 198) while you, O Blessed One, (assert that) all objects are neither born, nor destroyed, as their being and non-being is unattainable [i.e., due to impermanence]. And as the elements are indestructible, their own individuality [or intrinsic nature] is neither born, nor annihilated; having followed their various courses (of transformation), what constitutes their own essential nature is not abandoned.

Thus, in opposition to the Brahmanical belief that certain metaphysical entities are unborn, immutable, eternal, and indestructible (i.e., the atom, the Ātman, the primordial matter, Īśvara, the creator, and so on),[6] and also in contradistinction to the Theravādins who still held a few things as unconditioned and indestructible (the Asamskṛtadharmas, such as Nirvāṇa and Ākāśa, space),[7] the Mahāyānists made skillful use of the doctrine of Dependent Origination in order to discard the last illusions of permanency and ultimate cause.[8] Already in the second century A.D., the greatest Mādhyamika dialectician Nāgārjuna made the resounding statement in the Nirvāṇa chapter of the *Mūlamādhyamika-kārikā* 25.19:

na saṃsārasya nirvāṇāt kiṃ cid asti viśeṣaṇaṃ/
na nirvāṇasya saṃsārāt kim cid asti viśeṣaṇaṃ//

> There is no difference whatsoever between Nirvāṇa and Saṃsāra; there is no difference whatsoever between Saṃsāra and Nirvāṇa.

The implications of this verse to the doctrine of Causation, are made clear in his *Yuktiṣaṣṭikā* (k. 10-11 AB),[9] where the attainment of right knowledge is directly linked with the abandonment of (traditional) causal thinking, even in regard to the attainment of the stage of Nirvāṇa, from within the world of Saṃsāra:

> Having seen with the right knowledge (= clear vision) what has arisen with the condition of 'nescience' [i.e., 'motivation'], there is no apprehension at all of either arising or passing away. That very thing is Nirvāṇa as this life (= the *dharma* seen), and the requirement is done (*kṛta-kṛtya*). [Wayman, tr.]

In the *Laṅkāvatāra*, too, the monistic world view is given special emphasis, in connection with the Mahāyānic preference for the doctrine of Mutual Causation (II: 42; ll. 7-8):

> The Bodhisattvas, the Great Beings, O Mahāmati, will have come to the attainment of the sameness (or similarity) between Nirvāṇa and Saṃsāra.

And this is explained in detail elsewhere (*Laṅkā* II: 76; ll. 7-13):

> Again, Mahāmati, whatever is (meant by) the mark of non-duality? It means that black and white, long and short, light and shade, are rising relatively, Mahāmati, and not independently from one another. Just as Nirvāṇa (is dependent upon) Saṃsāra [i.e., for its existence], so, Mahāmati, all things are non-dual. There is no Nirvāṇa, Mahāmati, (except) where is Saṃsāra, and there is no Saṃsāra (except) where is Nirvāṇa; for the condition of existence is due to causation and the act of distinguishing [between opposite things, n.n.]. Therefore, it is said that all things are non-dual, as are Nirvāṇa and Saṃsāra. For this reason, Mahāmati, the discipline should be exercised in (the realization of) no-Self-nature, non-duality, no-birth, and Voidness.

This monistic view gradually gained influence throughout the Mahāyāna literature, as may be seen from the following excerpts quoted by Wayman in his article "Dependent Origination—The

Indo-Tibetan Tradition." First, here is a significant passage from a scripture called the *Bodhisattvapiṭaka-sūtra:*[10]

> Whatever is the meaning of Dependent Origination, is the meaning of Dharma; whatever is the meaning of Dharma, is the meaning of Tathāgata. Therefore, whoever sees Dharma, sees the Tathāgata. Also, seeing that way, and accordingly fully understanding in the sense of Thusness, still one sees scarcely anything. What is that "scarcely anything?" It is the Signless and the Non-Apprehension; the one who sees in the manner of the Signless and the Non-Apprehension, sees rightly.

Later, in 14th century Tibet, Tsoṅ-kha-pa, the great reformer and synthesizer of both Mādhyamika and Yogācāra thought, made the following comment regarding the doctrine of Dependent Origination as set forth in Asaṅga's *Daśabhūmika-sūtra* and in Candrakīrti's *Mādhyamakāvatāra:*[11]

> (The Bodhisattva on the Sixth Stage) reflects on Dependent Origination (*pratītya-samutpāda*) in the forward direction . . . (and so on down to:) Thus he thinks:
>
> "Only this heap of suffering, this tree of suffering develops, devoid of a creator, a feeler (*kāraka-vedaka*)." This occurs to him: "Because of the clinging to a creator, activites are known; whenever there is no creator, there also activities are not perceptively reached in the absolute sense." This occurs to him:
>
> "These three realms are this Mind-only; whatever those twelve members of generation, all those, while explained by the Tathāgata in mutiple aspect (*prabhedasas*), in fact depend on a single *citta* (*ekacitta*)."

Along with the passages cited previously, these lines too point in the direction of Monism, derived from the doctrine of Causation, when construed as a cosmic, unifying link between all levels of existence, crisscrossing both time and space, both inner and outer dimensions of Being. Thus, gradually, as one's cosmic awareness increases, the sharp separating line between the observer and the observed, between subject and object, becomes less obvious, thereby reducing all theories to didactic stepping stones on the path towards detachment from self and of oneness with a larger Self, the universe as a whole (*samatā, tathatā, buddhatā, dharmatā,* etc.). Let us see now how the *Sūtra* addresses the finer theoretical implications of this fact.

Causation as a Teaching Device

This is yet another strand in the exposition of causality in the *Laṅkāvatāra-sūtra*. As we have pointed out in the preceding section on Citta-mātra (ch. 2.1.), the idea of Causation also may be regarded as a mere teaching device within the meditational context, the purpose of which is to help the practitioner rid his mind of attachment to the illusion of permanence, of a creator, of original cause, and other such erroneous views. Thus, we read in the *Laṅkā* II: 103, ll. 7-17:

> Now then, the Bodhisattva Mahāmati further spoke to the Blessed One thus: "Dependent Origination if further explained by the Blessed One (by saying that) what is designated as cause is (merely) an effect (and that) this is not a theory established (on the principle of) a self-animating substance" [*svanaya-prakṛti*, i.e., an allusion to the Sāṃkhya principles, here rejected].
>
> The philosophers also, O Lord, describe a (form of) causal origination when they say that the rising of (all) things is due to causes (such as): Supreme Spirit, Īśvara (Lord), a personal spirit, time, or atom. Still, the rise of all things is described by the Blessed One, through a different formula of Causation, and yet not so different in its essence and [or, excellence of] purpose? On account of (the duality of) Being and non-Being, O Blessed One, the philosophers also explain the rising of (all) things through causal factors, and having come [into existence through causation], they also disappear (by causation).
>
> That is explained by the Blessed One (thus:): "The causal factors (beginning with) ignorance, are: predispositions [*samskāra*, explained by Edgerton, op. cit., p. 542, as 'the effects of past deeds'], (which lead to) birth, old age and death. This (teaching) is described by the Blessed One as not pointing to the doctrine of Non-causality, nor is it really a doctrine of Causality."

So far, the explanation is restricted to the realm of human experience, although the refutation is supposed to be addressed to the Brahmanic philosophers (mainly Sāṃkhya-Yoga deists). However, in the second part of the dialogue, the scope of the discourse is expanded to included a general exposition of causal relations, both psychological and physical, both sudden and gradual (*Laṅkā* II: 103-104; ll. 17-18, 1-11):

> "According to the Blessed One, this (formula) is given, signifying simultaneous (causation): 'That being so, this is.' It is not used with the meaning of gradual development [or, evolution in the sense of Causality].
>
> Nevertheless, this is merely the teaching of the philosophers (which) does not surpass yours, O Blessed One. Why? Because the cause of the philosophers, O Lord, does not produce an effect (*kārya*) (in the manner of) Dependent Origination, as (your) cause (*kāraṇa*) does.
>
> For, O Blessed One, your cause has reference to its effect (*kārya*), and likewise, the effect has reference to its cause (*kāraṇa*); thus, there is an interconnection of causal links (*hetu-pratyaya-saṃkara*) and from this mutuality follows (the condition of) non-finality [or, un-settled-ness, *anavasthā*].
>
> Consequently, when someone tells you, O Blessed One, 'That being so, this is,' (it means that) in the world there is (a state of) causelessness (*ahetutvaṃ*)."
>
> The Blessed One replied: "Not so, Mahāmati, mine is not a causeless doctrine of Causation (which) is applicable to [or, results in] the comingling [or, an intermixture] of causes and conditions. When I say: 'That being so, this is,' it is because of the understanding of the unreality (*abhāvāt*) of the object [lit., grasped, *grāha*] and the subject [lit., grasping, *grāhya*], and (because of the awakening to the notion that) this is merely the seeing of one's own mind (*svacitta-dṛśya-mātra*).
>
> However, Mahāmati, when people become attached to (the duality of) object and subject, they fail to recognize that there is nothing (to be seen) but one's own mind. Their fault, Mahāmati, follows from (taking) the (duality of) Being and non-Being—which is one's own reality—as the external (Reality); in contrast, my indication is made (toward the view of) Dependent Causation (instead)."

The causation through Dependent Origination (*pratītya-samutpāda*) is here contrasted to other, non-Buddhist theories of Causation, whose one common feature was the assumption of a Self and of something other than Self (subject and object). These theories have been analysed in great detail, as well as contrasted to the Buddhist view, by David J. Kalupahana.[12] In his book on the important subject of causality, he divides the non-Buddhist theories into four major categories, as follows:

(1) **Self-causation** (*sayaṃ kataṃ, attakataṃ*), which assumes that the cause and the effect are identical in essence. It is based upon

the principle of creative evolution due to the immanent energy (*svadhā*) of nature, as presented in the Vedic and Upaniṣadic tradition (*Ṛgveda*, tenth book, *Śatapatha Brāhmaṇa*, *Aitareya Āraṇyaka*, *Śvetāśvatara*, *Kaṭha* and *Chāndogya Upaniṣads*).[13]

(2) **External causation** (*paraṃ kataṃ*), which postulates a causal factor outside the subject which experiences it, such as: Time (*kāla*), God (*Īśvarakṛtaka*), inherent nature (*svabhāva*), or natural determinism (*svabhāvavāda*), action or behavior (*karma*), and Fate (*niyativāda*). These principles were held by various naturalistic schools belonging to the non-Vedic tradition, such as the Cārvākas, the Lokāyata, the Bārhaspatya, the Ājīvikas, and even certain Buddhist sects.[14]

(3) **Internal**, as well as **external** causation (*sayaṃ katañ ca paraṃ katañ ca*), a combination of the first two theories, propounded by the Jaina relativists in the *Sūtrakṛtaṅga* and its commentary by Śilāṅka.[15] While the Jainas posited *karma* as the external cause and human exertion as an internal cause, a certain group of Theists mentioned in the *Śvetāśvatara Upaniṣad* (5.11) (according to Jayatilleke) assumed that God is the external cause and the person undergoes changes on account of his own good and evil actions.[16]

(4) **Neither internal nor external** (*asayamkāraṃ aparamkāraṃ*), or indeterminism (*adhiccasamuppanna*), which denies any form of causation. It was explained by the Buddhist commentator Dhammapāla with the following words: "*Adhiccasamuppanna* means 'arisen by chance' (*yadicchāya*); it is called the theory of 'fortuitous origination' because events arise without any cause. Therefore, even *ahetukavāda* ('the theory of no-cause') is to be included in it."[17] Jayatilleke identifies this theory with the *niyativāda* of the Ājīvikas, but his attribution is questioned by Kalupahana.[18]

At any rate, *all* these theories are rejected by the two major Mahāyāna schools. In the very first verse of the *Mūlamādhyamika-kārikā* 1.1, Nāgārjuna states:[19]

> na svato nāpi parato na dvābhyāṃ nāpy ahetutaḥ/
> utpannā jātu vidyante bhāvāḥ kva cana ke cana//
>
> At nowhere and at no time can entities (*bhāva*) ever be found to exist by originating out of themselves, from other (than themselves), from both (self and other), or from lack of cause(s).

The position adopted by the *Laṅkāvatāra* is not dissimilar to that presented in the earlier Mādhyamika writings of teachers such as Nāgārjuna. For its author, like for Nāgārjuna, the question regarding the gradual or simultaneous rising of the effect from its cause, does not represent a problem. This is because they are both rejected, just as the entire system of causal relations is ultimately discarded as mental fabrication without corresponding reality in the external world. Therefore, one may safely assume that, from the vantage point expressed in the *Laṅkāvatāra*, the value of any causal theory is not so much ontological, or even epistemological, but rather, and ultimately, soteriological. In the end, it is the experience of spiritual freedom from the anguish caused by ignorance, mental habits of discrimination, speculation, etc., that matters for the Yogācāra Buddhist.

To be sure, in order to prove this point, the author develops a complex argument that runs in several stages, skillfully leading the reader from one level of understanding of causality to the next. First, there is an enumeration of six types of causal situations or processes that may occur among phenomena. These six types are apparently found only in the *Laṅkāvatāra*. They seem to indicate that during the early phase of the development of the Mahāyāna thought, there was no unified theory of Causation as such, except perhaps for the general agreement regarding the principle of Dependent Origination (*pratītya-samutpāda*). Various detailed interpretations of this broad principle were adopted independently from one another.[20] Even among the Yogācāra authors, the types of causation varied not only in number, but also in terminology.[21] Therefore, one can say that the causal terms used in the *Laṅkā* are not representative for the Yogācāra as a whole, but rather they are one variation among several others. Here is the list of the six types of causes (according to circumstances), and their respective explanations (*Laṅkā* II: 83-84; ll. 8-17, 1):

> Now, Mahāmati, the cause [or causation, *hetu*] is of six kinds, namely: (1) Impending-cause, (2) Dependence-cause, (3) Characteristic-cause, (4) Instrument-cause, (5) Manifesting-cause, and (6) Abandonment-cause.
>
> Therefore: (1) The Impending-cause (*bhaviṣya-hetu*), Mahāmati, (means that) when a cause is to become effective, there is the rising of things, internally and externally [or, inner and outer];
>
> (2) Further, Mahāmati, the Dependence-cause (*saṃbandha-hetu*) (means that) when the dependent condition is to become effective, there is the rising of the seeds of the personality-aggregates, inner and outer;
>
> (3) Furthermore, Mahāmati, the Characteristic-cause (*lakṣaṇa-hetu*) (means that) an uninterrupted indication of continuity of action is produced;

(4) Again, Mahāmati, the Instrumental-cause (*kāraṇa-hetu*) (means that) when a cause is invested with supreme authority, it becomes effective [or, asserts itself] like a sovereign ruler;

(5) Further, Mahāmati, the Manifesting-cause (*vyañjana-hetu*) (means that) on account of the rising of the state of discrimination, there is the rising of individual marks, which become effective just as the forms, etc., are produced out of a lamp;

(6) Lastly, Mahāmati, the Abandonment-cause (*upekṣa-hetu*) (means that) when there is the rising of the state of non-discrimination, there is an interruption of the activity of the system [or combination of *vijñānas*] (and) in time, their (complete) discontinuance takes place [or, is effectuated].

Having outlined these six types of causal categories, the *Sūtra* goes on to the next step of unequivocally denying their absolute validity. This is accomplished by means of a skillfully argued rejection of both the gradual and simultaneous rising of the effects from their causes (*Laṅkā* II: 84; ll. 2-15):

These, Mahāmati, [i.e., the six causal categories] are fabricated through one's discrimination by the immature and the commoners, and there is neither gradual evolving [or evolution], nor do they [i.e., the effects from causes] occur simultaneously [i.e., through sudden revolution]. Why? Because again, Mahāmati, if there were a simultaneous development, there would be no shared portion between cause and effect, and there would be nothing to characterize a cause (as such).

Now, if there is gradual development, there would evolve out of the inherent nature of the individual forms (something) incongruous [lit., un-met with previously]; (therefore), gradual development does not occur.

Like the term "father" to the unborn child, Mahāmati, the simultaneous, together with the gradual rising, are not possible. (According to) the logicians, there is a cause, a beginning, continuation, and climax; (there are) generated (effects) and generating (cause), along with causal conditions, and so on; (but) Mahāmati, these do not rise in gradual evolution (*krama-vṛttyā*).

> Nor does the simultaneous rising take place, Mahāmati, (except on account of) one's individual attachment to one's own nature of discrimination. (Categories discriminated as): existence and non-existence of the external (world), one's specific and generic (attributes), one's material existence (composed of) body, food and habitat, (are only) seen in one's own mind, (and therefore), O Mahāmati, the simultaneous, along with the gradual [types of causation] do not take place (in actuality). Otherwise, the perception (*vijñāna*) (of categories) develops on account of discrimination which discriminates what is (only) seen in one's own mind. Consequently, Mahāmati, you must become (free) by desisting from the views of simultaneous and gradual (causation), characterized by the combination of (causal) agent (*kriyā*), (causal) conditions (*pratyaya*), and (principal, or main) cause (*hetu*).

After denying the reality of the six types of causal situations, and now the possibility of their sudden or gradual emergence, the author, in a relentless display of dialectical vigor, will reach the climax of his argument, namely, the refutation of the idea of Causality itself. Coincidently or not, the discourse shifts at this point (as if caught in a flight of inspiration) from argumentative prose to metaphysical poetry. Here are the gāthas which follow immediately after the above citation (*Laṅkā* II: 84-85, gāthas 140-144):

> Thus it is said:
>
> "Indeed, nothing whatever rises or disappears through [or, by reason of] causal factors [or, conditions, *pratyaya*]. (For), it is merely when causal conditions are discriminated that they [or, things?] rise and disappear.
>
> (On account of) causal relations [i.e., discriminated as such], the affliction (*saṃkleśa*) of birth and destruction is not stopped; (But) wherever the immature discriminate, that (affliction, or pain) is stopped along with (the stopping of) causal conditions.
>
> The Being and non-Being of things subject to [or, produced from] causal conditions do not exist; It is by reason of habit-energy that the mind is erroneously known as the triple world.
>
> Not being existent, nothing whatever is born or disappears through causal conditions; When one regards the effect-producing cause (*saṃskṛta*) like a flower in the sky, or (like a) barren woman's child, then one having perceived the subject

> [lit., grasping, *grāhya*] and the object [lit., the grasped, *grāha*] as an error (*bhrānti*), one turns away (from it).
>
> And there is nothing to be born, and nothing that has been born, nor is there even something (called) Causation; Then where and whence is the (causal) action said to be found?"

The answer to this paramount question is contained in the quintessential expression of the Yogācāra-Vijñānavāda school, namely Mind-only, or Representation-only (*Citta-mātra, Vijñapti-mātra*), elucidated in the preceding chapter with the same title (see: ch. 2.1.). This expression points out, as we have shown, the continuous evaluative, and yet deluding activity of the mind, the source of suffering which needs to be transcended in order to achieve true insight into the nature of Reality, free from discrimination (here called *tathatā, bhūtatā,* or *śūnyatā*). These examples from the *Sagāthakam* illustrate the point (p. 312 gāthas 366-68):

> Nothing is produced, and yet things are being set in motion; nothing disappears, and yet things are falling away (from sight); it (all) resembles the simultaneous (reflections of the) moon in the water, seen over a multitude of sites.
>
> Unity [or, oneness] having become plurality [or, manyness, multiplicity], and the rains falling, or the fires burning; having (all) thoughts produced in the mind, they [i.e., the Tathāgatas] declare that there is nothing but the mind.
>
> The (idea of) Mind-only is in the mind, and the (idea of) No-mind is also produced by the mind; (thus) understood, the appearances of various forms are produced in the mind only.

If both *Mind* and *No-mind* ideas are nothing but mental products, and the concept of *Mind-only* refers to the unifying vision acquired in the process of yogic contemplation, as a result of the immediacy of the experience of Enlightenment (as previously indicated in our discussion of the Citta-mātra concept, chapter 2.1.), then on the discursive, philosophical plane, the idea of *Mind-only* can best be understood in relation to the Dependent Origination (*pratītya-samutpāda*) and the Middle Way (*madhyamā-pratipad*) concepts about the nature of Reality, as expounded in many Mādhyamika and Yogācāra works, including the *Laṅkāvatāra*. Thus, in the *Sagāthakam*, certain verses seem to underscore the distinction between the self-deluding mental activity and the external Reality as such by means of the correct understanding of the Middle Path (with respect to causation).

First, we find the following exposition of the philosophers' mistaken apprehension of the nature of causality through the Middle Path (*Sagāthakam:* 310 vv. 355-57):

> [According to the philosophers] there is an entity (born of) no cause, which is free from either permanency or impermanency and removed from the alternatives of Being and non-Being; this they imagine to be the Middle Path (of causation).
>
> They (also) imagine the theory of No-cause; (but their) No-cause is (the equivalent of) the doctrine of Nihilism. As they fail to comprehend the real nature of the external (world), they destroy [or, miss entirely the meaning of] the Middle Path.
>
> The attachment to existence is not relinquished, lest they be considered Nihilists; (so) they try to teach the (meaning of) the Middle Path by means of denial and affirmation [i.e., in a contradictory manner].

The author then goes on to explain the meaning of the Middle Path in connection with the view of Dependent Origination of all things, and their lack of Self-nature (*naiḥ-svabhāvyam*) (gāthas 358-61):

> Through the understanding of Mind-only, (the attachment to) the external objects (is/) are abandoned; (this is) the end [or, completion] of discrimination, and (thus) the Middle Path is entered upon.
>
> They [the philosophers] do not understand Mind-only (which) is not produced by the visible objects; this is taught by myself and other [Tathāgatas] as the attainment of the Middle (Path).
>
> Birth and No-birth, existence and non-existence—the lack of self-nature of (all) things (is called) Voidness; (therefore) the two-fold nature (of things) is not possible [or, is not to be conceived].
>
> The condition of the activity of discrimination is not the emancipation that the immature ones imagine; (for) without understanding (the nature of) mental activity, the attachment to duality is not destroyed.

Lastly, the author states that it is only by renouncing this intellectual attachment to the mode of cognition characterized by dividing, or discriminating the world through mutually definable categories, that the true nature of reality (here called Suchness, *tathatā*) can reveal itself (gāthas 362-63):

> (But) as it is understood that the seeing is of one's own mind (only), the attachment to duality is destroyed; thorough knowledge, indeed, is the abandonment, not the destruction of the discriminated (object).
>
> As it becomes thoroughly known that the seeing is of the mind (only), discrimination is stopped; (and) as the stopping of discrimination (occurs), Suchness is relinquished from the intellect (*citta*).

This criticism was not new, however, since Buddha himself warned against discriminating views (Pāli: *diṭṭhi*).[22] Its full development is found in the radical critique of all philosophical positions which characterizes the Mādhyamika school, beginning with Nāgārjuna. It may be helpful, therefore, to pause for a moment and contrast Nāgārjuna's position regarding Causality to that expressed in the *Laṅkāvatāra*. The similarity between the two may thus come to the fore, which would indicate that the author of the *Sūtra* was not only familiar with, but had thoroughly assimilated, the teachings of this most celebrated Mahāyāna master.

Excursus: Highlighting Nāgārjuna's Thought in Respect to Causation

We pointed out earlier in the first sub-section that the Buddhist theory of Causation was first formulated at the empirical, psychological level in the form of the twelve-fold Chain of Causation and only later expanded to cover the nature of the world as such, in the ontological sense.[23] It is also important to note that from its very beginnings, the theory of Causation was associated with the concept of the Middle Path between the two extremes, such as the belief in existence (*atthitā*) and non-existence (*natthitā*). Both were rejected by the Buddha as leading to two equally wrong doctrines, those of Eternalism (*sassatavāda*) and Annihilationism (*ucchedavāda*), respectively. This position was maintained continuously throughout the development of Buddhist thought, from the early Abhidharmists to the later Mahāyāna writers.[24] The Mādhyamikas, in particular, made the Middle Way (*madhyamā pratipad*) the cornerstone of their teachings.

Nāgārjuna, for instance, in his celebrated *Mūlamadhyamika-kārikās* (15.10), states:[25]

astīti śāśvatagrāho nāstīty ucchedadarśanaṃ/
tasmād astitvanāstitve nāśrīyata vicakṣaṇaḥ//

(The theory that everything) exists is the adherence to Eternalism; (the theory that) nothing exists is the doctrine of Annihilationism. Therefore, the wise should not adhere to either of these (two views of) existence and non-existence.

According to Nāgārjuna, the only acceptable alternative to these two views is the Relational Origination (*pratītya-samutpāda*). This is clearly stated in the opening dedicatory verses of the *kārikās*, the so-called Mādhyamika Creed:[26]

anirodham anutpādam anucchedam aśāśvataṃ/
anekārtham anānārtham anāgamam anirgamaṃ//

yaḥ pratītyasamutpādaṃ prapañcopaśamaṃ śivaṃ/
deśayāmāsa saṃbuddhastaṃ vande vadatāṃ varaṃ//

I pay homage to the Fully Awakened One,
the supreme teacher who has taught
the doctrine of Dependent Origination,
the cessation [lit., calming] of (all)
deceitful thought-constructions,

which is (characterized by both):
non-origination (and) non-extinction,
non-destruction (and) non-permanence,
non-identity (and) non-differentiation,
non-coming (into being, and) non-going (out of being).

Furthermore, in the first verse of the first chapter on Causal Relation (or, Condition, *pratyaya*), this denial of opposite alternatives is extended to all possible relational conditions between cause and effect, by means of the fourfold negation formula (*catuṣkoṭi*):

na svato nāpi parato na dvābhyāṃ nāpy ahetutaḥ/
utpannā jātu vidyante bhāvāḥ kvacana ke cana// (1.1)

Nowhere and at no time can objects be found to originate from themselves, from something else, from both (self and other), or from no cause. (1.1)

As the common notion of a primary causal condition (*hetu-pratyaya*) is found without real support in reality, the very idea of Causation, in the simplistic sense in which it is asserted by the speculative philosophers (Buddhist and non-Buddhist), is utterly rejected by Nāgārjuna:

> na san nāsan na sad asan dharmo nirvartate yadā/
> kathaṃ nirvartako hetur evaṃ sati hi yujyate// (1.7)
>
> If an element of existence does not evolve from Being, or non-Being, nor from both Being and non-Being, how can a cause be referred to [lit., abolished], or, indeed, even thought upon [or, meditated upon]? (1.7)

In the seventh chapter of the *Kārikās*, devoted to the analysis of the composite nature of Reality (*Saṃskṛta-parīkṣā*), Nāgārjuna arrives at the following conclusions regarding the triple nature of the causal process (i.e., origination, *utpāda*, duration, *sthiti*, and cessation, *bhaṅga*):

> yadaiva sarvadharmāṇāṃ utpādo nopapadyate/
> tadaivaṃ sarvadharmāṇāṃ nirodho nopapadyate// (7.29)
>
> utpādasthitibhaṅgānām asiddher nāsti saṃskṛtaṃ/
> saṃskṛtasyāprasiddhau ca kathaṃ setsyaty asaṃskṛtaṃ// (7.33)
>
> yathā māyā yathā svapno gandharvanagaraṃ yathā/
> tathotpādastathā sthānaṃ tathā bhaṅga udāhṛtaṃ// (7.34)
>
> Since the origination of all elements of existence does not occur, so (also) the cessation of all elements [of existence, *dharmas*] is not possible. (7.29)
>
> Because of the non-substantiation of [the factuality of] origination, duration, and destruction, and without the establishment of the composite Reality, how could a non-composite Reality be proven? (7.33)
>
> So, just like an illusion, a dream, or a city in the sky, in the same manner the (concepts of) origination, duration and cessation have been named [or, set up]. (7.34)

In another, lesser known work, the *Mahāyānaviṃśaka*, which appears very close to the *Laṅkāvatāra* in conceptual outlook, Nāgārjuna reiterates this denial of absolute, independent reality of either origination (*utpāda*) or cessation (*nirodha*), and reasserts the fictitious nature of all mental constructs:[27]

> māyaiva dṛśyate māyānirmitaṃ saṃmskṛtam yadā/
> naiva kiṃ cit tadā bhāvo dharmāṇāṃ sarva dharmatā// (18)
>
> cittramātraṃ idaṃ sarvaṃ māyāvad avatiṣṭhate/
> tataḥ śubhāśubhaṃ karma tato jātiḥ śubhāśubhā// (19)
>
> If the composite nature of Reality is (only) imagined, and even the illusion (itself) is regarded as illusion, then there is nothing whatever (which can be regarded, or called as) "the real thing" —Such is the nature of all elements of existence. (18)
>
> All this is nothing but thought [or mind, *citta*] and exists only as an illusion. Hence, the good and evil action, and from them the auspicious and inauspicious birth. (19)

Clearly, we can observe here that quite early in the Mahāyāna literature, the Citta-mātra concept was used with the equivalent sense of illusion (*māya*), ignorance, error, delusion (*moha*, verse 17), fancy, imagination, false discrimination, or notion (*vikalpa, vikalpitā*, verse 18b). The real truth (*bhūta-ārtha*), however, says Nāgārjuna (verse 15) is the Dependent Origination (*pratītya-samutpāda*), which is the same as the Void, without beginning, middle or end (*śūnyam ādimadhyānta-varjitam*, verse 15). It resembles the sky in that it has neither origination nor cessation (verse 2), "it is devoid of any duality and remains always and in all circumstances in the same way" (*tathatā*, verse 4). The world being made of appearances is perceived as "illusory and it exists only on account of its cause and conditions" (verse 9).

From this brief excursion into the thought of Nāgārjuna, it appears obvious that the Yogācāra writers did not really invent the Citta-mātra concept, nor were they the first in establishing the discrepancy between the mental habit of discrimination (through dual categories of thought), on the one hand, and the integral, non-dual, monistic nature of Reality, on the other. It was the merit of the Yogācāras, however (such as the author of the *Laṅkāvatāra*), to have fully developed the epistemological implications of these concepts, especially in relation to the theory of Causation (*hetu-pratyaya*).

The Soteriological Value of the Theory of Causation

Having pointed out the essential empirical fact that all processes of discrimination take place in the mind, the late Abhidharmists arrived at the idea of Mind-only in regard to the interpretation of the interaction between various phenomena. From here, some late Mahāyāna philosophers or commentators, as well as certain modern interpreters or translators, made the misleading assumption (by obviously extrapolating from the mental onto the metaphysical, existential level of reference) that the entire external world was made up of fleeting appearances that lacked objective reality, or existence.[28] However, as I have previously argued, contending that the world evinces an illusory character does not necessarily mean that the objective universe is unreal, just as the idea that the world is devoid of self-existence (*niḥsvabhāva*) does not imply that it is devoid of existence altogether, or that it is non-existent. This is the point which Nāgārjuna, along with his disciples Āryadeva and Candrakīrti (and certain Yogācāra writers as well) never tire of making, thereby refuting all accusations of nihilism.[29]

The *Laṅkāvatāra*, too, insists on this subtle but crucial distinction, as illustrated by the following verses (III: 200-1; vv. 86-87, 92-94, 96-97):

> For the sake of removing (the notion of) birth [or causal origination, *utpāda*], and rendering clear (the notion of) no-birth [or non-production, *anutpāda*], I teach the doctrine of No-cause [or Non-Causation, *ahetu-vāda*]; but (this) is not comprehended by the immature (ones).
>
> All this (world) is un-originated [or, un-created], but that does not mean that there are no earthly objects (*bhāva*); they seem like an illusion, a dream, a phantasm, (for) the objects are found (to be) causeless (*ahetuka*).
>
> If compounded things are perceived as (arising) neither from causes, nor without cause [or, are neither subject to causation, nor above it], then the view (maintained by) the opponent (teachers) about origination and destruction is averted [or layed aside].
>
> Is non-existence really no-birth? That is, is an investigation of

causal relations (*pratyaya*) (really possible)? Therefore, is this being's name without object? Please, tell me!

Truly, non-existence is not no-birth, nor is the investigation of causal factors (possible); however, this being's name is not a name without a (corresponding) object (behind it).

The removal of the (notion of) (primary) cause and of causal conditions, the cessation of the instrumental cause [or, causal agent, *kāraṇa*], and the establishment of nothing but the mind [as the source of the notion of Causality]—this I call Non-origination.

The practice of non-cause (means) freeing oneself from [the duality, or the idea of] imagined and imagining of objects; (it means) liberating oneself from the alternatives of Being and non-Being—this I call the doctrine of Non-origination.

From this assessment of the futility of entertaining any causal notions to the complete abandonment of all philosophical views, there seems indeed to emerge in the *Laṅkāvatāra-sūtra* (and later in the development of Ch'an Buddhism) a relentless drive toward a certain kind of spiritual condition which is absoutely free from any cognitive associations. There is, however, a pragmatic motivation behind such denial, for, in India, the pursuit of knowledge never lacked the depth of the existential concern for self-fulfillment and inner realization. Here is how the *Sūtra* sums up its considerations regarding Causation (III: 202-203; vv. 99, 100, 103-104):

There is no external existence, nor non-existence, and not even comprehension through the mind, (for they are like) a dream, a hair net-like apparition, an illusion, a phantasm, a mirage [lit., a "deer-thirst"]; rather, the abandonment of all (philosophical) views [about Causation?]—this is what characterizes No-birth.

And the bundle of causal relations is rising and falling, but by becoming separated from the bundle, one is neither born, nor annihilated.

Nothing is generated, there is neither Being nor non-Being, nowhere is there Being-and-non-Being (found by themselves), except when there is a system [of causal relations, or conditions], within which there is (only) the rising and dissolution (of things).

> Even this chain of mutual (origination) is to be regarded as a mere convention, (for) apart from the chain of causal relations, the (idea of) origination does not even make sense [lit., there is not even meaning in the notion of birth].

And this is how the author of the *Sūtra* justifies the rejection of all explanations of Causality, namely on salvific rather than epistemic ground (*Laṅkā* III: 204; vv. 113-15, 117):

> When what is born is non-existent, from what causal relation would it be understood? Things are indeed mutually originating and it is by that (mutual origination) that causal conditions are being taught (to arise).
>
> Heat, fluidity, solidity—these are things discriminated (only) by the immature; (for) this is a system (of relations) and not (of individual) entities; hence the denial of self-nature-hood (of things).
>
> The physician renders his treatment differentially, according to his strong authority [or, quick wish]; (for), although there is no variety of principles [or doctrines of healing], the treatment does differ, however, on account of the variety of diseases.
>
> My doctrine [or, teaching, correction, *śāsana*] does not vary with the differentiated power of the senses (*indriya*) and of (different) afflictions (of people, *kleśas*); (for) even though there is only one vehicle [of salvation, *yāna*], there may be an auspicious eightfold path (*mārga*).

Thus, in the ultimate sense, the system of causes and conditions (*hetu-pratyaya*) is to be regarded as just another teaching device employed by the master for the purpose of closing the gap between the inner and outer realities. The denial of birth and annihilation is a display of the teacher's skill in means (*upāya-kauśalya*) aimed at removing the faulty views of causation, such as the emergence of one separate entity from another, apart from causal conditions. Causality proves itself to be an ultimately intractable network of causal relations between a multiplicity of external factors and compounded objects. Therefore, the investigation of the entire system (or bundle) of causal conditions is not really possible (*na pratyayavīkṣaṇam*). The religious goal, however, means to free oneself from such futile, and tormenting pursuits, as speculating about various views and theories of Causation.

Concluding Observations

This differentiated teaching in regard to causality (i.e., the multiplicity of causal relations, *hetu-pratyaya,* on the one hand, and the denial of the possibility, as well as the validity of a thoroughgoing causal theory, on the other), gave rise to a certain epistemological inconsistency, or unresolved tension between the two points of view, namely: the immediate, or empirical, and the ultimate, or transcendental (here called *āryajñāna,* as opposed to *vijñāna,* or discriminative knowledge). The solution to this problem is best described by Suzuki in the following lines (of his *Studies,* p. 300):

> . . . It is from this point of view [i.e., of the absolute, supreme wisdom, *āryajñāna,* n.n.] that the world is now describable as unborn, with no self-substance, and unconditionally empty and not at all limited by causation. Birthlessness (*anutpāda*) or emptiness does not belong to the domain of our relative consciousness. The sutra in this respect is quite explicit lest the unwary should slip at this point. The development and definite assertion later in the Mādhyamika school of the conception of twofold truth, Saṃvṛti and Paramārtha, or worldly and transcendental, is the natural consequences of the positions taken up by the *Laṅkāvatāra.*

In other words, according to Suzuki, in their obstinate efforts to achieve an unqualified unifying vision of Reality (monism), the author(s) of the *Laṅkāvatāra* were forced to admit the *epistemic* duality in regard to perception. For, the ontic domain (which includes here both Being and non-Being) only *appears* to be multi-faceted, or multi-phenomenal (to the empirical mind), when under ultimate analysis it is void (of self-existence, *svabhāva*), and therefore, unborn, unoriginated, uncreated (*anutpāda*).

Indeed, according to the *Laṅkāvatāra,* the notion of a Creator (such as Īśvara, Pradhāna, or Brahmā) is due to mental activity of imagination, or discrimination (*vikalpa, vikalpitā*). The analysis of Causation with its three distinct aspects (namely, primary cause, *hetu;* causal conditions, *pratyaya,* and instrumental, or agency cause, *kāraṇa,* or *karyā*) is itself a mental construct due to imagination. Therefore, the reader is urged throughout the *Sūtra* to attain the transcendental mental state of pure concentration (*prajñā, parijñā, samatā-jñāna, abhisaṃbodha,* etc.),[30] the only state of consciousness that can *perceive* the primal condition of Non-origination, or Non-causation, that is to say, the primal *unity* behind the diversity of the phenomenal world. *This* is the state of Mind-only, as we have indicated above (vide: *Laṅkā* III: 201, gātha 96).[31]

But Suzuki, on the other hand, goes one step further, by interpreting the whole matter in a different light, when he concludes the following (in *Studies,* 272):

> The logical necessity of reaching the ultimate notion of unity has made the author of the *Laṅkāvatāra* accept the doctrine of "Mind-only" instead of that of "matter-only." When no creator is recognised and all forms of dualism are set aside as not in accord with the real state of things, there remain two ways for achieving the unification of thought, realism and idealism; and as the *Laṅkāvatāra* denies the reality of an external world (*vishaya*), or outside objects (*bāhyabhāva*) that are characterised with multitudinousness (*vicitratā*), the doctrine of "Mind-only" seems to be the natural conclusion. The philosophical thesis of the present sutra is thus an *absolutely idealistic monism.* (Italics mine, n.n.)

Our analysis, however, led us to different conclusions, for there are ways of solving this classical dilemma (between unmitigated realism and uncompromizing idealism) without taking recourse to such clearcut "either/or" absolutisms. For instance, as far as the concepts put forth in the *Laṅkāvatāra* are concerned, one may very well say that its author(s) asserted an *epistemological dualism* (true, of a very biased idealistic sort, by emphasizing the Citta-mātra state of knowing over the empirical Vijñāna state), while becoming *dialectical relativists* (i.e., *quasi*-dualists, or *almost* monists) in respect to their *ontology.* This we have already demonstrated by developing at some point or another, the following three arguments:

(1) The external, objective world (*traidhātuka*) is never clearly denied in the *Laṅkāvatāra,* in spite of its illusory character, due to the fallibility of empirical perception, and the super-imposition of our misconstructed judgments;

(2) If the world were nothing but Mind (Citta-mātra), why would Enlightenment (*pratyaksaṃbodhi*) be needed? And, as a corrolary of that, whence would ignorance, the impure accretions (*kleśas*), and the evil deeds (*karma*) originate? For, indeed, there must be somewhere in the world (which is supposedly "nothing but Mind") something which is essentially different (i.e., other than Mind), to account for their existence and continuous efficacy; and finally,

(3) To assert that the Yogācāra philosophy is an absolute monistic idealism would amount to attributing to the Yogācāras a

specific philosophical point of view, which would be against their transcendental position based upon the tetralemma logic, and sustained throughout the *Sūtra*, as we have seen.

Thus, in regards to causation, the Mind (*citta*) *neither is, nor is not* identical with the external world, since the two are in a relation of mutual dialectical interaction and dynamic interdependence. For, just as Nirvāṇa cannot be conceived without Saṃsāra, so does the reflecting Subject (i.e., Mind, *citta*) exist because of the Object (i.e., the external world, *loka, tribhava, traidhātuka*), and conversely, the Object is defined as such due to the existence of a Subject which perceives it (apart from itself). Consequently, to affirm the *absolute* existence of one over the other (i.e., Subject only = absolute idealism; Object only = absolute realism) would be in direct contradiction with the most fundamental Buddhist idea of causality through Interdependent Origination of all things (*pratītya-samutpāda*), as well as against the concept of the Middle Way between extreme philosophical views.

Therefore, in light of the above analysis, one is forced to conclude that the Yogācāra author(s) of the *Laṅkāvatāra-sūtra* did not ultimately intend to present a water-tight monistic, or any other one-sided view of the universe. The philosophical thesis of this sūtra *is not* (as Suzuki said) "an absolutely idealistic monism," but rather a radical *critique* of the absolutizing tendency of the mind (i.e., of the habit of reification of concepts) mounted from the point of view of the Mahāyāna dialectical relativism (both logical and ontic) and soteriology. The form of *qualified monism* it developed should *not* be regarded as an *absolutism* based upon the Mind-only doctrine writ large, but as yet another kind of Mahāyāna *relativism* (along with that developed by Nāgārjuna and his followers) based upon the causal theory of Dependent Origination (of the mind vis-à-vis the world) and dialectical logic.[32]

To say, as Suzuki does (and there are others as well, as I had the opportunity to indicate above), that "it would be unreasonable of us to expect anything systematically or logically thoroughgoing in the *Laṅkāvatāra*" (*Studies*, p. 276), would mean to throw in the hermeneutical towel, something which he himself, obviously, was not willing to do.

3.0. Final Overview

During the last one hundred years or so, Western philosophy has become increasingly preoccupied with problems of logic, language, and meaning, thereby relaxing the traditional focus on ontological categories, such as: mind-matter, time-space, determinism-freedom, relative and absolute principles, and so forth. In this modern context, the so-called Oxford, Cambridge, and Vienna schools of philosophy have been instrumental in advancing a new methodological outlook, based on logical analysis (whether mathematically or linguistically oriented), which from its beginnings has never ceased to affect, one way or another, all fields of human inquiry. Linguistic analysis, particularly (i.e., the study of the value and meaning of words and of their usefulness in knowing reality) has been held by some to be heralding an epoch-making, true Copernican "revolution in philosophy."[1]

With all due respect for the remarkable clarification concerning the modes and the limits of knowledge, brought about by this presumably modern shift of perspective from the ontological to the epistemological domain (Kant is believed to have been the first to proceed upon this path), may we suggest that from the larger standpoint of the history of human thought, such radical turn is neither so new, nor so revolutionary as it may seem. For Buddhism, a culture with an effervescent development spanning twenty-five centuries of continuous history, has known even more radical solutions to similar problems confronting all mankind, namely: the relation between substance and appearance, between Being and Becoming, between logical Truth and objective Reality, between cause and effect, between self and the world, on the one hand, and the question of reconciliation of contradictory claims set forth by various schools of thought, on the other. And as we have already pointed out, some of the Buddhist answers to all these questions were at least as radical, as new and original, as the Western world has seen in the last hundred years or so of intellectual innovation and discovery.

Moreover, Buddhism, as a particular type of religio-philosophical mode of interpreting the world, did not suddenly appear out of a cultural vacuum. Rather, it gradually emerged, meandering over a fertile soil of competing ideas more or less crystallized into various schools of thought, some orthodox (i.e., maintaining continuity with the ancient Vedic and Brahmanic tradition), some radically antinomian. Out of this rich cultural environment, over the centuries, a process of creative selection took place which at some point in time, under the nourishing influence of certain powerful personalities, blossomed out into a world of ideas as magnificent and profound as they were new and original.

Now, the highest point, or better yet, the highest plateau in this historical development, was the creative synthesis that can be placed chronologically some time between the first and the fifth centuries A.D. in Indian history. By this time, all important ideas (i.e., the impermanent and the ever-evolving nature of Reality, the non-substantial and dynamic nature of Self, the universal Void, the fourfold dialectics or tetralemma, the Dependent Origination of all things, the cognitive and depth psychology of Enlightenment, the primacy of Self-realization and of practical experience over theoretical speculation), have already been formulated in one form or another. This was also the period when Buddhist ideas began to exert a powerful and long-lasting impact upon other cultures as well, not only in India, but, more importantly, outside the subcontinent, stretching its far-reaching influence in all four directions: from Indonesia in the South to Mongolia in the North, and from Japan in the East to Greece and Egypt in the West.

It was also at this time that the *Laṅkāvatāra-sūtra* was written and compiled as a major synthesis of the most widely circulating ideas of both the Hīnayāna and the Mahāyāna branches of Buddhism. It was to have a great impact on the subsequent development of the last truly creative and influential school of Mahāyāna Buddhism in India, that of the Yogācāra. Later on, following Buddhist missionary activities in China and beyond, it contributed to the foundation of one of the most popular and original currents of thought in Asia: Zen (Ch'an) Buddhism. Its impact upon the medieval and modern history of Japan, for instance, cannot be underestimated.

That is why we have attempted in this work the immensely difficult task of bringing into clear focus the two pillars of thought upon which the Yogācāra philosophy rests, as preserved in the *Laṅkāvatāra* and other related texts. These two main pillars (which define the essential outline of any coherent worldview, for that matter) are: (1) its description of Being, its **ontology**, and (2) its mode of Knowing, its **epistemology**, broadly defined.

In pursuing the **former**, we found it useful to follow certain guidelines laid out by the German existentialist philosopher Edmund Husserl, the founder of phenomenology. According to him, Being as such, or to use his expression, Being-in-the-world (*Dasein*) can be defined along three dimensions, namely, its *essence*, its *temporal*, and its *spatial* coordinates. Therefore, we have selected, perhaps somewhat arbitrarily (but does not any hermeneutical effort involve a good measure of subjective selection of data, method, and focus?) three distinctive Buddhist concepts treated in the *Laṅkāvatāra* at great length, namely: the Tathāgata-garbha, the five Skandhas, and the Dharmadhātu.

First, the inner "essence" of Being is symbolized in Mahāyāna metaphysics by the technical term: Tathāgata-garbha (ch. 1.1.). It has broad usage in the *Laṅkā*, as well as other related texts. Its meaning varies, however, depending upon the context. Thus, as "essential, supramundane pure dharma," it is constantly being compared and contrasted with the Upaniṣadic (Hindu) notion of Ātman. It is pointed out that it does *not* represent a metaphysical "substance," or "substratum" underlying the universe, as Ātman does, but rather it is to be understood as a merely metaphysical construct, without ontological validity *per se*, devised by the Master as a didactic tool for the benefit of those who cannot yet grasp the terrifying truth of the ego-lessness of all things (*dharma-nairātmya*) and of Voidness (Śūnyatā).

As "embryo," "womb," and "matrix" of Buddhahood, the concept can also provide the disciple with a great deal of inspirational power, since it symbolically represents the "seed" of Buddhahood present in all things, as well as the ideal embodied in the religious Law, or Dharma, which envelops the entire universe with its receptive, womb-like quality.

Next follows the "temporal" manifestation of Being as the ever-evolving psycho-physical aggregates which make up the human personality, the five Skandhas (ch. 1.2.). Unlike the *inner* "essence" which is not directly manifested, the Skandhas along with the Dharmadhātu, which we have designated as their "spatial" correlate, represent the concrete, direct *outer* manifestations of Being in the physical world.[2] The Skandhas, of course, represent one of the most radical and original contributions made by Buddhist thought to the age-old effort of man towards a better understanding of himself. Instead of a rigid, indivisible metaphysical entity called Self, soul, or Ātman, the Buddhists introduced the dynamic, empirical notion of five interwoven strands, or streams of events, which together form a dynamic river of energy, accounting for the baffling mystery of human personality.

Now, while the Skandhas stand for the *personal* aspect of the manifestation of Being, Dharmadhātu (lit., the "Realm-of-the-existential-elements") indicates its *impersonal*, cosmic manifestation (ch. 1.3.). Therefore, they are to be seen in a complementary relationship to one another, one being the more subjective aspect of Being, the other its objectification in "space" (both physical, the Cosmos as a whole with its natural Law, and metaphysical, as the cosmic Void, Śūnya, the very ground of Being). Naturally, since Buddhism is a *religious* philosophy, both Dharmadhātu and the Skandhas are treated in their dual dimensions: both empirical and trans-empirical.

The **second** part of the study sets out to systematize the essential epistemic structure underlying the Buddhist worldview by using as paradigm, or key to its understanding, a revolutionary form of dialectical reasoning, developed by the Buddhists themselves: the tetralemma (*catuṣkoṭi*). The four limbs of the Buddhist form of dialectics are: (1) Affirmation; (2) Negation; (3) Conjunction of both; and (4) Disjunction (i.e., neither affirmation nor negation, hedging). Subsequently, we have selected four crucial epistemological concepts which not only define the Yogācāra school and its place in Buddhist history, but also beautifully illustrate particular doctrinal instances in which the four alternatives of the tetralemma may be applied.

Thus, the first *affirmative* alternative is exemplified by the much debated notion of "Mind-only" (Citta-mātra) (ch. 2.1.). We have shown that, while it is true that it dominates the Yogācāras' epistemological outlook, it does not represent (as many believe) a forthright denial of the external world. It rather underscores the role of the *subjective* factors in our perception of Reality, and the way in which our own preconceived notions limit and define the kind of "reality" we are able to see. Truly, as the saying goes, "perception is reality," and Reality is "made of mind," that is, of our perceptions ("Mind-only").

If this is true, then a transcendental leap from "Mind" to "No-mind" is necessary to overcome and expand the barriers to perception and to transgress our self-built limitations. This can be done through a fundamental understanding of the process of cognition, its Categories and Modes, which will bring about an inner Revolution (*parāvṛtti*), and ultimately, the attainment of Transcendental Wisdom or Gnosis (Āryajñāna). This constitutes the subject of the next section (ch. 2.2.), which, from the epistemic point of view, is nothing but the clearing of the clutter of preconceived erroneous notions that our mind has accumulated "since beginningless time." Therefore, this state may be called "No-mind," free from discriminations (*nirvikalpa*) and imaginations (*nirābhāsa*), and it illustrates the second, opposite limb of the tetralemma, *the negation.*

The third, *conjunctive* alternative is instantiated when the first two (Affirmation and Negation, Mind and No-mind) are integrated in a functioning manner, such as is the case with the psychological system of the eight States-of-perception (Vijñānas) (ch. 2.3.). This system, of which the deepest state of subliminal perception, or unconsciousness (Ālaya-vijñāna), is an integral part, represents yet another original creation of the Yogācāras. It is, certainly, the *first empirical* mapping of the various levels of consciousness, long before anything similar in precision and depth has even been attempted anywhere else in the world.

Finally, the fourth, *disjunctive* alternative is exemplified by the last section on the doctrine of Causation (ch. 2.4.), which lays down the foundation for a unifying view of the world by means of negating the *static* view of things (this being "neither this, nor that") in favor of their constant *dynamic* interaction, inter-dependence, and transformation. Therefore, the unifying link between phenomena and events can possibly be found only when the doctrine of Causality is understood as a complex network of causes and conditions (*hetu-pratyaya*). The soteriological value of this doctrine is provided by the following factual observation: since all things arise by virtue of their mutual conditioning and through dual discrimination (i.e., between Being and non-Being, high and low, Saṃsāra and Nirvāṇa, and so on), spiritual freedom can only be obtained from the understanding that no one-sided dogmatism, or absolutism, can be sustained for long ("neither this, nor that"), and only integrative dialectics can prevail over dualistic thinking in interpreting the world "as it is," in its "facticity," or "suchness" (Tathatā).

That brings us to the final questions that need to be addressed at the conclusion of this study on Yogācāra Buddhism, namely: (1) Should the Yogācāras' world of ideas be regarded as a rational, analytic philosophy, or as a religious transcendentalism with mystical overtones? and (2) Whatever the answer to the first question might be, does Yogācāra Buddhism have any value in helping us, free-thinkers, multi-cultural seekers of the twentieth century, with our own different set of problems, to find a new paradigm by means of which we might try to reformulate our own vision of a changing world?

Addressing the first question, let us first consider the widespread criticism raised in the West against Buddhist philosophy in general on the ground that it is *not really* a philosophy on a par with the Western tradition, since it lacks analytical rationality and detached intellectual discipline as understood in the West. Therefore, at best one may regard it as closer to theology, or philosophy of religion.

To that one can reply that, although the Yogācāras' outlook is certainly not a purely *analytical* philosophy, it cannot be considered as a full-fledged *religious* philosophy either, since its radical critique of knowledge is equally directed, as I had the opportunity to demonstrate above, against both Hindu and Buddhist doxologies, as well as against Indian philosophical Materialism (Lokayata). Indeed, one may say that it does not offer ground of support to any reified, absolutized concept, or idealized being (such as a creator God, Allah, or Īśvara-Lord), nor does it accept the limitations imposed upon experience by the purely rationalistic philosophical analysis based solely upon the inference derived from the senses, as the materialists would have it. As we have seen, it advocates transcendence of both "pure" reason and "irrational" belief. So, while it has certain elements of both religious and analytical philosophy, the Yogācāras' worldview can be said to be neither. At most, the only absolute one can speak of in this case, is *the Goal* (of Enlightenment, or Self-realization) which, if interpreted transcendentally, can be said to be of a spiritual nature, but only in the most general sense.

Basically, however, if our ultimate notions of Reality are, according to the Yogācāras, hopelessly clouded by distorted conceptualization and misleading dualistic logic, how can one speak of either a Yogācāra "philosophy," or a "theology," when both disciplines are dependent upon definite statements and confident affirmations, without even mentioning their undaunted reliance upon the infallibility of language and of conventional logic? For, as indicated in this book, the Yogācāra Buddhist believed only in the power of direct, intuitive wisdom, or insight, which, by going beyond conceptual discourse, can put us back in touch with ourselves, our deepest aspirations, our Reality "as it really is."

Consequently, in answer to the second question raised above, the so-called "New paradigm" that the Yogācāras' worldview might help us construct today, is a "No paradigm," since another iron-clad paradigm would be yet another case of self-hypnosis, as was the Old paradigm. The reason for this is quite simple: there is no one model of Reality that will solve all our present existential problems and aspirations. Indeed, we do not need anther "tunnel" reality to narrow our options for an unpredictable future. Reality, "as it really is," cannot fit into the Procrustean bed of our mental fabrications, no matter how ambitious, or ingenious, they might be. This is, perhaps, the most important, and paradoxically, the most rational lesson the Yogācāras can teach us today.

Another, no less paradoxical lesson the Yogācāras can teach us, is that it is precisely in the transcendence of our own conditioned "realities" (through Enlightenment), that we can directly experience Reality "as it really is." It is in this directly experienced Reality that the Buddhist epistemological endeavor is ultimately validated. It is also here, one may add, that Buddhist existentialism and soteriology can be said to truly differ from their Western counterparts, namely: philosophical existentialism and ethical theology.

And yet, as I had the opportunity to suggest in the course of this book, there are also areas of unexpected convergence between ancient Buddhist thought, on the one hand, and evolving modern philosophy, on the other hand. For example, as far as the Yogācāra *critique* of the fundamental inadequacies of language and of metaphysical speculations is concerned, it may also apply to most of the philosophical activities we tend to engage in, here in the West, as Wittgenstein's "language games" theory has so well demonstrated.

On the other hand, Sartre's and other modern philosophers' and theologians' attitude of "commitment to," or "engagement in" the life process rings like a distant echo of the Yogācāras' extollment of self-transcendence and of direct experience of life. But I shall leave to the reader the pleasure of drawing parallels and of deciding upon the place the Yogācāra philosophy deserves in the larger picture of the history of ideas, or, for that matter, its usefulness for his or her own personal aspirations.

In as far as the difficulties inherent in understanding the ultimate meaning and significance of the Yogācāra school of Buddhism are concerned (to which I have briefly alluded above, and which are only in part due to the great distance from us in both time and space), suffice it to say that, from a historian's perspective, in the West, too, from Plato to Kant, from Augustine to Spinoza and Hegel, philosophy has been "tainted" by more than a touch of mystical "irrationalism" which, when garbed in poetic, metaphorical, or symbolic language (as has often been the case), has appeared just as cryptic to the uninitiated as the ancient Oriental gnosis (such as that contained in the *Laṅkāvatāra-sūtra*) may seem to us today. That is not to say that the germs planted by such great minds of the past have been sterile and have not borne rich fruits, in spite of their initial limited appeal, for these fruits are today visible all around us in subtle and not so subtle ways.

Therefore, having presented in this book some of the more

disturbing aspects of the Yogācāras' world of ideas, I shall now entrust the reader to decide for himself, or herself, whether Yogācāra thought is primarily a rational philosophy of language, a mystical transcendentalism, both, or neither. And may the seeds of wisdom, planted by the Yogācāra Buddhists many centuries ago and carefully nourished over the years by scholars and practitioners of many generations and nationalities, continue to bear fruit in the minds of those who, courageously, dare to fathom such difficult and fascinating issues. For, ultimately, the results of this process of enlightenment, although not immediately visible, cannot but help increase the degree of open-mindedness and of the general livability of our planet, where mutual tolerance in the ideological realm is increasingly becoming *the* most essential ingredient of a realistic prescription for survival.

Appendix

Containing
The *Laṅkāvatāra-sūtra* excerpts quoted in the book
(arranged in the order in which they appear).

Introduction

0.1. The Purpose of the Study and the Significance of the *Laṅkāvatāra-sūtra* within Buddhist Doctrinal History

III: 194 (1-2):

rutaṃ mahāmate akṣarapatitam artho 'nakṣarapatitaḥ/

III: 195 (1-3):

vyañcanānusārī mahāmate kulaputro vā kuladuhitā vā svātmānaṃ ca nāśayati paramārthaṃś ca nāvabodhayati/

III: 196 (4-8):

tena na mahāmate kulaputreṇa vā kuladuhitrā vā yathā rutārthābhiniveśakuśalena navitavyam/ nirakṣaratvāt tattvasya/ na cāṅguliprekṣakena navitavyam/ tad yathā mahāmate aṅgulyā kaścit kasyacit kiṃcid ādarśayet sa cāṅgulyagram eva pratisared vīkṣitum/

III: 197 (1-8):

artho mahāmate vivikto nirvāṇahetuḥ/ rutaṃ vikalpasaṃbaddhaṃ saṃsārāvāhakam/ arthaś ca mahāmate bahuśrutānāṃ sakāśāl labhyate/ bāhuśrutyaṃ ca nāma mahāmate yad utārthakauśalyam na rutakauśalyam/ tatrārthakauśalyaṃ yat sarvatīrthakaravādāsaṃsṛṣṭaṃ darśanaṃ yada svayaṃ ca na patati parāṃś ca na pātayati/ evaṃ satyarthe mahāmate bāhuśrutyaṃ bhavati/ tasmād arthakāmena te sevanīyāḥ ato viparītā ye yathārutārthābhiniviṣṭās te varjanīyās tattvān veṣiṇā//

VI: 223-24 (gātha 3):

aṅgulyagraṃ yathā balo na gṛhṇāti niśākaram/
tathā hy akṣarasaṃsaktās tattvaṃ na vetti māmakam//

Part One: Concepts of Being

1.0. The Nature of Buddhist Ontology

III: 176-77 (19-20, 1-4):

punar api bho gautama sarvam avyākṛtaṃ sarvaṃ vyākṛtam asty ātmā nāsty ātmāsty ayaṃ loko nāsty ayaṃ loko 'sti paro loko nāsti paro loko nāsty asti ca paro loko 'sti mokṣo nāsti mokṣaḥ sarvaṃ kṣaṇikaṃ sarvam akṣaṇikam ākāśam pratisaṃkhyā nirodho nirvāṇaṃ bho gautama kṛtakam akṛtakam asty antarābhavo nāsty antarābhava iti/

III: 177 (5-16):

tasyaitad uktaṃ mahāmate mayā/ yadi bho brāhmaṇa evam idam api brāhmaṇa lokāyatam eva bhavatīti/ na mad īyaṃ tvad īyam etad brāhmaṇa lokāyatam/ ahaṃ bho brāhmaṇa anādikālaprapañcavikalpavāsanādauṣṭhulyahetukaṃ tribhavaṃ varṇayāmi svacittadṛśyamātrānavabodhād brāhmaṇa vikalpaḥ pravartate na bāhyabhāvopalambhāt/ yathā tīrthakarāṇām ātmendriyārthasaṃnikarṣāt trayāṇāṃ na tathā mama/ ahaṃ bho brāhmaṇa na hetuvādī nāhetuvādī anyatra vikalpam eva grāhyagrāhakabhāvena prajñāpya pratītyasamutpādaṃ deśayāmi/ na ca tv ādṛśā anye vā budhyanta ātmagrāhapatitayā saṃtatyā/ nirvāṇākāśanirodhānāṃ mahāmate tattvam eva nopalabhyate saṃkhyāyām/ kutaḥ punaḥ kṛtakatvam//

II: 80-81 (14-17, 1-3):

yaduta māyāsvapnarūpajanmasadṛśāḥ sarvabhāvāḥ svaparobhayābhāvān notpadyante/ svacittamātrānusāritvād bāhyabhāvābhāvadarśanād vijñānānām apravṛttiṃ dṛṣṭvā pratyayānām akūṭarāśitvaṃ ca vikalpapratyayodbhavaṃ traidhātukaṃ paśyanto 'dhyātmabāhyasarvadharmānupalabdhibhir niḥsvabhāvadarśanād utpādadṛṣṭivinivṛttau māyādidharmasvabhāvānugamānutpattikadharmakṣāntiṃ pratilabhante/

II: 52 (1-3):

dehabhogapratiṣṭhāgativikalpamātre mahāmate śaśaśṛṅgaṃ nāsty asti vinivṛttaṃ na kalpayet tathā mahāmate sarvabhāvānāṃ nāsty asti vinivṛttaṃ na kalpayitavyam/

II: 54 (vv. 125, 127, 128):

dṛśyaṃ na vidyate citraṃ cittaṃ dṛśyāt pravartate/
dehabhogapratiṣṭhānam ālayaṃ khyāyate nṛṇām//
dīrghahrasvādisaṃbandham anyonyataḥ pravartate/
astitvasādhakaṃ nāsti asti nāstitvasādhakam//
aṇuso bhajyamānaṃ hi naiva rūpaṃ vikalpayet/
cittamātraṃ vyavasthānaṃ kudṛṣṭyā na prasīdati//

1.1. The Threefold Meaning of Tathāgata-garbha and its Relation to Ālaya-vijñāna: the *Essence* of Being

II: 77-78 (13-18, 1):

atha khalu mahāmatir bodhisattvo mahāsattvo bhagavantam etad avocat/ tathāgatagarbhaḥ punar bhagavatā sūtrāntapāṭhe 'nuvarṇitaḥ/ sa ca kila tvayā prakṛtiprabhāsvaraviśuddhyādiviśuddha eva varṇyate dvātriṃśal-lakṣaṇadharaḥ sarvasattvadehān targato mahārghamūlyaratnamalinavastu-pariveṣṭitam iva skandhadhātvāyatanavastuveṣṭito rāgadveṣamohābhūta-parikalpamalamalino nityo dhruvaḥ śivaḥ śāśvataś ca bhagavatā varṇitaḥ/

II: 78 (1-4):

tatkathamayaṃ bhagavaṃstīrthakarātmavādatulyastathāgatagarbhavādo na bhavati/ tīrthakarā api bhagavan nityaḥ kartā nirguṇo vibhūravyayaity ātmavādopadeśaṃ kurvanti//

II: 78 (5-18):

bhagavān āha/ na hi mahāmate tīrthakarātmavādatulyo mama tathāgata-gārbhopadeśaḥ/ kiṃ tu mahāmate tathāgatāḥ śūnyatābhūtakoṭinirvāṇānut-pādānimittāpraṇihitādyānāṃ mahāmate padārthānāṃ tathāgatagarbhopa-deśaṃ kṛtvā tathāgatā arhantaḥ samyaksaṃbuddhā bālānāṃ nairātmyasaṃ-trāsapadavivarjitārthaṃ nirvikalpanirābhāsagocaraṃ tathāgatagarbha-mukhopadeśena deśayanti/ na cātra mahāmate anāgatapratyutpannaiḥ bodhisattvair mahāsattvair ātmābhiniveśaḥ kartavyaḥ/ tadyathā mahāmate kumbhakāra ekasmāṇmṛtparamāṇurāśervividhāni bhāṇḍāni karoti hasta-śilpadaṇḍodakasūtraprayatnayogāt evameva mahāmate tathāgatās tad eva dharmanairātmyaṃ sarvavikalpalakṣaṇavinivṛttaṃ vividhaiḥ prajñopāya-kauśalyayogair garbhopadeśena vā nairātmyopadeśena vā kumbhakāravac-citraiḥ padavyañjanaparyāyair deśayante/ etasmāt kāraṇān mahāmate tīrthakarātmavādopadeśatulyas tathāgatagarbhopadeśo na bhavati/

X: 358 (vv. 750, 751):

prakṛtiprabhāsvaram cittaṃ garbhaṃ tathāgataṃ śubham/
upādānaṃ hi sattvasya antānantavivarjitam//
kāntir yathā suvarṇasya jātarūpaṃ ca śarkaram/
parikarmeṇa paśyanti sattvaṃ skandhālayais tathā//

II: 79 (1-13; gātha 139):

evaṃ hi mahāmate tathāgatagarbhopadeśam ātmavādābhiniviṣṭānāṃ tīrthakarāṇām ākarṣaṇārthaṃ tathāgatagarbhopadeśena nirdiśanti/ kathaṃ vatābhūtātmavikalpadṛṣṭipatitāśayā vimokṣatrayagocarapatitāśayopetāḥ kṣipram anuttarāṃ samyaksaṃbodhim abhisaṃbudhyerann iti/ etad arthaṃ mahāmate tathāgatā arhantaḥ samyaksaṃbuddhās tathāgatagarbhopadeśaṃ kurvanti/ ata etan na bhavati tīrthakarātmavādatulyam/ tasmāt tarhi mahāmate tīrthakaradṛṣṭivinivṛttyarthaṃ tathāgatanairātmyagarbhānu-sāriṇā ca te bhavitavyam//

atha khalu bhagavāṃs tasyāṃ velāyām imāṃ gāthām abhāṣata//
pudgalaḥ saṃtatiḥ skandhāḥ pratyayā aṇavastathā/
pradhānam īśvaraḥ kartā cittamātraṃ vikalpyate//

VI: 236 (4-8):

asaṃsāriṇo mahāmate pañcavijñānakāyā ananubhūtasukhaduḥkhā anirvāṇahetavaḥ/ tathāgatagarbhaḥ punar mahāmate anubhūtasukhaduḥkhahetusahitaḥ pravartate nivartate ca catasṛbhir vāsanābhiḥ saṃmūrcchitaḥ/ na ca bālā avabudhyante kṣaṇikadṛṣṭivikalpavāsitamatayaḥ//

VI: 221 (12-19):

aparāvṛtte ca tathāgatagarbhaśabdasaṃśabdita ālayavijñāne nāsti saptānāṃ pravṛttivijñānānāṃ nirodhaḥ/ tat kasya hetos tad dhetv ālambanapravṛttatvād vijñānānām aviṣayatvāc ca sarvaśrāvakapratyekabuddhatīrthyayogayogināṃ svapudgalanairātmyāvabodhāt svasāmānyalakṣaṇaparigrahāt skandhadhātvāyatanānāṃ pravartate tathāgatgarbhaḥ pañcadharmasvabhāvadharmanairātmyadarśanān nivartate bhūmikramānusaṃdhiparāvṛttyā nānyatīrthyamārgadṛṣṭibhir vicārayituṃ śakyate/

VI: 221-22 (19, 1-8):

tato 'calāyāṃ bhūmau bodhisattvabhūmau pratiṣṭito daśasamādhisukhamukhamārgān pratilabhate/ samādhibuddhaiḥ saṃdhāryamāṇo 'cintyabuddhadharmasvapraṇidhānavyavalokanatayā samādhisukhabhūtakoṭyā vinivārya pratyātmāryagatigamyaiḥ sarvaśrāvakapratyekabuddhatīrthyakarāsādhāraṇair yogamārgair daśāryagotramārgaṃ pratilabhate kāyaṃ ca jñānamanomayaṃ samādhyabhisaṃskārarahitam/ tasmāt tarhi mahāmate tathāgatagarbha ālayavijñānasaṃśabdito viśodhayitavyo viśeṣārthibhir bodhisattvair mahāsattvaiḥ//

VI: 220-21 (13-16, 1):

anādikālavividhaprapañcadauṣṭhulyavāsanāvāsita ālayavijñānasaṃśabdito 'vidyāvāsanabhūmijaiḥ saptabhir vijñānaiḥ saha mahodadhitaraṅgavan nityam avyucchinnaśarīraḥ pravartate anityatādoṣarahita ātmavādavinivṛtto 'tyantaprakṛtipariśuddhiḥ/

II: 37 (12-15)

trividhaṃ vijñānaṃ pravṛttilakṣaṇaṃ karmalakṣaṇaṃ jātilakṣaṇaṃ ca/

II: 38-39 (13-19, 1-2):

evam eva mahāmate pravṛttivijñānāny ālayavijñānajātilakṣaṇād anyāni syur anālayavijñānahetukāni syuḥ/ athānanyāni pravṛttivijñānanirodha ālayavijñānanirodhaḥ syāt sa ca na bhavati svajātilakṣaṇanirodhaḥ/ tasmāt mahāmate na svajātilakṣaṇanirodho vijñānānāṃ kiṃ tu karmalakṣaṇanirodhaḥ/ svajātilakṣaṇe punar nirudhyamāna ālayavijñānanirodhaḥ syāt/ ālayavijñāne punar nirūpyamāṇe nirviśiṣṭas tīrthakarocchedavādena ayaṃ vādaḥ syāt/

II: 46 (vv. 102, 103, 104):

na cānyena ca nānanyena taraṅgā hy udadher matā/
vijñānāni tathā sapta cittena saha saṃyutāḥ//
udadheḥ pariṇāmo 'sau taraṅgāṇāṃ vicitratā/
ālayaṃ hi tathā citraṃ vijñānākhyaṃ pravartate//
cittaṃ manaś ca vijñānaṃ lakṣaṇārthaṃ prakalpyate/
abhinnalakṣaṇā hy aṣṭau na lakṣya na ca lakṣaṇam//

VI: 222 (9-14):

yadi hi mahāmate ālayavijñānasaṃśabditas tathāgatagarbho 'tra na syād ity asati mahāmate tathāgatagarbha ālayavijñānasaṃśabdite na pravṛttir na nivṛttiḥ syāt/ bhavati ca mahāmate pravṛttir nivṛttiś ca bālāryāṇām/ svapratyātmāryagatidṛṣṭadharmasukhavihāreṇa ca viharanti yogino 'nikṣiptadhurā duṣprativedhāś ca/

VI: 222 (14-19):

mahāmate ayaṃ tathāgatagarbhālayavijñānagocaraḥ sarvaśrāvaka-pratyekabuddhatīrthayavitarkadarśanānāṃ prakṛtipariśuddho 'pi san na śuddha ivāgantukleśopakliṣṭatayā teṣām ābhāti na tu tathāgatānām/ tathāgatānāṃ punar mahāmate karatalāmalakavat pratyakṣagocaro bhavati//

VI: 222-23 (20, 1-13):

etad eva mahāmate mayā srīmālāṃ devīm adhikṛtya deśanāpāthe 'nyāṃś ca sūkṣmanipuṇaviśuddhabuddhīn bodhisattvān adhiṣṭhāya tathāgatagarbha ālayavijñāna śabditaḥ saptabhir vijñānaiḥ saha pravṛtty abhiniviṣṭāṇāṃ śrāvakāṇāṃ dharmanairātmyapradarśanārthaṃ śrīmālāṃ devīm adhiṣṭhāya tathāgataviṣayo deśito na śrāvakapratyekabuddhānyatīrthakaratarkaviṣayo 'nyatra mahāmate tathāgataviṣaya eva tathāgatagarbha ālayavijñānaviṣayas tvatsadṛśānāṃ ca sūkṣmanipuṇamatibuddhiprabhedakānāṃ bodhisattvānāṃ mahāsattvānām arthapratisaraṇānāṃ no tu yathārutadeśanāpāṭhābhi-niviṣṭānāṃ sarvānyatīrthyaśrāvakapratyekabuddhānām/ tasmāt tarhi mahāmate tvayānyaiś ca bodhisattvair mahāsattvaiḥ sarvatathāgataviṣaye 'smiṅs tathāgatagarbhālayavijñānaparijñāne yogaḥ karaṇīyo na śrutamātra-saṃtuṣṭair bhavitavyam//

VI: 223-24 (vv. 1-4):

garbhas tathāgatānāṃ hi vijñānais saptabhir yutaḥ/
pravartate dvayo grāhāt parijñānān nivartate//
vimbavad dṛśyate cittamanādimatibhāvitam/
arthākāro na cārtho 'sti yathā bhūtaṃ vipaśyataḥ//
aṅgulyagraṃ yathā bālo na gṛhṇāti niśākaram/
tathā hy akṣarasaṃsaktās tattvaṃ na vetti māmakam//
naṭavan nṛtyate cittaṃ mano vidūṣasādṛśam/
vijñānaṃ pañcabhiḥ sārdhaṃ dṛśyaṃ kalpeti raṅgavat//

1.2. The Five Skandhas: the *Temporal* Manifestation of Being

II: 124 (2-10):

tatra mahāmate mahābhūteṣu kathaṃ bhautikaṃ bhavati yaduta snehavikalpamahābhūtaṃ mahāmate abdhātuṃ niṣpādayaty adhyātmabāhyam/ utsāhavikalpamahābhūtaṃ mahāmate tejodhātuṃ niṣpādayaty adhyātmabāhyam/ samudīraṇavikalpamahābhūtaṃ mahāmate vāyudhātuṃ niṣpādayaty adhyātmabāhyam/ rūpaparicchedavikalpamahābhūtaṃ punar mahāmate pṛthivīdhātuṃ janayaty ākāśasahitam adhyātmabāhyam/ mithyāsatyābhiniveśāt pañcaskandhakadambakaṃ mahābhūtabhautikaṃ pravartate/

II: 124 (10-16):

vijñānaṃ punar mahāmate vicitrapadaviṣayābhiniveśābhilāṣahetutvād vijñānaṃ pravartate 'nyagatisaṃdhau/ pṛthivībhūtabhautikānāṃ mahāmate kāraṇam asti mahābhūtāni na tu mahābhūtānām/ tat kasya hetor yad uta bhāvaliṅgalakṣaṇa[m] grahaṇasaṃsthānakriyāyogavatāṃ mahāmate kriyāsaṃyogotpattir bhavati nāliṅgavatām/ tasmād etan mahāmate mahābhūtabhautikalakṣaṇaṃ tīrthakarair vikalpyate na tu mayā//

II: 124-25 (17-18, 1-4):

punar aparaṃ mahāmate skandhānāṃ skandhasvabāvalakṣaṇaṃ nirdekṣyāmaḥ/ tatra mahāmate pañcaskandhāḥ katame yaduta rūpavedanāsaṃjñāsaṃskāravijñānāni/ tatra mahāmate catvāraḥ skandhā arūpiṇo vedanā saṃjñā saṃskārā vijñānaṃ ca/ rūpaṃ mahāmate cāturmahābhautikaṃ bhūtāni ca parasparavilakṣaṇāni/

II: 125 (4-15):

na ca mahāmate arūpiṇāṃ catuṣkasaṃkhyā bhavaty ākāśavat/ tadyathā mahāmate ākāśam saṃkhyālakṣaṇātītamatha ca vikalpyata evam ākāśaṃ iti evam eva mahāmate skandhāḥ saṃkhyālakṣaṇagaṇanātītā bhāvābhāvavivarjitāś catuṣkoṭi karahitāḥ saṃkhyāgaṇanānir deśena nirdaśyante bālair na tv āryaiḥ//

āryaiḥ punar mahāmate māyāvicitrarūpākṛtivadanyānany avarjitāḥ prajñāpyante svapnavimbapuruṣavat/ āsrayānanyatvād āryajñānagatisaṃmohān mahāmate skandhavikalpaḥ khyāyate/ etan mahāmate skandhānāṃ skandhasvabhāvalakṣaṇam/ sa ca vikalpas tvayā vyāvartanīyaḥ vyāvṛtya viviktadharmopadeśaḥ karaṇīyaḥ/

II: 125-26 (15-18, 1-5):

sarvabuddhaparṣanmaṇḍaleṣu tīrthyadṛṣṭinivāraṇāya viviktadharmopadeśena mahāmate kriyamāṇena dharmanairātmyadarśanaṃ viśudhyate dūraṃgamābhūmipraveśaś ca bhavati/ sa dūraṃgamāṃ mahābhūmim anupraviśyānekasamādhivaśavartī bhavati/ manomayakāyapratilambhāc ca samādhiṃ māyopamaṃ pratilabhate/ balābhijñāvaśitāgatiṃgataḥ sarvasattvopajivyo bhavati pṛthivīvat/ yathā mahāmate mahāpṛthivī sarvasattvopajīvyā bhavati evam eva mahāmate bodhisattvo mahāsattvaḥ sarvasattvopajīvyo bhavati//

III: 146-47 (17, 1):

skandhādhatvāyatanāni saṃtitiprabhadhena vinivṛtya vinivartanta/

X: 358-59 (vv. 752-761):

na pudgalo na ca skandhā buddho jñānam anāsravam/
sadāśantiṃ vibhāvitvā gacchāmi śaraṇaṃ hy aham//
prakṛtiprabhāsvaraṃ cittam upakleśair manādibhiḥ/
ātmanā saha saṃyuktaṃ deśeti vadatāṃvaraḥ//
prakṛtiprabhāsvaraṃ cittaṃ manādyas tasya vai paraḥ/
tair ācitāni karmāṇi yataḥ kliśyanti tāv ubhau//
āgantukair anādyaiś ca kleśair ātmā prabhāsvaraḥ/
(p. 359)
saṃkliśyate upetaś ca vastravat pariśudhyate//
malābhāvād yathā vastraṃ hemaṇ vā doṣavarjitam/
tiṣṭhanti na ca naśyante ātmā doṣais tathā vinā//
vīnāśaṅkhe 'tha bheryām ca mādhuryasvarasaṃpadā/
mṛgayed dhy akovidaḥ kaścit tathā skandheṣu pudgalam//
nidhayo maṇayaś cāpi pṛthivy āmudakaṃ tathā/
vidyamānā na dṛśyanti tathā skandheṣu pudgalam//
cittacaittakalāpāṃś ca svaguṇāṃ skandhasaṃyutām/
akovidā na gṛhṇanti tathā skandheṣu pudgalam//
yathā hi garbho garbhiṇyā vidyate na ca dṛśyate/
ātmā hi tadvat skandheṣu ayuktijño na paśyati//
auṣadhīnāṃ yathā sāram agniṃ vā indhanair yathā/
na paśyanti ayuktijñās tathā skandheṣu pudgalam//

X: 359-60 (vv. 762-71):

anityatā sarvabhāveṣu śūnyatāṃ ca yathābudhāḥ/
vidyamānāṃ na paśyanti tathā skandheṣu pudgalam//
bhūmayo viśitābhijñā abhiṣekaṃ ca uttaram/
samādhayo viśeṣāś ca asaty ātmani nāsti vai//
(p. 360)
vaināśiko yadā gatvā brūyād yady asti deśyatām/
sa vaktavyo bhaved vijñaḥ svavikalpaṃ pradarśayam//
nairātmyavādino 'bhāṣyā bhikṣukarmāṇi varjaya/
bādhakā buddhadharmāṇāṃ sadasatpakṣadṛṣṭayaḥ//
tīrthadoṣair vinirmuktaṃ nairātmyavanadāhakam/
jājvalaty ātmavādo 'yaṃ yugāntāgnirivotthitaḥ//
khaṇḍekṣuśarkaramadhvādidadhitilaghṛtādiṣu/
svarasaṃ vidyate teṣu anāsvādyaṃ na gṛhyate//
pañcadhā gṛhyamānaś ca ātmā skandhasamucchrayate/
na ca paśyanty avidvāṃso vidvān dṛṣṭvā vimucyate//
vidyādibhiś ca dṛṣṭāntaiś cittaṃ naivāvadhāryate/

yatra yasmād yad artham ca samūham nāvadhāryate//
vilakṣaṇā hi vai dharmāś cittam ekaṃ na gṛhyate/
ahetur apravṛttiś ca tārkikāṇāṃ prasajyate//
cittānupaśyī ca yogī cittaṃ citte na paśyati/
paśyako dṛśya nirjāto dṛśyaṃ kiṃ hetusaṃbhavam//

X: 357-58 (vv. 746, 748):

pratyātmagatigamyaś ca ātmā vai śuddhilakṣaṇam/
garbhas tathāgatasyāsau tārkikānām agocaraḥ//
ālayaṃ garbhasaṃsthānaṃ mataṃ tīrthyānuvarṇitam/
ātmanā saha saṃyuktaṃ na ca dharmāḥ prakīrtitāḥ//

III: 88-89 (16-17, 1-7):

evaṃ skandhebhyo nānyo nānanyas tathāgataḥ/ yady ananyaḥ skandhebhyaḥ syād anityaḥ syāt kṛtatvāt skandhānām/ athānyaḥ syād dvaye satyany athā bhavati goviṣāṇavat// tatra sādṛśyadarśanād ananyatvaṃ hrsvadīrghadarśanād anyatvaṃ sarvabhāvānāṃ/ dakṣiṇaṃ hi mahāmate goviṣāṇaṃ vāmasyānyad bhavati vāmam api dakṣiṇasya evaṃ hrsvadīrghatvayoḥ parasparataḥ evaṃ varṇavaicitryataś ca/ ataś cāparasparato 'nyo na cānyas tathāgataḥ skandhadhātvāyatanebhyaḥ/

II: 114-15 (12-17, 1-6):

avyākṛtāny api ca mahāmate tīrthakaradṛṣṭivādavyudāsārthaṃ nopadiśyante tathāgataiḥ/ tīrthakarā hi mahāmate evaṃ vādino yaduta sa jīvas tac charīram anyo jīvo 'nyac charīram ity evam ādye 'vyākṛtavādaḥ/ tīrthakarāṇāṃ hi mahāmate kāraṇavisaṃmūḍhānām avyākṛtaṃ na tu mat pravacane/ mat pravacane tu mahāmate grāhyagrāhakavisaṃyukte vikalpo na pravartate/ teṣāṃ kathaṃ sthāpyaṃ bhavet/ ye tu mahāmate grāhyagrāhakābhiniviṣṭāḥ svacittadṛśyamātrānavadhāritamatayas teṣāṃ sthāpyaṃ bhavati/ caturvidhapadapraśnavyākaraṇena mahāmate tathāgatā arhantaḥ samyaksaṃbuddhāḥ sattvabhyo dharmaṃ deśayanti/ sthāpanīyam iti mahāmate kālāntara deśanaiṣā mayā kṛtāparipakvendriyāṇāṃ na tu paripakvendriyāṇāṃ sthāpyaṃ bhavati/

II: 116 (vv. 173, 175):

caturvidhaṃ vyākaraṇam ekāṃśaṃ paripṛcchanam/
vibhajyaṃ sthāpanīyaṃ ca tīrthavādanivāraṇam//
buddhyā vivecyamānānāṃ svabhāvo nāvadhāryate/
tasmād anabhilāpyās te niḥsvabhāvāś ca deśitāḥ//

III: 188 (7-16):

yad apy uktaṃ mayā nirātmānaḥ sarvadharmā iti tasyāpy arthaṃ nibodhavyaṃ mahāmate nirātmabhāvo mahāmate nairātmyaṃ svātmanā sarvadharmā vidyante na parātmanā go 'śvavat/ tad yathā mahāmate na gobhāvo 'śvātmako na cāśvabhāvo gavātmako na san nāsan na ca tau svalakṣaṇato na vidyate eva tau svalakṣaṇataḥ evam eva mahāmate sarvadharmā na ca svalakṣaṇena na saṃvidyante vidyanta eva tena ca bālapṛthagjanair nirātmārthatāv abudhyate vikalpam upādāya na tva vikalpam evaṃ śūnyānutpādāsvābhāvyaṃ sarvadharmānāṃ pratyavagantavyam/

X: 266 (vv. 19, 20):

saṃskṛtāsaṃskṛtaṃ nāsti anyatra hi vikalpanāt/
bālā gṛhnanti dhiṅmūdā bandhyāḥ svapne yathā sutam//
naiḥsvābhāvyam anutpādo pudgalaḥ skandhasaṃtatiḥ/
pratyayā dhātavo jñeyā śūnyatā ca bhavābhavam//

III: 189 (13-17):

yaddhi mahāmate na nityaṃ nānityaṃ na kāryaṃ na kāraṇaṃ na saṃskṛtaṃ nāsaṃskṛtaṃ na buddhir na boddhavyaṃ na lakṣyaṃ na lakṣaṇaṃ na skandhā na skandhebhyo 'nyan nābhidheyaṃ nābhidhānaṃ naikatvānyatvobhayatvānubhayatvasaṃbaddhaṃ tat sarvapramāṇavinivṛttaṃ yat sarvapramāṇavinivṛttaṃ tad vāṅmātraṃ saṃpadyate/

II: 43 (2-6):

tasmāt tarhi mahāmate te bodhisattvair mahāsattvaiḥ tathāgatakāyānugamena pratilābhinā skandhadhātvāyatanacittahetupratyayakriyāyogotpādasthitibhaṅgavikalpaprapañcarahitair bhavitavyaṃ cittamātrānusāribhiḥ//

1.3. Dharmadhātu: the *Spatial* or Cosmic Dimension of Being

III: 140 (9-17):

punar api mahāmatir āha/ deśayatu me bhagavān buddhānāṃ bhagavatāṃ kathaṃ bhagavān buddhānāṃ buddhatā bhavati/ bhagavān āha/ dharmapudgalanairātmyāvabodhān mahāmate āvaraṇadvayaparijñānāvabodhāc ca cyutidvayādhigamāt kleśadvayaprahāṇāc ca mahāmate buddhānāṃ bhagavatāṃ buddhatā bhavati/ eteṣām eva mahāmate dharmāṇām adhigamāc chrāvakapratyekabuddhasaṃbuddhatā bhavati/ atha etasmān mahāmate ekayānaṃ deśayāmi// tatredam ucyate// nairātmyasya dvayaṃ kleśās tathaivāvaraṇadvayam/ acintya pariṇāminyāś cyuter lābhāt tathāgataḥ//

III: 142-43 (16-17, 1-3):

punar api mahāmatir āha/ yad idam uktaṃ bhagavatā yāṃ ca rātriṃ tathāgato 'bhisaṃbuddho yāṃ ca rātriṃ parinirvāsyati atrāntara ekam apyakṣaraṃ tathāgatena nodhāhṛtaṃ na pravyāhariṣyati avacanaṃ buddhavacanam iti tat kim idaṃ saṃdhāyoktaṃ tathāgatenārhatā samyaksaṃbuddhenāvacanaṃ buddhavacanam iti/

III: 143 (3-14):

bhagavān āha/ dharmadvayaṃ mahāmate saṃdhāya mayaitad uktaṃ katamad dharmadvayaṃ yaduta pratyātmadharmatāṃ ca saṃdhāya paurāṇasthitidharmatāṃ ca/ idaṃ mahāmate dharmadvayaṃ saṃdhāyedam uktaṃ mayā/ tatra svapratyātmadharmatānusaṃdhiḥ katamattais tathāgatair adhigataṃ tan mayāpy adhigatam anūnam anadhikaṃ svapratyātmagatigocaraṃ vāgvikalparahitam akṣaragatidvayavinirmuktam/ tatra paurāṇasthitidharmatā katamā yaduta paurāṇam idaṃ mahāmate dharmatāvan me hiraṇyarajatamuktākaravan mahāmate dharmadhātu sthititotpādād va tathāgatānām anutpādād vā tathāgatānāṃ sthitaivaiṣāṃ dharmāṇāṃ dharmatā dharmasthititā dharmaniyāmatā paurāṇanagarapathavan mahāmate/

III: 143-44 (14-16, 1-13; vv. 7-8):

tad yathā mahāmate kaścid eva puruṣo 'ṭavyāṃ paryaṭan paurāṇaṃ nagaram anupaśyed avikalpathapraveśaṃ sa taṃ nagaram anupraviśet tatra praviśya pratiniviśya nagaraṃ nagarakriyā sukham anubhavet/ tat kiṃ manyase mahāmate api nu tena puruṣeṇa sa panthā utpādito yena pathā taṃ nagaram anupraviṣṭo nagaravaicitryaṃ ca/ āha/ no bhagavan/ bhagavān āha/ evam eva mahāmate yan mayā taiś ca tathāgatair adhigataṃ sthitaivaiṣā dharmatā dharmasthititā dharmaniyāmatā tathatā bhūtatā satyatā/ ata etasmāt kāraṇān mahāmate mayedam uktaṃ yāṃ ca rātriṃ tathāgato 'bhisaṃbuddho yāṃ ca rātriṃ parinirvāsyati atrāntara ekam apy akṣaraṃ tathāgatena nodāhṛtaṃ nodāhariṣyati// tatredam ucyate//
yasyāṃ ca rātryāṃ dhigamo yasyāṃ ca parinirvṛtaḥ/
etasmin nantare nāsti mayā kiṃcit prakāśitam//
pratyātmadharmasthititāṃ saṃdhāya kathitaṃ mayā/
taiś ca buddhair mayā na ca kiṃcid viśeṣitam//

II: 73, 74 (12-16, 1-8):

deśayatu bhagavāñ chūnyatānutpādādvayaniḥsvabhāvalakṣaṇaṃ sarvadharmāṇāṃ yena śūnyatānutpādādvayaniḥsvabhāvalakṣaṇāvabodhenāhaṃ cānye ca bodhisattvā mahāsattvā nāstyastivikalpavarjitāḥ kṣipram anuttarāṃ samyaksaṃbodhim abhisaṃbudheran//
bhagavān etad avocat/ śūnyatā śūnyateti mahāmate parikalpitasvabhāvapadam etat/ parikalpitasvabhāvābhiniveśena punar mahāmate śūnyatānutpādābhāvādvayaniḥsvabhāvabhāvavādino bhavanti/ tatra mahāmate saṃkṣepeṇa saptavidhā śūnyatā yaduta lakṣaṇaśūnyatā bhāvasvabhāvaśūnyatāpracaritaśūnyatā pracaritaśūnyatā sarvadharmanirabhilāpyaśūnyatā paramārthāryajñānamahāśūnyatetaretaraśūnyatā ca saptamī//

X: 289-90 (vv. 185, 190-93):

dharmasaṃketa evāyaṃ tasmiṃs tad idam ucyate/
saṃketāc ca pṛthagbhūto na jāto na nirudhyate//
ekatvena pṛthaktvena bhāvo vai pratyaye na tu/
janma samāsamevoktaṃ nirodho nāśa eva hi//
ajātaśūnyatā caikam ekaṃ jāteṣu śūnyatā/
ajātaśūnyatā śreṣṭhā naśyate jātaśūnyate//
tathatā śūnyatā koṭī nirvāṇaṃ dharmadhātuvat/
kāyo manomayaṃ citraṃ paryāyair deśitaṃ mayā//

sūtravinayābhidharmeṇa viśuddhiṃ kalpayanti ye/
granthato na tu arthena na te nairātmyam āśritāḥ//

II: 87-88 (8-17, 1-13; vv. 145-48):

bhagavān āha/ na mahāmate vacanaṃ paramārthaḥ na ca yad vacanenābhilapyate sa paramārthaḥ/ tat kasya hetor yaduta paramārthāryasukhābhilāpapraveśitvāt paramārthasya vacanaṃ na paramārthaḥ/ paramārthas tu mahāmate āryajñānapratyātmagatigamyo na vāgvikalpabuddhigocaraḥ tena vikalpo nodbhāvayati paramārtham/ vacanaṃ punar mahāmate utpannapradhvaṃsi capalaṃ parasparaṃ pratyayahetusamutpannaṃ yac ca mahāmate parasparaṃ pratyayahetusamutpannaṃ tat paramārthaṃ nodbhāvayati svaparalakṣaṇābhāvān mahāmate vāglakṣaṇaṃ nodbhāvayati//

punaraparaṃ mahāmate svacittadṛśyamātrānusāritvād vividhavicitralakṣaṇabāhyabhāvābhāvād vāgvikalpaḥ paramārthaṃ na vikalpayati/ tasmāt tarhi mahāmate vāgvicitravikalparahitena te bhavitavyam//

tatredam ucyate//

sarvabhāvo 'svabhāvo hi san vacanaṃ tathāpy asat/
śūnyatā śūnyatārtham vā bālo 'paśyan vidhāvati//
sarvabhāvasvābhāva ca vacanam api nṛṇām/
kalpanā sāpi nāsti nirvāṇaṃ svapnatulyam/
bhavaṃ parīkṣeta na saṃsāre nāpi nirvāyāt//
rājā śreṣṭhī yathā putrān vicitrair mṛnmayair mṛgaiḥ/
pralobhya krīḍayitvā ca bhūtān dadyāt tato mṛgān//
tathāhaṃ lakṣaṇaiś citrair dharmāṇāṃ prativimbakaiḥ/
pratyātmavedyāṃ putrebhyo bhūtakoṭim vadāmy aham//

Part Two: Concepts of Knowing

2.0. Buddhist Epistemology, Buddhist Dialectics

II: 79 (5-11):

bhagavān āha/ na hi mahāmate tīrthakarātmavādatulyo mama tathāgatagarbhopadeśaḥ/ kiṃ tu mahāmate tathāgatāḥ śūnyatābhūtakoṭinirvāṇānutpādānimittāpraṇihitādyānāṃ mahāmate padārthānāṃ tathāgatagarbhopadeśaṃ kṛtvā tathāgatā arhantaḥ samyaksaṃbuddhā bālānāṃ nairātmyasaṃtrāsapadavivarjitārthaṃ nirvikalpanirābhāsagocaraṃ tathāgatagarbhamukhopadeśena deśyanti/

II: 80 (13-15):

kathaṃ punar mahāmate bodhisattvo mahāsattva utpādasthitibhaṅgadṛṣṭivivarjito bhavati/ yad uta māyāsvapnarūpajanmasadṛśāḥ sarvabhāvāḥ svaparobhayābhāvān notpadyante/

V: 217, 218 (3-5, 14-16; 1-2, 5-8):

bhagavān āha/ na mahāmate
tathāgato nityo nānityaḥ/ tat kasya hetor yad utobhayadoṣaprasaṅgāt/ . . . / punar api mahāmate na nityas tathāgataḥ kasmād ākāśasaṃbhāraivayarthya-

prasaṅgāt/ tad yathā mahāmate ākāśaṃ na nityaṃ nānityaṃ nityānityavyudasad ekatvānyatvobhayatvānubhayatvanityānityatvadoṣair vacanīyaḥ/ . . .

punar aparaṃ mahāmate astyasau paryāyo yena nityas tathāgataḥ/ tat kasya hetor yad utābhisamayādhigamajnānanityatvān nityas tathāgataḥ/ abhisamayādhigamajñānaṃ hi mahāmate nityaṃ tathāgatānām arhataṃ samyaksaṃbuddhānām/

V: 219 (1-9; vv. 1-3):

vikalpabuddhikṣayān mahāmate nityānityagrāho nivāryate bālānāṃ na tu viviktadṛṣṭi buddhikṣāyāt/ tatredam ucyate//

nityānityavinirmuktān nityānityaprabhāvitān/
ye paśyanti sadā buddhān na te dṛṣṭivaśaṃ gatāḥ//
samudāgamaivayarthyaṃ nityānitye prasajyate/
vikalpabuddhivaikalyān nityānityaṃ nivāryate//
yāvat pratijñā kriyate tāvat sarvaṃ sasaṃkaram/
svacittamātraṃ saṃpaśyan na vivādaṃ samārabhet//

III: 176, 177 (16-20, 1-5):

punar api mahāmate māmevam āha brāhmaṇo lokāyatikaḥ/ sarvaṃ bho gautama ekatvaṃ sarvam anyatvaṃ sarvam ubhayatvaṃ sarvam anubhayatvaṃ sarvaṃ kāraṇādhīnaṃ vicitrahetūpapattidarśanāt/ idam api brāhmaṇa ekādaśaṃ lokāyatam/ punar api bho gautama sarvam avyākṛtaṃ sarvaṃ vyākṛtam astyātmā nāstyātmāstyayaṃ loko nāstyayaṃ loko 'sti paro loko nāsti paro loko nāstyasti ca paro loko 'sti mokṣo nāsti mokṣaḥ sarvaṃ kṣaṇikaṃ sarvam akṣaṇikam ākāśam pratisaṃkhyānirodho nirvāṇaṃ bho gautama kṛtakam akṛtakam astyantarābhavo nāstyantarābhava iti/

III: 177 (15-16):

nirvāṇākāśanirodhānāṃ mahāmate tattvam eva nopalabhyate saṃkhyāyām/ kutaḥ punaḥ kṛtakatvam//

II: 76-77 (7-17, 1-2; vv. 137, 138):

advayalakṣaṇaṃ punar mahāmate katam adyad uta cchāyātapavaddhīrghahrasvakṛṣṇaśuklavan mahāmate dvayaprabhāvitā na pṛthakpṛthak/ evaṃ saṃsāranirvāṇavan mahāmate sarvadharmā advayāḥ/ na yatra mahāmate nirvāṇaṃ tatra saṃsāraḥ/ na ca yatra saṃsāraḥ tatha nirvāṇaṃ vilakṣaṇahetusadbhāvāt/ tenocyante 'dvayā saṃsāraparinirvāṇavat sarvadharma iti/ tasmāt tarhi mahāmate śūnyatānutpādādvayaniḥsvabhāvalakṣaṇe yogaḥ kalaṇīyaḥ//

atha khalu bhagavāṃs tasyāṃ velāyām ime gāthe 'bhāṣata//
deśemi śūnyatāṃ nityaṃ śāśvatocchedavarjitāṃ/
saṃsāraṃ svapnamāyākhyaṃ na ca karma vinaśyati//
ākāśam atha nirvāṇaṃ nirodhaṃ dvayam eva ca/
bālā kalpentyakṛtakānāryā nāstyastivarjitāḥ//

III: 172 (10-14):

yad utaikatvānyatvobhayatvānubhayatvapakṣāpatanatācittamanomanovijñānātītaṃ svapratyātmāryagatigocaraṃ hetuyuktidṛṣṭilakṣaṇavinivṛttamanālīḍhaṃ sarvakutārkikais tīrthakaraśrāvakapratyekabuddhayāni kair nāstyastitvāntadvayapatitais tam ahaṃ siddhānta iti vadāmi/

III: 202-203 (13-15; vv. 103, 104):

asan na jāyate bhāvo nāsan na sadasat kvacit/
anyatra hi kalāpo 'yaṃ pravartate nivartate//
saṃketamātram evedam anyonyāpekṣasaṃkalā/
janyam arthaṃ na caivāsti pṛthakpratyayasaṃkalāt//

2.1. The Epistemological Reduction of the Citta-mātra (*Mind-only*) Doctrine

X: 322-23 (gātha 459):

cittaṃ vikalpo vijñaptir mano vijñānam eva ca/
ālayaṃ tribhavaś ceṣṭā ete cittasya paryāyāḥ//

II: 130 (gātha 182):

cittaṃ viṣayasaṃbandhaṃ jñānaṃ tarke pravartate/
nirābhāse viśeṣe ca prajñā vai saṃpravartate//

III: 200 (5-8):

tatra nirvāṇam iti mahāmate yathābhūtārthasthānadarśanaṃ vikalpacittacaittakalāpasya parāvṛttipūrvakaṃ tathāgatasvapratyātmāryajñānādhigamaṃ nirvāṇam iti vadāmi/

X: 311 (gātha 358):

cittamātrāvabodhena bāhyabhāva vyudāśrayā/
vinivṛttir vikalpasya pratipatsu ca madhyamā//

X: 276 (gātha 93):

sarvarūpāvabāsaṃ hi yadā cittaṃ pravartate/
nātra cittaṃ na rūpaṇi bhrāntaṃ cittam anādikam/
tadā yogī hy anābhāsaṃ prajñayā paśyate jagat//

II: 42 (vv. 99, 100):

taraṅgā hy udadher yadvat pavanapratyayeritāḥ/
nṛtyamānāḥ pravartanta vyucchedaś ca na vidyate//
ālayaughas tathā nityaṃ viṣayapavaneritaḥ/
cittais taraṅgavijñānair nṛtyamānaḥ pravartate//

II: 46 (vv. 102, 105):

na cānyena ca nānanyena taraṅgā hy udadher matā/
vijñānāni tathā sapta cittena saha saṃyutāḥ//

udadheś ca taraṅgāṇāṃ yathā nāsti viśeṣaṇam/
vijñānānāṃ tathā citte pariṇāmo na labhyate//

II: 46 (gātha 106):

cittena cīyate karma manasā ca vicīyate/
vijñānena vijānāti dṛśyaṃ kalpeti pañcabhiḥ//

II: 47 (gātha 111):

udadhis taraṅgabhāvena nṛtyamāno vibhāvyate/
ālayasya tathā vṛttiḥ kasmād buddhyā na gamyate//

X: 335 (gātha 569):

na paraṃ na ca vai tantraṃ kalpitaṃ vastum eva ca/
pañcadharmā dvicittaṃ ca nirābhāse na santi vai//

IV: 215 (gātha 1):

cittamātre nirābhāse vihārā buddhabhūmi ca/
etad dhi bhāṣitaṃ buddhair bhāṣante bhāṣayanti ca//

IV: 215 (gātha 2):

cittaṃ hi bhūmayaḥ sapta nirābhāsā tv ihāṣṭamī/
dve hi bhūmī vihāro 'tra śeṣā bhūmir mamātmikā//

VI: 221 (12-13):

aparāvṛtte ca tathāgatagarbhaśabdasaṃśabdita ālayavijñāne nāsti saptānāṃ pravṛttivijñānānāṃ nirodhaḥ/

II: 54 (vv. 125, 127, 128):

dṛśyaṃ na vidyate citraṃ cittaṃ dṛśyāt pravartate/
dehabhogapratiṣṭānam ālayaṃ khyāyate nṛṇām//
dīrghahrasvādisaṃbandham anyonyataḥ pravartate/
astitvasādhakaṃ nāsti asti nāstitvasādhakam//
anuśo bhajyamānaṃ hi naiva rūpaṃ vikalpayet/
cittamātraṃ vyavasthānaṃ kudṛṣṭyā na prasīdati//

II: 121 (vv. 176, 178):

dhyānāni cāpramāṇāni ārūpyāś ca samādhayaḥ/
saṃjñānirodho nikhilaś cittamātre na vidyate//
dhyātā dhyānaṃ ca dhyeyaṃ ca prahāṇaṃ satyadarśanam/
kalpanāmātram evedaṃ yo budhyati sa mucyate//

X: 335 (gātha 568):

svadhāraṃ hi yathā khaṅgaṃ svāgraṃ vai aṅgulir yathā/
na cchindate na spṛśate tathā cittaṃ svadarśane//

III: 223-24 (gātha 3):

aṅgulyagraṃ yathā bālo na gṛhṇāti niśākaram/
tathā hy akṣarasaṃsaktās tattvam na vetti māmakam//

II: 49 (gātha 123):

āture āture yadvad bhiṣag dravyam prayacchati/
buddhā hi tadvat sattvānāṃ cittamātraṃ vadanti vai//

II: 73 (gātha 136):

cittamātraṃ yadā lokaṃ prapaśyanti jinātmajāḥ/
tadā nairmāṇikaṃ kāyaṃ kriyāsaṃskāravarjitam/
labhante te balābhijñāvaśitaiḥ saha saṃyutam//

II: 42 (10-13):

cittābāhyadarśanatayānimittādhiṣṭhānānugatā anupūrveṇa bhūmikramasamādhiviṣayānugamanatayā traidhātukasvacittatayādhimuktitāḥ prativibhāvayamānā māhopamasamādhiṃ pratilabhante/

II: 80 (5-10):

tatra kathaṃ mahāmate bodhisattvo mahāsattvaḥ svacittadṛśyavibhāvanākuśalo bhavati/ yad uta sa evaṃ pratyavekṣate svacittamātram idaṃ traidhātukam ātmātmīyarahitaṃ nirīham āyūhaniryūhavigatam anādikālaprapañcadauṣṭhulyavāsanābhiniveśavāsitaṃ traidhātukavicittarūpopacāropanibaddhaṃ dehabhogapratiṣṭhāgativikalpānugataṃ vikalpyate khyāyate ca/

II: 123-24 (15-17, 1-2):

evaṃ prativipaśyan nāma vikalpamātram svacittadṛśyamātrāvabodhād bāhyabhāvābhāvān nāma cittadṛśyavikalpamātram idaṃ yad uta traidhātukaṃ mahābhūtabhautikarahitaṃ prativipaśyati cātuṣkoṭikanayaviśuddhim ātmātmīyarahitaṃ yathābhūtasvalakṣaṇāvasthānāvasthitam anutpādasvalakṣaṇasiddham/

II: 112 (6-7):

tatra yathābhūtāvasthānadarśanaṃ mahāmate sarvadharmāṇāṃ yad uta svacittadṛśyamātrāvatāraḥ//

IV: 213 (10-13):

na tu mahāmate 'tra kaścit pravartate vā nivartate vānyatra svacittadṛśyamātram idaṃ yad uta bhūmikramānusaṃdhis traidhātukavicitropacāraś ca/

X: 269 (gātha 36):

cittaṃ hi traidhātukayonir etat bhrāntaṃ hi cittaṃ ihamutra dṛśyate/
na kalpayel lokam asatta eṣāṃ etādṛśīṃ lokagatiṃ viditvā//

III: 208 (12-13):

mama tu mahāmate na nityā nānityā/ tat kasya hetor yad uta bāhyabhāvānabhyupagamāt tribhavacittamātropadeśāt/

III: 208 (16-17):

vikalpasya pravṛttidvayaparijñānād bāhyabhāvābhāvadṛṣṭivigamāt svacittamātrāvabodhād/

X: 282 (gātha 134):

cittaṃ hi sarvaṃ sarvatra sarvadeheṣu vartate/
vicitraṃ gṛhyate 'saddhiś cittamatraṃ hy alakṣaṇam//

II: 69 (11-13):

cittamanomanovijñānapañcadharmasvabhāvarahitān mahāmate sarvadharmān vibhāvayan bodhisattvo mahāsattvo dharmanairātmyakuśalo bhavat/

X: 282 (vv. 132, 133):

na bhūmayo na satyāni na kṣetrā na ca nirmitāḥ/
buddhāḥ pratyekabuddhāś ca śrāvakāś cāpi kalpitāḥ//
pudgalasaṃtatiskandhāḥ pratyayā hy aṇavastathā/
pradhānam īśvaraḥ kartā cittamātre vikalpyate//

X: 276 (vv. 93-94):

sarvarūpāvabhāsaṃ hi yadā cittaṃ pravartate/
nātra cittaṃ na rūpaṇi bhrāntaṃ cittam anādikam//
tadā yogī hy anābhāsaṃ prajñayā paśyate jagat/

X: 353 (vv. 708, 709):

bimbavad dṛśyate cittam anādim abhibhāvitam/
arthākāraṃ na cārtho 'sti yathā bhūtaṃ vibhāvayet//
yathā hi darpaṇe rūpam ekatvānyatvavarjitam/
dṛśyate na ca tan nāsti tathā cotpādalakṣaṇam//

III: 154 (vv. 32, 33):

vikalpavāsanābaddhaṃ vicitraṃ cittasaṃbhavam/
bahir ākhyāyate nṛṇāṃ cittamātraṃ hi laukikam//
dṛśyaṃ na vidyate bāhyaṃ cittaṃ citraṃ hi dṛśyate/
dehabhogapratiṣṭhānaṃ cittamātraṃ vadāmy aham//

X: 374 (gātha 872):

kṣaṇabhedasaṃkalābaddhāḥ svacittārthavigrāhiṇaḥ/
saṃsthānalakṣaṇākārā manocakṣvādisaṃbhavāḥ//

III: 153 (vv. 25, 29):

ālambālambyavigataṃ yadā paśyati saṃskṛtam/
niścitaṃ cittamātraṃ hi cittamātraṃ vadāmy aham//

vyāvṛttiḥ sarvadṛṣṭīnām kalpyakalpanavarjitā/
anupalambo hy ajātiś ca cittamātrām vadāmy aham//

III: 153-54 (vv. 30, 31):

na bhāvam nāpi cābhāvaṃ bhāvābhāvavivarjitam/
tathā cittavinirmuktaṃ cittamātraṃ vadāmy aham//
tathatāsūnyatākoṭi nirvāṇaṃ dharmadhātukam/
kāyaṃ manomayaṃ citraṃ cittamātraṃ vadāmy aham//

X: 335 (gātha 565):

tathatā cittamātraṃ ca āryavastunayasya tu/
vidyante na ca vidyante na te mannayakovidāḥ//

2.2. From Mind to *No-mind:* the Transcendental Leap beyond Empirical Cognition

I: 17 (11-13):

asti dharmādharmayoḥ prativibhāgo bālaprativikalpam upādāya na tvāryajñānādhigamaṃ pratidarśanena.

VI: 224-25 (15-17, 1-2):

yad uta nāma nimittaṃ vikalpaḥ samyagjñānaṃ tathatā ca tathāgatapratyātmāryagatipravesaḥ śāśvatocchedasad asad dṛṣṭivivarjitaḥ dṛṣṭadharmasukhasamāpattisukhavihāra āmukhībhavati yogayogināṃ/

VI: 225 (6-7):

nāmasaṃjñāsaṃketābhiniveśena mahāmate bālāś cittam anusaranti/

VI: 225-26 (18, 1-2):

tatra nimittaṃ punar mahāmate yac cakṣurvijñānasyābhāsam āgacchati rūpasaṃjñakam evaṃ śrotraghrāṇajihvākāyamanovijñānānāṃ śabdagandharasaspraṣṭavyadharmasaṃjñakam etaṇ nimittam iti vadāmi/

VI: 228 (7-9):

yat tasmin nimitte ghaṭādisaṃjñākṛtakam evam idaṃ nānyatheti tan nāma/

VI: 228 (10-12):

yan nāmanimittayoratyantānupalabdhitā buddhipralayādanyonyānanubhūtāparikalpitatvād eṣām dharmāṇāṃ tathateti/

VI: 226 (3-5):

tatra vikalpaḥ punar mahāmate yena nāma samudīrayati/ nimittavyañjakam idam enam idaṃ nānyatheti hastyaśvarathapadātistrīpuruṣādisaṃjñakaṃ tat vikalpaḥ pravartate/

VI: 226 (5-8):
samyagjñānaṃ punar mahāmate yena nāmanimittayor anupalabdhir anyonyāgantukatvād apravṛttir vijñānasyānucchedāśaśvatataḥ sarvatīrthakaśrāvakapratyekabuddhabhūmyapātanatvāt samyagjñānam ity ucyate/

VI: 226 (8-10):
punar aparam mahāmate yena samyagjñānena bodhisattvo mahāsattvo na nāma bhāvī karoti na ca nimittam abhāvī karoti/

VI: 226 (10-14):
samāropāpavādāntadvayakudṛṣṭivivarjitaṃ nāmanimittārthayor apravṛttivijñānam evam etāṃ tathatāṃ vadāmi/ tathatāvyavasthitaś ca mahāmate bodhisattvo mahāsattvo nirābhasagocarapratilābhitvāt pramuditāṃ bodhisattvabhūmiṃ pratilabhate/

VI: 226 (15-16):
sa pratilabhya pramuditāṃ bodhisattvabhūmiṃ vyāvṛttaḥ sarvatīrthyāpāyagatibhyo bhavati lokottaradharmagatisamavasṛtaḥ/

VI: 226-27 (17-18, 1):
. . . vibhāvayan svapratyātmāryadharmagatilakṣaṇaṃ tarkadṛṣṭivinivṛttakautuko 'nupūrvena yāvad dharmameghā bhūmir iti/

VI: 227 (4-5):
aṣṭāpadasunibaddhadharmā nānādhimuktikatayā sattvebhyo dharmaṃ deśayati/

VI: 227 (5-7):
kāyaṃ manovijñaptirahitam etan mahāmate tathatāpraveśāt pratilabhante bodhisattvā mahāsattvāḥ//

II: 42 (4-7):
dehabhogapratiṣṭāsamālayavijñānaviṣayagrāhyagrāhakavisaṃyuktaṃ nirābhāsagocaram utpādasthitabhaṅgavarjyaṃ svacittotpādānugataṃ vibhāvayiṣyanti nacirātte/

II: 42 (7-8):
mahāmate bodhisattvā mahāsattvāḥ saṃsāranirvāṇa samatāprāptā bhaviṣyanti/

III: 157 (14-15):
punar aparam mahāmate asaṅgalakṣaṇaṃ jñānaṃ viṣayavaicitryasaṅgalakṣaṇaṃ ca vijñānam/

VI: 227 (9-12):

bhagavān āha/ atraiva mahāmate trayaḥ svabhāvā antargatā aṣṭau ca vijñānāni dve ca nairātmye (pañcasu dharmeṣu)/ tatra nāma ca nimittaṃ ca parikalpitaḥ svabhāvo veditavyaḥ/

VI: 227 (12-15):

yaḥ punar mahāmate tad āśrayapravṛtto vikalpaś cittacaittasaṃśabdito yugapatkālodita āditya iva raśmisahito vicittalakṣaṇasvabhāvo vikalpādhārakaḥ sa mahāmate svabhāvaḥ paratantra ity ucyate/

VI: 227 (15-17):

samyagjñānaṃ tathatā ca mahāmate avināśatvāt svabhāvaḥ pariniṣpanno vaditavyaḥ//

X: 293 (gātha 218):

madīyaṃ dṛśyate cittaṃ bāhyam arthaṃ na vidyate/
evaṃ vibhāvayed bhrāntiṃ tathatāṃ cāpy anusmaret//

X: 294 (gātha 222):

pratyekabodhiṃ buddhatvam arhattvaṃ buddhadarśanam/
gūḍhavījaṃ bhaved bodhau svapne vai sidhyate tu yaḥ//

X: 287-88 (vv. 173, 174):

pratibhāsavimbamāyābhamarīcyā supinene tu/
alātacakragandharvapratiśrutkāsamodbhavāḥ//
advayā tathatā śūnyā bhūtakoṭiś ca dharmatā/
nirvikalpaś ca deśemi ye te niṣpannalakṣaṇāḥ//

II: 67-68 (15-17, 1-7; gātha 134):

tatra mahāmate pariniṣpannasvabhāvaḥ katamo yad uta nimittanāmavastulakṣaṇavikalpavirahitaṃ tathatāryajñānagatigamanapratyātmāryajñānagatigocara eṣa mahāmate pariniṣpannasvabhāvas tathāgatagarbhahṛdayam//

atha khalu bhagavāṃs tasyāṃ velāyām imāṃ gāthām abhāṣata//
nimittaṃ nāma saṃkalpaḥ svabhāvadvayalakṣaṇam/
samyagjñānaṃ hi tathatā pariniṣpannalakṣaṇam//

eṣa mahāmate pañcadharmasvabhāvalakṣaṇapravicayo nāma dharmaparyāyaḥ pratyātmāryajñānagatigocaro yatra tvayānyaiś ca bodhisattvaiḥ śikṣitavyam//

II: 130-33 (vv. 182, 187, 196, 202):

cittaṃ viṣayasaṃbandhaṃ jñānaṃ tarke pravartate/
nirābhāse viśeṣe ca prajñā vai saṃpravartate//
saṃvṛtiḥ paramārthaś ca tṛtīyaṃ nāsti hetukam/
kalpitaṃ saṃvṛtir hyuktā tac chedād āryagocaram//

pañcadharmā bhavet tattvaṃ svabhāvā hi trayas tathā/
etad vibhāvayed yogī tathatāṃ nātivartate//
vikalpadvayanirmuktaṃ niṣpannaṃ syāt tad eva hi//

IV: 215 (vv. 1, 2):

cittamātre nirābhāse vihārā buddhabhūmi ca/
etad dhi bhāṣitaṃ buddhair bhāṣante bhāṣayanti ca//
cittaṃ hi bhūmayaḥ sapta nirābhāsā tv ihāṣṭamī/
dve hi bhūmī vihāro 'tra śeṣā bhūmir mamātmikā//

II: 39 (13-16):

punaraparaṃ mahāmate saptavidhaḥ paramārtho yad uta cittagocaro jñānagocaraḥ prajñāgocaro dṛṣṭidvayagocaro dṛṣṭidvayātikrāntagocaraḥ sutabhūmyanukramaṇagocaraḥ tathāgatasya pratyātmagatigocaraḥ//

II: 49-50 (15-17, 4-12):

tatropariṣṭādāryajñānalakṣaṇatrayaṃ mahāmate katam adyad uta nirābhāsalakṣaṇaṃ sarvabuddhasvapraṇidhānādhiṣṭānalakṣaṇaṃ pratyātmāryajñānagatilakṣaṇaṃ ca/ (. . .)

tatra nirābhāsalakṣaṇaṃ punar mahāmate sarvaśrāvakapratyekabuddhatīrthalakṣaṇaparicayāt pravartate/ adhiṣṭānalakṣaṇaṃ punar mahāmate pūrvabuddhasvapraṇidhānādhiṣṭānataḥ pravartate/ pratyātmāryajñānagatilakṣaṇaṃ punar mahāmate sarvadharmalakṣaṇān abhiniveśato māyopamasamādhikāyapratilambhād buddhabhūmigatigamanapracārāt pravartate/ etan mahāmate āryāṇāṃ lakṣaṇatrayaṃ yenāryeṇa lakṣatrayeṇa samanvāgatā āryāḥ svapratyātmāryajñānagatigocaram adhigacchanti/ tasmāt tarhi mahāmate āryajñānalakṣaṇatrayayogaḥ karaṇīyaḥ//

III: 172 (4-18; gātha 61):

bhagavāṃs tasyai tad avocat/ dviprakāro mahāmate 'tītānāgatapratyutpannānāṃ tathāgatānām arhatāṃ samyaksaṃbuddhānāṃ dharmanayo yad uta deśanānayaś ca siddhāntapratyavasthānanayaś ca/ tatra deśanāpāṭanayo mahāmate yad uta vicitrasaṃbhārasūtropadeśo yathā cittādhimuktikatayā deśayanti sattvebhyaḥ/ tatra siddhāntanayaḥ punar mahāmate katamo yena yoginaḥ svacittadṛśyavikalpavyāvṛttiṃ kurvanti yad utaikatvānyatvobhayatvānubhayatvapakṣāpatanatācittamanomanovijñānātītaṃ svapratyātmāryagatigocaraṃ hetudṛṣṭilakṣaṇavinivṛttamanālīḍhaṃ sarvakutārkikais tīrthakaraśrāvakapratyekabuddhayāni kair nāstyastitvāntadvayapatitais tam ahaṃ siddhānta iti vadāmi/

etan mahāmate siddhāntanayadeśanālakṣaṇaṃ yatra tvayā cānyaiś ca bodhisattvair mahāsattvair yogaḥ karaṇīyaḥ// tatredam ucyate//
nayo hi dvividho mahyaṃ siddhānto deśanā ca vai/
deśemi yā bālānāṃ siddhāntaṃ yogināṃ aham//

VI: 229 (15-18):
bhagavān āha/ na mahāmate yathā rutārthagrahaṇaṃ kartavyam/ na ca mahāmate gaṅgānadībālukāpramāṇatayā tryadhvakabuddhapramāṇatā bhavati/

II: 132 (vv. 198, 199):
buddhyā vivecyamānaṃ tu na tantraṃ nāpi kalpitam/
niṣpanno nāsti vai bhāvaḥ kathaṃ buddhyā vikalpyate//
niṣpanno vidyate bhāvo bhāvābhāvavivarjitaḥ/
bhāvābhāvavinirmukto dvau svabhāvau kathaṃ na tau//

2.3. The Conjunctive System of the Eight Vijñānas: the Integration of *Both Mind and No-mind* States of Consciousness

II: 37 (8-12):
dvividho mahāmate vijñānānām utpattisthitinirodho bhavati na ca tārkikā avabudhyante yad uta prabandhanirodho lakṣaṇanirodhaś ca/ dvividha utpādo vijñānānāṃ prabandhotpādo lakṣaṇotpādaś ca/ dvividha sthitiḥ prabandhasthitir lakṣaṇasthitiś ca/

II: 37 (12-15):
trividhaṃ vijñānaṃ pravṛttilakṣaṇaṃ karmalakṣaṇaṃ jātilakṣaṇaṃ ca/

III: 156-57 (14-15, 8-13):
tatra mahāmate triprakāraṃ jñānaṃ laukikaṃ lokottaraṃ ca lokottaratamaṃ ca// tatra laukikaṃ jñānaṃ sad asat pakṣābhiniviṣṭānāṃ sarvatīrthakarabālapṛthagjanānāṃ ca/ tatra lokottaraṃ jñānaṃ sarvaśrāvakapratyekabuddhānāṃ ca svasāmānyalakṣaṇapatitāsayābhiniviṣṭānāṃ/ tatra lokottaratamaṃ jñānaṃ buddhabodhisattvānāṃ nirābhāsadharmapravicayādanirodhān utpādadarśanāt sad asat pakṣavigataṃ tathāgatabhūminairātmyādhigamāt pravartate//

III: 157 (1-7):
tatrotpannapradhvaṃsi vijñānam anutpannapradhvaṃsi jñānam/ punar aparaṃ mahāmate nimittānimittapatitaṃ vijñānaṃ nāsty asti vaicitryalakṣaṇahetukaṃ ca nimittānimittavyatikrāntalakṣaṇaṃ jñānam/ punar aparaṃ mahāmate upacayalakṣaṇaṃ vijñānam apacayalakṣaṇaṃ jñānam/ tatra trividhaṃ jñānaṃ svasāmānyalakṣaṇavādhārakaṃ cotpādavyayāvadhārakaṃ cānutpādānirodhavadhārakaṃ ca//

III: 157-58 (14-17, 1):
punar aparam mahāmate asaṅgalakṣaṇaṃ jñānaṃ viṣayavaicitryasaṅgalakṣaṇaṃ ca vijñānam/ punar aparaṃ mahāmate trisaṅgatikṣayotpādayogalakṣaṇaṃ vijñānam asaṅgasvabhāvalakṣaṇaṃ jñānam/ punar aparaṃ mahāmate aprāptilakṣaṇaṃ jñānaṃ svapratyātmāryajñānagatigocaram apraveśānirgamatvād udakacandravajjale//

II: 68 (11-13):
ajñānakarmatṛṣṇāprabhavaṃ cakṣuṣā rūpādigrahaṇābhiniveśāt pravartamānaṃ vijñānaṃ sarvendriyaiḥ svacittadṛṣyabhājanadehālayasvacittavikalpavikalpitaṃ vijñāpayati/

II: 65 (11-14; vv. 131, 132):
triyānam ekayānaṃ ca ayānaṃ ca vadāmy ahaṃ/
bālānāṃ mandabuddhīnām āryāṇāṃ ca viviktatāṃ//
dvāraṃ hi paramārthasya vijñaptidvayavarjitam/
yānatrayavyavasthānaṃ nirābhāse sthite kutaḥ//

II: 37-38 (15-19, 1-2):
khyāsyati khyātivijñānaṃ ca mahāmate vastuprativikalpavijñānam ca dve 'pyete 'bhinnalakṣaṇe 'nyonyohetuke/ tatra khyātivijñānaṃ mahāmate 'cintyavāsanāpariṇāmahetukam vastuprativikalpavijñānaṃ ca mahāmate viṣayavikalpahetukam anādikālaprapañcavāsanāhetukaṃ ca//

II: 127 (gātha 180):
tadd hetukaṃ tad ālambya manogatisamāśrayam/
hetuṃ dadāti cittasya vijñānam ca samāśritam//

II: 46 (vv. 102, 103, 104):
na cānyena ca nānanyena taraṅgā hy udadher matā/
vijñānāni tathā sapta cittena saha saṃyutāḥ//
udadheḥ pariṇāmo 'sau taraṅgāṇāṃ vicitratā/
ālayaṃ hi tathā citraṃ vijñānākhyaṃ pravartate//
cittaṃ manaś ca vijñānaṃ lakṣaṇārthaṃ prakalpyate/
abhinnalakṣaṇā hy aṣṭau na lakṣya na ca lakṣaṇam//

X: 278 (gātha 103):
cittam avyākṛtaṃ nityaṃ mano hy ubhayasaṃcaram/
vartamānaṃ hi vijñānaṃ kuśalākuśalaṃ hi tat//

X: 293 (gātha 217):
ālayo muñcate kāyaṃ manaḥ prārthayate gatim/
vijñānaṃ viṣayābhāsaṃ bhrāntiṃ dṛṣṭvā pralabhyate//

X: 293 (gātha 216):
svacchaṃ cittaṃ svabhāvena manaḥ kaluṣakārakam/
manaś ca sahavijñānair vāsanā kṣipate sadā//

X: 330 (vv. 521, 523):
vyavṛtte rūpavijñāne yadi karma vinaśyati/
nityānityaṃ na prāpnoti saṃsāraś ca na vidyate//
pradhvaṃsi patitaṃ rūpaṃ vijñānaṃ ca bhavālaye/
rūpavijñānasaṃbaddhaṃ na ca karma vinaśyati//

II: 46 (vv. 105, 106):

udadheś ca taraṅgānāṃ yathā nāsti viśeṣaṇam/
vijñānānāṃ tathā citteḥ pariṇāmo na labhyate//
cittena cīyate karma manasā ca vicīyate/
vijñānena vijānāti dṛśyaṃ kalpeti pañcabhiḥ//

II: 47-48 (vv. 113-115, 121):

udeti bhāskaro yadvat samahīnottame jine/
tathā tvaṃ lokapradyota tattvaṃ deśesi bāliśān//
kṛtvā dharmeṣvavasthānāṃ kasmāt tattvaṃ na bhāṣase/
bhāṣase yadi vā tattvaṃ citte tattvaṃ na vidyate//
udadher yathā taraṅgā hi darpaṇe supine yathā/
dṛśyanti yugapat kāle tathā cittaṃ svagocare//
deśemi jinaputrāṇāṃ neyaṃ bālāna deśanāḥ/
vicitrā hi yathā māyā dṛśyate na ca vidyate//

II: 38 (3-8):

tatra sarvendriyavijñananirodho mahāmate yad utālayavijñānasyābhūtaparikalpavāsanāvaicitryanirodhaḥ eṣa hi mahāmate lakṣaṇanirodhaḥ/ prabandhanirodhaḥ punar mahāmate yasmāc ca pravartate/ yasmād iti mahāmate yad āśrayena yad ālambanena ca/ tatra yad āśrayam anādikālaprapañcadauṣṭhulyavāsanā yad ālambanaṃ svacittadṛṣyavijñanaviṣaye vikalpāḥ/

X: 354 (gātha 722):

cittam manaś ca ṣadvānyavijñānānyātmasaṃyutā/
ekatvānyatvarahitā ālayo 'yaṃ pravartatte//

II: 38-39 (13-19, 1-2):

evam eva mahāmate pravṛttivijñānānyālayavijñānajātilakṣaṇādanyāni syur anālayavijñānahetukāni syuḥ/ athānanyāni pravṛttivijñānanirodha ālayavijñānanirodhaḥ syāt sa ca na bhavati svajātilakṣaṇanirodhaḥ/ tasmāt mahāmate na svajātilakṣaṇanirodho vijñānānāṃ kiṃ tu karmalakṣaṇanirodhaḥ/ svajātilakṣaṇe punar nirudhyamāna ālayavijñānanirodhaḥ syāt/ ālayavijñāne punar nirūpyamāṇe nirviśiṣṭastīrthakarocchedavādenāyaṃ vādaḥ syāt/

II: 235-36 (12-17, 1):

pravṛtya ca vinaśyanti svacittadṛśyānavabodhāt samanantaranirodhe 'nyadvijñānaṃ pravartate saṃsthānākṛtiviśeṣagrāhakaṃ manovijñānaṃ pañcabhir vijñānakāyaiḥ saha saṃprayuktaṃ pravartate/ kṣaṇakālānavasthāyi tat kṣaṇikam iti vadāmi/ kṣaṇikaṃ punar mahāmate ālayavijñānaṃ tathāgatagarbhaḥ samśabditaṃ manaḥsahitaṃ pravṛttivijñānavāsanābhiḥ kṣaṇikamanāsravavāsanābhir akṣaṇikam/

VII: 242-43 (15-17, 1-3):

punar aparaṃ mahāmate ṣaṇām vijñānakāyānāṃ nirodhād ucchedadṛṣṭim-āśrayanti bālapṛthagjanā ālayānabodhāt śāśvatadṛṣṭayo bhavanti/ . . . / svamativikalpasyaiva vinivṛtter mokṣaḥ prajñāyate/ caturvāsanāprahāṇāt sarvadoṣaprahāṇam//

VII: 243 (vv. 4, 5):

bhāvakāmarūpadṛṣṭīnāṃ vāsanā vai caturvidhā/
manovijñānasaṃbhūtā ālayaṃ ca manaḥ sthitāḥ//
manovijñānanetrādyair ucchedaś cāpy anityataḥ/
śāśvataṃ ca anādyena nirvāṇamatidṛṣṭināṃ//

II: 48-49 (vv. 119-20, 122-23):

sattvānāṃ karṣaṇārthāya raṅgaiś citraṃ vikalpyate/
deśanā vyabhicāraṃ ca tattvaṃ hy akṣaravarjitam//
kṛtvā dharmeṣvavasthānaṃ tattvaṃ deśemi yoginām/
tattvaṃ pratyātmagatikaṃ kalpyakalpena varjitam//
deśanāpi tathā citrā deśyate vyabhicāriṇī/
deśanā hi yad anyasya tad anyasyāpy adeśanā//
āture āture yadvad bhiṣagdravyaṃ prayacchati/
buddhā hi tatvat sattvānāṃ cittamātraṃ vadanti vai//

III: 155-56 (13-17, 1-2):

punaraparaṃ mahāmate aniruddhā anutpannāḥ prakṛtiparinirvṛtās triyānam ekayānaṃ ca pañcacittasvabhāvādiṣu yathārutārthābhiniveśaṃ pratītyā-bhiniveśataḥ samāropāpavādadṛṣṭipatito bhavati/ anyathā vyavasthitān anyathā prativikalpayan māyāvaicitryadarśanavikalpanavat/ tad yathā mahāmate anyathā hi māyāvaicitryaṃ dṛṣṭavyam anyathā pratikalpyate bālair na tvāryaiḥ//

III: 156 (7-10; gāthas 36-37):

astitvaṃ sarvabhāvānāṃ yathā bālair vikalpyate/
yadi te bhaved yathā dṛṣṭyāḥ sarve syus tattvadarśinaḥ//
abhāvāt sarvadharmāṇāṃ saṃkleśo nāsti śuddhiś ca/
na te tathā yathā dṛṣṭā na ca te vai na santi ca//

2.4. The Disjunctive Theory of Causation: Things are *Neither this, Nor that,* for They Are All Subject to Causes and Conditions (Hetu-pratyaya)

II: 82-83 (9-18, 1-2):

deśayatu me bhagavān hetupratyayalakṣaṇaṃ sarvadharmāṇāṃ yena hetupratyayalakṣaṇāvabodhenāhaṃ cānye ca bodhisattvā mahāsattvā sad asad dṛṣṭivikalparahitāḥ sarvabhāvanākramaṃ yugapad utpattiṃ na kalpayeyuḥ//

bhagavān āha/ dviprakāraṃ mahāmate pratītyasamutpādahetulakṣaṇaṃ sarvadharmāṇāṃ yad uta bāhyaṃ cādhyātmikaṃ ca/ tatra bāhyapratītyasamutpādo mahāmate mṛtpiṇḍadaṇḍacakrasūtrodakapuruṣaprayatnādipratyayair mahāmate ghaṭa utpadyate/ yathā ca mahāmate ghaṭo mṛtpiṇḍād eva tantubhyaḥ paṭaḥ vīraṇebhyaḥ kaṭā vījād aṅkuraḥ khaṇḍādipuruṣaprayatnayogād dadhno navanīta utpadyate evam eva mahāmate bāhyaḥ pratītyasamutpādaḥ pūrvottarottaro dṛṣṭavyam//

II: 83 (3-7):

tatrādhyātmikaḥ pratītyasamutpādo yad utāvidyā tṛṣṇā karmety evam ādhyā mahāmate dharmāḥ pratītyasamutpādasaṃjñāṃ pratilabhante/ ebhya utpannā mahāmate skandhadhātvāyatanākhyā dharmāḥ pratītyasamutpādasaṃjñāṃ pratilabhante/ te cāviśiṣṭāḥ kalpyante ca bālaiḥ//

III: 203 (vv. 110-111):

yadā sarvam imaṃ lokaṃ saṃkalām eva paśyati/
saṃkalāmātram evedaṃ tadā cittaṃ samādhyate//
ajñānatṛṣṇākarmādiḥ saṃkalādhyātmiko bhavet/
khejamṛddhāṇḍacakrādi vījabhūtādi bāhiram//

III: 197-98 (9-19, 1-4):

na bhavatānirodhānutpādadaśanena kiṃcid viśiṣyate/ tat kasya hetoḥ sarvatīrthakarāṇām api bhagavan kāraṇāny anutpannānyaniruddhāni tavāpi bhavannākāśam apratisaṃkhyānirodho nirvāṇadhātuś cānirodho 'nutpannaḥ/ tīrthakarā api bhagavan kāraṇapratyayahetukīṃ jagata utpattiṃ varṇayanti/ bhagavān apyajñānatṛṣṇākarmavikalpapratyayebhyo jagata utpattim varnayati/ tasyaiva kāraṇasya saṃjñāntaraviśeṣam utpādya pratyayā iti/ evaṃ bāhyaiḥ pratyayair bāhyānāṃ te ca tvaṃ ca bhāvānām utpattaye/ ato nirviśiṣṭo 'yaṃ bhagavan vādastīrthakaravādena bhavati/ aṇupradhāneśvaraprajāpatiprabhṛtayo navadravyasahitā aniruddhā anutpannāḥ tavāpi bhagavan sarvabhāvā anutpannāniruddhāḥ sad asato 'nupalabdheḥ/ bhūtāvināśāc ca svalakṣaṇaṃ notpadyate na nirudhyate yāṃ tāṃ gatiṃ gatvā bhūto bhūtasvabhāvaṃ na vijahāti/

II: 42 (7-8):

mahāmate bodhisattvā mahāsattvāḥ saṃsāranirvāṇasamatāprāptā bhaviśyanti/

II: 76 (7-13):

advayalakṣaṇaṃ punar mahāmate katamad yad uta cchāyātapavaddīrghahrsvakṛṣṇaśuklavan mahāmate dvayaprabhāvitā na pṛthakpṛthak/ evaṃ saṃsāranirvāṇavan mahāmate sarvadharmā advayāḥ/ na yatra mahāmate nirvāṇaṃ tatra saṃsāraḥ/ na ca yatra saṃsāraḥ tatra nirvāṇaṃ vilakṣaṇahetusadbhāvāt/ tenocyante 'dvayā saṃsāraparinirvāṇavat sarvadharmā iti/ tasmāt tarhi mahāmate śūnyatānutpādādvayaniḥsvabhāvalakṣaṇe yogaḥ karaṇīyaḥ//

II: 103 (7-17):

atha khalu mahāmatir bodhisattvaḥ punar api bhagavan tam etad avocat/ pratītyasamutpādaṃ punar bhagavatā deśayatā kāraṇavyapadeśa eva kṛto na svanayaprakṛtyavasthānakathā/ tīrthakarā api bhagavan kāraṇata utpattiṃ varṇayanti yad uta pradhāneśvarapuruṣakālāṇupratyayebhyo bhāvānām utpattayaḥ/ kiṃ tu bhagavatā pratyayaparyāyāntareṇa utpattir varṇyate bhāvānāṃ na ca siddhāntaviśeṣāntaram/ sad asato hi bhagavaṃs tīrthakarā apy utpattiṃ varṇayanti bhūtvā ca vināśaṃ pratyayair bhāvānām/ yad apy uktaṃ bhagavatāvidyāpratyayāḥ saṃsārā yāvajjarāmaraṇamati ahetuvādavyapadeśa eṣa bhagavatānuvarṇito na sa hetuvādaḥ/

II: 103-104 (17-18, 1-11):

yugapad vyavasthitānāṃ bhagavann etad dhavati/ asmin satīdaṃ bhavatīti na kramavṛttyapekṣāvasthitānām/ kiṃ tu tīrthyakaravyapadeśa eva bhagavan viśiṣyate na tvadīyam/ tat kasya hetos tīrthyakarāṇāṃ hi bhagavan kāraṇamapratītyasamutpannaṃ kāryam abhinivartayati/ tava tu bhagavan kāraṇam api kāryāpekṣaṃ kāryam api kāraṇapekṣaṃ hetupratyayasaṃkaraś caivam anyonyānavasthā prasajyate/ ahetutvam ca bhagavaṃl lokasyāsmin satīdaṃ bruvataḥ/ bhagavān aha/ na mahāmate mamāhetukakāraṇavādo hetupratyayasaṃkaraś ca prasajyate/ asmin sat īdaṃ bruvato grāhya-grāhakābhāvāt svacittadṛśyamātrāvabodhāt/ ye tu mahāmate grāhya-grāhakābhiniviṣṭāḥ svacittadṛśyamātraṃ nāvabudhante bāhyasvaviṣaya-bhāvātvena teṣāṃ mahāmate eṣa doṣaḥ prasajyate na tu mama pratīya-kāraṇavyapadeśaṃ kurvataḥ//

II: 83-84 (8-17, 1):

tatra hetur mahāmate ṣadvidho yad uta bhaviṣyadd hetuḥ saṃbandhahetur lakṣaṇahetuḥ kāraṇahetur vyañjanahetur upekṣāhetur mahāmate ṣaṣṭhaḥ/ tatra bhaviṣyadd hetuḥ mahāmate hetukṛtyaṃ karoty adhyātmabāhyot-pattau dharmāṇām / saṃbandhahetuḥ punar mahāmate alambanakṛtyaṃ karoty adhyātmikabāhyotpattau skandhavījādīnām/ lakṣaṇahetuḥ punar aparaṃ mahāmate anantarakriyālakṣaṇoparibaddhaṃ janayati/ kāraṇahetuḥ punar mahāmate ādhipatyādhikārakṛtyam karoti cakravartinṛpavat/ vyañjanahetuḥ punar mahāmate utpannasya vikalpasya bhāvasya lakṣaṇa-dyotanaṃ kṛtyaṃ karoti pradīpavadrūpadīnām/ upekṣāhetuḥ punar mahāmate vinivṛttikāle prabandhakriyāvyucchittiṃ karoty avikalpotpattau//

II: 84 (2-15):

ete hi mahāmate svavikalpakalpitā bālapṛthagjanair na kramavṛttyā na yugapat pravartante/ tat kasya hetor yadi punar mahāmate yugapat pravarteran kāryakāraṇavibhāgo na syād apratilabdhahetulakṣaṇatvāt/ atha kramavṛttyā pravarteran alabdhasya lakṣaṇātmakatvāt kramavṛttyā na pravartate/ ajātaputrapitṛśabdavan mahāmate kramavṛttisaṃbandhayogā na ghaṭante/ tārkikāṇāṃ hetvārambaṇanirantarādhipatipratyayādibhir janyajanakatvān mahāmate kramavṛttyā notpadyante/ parikalpitasvabhāvā-bhiniveśalakṣaṇān mahāmate yugapannotpadyate svacittadṛśyadehabhogapraviṣṭānatvāt svasāmānyalakṣaṇabāhyabhāvābhāvān mahāmate krameṇa yugapadvā notpadyante/ anyatra svacittadṛśyavikalpavikalpitatvād vijñānaṃ pravartate/ tasmāt tarhi mahāmate hetupratyayakriyāyogalakṣaṇakrama-yugapaddṛṣṭivigatena te bhavitavyam//

II: 84-85 (vv. 140-44):

tatredam ucyate//
na hy atrotpadyate kiṃcit pratyayair na virudhyate/
utpadyante nirudhyante pratyayā eva kalpitāḥ//
na bhaṅgotpādasaṃkleśaḥ pratyayānām nivāryate/
yatra bālā vikalpanti pratyayaiḥ sa nivāryate//
yac cāsataḥ* pratyayeṣu dharmāṇāṃ nasti saṃbhavaḥ/
vāsanair bhrāmitaṃ cittaṃ tribhave khyāyate yataḥ//
nābhūtvā jāyate kiṃcit pratyayair na virudhyate/
bandhyāsutākāśapuṣpaṃ yadā paśyanti saṃskṛtam//
tadā grāhaś ca grāhyaṃ ca bhrāntiṃ dṛṣṭvā nivartate/
na cotpādyaṃ na cotpannaḥ pratyayo 'pi na kiṃcana/
saṃvidyante kvacit kecid vyavahāras tu kathyate//

X: 312 (vv. 366-68):

ajāḥ prasūtajanmā vai acyutāś ca cyavanti ca/
yugapajjalacandrābhā dṛśyante kṣetrakoṭiṣu//
ekadhā bahudhā bhūtvā varṣanti ca jvalanti vai/
citte cintamayā bhūtvā cittamātraṃ vadanti te//
citte cittamātraṃ ca acittā cittasaṃbhavā/
vicitrarūpasaṃsthānāś cittamātre gatiṃgatāḥ//

X: 310 (vv. 355-57):

asty anākārato bhāvaḥ śāśvatocchedavarjitaḥ/
sad asat pakṣavigatāḥ kalpayiṣyanti madhyamam//
ahetuvāde kalpyante ahetūcchedadarśanam/
vāhyabhāvāparijñānān nāśayiṣyanti madhyamam//
bhāvagrāhaṃ na mokṣate mā bhūducchedarśanam/
samāropāpavādena deśayiṣyanti madhyamam//

X: 311 (vv. 358-61):

cittamātrāvabodhena bāhyabhāvā vyudāśrayā/
vinivṛttir vikalpasya pratipatsye ca madhyamā//
cittamātraṃ na dṛśyanti dṛśyābhāvān na jāyate/
pratipanmadhyamā caisā mayā cānyaiś ca deśitā//
utpādaṃ cāpy anutpādaṃ bhāvābhāvaś ca śūnyatā/
naiḥsvabhāvyaṃ ca bhāvānāṃ dvayam etan na kalpayet//
vikalpavṛttya bhāvo na mokṣaṃ kalpenti bāliśāḥ/
na cittavṛttyasaṃbodhād dvayagrāhaḥ prahīyate//

---

* Rather, *sadasataḥ* or *yaccāsadasataḥ*, according to Nanjio ed.

X: 311 (vv. 362-63):

svacittadṛśyasaṃbodhād dvayagrāhaḥ prahīyate/
prahāṇaṃ hi parijñānaṃ vikalpyasyāvināśakam//
cittadṛśyaparijñānād vikalpo na pravartate/
apravṛttir vikalpasya tathatā cittavarjitā//

III: 200-201 (vv. 86-87, 92-94, 96-97):

utpādavinivṛtty artham anutpādaprasādhakam/
ahetuvādaṃ deśemi na ca bālair vibhāvyate//
anutpannam idaṃ sarvaṃ na ca bhāvā na santi ca/
gandharvasvapnamāyākhyā bhāvā vidyanty ahetukāḥ//
nāhetuko na hetubhyo yadā paśyanti saṃskṛtam/
tadā vyāvartate dṛṣṭir vibhaṅgotpādavādinī//
kim abhāvo hy anutpāda uta pratyayavīkṣaṇam/
atha bhāvasy nāmedaṃ nirarthaṃ vā bravīhi me//
na cābhāvo hy anutpādo na ca pratyayavīkṣaṇam/
na ca bhāvasya nāmedaṃ na ca nāma nirarthakam//
hetupratyayavyāvṛttiṃ kāraṇasya nirodhanam/
cittamātravyavasthānam anutpādaṃ vadāmy aham//
ahetuvṛttir bhāvānāṃ kalpyakalpanavarjitam/
sad asat pakṣanirmuktam anutpādaṃ vadāmy aham//

III: 202-203 (vv. 99, 101, 103, 104):

na bāhyabhāvaṃ nābhāvaṃ nāpi cittaparigrahaḥ/
svapnaṃ keśoṇḍukaṃ māyā gandharvaṃ mṛgatṛṣṇikā/
sarvadṛṣṭiprahāṇaṃ ca tad anutpādalakṣaṇam//
kalāpaḥ pratyayānāṃ ca pravartate nivartate/
kalāpāc ca pṛthagbhūtaṃ na jātaṃ na nirudhyate//
asan na jāyate bhāvo nāsan na sad asat kvacit/
anyatra hi kalāpo 'yam pravartate nivartate//
saṃketamātram evedam anyonyāpekṣasaṃkalā/
janyam arthaṃ na caivāsti pṛthakpratyayasaṃkalāt//

III: 204 (vv. 113-15, 117):

yadi janyo na bhāvo 'sti syād buddhiḥ kasya pratyayāt/
anyonyajanakā hy ete tanaite pratyayāḥ smṛtāḥ//
uṣṇadravacalakaṭhinā dharmā bālair vikalpitāḥ/
kalāpo 'yaṃ na dharmo 'sti ato vai niḥsvabhāvatā//
vaidyā yathāturavaśāt kriyābhedaṃ prakurvate/
na tu śāstrasya bhedo 'sti doṣabhedāt tu bhidyate//
na kleśendriyabhedena śāsanaṃ bhidyate mama/
ekam eva bhaved yānaṃ mārgam aṣṭāṅgikam śivam//

Notes

Introduction

0.1. The Purpose of the Study

1. Ed. J. Thomas, in his *History of Buddhist Thought* (London: 1933, reprint: 1971), p. 230, refers to this sūtra as "the chief canonical text for the doctrine of subjective idealism." Ed. Conze calls it "a work of quite exceptional spiritual profundity," in his *Buddhist Thought in India* (London: 1962, reprint: 1973), p. 251. In addition, D. T. Suzuki considers it "the sūtra par excellence in relation to the Zen teaching of Buddhism;" see his *Studies in the Laṅkāvatāra Sūtra* (London: 1930, reprint: 1968), p. 90. More recently, Heinrich Dumoulin, yet another major European scholar, reinforces this high regard for and general agreement on the importance of this text in the history of Buddhism: "Of all the sacred scriptures of Buddhism, this sūtra comes closest to Zen;" see *A History of Zen Buddhism* (Berlin: 1959, Boston: 1963), p. 45.

2. Wm. M. McGovern, *A Manual of Buddhist Philosophy* (London, New York: 1923), vol. 1 "Cosmology," p. 20. E. Frauwallner also regards the Yogācāras as "the most important school of the Mahāyāna," in *Die Philosophie des Buddhismus* (1956), p. 264.

3. See the introduction to Silvain Lévi's translation of Asaṅga's major opus *Mahāyāna-Sūtrālaṃkāra* (Paris: 1907 & 1911). For details concerning the lives of Vasubandhu and Asaṅga, see Takakusu's translation of "The Life of Vasu-bandhu by Paramārtha (499-569)," *T'oung Pao*, ser. 2, 5 (1904), pp. 269-96; and E. Frauwallner, "On the Date of the Buddhist Master of the Law, Vasubandhu," *Serie Orientale Roma*, 3 (1951). More recently, Stefan Anacker suggested A.D. 316 in Gandhāra as the time and place of his birth, in *Seven Works of Vasubandhu, The Buddhist Psychological Doctor* (Delhi: 1984), p. 11; for an extensive discussion, see Chapter II, "Vasubandhu, His Life and Times," pp. 7-28.

4. See also Alex and Hideko Wayman, *The Lion's Roar of Queen Śrīmālā* (New York, London: 1974), p. 6. The historicity of Asaṅga's teacher Maitreya (-nātha), the founder of the Yogācāra school, is accepted only by some scholars, e.g., T. R. V. Murti, *The Central Philosophy of Buddhism* (London: 1955, 1980), p. 107 & n. 6.

5. See also Ed. Conze, *Buddhism: Its Essence and Development* (New York: Harper Torchbooks, 1975), pp. 119-24; Ed. Conze, *The Prajñāpāramitā Literature* (The Hague: 1960) (Indo-Iranian Monographs), p. 9; Nalinaksha Dutt, *Aspects of Mahāyāna Buddhism and its Relation to Hīnayāna* (London: 1930), pp. 28-43; Sarvepalli Radhakrishnan (gen. ed.), *The Cultural Heritage of India*, vol. 1: *The Early Phases: Prehistoric, Vedic, and Upanishadic, Jaina, and Buddhist* (Calcutta: 1937), p. 517; Kajiyama Yuichi, "Hannya-gyō" (Prajñā literature) in *Nihon no buten (Buddhist Literature of Japan)*, ed. by Toshinori Takeuchi and Takeshi Umehara (Tokyo: 1969), (Chūkō shinshō No. 179 in a series), p. 25; A. K. Warder, *Indian Buddhism* (Delhi: 1970), pp. 352-53; Diana Mary Paul, *The Buddhist Feminine Ideal: Queen Srīmālā and the Tathāgatagarbha*, AAR Dissertation Series No. 30 (Ann Arbor: 1980), pp. 9-10 & 34; and Étienne Lamotte, *Histoire du Bouddhisme Indien* (Louvain: 1958), pp. 580-82.

6. See also Bhikshu Sangharakshita, *A Survey of Buddhism* (Bangalore: 1957), p. 332; E. Obermiller, *History of Buddhism (Chos-hbyung)* by Bu-ston (Heidelberg: 1931; repr. 1965), pp. 110 & 120.

7. See Diana M. Paul, op. cit., p. 10 & p. 38, nn. 10 & 11.

8. According to Paramārtha and from inscriptions at Amarāvatī, quoted by André Bareau in *Les Sectes Bouddhiques du Petit Véhicule* (Saigon: 1955), pp. 32-33.

9. This introductory chapter is best understood in light of the Buddhist tradition, according to which: " . . . the Conqueror, in the ninth month of his buddhahood, at the full moon of Phussa, himself set forth for the isle of Laṅkā, to win Laṅkā for the faith. For Laṅkā was known to the Conqueror as a place where his doctrine should (thereafter) shine in glory; and (he knew that) from Laṅkā, filled with the yakkhas, the yakkhas must (first) be driven forth." Cf. *Mahāvaṃsa*, or *The Great Chronicle of Ceylon* 1.19-20, vol. 3, Wilhelm Geiger, tr. (London: 1912), "The Visit of the Tathāgata," p. 3.

10. See Suzuki, *Studies*, p. 4.

11. Aside from the continual migration between north and south, in many places various Buddhist sects co-existed rather successfully. Bareau writes (op. cit., pp. 38-39, my translation):

"Certain regions, where it (Buddhism) thrives, seem characterized by the fact that very diverse sects and both Vehicles live there side by side" (This is based on Hsüan-tsang's observations).

12. See also Lama Chimpa and Alaka Chattopadhyaya, tr., *Tāranātha's History of Buddhism in India*, Debiprasad Chattopadhyaya, ed. (Calcutta: 1980, reprint Atlantic Highlands, N. J.: 1981), pp. 18, 325. An interesting parallel may be noted here between the personal history of this Buddhist teacher and the textual history of the *Laṅkāvatāra-sūtra*, as reflected in its internal eclectic structure, a composite of early Hindu mythology (Ch. I), middle Mahāyāna doctrine (Chapters II—VII), and late Tantric ideas (Chapters VII-IX).

13. According to Philip B. Yampolsky, this story is fictional, since

Guṇabhadra must have been dead by the time Bodhidharma came to the Middle Kingdom from South India; hence, the recognition of Bodhidharma as the first patriarch by most Chinese writers. See Ph. B. Yampolsky, *The Platform Sūtra of the Sixth Patriarch* (New York: 1967), p. 20-21 & n. 55, p. 20.

14. Ibid., p. 20, n. 57. This attribution may be spurious, according to Prof. Yampolsky, who says: "Many works are attributed to Bodhidharma; almost all of them are products of a later age."

15. Again, I am indebted to Prof. Yampolsky for pointing out to me the thorough investigation of this obscure phase of Ch'an history done by John Robert McRae in "The Northern School of Chinese Ch'an Buddhism," unpublished *Ph.D. dissertation* at Yale University (New Haven: 1983), pp. 86-92.

16. Ibid., p. 92. The complex issues involved in authenticating hagiographical accounts are explored by Bernard Faure in his article "Bodhidharma as Textual and Religious Paradigm," found in *History of Religions* 25, no. 3 (Feb. 1986): 187-98.

17. McRae, op. cit., p. 105.

18. Ibid., p. 104. The history of patriarchal transmission is reproduced and commented upon by McRae between pp. 100-104, and by Faure, op. cit., pp. 188-90 & 197-98.

19. McRae, op. cit., pp. 104-105.

20. See McRae, op. cit., p. 105, & nn. 57, 58 & 59, p. 505. Aside from the *Laṅkāvatāra*, three other Mahāyāna sūtras are usually mentioned in connection with the Zen teachings of sudden enlightenment: the *Prajñāpāramitā* (for the Voidness doctrine), the *Avataṃsaka* (for its cosmotheism), and the *Vimalakīrti* (for its emphasis on the undogmatic and non-verbal essence of enlightenment). See also Heinrich Dumoulin, *Zen Enlightenment, Origins and Meaning* (N.Y.: 1979), pp. 26-28.

21. McRae, op. cit., pp. 106-107.

22. D. T. Suzuki, *Essays in Zen Buddhism* (First Series) (London: 1927, reprint: 1933), pp. 87-88.

23. Bernard Faure, "La Volonté d'Orthodoxie," unpublished *Ph.D. Dissertation*, Tome 1 (Paris: Collége de France, 1984), p. 353 (my translation from the original French manuscript).

24. Ibid. (my translation from the French manuscript).

25. Ibid., pp. 464-66.

26. Suzuki, *Studies*, p. 53. For a doctrinal history of the *Saṃparigraha* (Shelun) school, see also Junjirō Takakusu, *The Essentials of Buddhist Philosophy* (Honolulu: 1947, reprints, Bombay: 1956; Delhi: 1975, 1978), pp. 82f.

27. See Suzuki's *Studies*, p. 55.

28. Ibid.

29. *Ibid.*, pp. 53 & 55.

30. Jikidō Takasaki, *A Study on the Ratnagotravibhāga* (*Uttaratantra*) (Roma: 1966), p. 53.

31. See Bunyiu Nanjio's Preface to his edition of *The Laṅkāvatāra Sūtra* (Kyoto: 1923), pp. 8-9. For a detailed account of the history and the compartive textual condition of the three extant Chinese versions, see D. T. Suzuki's *Studies*, pp. 4-37. The three translations are referred to as the Sung, the Wei, and the Tang (according to the ruling dynasty), or simply, the Four, the Ten, and the Seven Fasciculi (p. 15, n. 1). They are mentioned in the *Kai-yuan Lu* records (Fascicule 4, 38a. Kōkyō Shoin edition).

32. Suzuki, *Studies*, pp. 12-13.

33. According to Suzuki (Ibid., p. 63), these "are still in current circulation, as they are all included in the supplementary part of the Tripiṭaka compiled by Mr. Tatsuye Nakano, Kyoto, 1905-12, and one is in the Chinese Tripiṭaka itself." The existence of only two T'ang commentaries may indicate the relative unimportance of the text in China at that time.

34. See Faure, "Bodhidharma as Paradigm, op. cit., pp. 195-96.

35. Suzuki, *Studies*, pp. 63-65.

36. D. T. Suzuki, tr., *The Laṅkāvatāra Sūtra, A Mahāyāna Text* (London: 1932, reprint Boulder: 1978).

37. See B. Nanjio, ed., op. cit., p. 9; see also pp. 12-13 for a reproduction of Mitsui's tabulation of the chapter divisions found in the Sanskrit and the three Chinese translations.

38. According to an anthropological study by Todd T. Lewis, "The Tuladhars of Kathmandu: A Study of Buddhist Tradition in a Newar Merchant Community," unpublished *Ph.D. dissertation* at Columbia University (New York: 1984), pp. 3 & 448.

39. Suzuki, *Studies*, pp. 54-55.

40. For a continuous rendition of the text, see Suzuki's translation of *The Laṅkāvatāra Sūtra*, pp. 166-69.

41. Ibid., ch. VI, pp. 223-24, *gātha* 3.

42. Suzuki, *Studies*, pp. 50-51.

43. Suzuki's account of the history of Zen in relation to the *Laṅkāvatāra* is given in his *Studies*, pp. 56-63 and 96f.

44. Faure, "La Volonté d'Orthodoxie," (op. cit.), pp. 291-93; for the description of the three Ch'an schools and their evolution in five stages, see pp. 5-7 and Tableaux 1 & 2.

45. Suzuki, *Studies*, p. 56.

46. Ibid., p. 57 and Faure, op. cit., p. 292.

47. Suzuki, *Studies*, pp. 60-61.

0.2. Dating the Text

1. For Sthiramati, see *Sūtrālaṃkāra-bhāṣyaṭīka*, XI, v. 40 (Peking Edition reprint), vol. 108, p. 283-2-7 (quoting Laṅkā., III, v. 33); for Dharmapāla, see *Tattva-saṃgraha*, vol. 31, p. 10c, and others.

2. This article first appeared in *Indological and Buddhist Studies in Honour of Prof. J. W. de Jong* (Canberra: 1982), 545-67.

3. Ui, *Indotetsugaku kenkyū*, 1 (1924): 406, quoted by Takasaki, op. cit., p. 546.

4. S. Yamaguchi, *Bunshū* (Collection of Minor Works), vol. 2, p. 312. (Originally in *Tōhōgaku Ronshū*, July, 1962), cited by Takasaki, op. cit., p. 546.

5. Takasaki, op. cit., p. 545 and Takasaki, *A Study on the Ratnagotravibhaga (Uttaratantra)* (Roma: 1966), p. 53.

6. Suzuki, tr., *The Laṅkāvatāra Sūtra*, Introduction, p. 42.

7. Takasaki, "Sources of the Laṅkāvatāra," op. cit., pp. 547-50.

8. Ibid., pp. 550-58.

9. Ibid., pp. 558-63.

10. Ibid., p. 564.

11. D. J. Kalupahana, *Buddhist Philosophy, A Historical Analysis* (Honolulu: 1976, reprint: 1982), p. 150.

12. Quoted by Ashok Kumar Chatterjee in *The Yogācāra Idealism* (Varanasi: 1962), p. 38.

13. Suzuki, *Studies*, p. 17; see also his *Essays in Zen Buddhism*, vol. 1 (Tokyo: 1927), p. 75 and his tr., *The Laṅkāvatāra Sūtra*, Introduction, pp. 41-43.

14. J. Takasaki, "Analysis of the *Laṅkāvatāra*, In search of its original form," in *Indianisme et Bouddhisme, Mélanges offerts à Mgr. Étienne Lamotte* (Louvain: 1980), pp. 339-52.

15. Ibid., p. 345. See also Suzuki's sixfold division of the text according to its prose/verse structure in *Studies*, p. 24. For the reproduction of Kokwan Shiren's division into 86 parts, and the verse correspondences between the *Sagāthakam* and the other chapters, see Takasaki's "Analysis," op. cit., pp. 347-52.

16. Cf. Takasaki, "Analysis," op. cit., pp. 341-45; see also Suzuki, *Studies*, pp. 37-44.

17. At least two topics (the characteristic marks, and the arts and

sciences, *lakṣaṇapadam* and *kalāvidyāpadam*) are repeated in the *pada* section (Nanjio edition, pp. 34-36, ll. 13, 11-12, 7-8).

18. See Suzuki, *Studies*, pp. 20, & 65-85, for an in-depth study of the first chapter and its relation to the *Rāmāyaṇa* epic.

19. J. W. Hauer, "Das *Laṅkāvatāra-Sūtra* und das Sāṃkhya," *Beiträge zur Indischen Sprachwissenschaft und Religionsgeschichte* (Stuttgart: 1927), p. 3.

20. See also Suzuki, *Studies*, p. 16.

21. See Hauer, op. cit., pp. 2-6, and n. 10, pp. 3-4.

22. Suzuki gives a thoroughly Buddhist interpretation of this chapter in his *Studies*, pp. 368-71 (i.e., ethical rather than text-critical).

23. Takasaki, "Analysis," pp. 345-47.

24. See also Suzuki, *Studies*, pp. 21-24. For an illuminating discussion of the polemics in the *Sagāthakam*, see Arnold Kunst, "Some of the Polemics in the *Laṅkāvatārasūtra*," in *Buddhist Studies in Honour of Walpola Rahula* (London: 1980), pp. 103-12.

25. Suzuki, *An Index to the Laṅkāvatāra Sūtra (Nanjio Ed.) with the Chinese and Tibetan Equivalents* (Kyoto: 1933).

26. Suzuki, tr., *The Laṅkāvatāra Sūtra*, Introduction, pp. 47-48. See also, *Studies*, p. 65, n. 1.

27. See Suzuki's *Studies*, p. 181.

28. Apparently, this text is the same as the *Mahāyāna-saṃgraha;* see also Chandradhar Sharma, *A Critical Survey of Indian Philosophy* (Delhi: 1960, reprint: 1976), p. 109.

29. Sir M. Monier-Williams, *A Sanskrit-English Dictionary* (Oxford: 1899, reprint: 1964), p. 154.

0.3. Methodology and Outline

1. The largest such MS used for this Sanskrit version is No. 3 in the Sanskrit Catalogue of the Asiatic Society, London, in six volumes, which was collated with MSS, Add. 915 & 1607 from the Cambridge University Library, as well as with Kawaguchi MS and some palm leaf fragments found in Nepal by J. Takakusu, in 1914. See Preface to B. Nanjio's edition of *The Laṅkāvatāra Sūtra* (Kyoto: 1923), p. 6-7.

2. Ibid., pp. 7-8.

3. See Wm. Barrett's Introduction to *Zen Buddhism, Selected Writings of D. T. Suzuki* (New York: Doubleday & Co., 1956), p. 11.

4. I would like to express my special debt of gratitude and sincere appreciation to Professor Alex Wayman of Columbia University, whose

generous suggestions and overall critique greatly enhanced the clarity of my work. In addition, his many books and articles on Yogācāra scriptures and ideas have offered an invaluable wealth of information and insight to anyone daring to venture upon the forbidding domain of Mahāyāna esotericism.

5. The term *enlightenment* used in the title of this book circumscribes more appropriately, in my opinion, the pursuit of *religious* truth, with its own sphere of specific concerns, quite distinct from other kinds of epistemological enterprises (e.g., empirical-scientific, aesthetic, or social). This term is particularly appropriate in the context of Oriental religio-philosophical systems, where it is not *Who* you know, but *What* you know (i.e., Gnosis, Jñāna, or enlightenment) that ensures the attainment of the final goal of liberation.

6. Perhaps an in situ investigation of the way in which the teachings of the *Laṅkāvatāra* are still being followed today in Buddhist communities, such as the Newaris of Nepal, or the Tibetan refugees settled in India and around the world, might shed more light on the practical aspects of this ancient Mahāyāna text.

7. Given in the *Madhyāntavibhāga-bhāṣya,* 3, K.3 (R. C. Pandeya's ed., p. 38).

8. This term has been used before by Buddhist, as well as non-Buddhist scholars. See Suzuki, *The Zen Doctrine of No Mind* (London: 1969), p. 43; also H. Benoit, *The Supreme Doctrine, Psychological Studies in Zen Thought* (N.Y.: 1955, 1959), pp. 72-78, where he speaks of "the Fundamental Unconscious (No-Mind of Zen);" and H. Dumoulin, who in *Zen Enlightenment* (N.Y.: 1979), pp. 50-52, has a section on "The Doctrine of No Mind."

9. These five steps are yet another original contribution of the *Laṅkā,* for it differs from both the Five Paths theory (*pañcamārga*) of the Sarvāstivāda Abhidharmists, and from the Ten Bodhisattva Stages (*bhūmis*), as outlined by the Mahāsāṅghikas in the *Mahāvastu* and the *Daśabhūmika-sūtra.*

1.0. The Nature of Buddhist Ontology

1. See also, Th. F. Carter, *The Invention of Printing and its Spread Westward* (2d ed.) (New York: 1955), pp. 54-56; Paul Pelliot, *Les Débuts de l'imprimerie en Chine* (Paris: 1953), pp. 47-48.

An unconfirmed newspaper report (*Canberra Times,* 16 Feb. 1967) mentions the finding of a scroll, printed from 12 wooden blocks, in the stonework of a South Korean pagoda built in 751. The date of the translation can be no later than 704, according to a reference given by J. W. de Jong in *Buddhist Studies,* ed. by Gregory Schopen (Berkeley, Ca.: 1979), p. 100, n. 56.

2. The Greek contemporary of the Buddha, Heraclitus of Ephesus (c. 540-470 B.C.) also developed a cosmology of process ("All things are flowing," *panta rhei*), but his leanings were materialistic and the impact of

his teachings was rather limited, due to the oracular character of his utterances. Cf. G. S. Kirk, "Natural Change in Heraclitus" in *The Pre-Socratics*, A. P. D. Mourelatos, ed. (New York: 1974), pp. 189, 195 & 229f.

3. See *Milindapañha* 25, 28; *Visuddhi-Magga*, Ch. 17, *Mahā-Nidāna-Sutta* of the *Dīgha-Nikāya; Saṃyutta-Nikāya* 22. 85; *Visuddhi-Magga*, Ch. 21; *Saṃyutta-Nikāya* 12. 62, etc. in H. C. Warren, *Buddhism in Translations* (New York: 1977), pp. 128-52.

4. For a detailed presentation of the development of substance and process (or modal) philosophies in India, see T. R. V. Murti, *The Central Philosophy of Buddhism* (London: 1980), Ch. 3.

5. For a succint review of the history of the term, the authors and the relevant literature, see the first chapter "Ontology and the Ontological Question" in Adrian Thatcher, *The Ontology of Paul Tillich* (Oxford: 1978), pp. 1-24.

6. See Eisler, R., *Kant Lexicon* (Berlin: 1930), p. 400.

7. G. W. F. Hegel, *The Science of Logic* (London: 1969), Foreword §33.

8. M. Heidegger, *Being and Time*, J. Macquarrie & E. Robinson, tr. (Oxford: 1967), p. 13 (German pagination number).

9. This emphasis upon the role of subjectivity in defining Reality, along with the consequent low regard for conceptual language and high regard for the totality of "pure" experience, have led to many misunderstandings of Buddhism as a valid philosophical way of interpreting the world in general, and of Yogācāra thought in particular, as a radical denial of the objective status of Reality. Prof. Robert Thurman, in his book *Life and Teachings of Tsong Khapa* (New Delhi: 1982), p. 97, commenting on the philosophical works of the celebrated 16th-century Tibetan master Je Rinpoche Tsong Khapa, says the following:

" . . . They conclusively disprove the popular misconception that Buddhism has no philosophy, no refined conceptual thinking, since its goal is non-conceptual realization. The fact is that truly insightful conceptual thought brings the philosophical meditator to the ultimate confrontation with reality, where even conceptuality is transcended."

10. Unless one is willing to accept the meditational process as an empirical activity of self-exploration. For further elaboration on this viewpoint, see Alex Wayman, *Buddhist Insight*, George Elder, ed. (Delhi: 1984), pp. 69-117.

11. I follow, in this essential distinction, the views of a number of modern existentialist philosophers, such as: Guido Küng, *Ontology and the Logical Analysis of Language, An Enquiry into the Contemporary Views on Universals* (Wien: 1963, repr. Dordrecht, Holland: 1967), esp. pp. 9-10, n. 30; R. Ingarden, *Der Streit um die Existenz der Welt*, 2 vols. (Tübingen: 1964/65, repr.

of Kraków: 1947/48 and Warszawa: 1960), vol. 1, §5, reprinted in English only partially as *Time and Modes of Being*, ed. H. R. Michejda (Springfield, Ill.: 1960).

12. These ontic categories are: 1) the Essential Being (*Wesen, Essenz*) or Eidos; 2) the Temporal Horizon manifesting in a continuous succession of content, forms, and relationships; and 3) the Spatial Order of the world, which can be "objective" (physical) and "perceptual" (symbolic representation of the first). See for (1) Husserl's *Ideas*, pp. 56-59, 161-65; for (2) ibid., pp. 92-93, 215-18; and for (3) ibid., pp. 116, 383, which summarizes all three dimensions of existence.

13. D. T. Suzuki, *Studies*, op. cit., p. 412.

1.1. Tathāgata-garbha

1. See the most comprehensive monograph to date written by David Seyfort Ruegg, *La Théorie du Tathāgatagarbha et du Gotra, Études sur la Sotériologie et la Gnoséologie du Bouddhisme* (Paris: 1969), Conclusion, pp. 499-516 (esp. p. 504, n. 1), where the numerous renditions of the term—in both Eastern and Western languages, old and new—are presented. Here, Ruegg divides all possible meanings into two categories: "contenu" and "contenant;" examples of the former would be "embryo," "essence," "nature," "germ," "seed," and of the latter, "womb" "matrix," "receptacle," "heart," "shrine," granary," etc.

Other synonyms and alternate references are given by A. Wayman following Abhayākaragupta's *Munimatālaṃkāra*, *Ratnagotravibhāga*, and *Śrī-Mālā-sūtra*, in Alex and Hideko Wayman, *The Lion's Roar of Queen Śrīmālā, A Buddhist Scripture on the Tathāgatagarbha Theory* (New York and London: 1974), pp. 44-46.

See also Jikidō Takasaki, *A Study on the Ratnagotravibhāga (Uttaratantra), Being a Treatise on the Tathāgatagarbha Theory of Mahāyāna Buddhism* (Rome: 1966), esp. Ch. 4 "Genealogy of Tathāgatagarbha," pp. 32ff.

2. Suzuki, *Studies*, p. 177 and in the Glossary, p. 405.

3. Published in *Daijō Bukkyō kara Mikkyō e* (From Mahāyāna Buddhism to Tantra); Hon. vol. for Dr. Shunkyō Katsumata (Shunjusha, Tokyo, Sept. 20, 1981), pp. 1320-34 (Japanese order), pp. (1)-(15) (English order).

4. Louis de La Vallée Poussin, *Vijñaptimātratāsiddhi, La Siddhi de Hiuan-Tsang* (Paris: 1929), "Appendice," p. 755.

5. Ibid. For a discussion of the 32 *mahāpuruṣalakṣaṇas* in the *Ratnagotra-vibhāga*, see V. S. Agrawala, "The Thirty-two Marks of the Buddha-Body," *Journal of the Oriental Institute*, M. S. University of Baroda, vol. I, no. 1 (Sept. 1951), pp. 20-22.

6. Poussin, op. cit., pp. 755-56.

7. These lines may be translated as follows: 1) "All these sentient beings

have the embryo of Tathāgata" (i.e., the potential of fulfilling the teaching of the Buddha, *dharmakāya*); 2) "The Tathāgata's embryo is the Thusness of all beings" (i.e., Thusness, *tathatā*, can be taken here as the "essence"); 3) "The realm of Tathāgata is the womb of all these beings" (i.e., *dhātuḥ*, 'realm, domain, place', may be the equivalent of 'womb, matrix, family, lineage', *gotra*).

8. Takasaki, *A Study on the Ratna*, op. cit., p. 198.

9. Ibid.

10. Ibid.

11. See J. W. de Jong, *Buddhist Studies*, Gregory Schopen, ed. (Berkeley, Ca.: 1979), p. 40.

12. The most obvious Buddhist borrowings are the references to the Hindu myths, e.g., the myth of Rāma, which found its way into the first chapter of the *Laṅkāvatāra*, and into the *Buddhacarita* of Aśvaghoṣa (see chs. 6.36; 7.8; 9.9, 59; 13.11, etc.).

13. The problem arises only if Tathāgata-garbha is taken as a real ontological substance (named *prakṛti* in the passage quoted here), existing independently (*svabhāva*) as the common essence of all sentient beings, and yet transcendent to them.

However, this would be a literal interpretation of the term, discouraged by the authority of the text, who uses it—as we shall see—with didactic and soteriological purpose in mind.

14. According to *Mahābhārata* 12, 312, 1-7, quoted by E. W. Hopkins in *Epic Mythology* (Varanasi: 1968, reprint).

15. See S. Dasgupta, *A History of Indian Philosophy*, vol. 1 (Cambridge: 1963), pp. 25-27; 45-48; 52.

16. See Radhakrishnan, *The Principal Upaniṣads* (London, New York: 1974 reprint), pp. 793, 837. Common Buddhist-Hindu ideas shown here are "the illusory character of the world, momentariness of phenomena," as well as such technical terms as *āśraya* and *ālaya*.

17. See Paul Deussen, *The Philosophy of the Upanishads.* The Religion and Philosophy of India Series (Edinburgh, New York: 1906, 1908), p. 201. Quoted by Dasgupta, op. cit., v. 1, p. 52.

18. E. B. Cowell, ed., *The Buddha-karita of Asvaghosha* (Oxford: 1893), pp. 4 and 9.

19. Mrs. C. A. F. Rhys Davids, *The Milinda-Questions* (London: 1930), p. 23.

20. See *Sacred Books of the East*, tr. vols. 35-36 (t. 2, 15).

21. Paul Demiéville, 'Sandhinirmocanasūtra,' *Bulletin de l'École Française*

des Études Orientales, 24, 1-2, 53 (my own translation from the French original text).

22. Paul Masson-Oursel, 'Tathāgatagarbha et Ālayavijñāna,' *Journal Asiatique* 210 (Paris: 1927), 297-98.

23. La Vallée Poussin, op. cit., p. 754 (my English rendition).

24. Ibid.

25. Gishin Tokiwa, "Tathāgata Garbha," *Journal of the Indian and Buddhist Studies*, Vol. 22, No. 1 (Dec. 1973): pp. (11)-(15) (Engl.).

26. Ibid., p. (11) and n. 5 (English order); Chinese version, Tokiwa tr.

27. Ibid., pp. (11)—(12) (English order); Chinese version, Tokiwa tr.

28. Tokiwa, op. cit., p. (13) (Engl. order), n. 12.

29. Alex Wayman, "The Title and Textual Affiliation of the Guhya-garbhatantra," in *Daijō Bukkyō kara Mikkyō e (From Mahāyāna Buddhism to Tantra)*, Hon. vol. for Dr. Shunkyo Katsumata. Tokyo, Set. 20, 1981: p. 4, n. 5 (English order).

30. Quoted by Tokiwa, op. cit., p. (22) (Engl. order), n. 8.

31. Takasaki, *A Study on the Ratna*, p. 290.

32. Ibid., pp. 53, 61.

33. See N. Takata, "On the *Āryacandrottaradārikāvyākaraṇa-nāma-mahāyāna-sūtra* (Japanese)," *Journal of Indian and Buddhist Studies*, vol. 5, No. 1 (1957), pp. 83-86.

34. Takasaki, op. cit., pp. 53-54.

35. Nakamura's edition, p. 89, Tokiwa's translation.

36. Takasaki's translations, from here on, op. cit., p. 291.

37. Ibid., p. 197.

38. Ibid., p. 259.

39. Wayman, *The Lion's Roar*, pp. 104-105.

40. In the *Brahmā-jāla Sutta* of the *Dīgha-Nikāya* 1.34, the Buddha upholds the higher truth over against the seven different sorts of Nihilist doctrines, among which two (*Uccheda-diṭṭhi* and the *Ātta-diṭṭhi*) are the illusions regarding personality.

41. For a more extensive discussion of the system of Vijñānas, see infra, Ch. 2.3 on "The Eight Vijñānas."

42. Wayman, *The Lion's Roar*, op. cit., p. 45.

43. Ibid.

44. Ibid., p. 46, quoting Johnston, ed., *Ratnagotravibhāga* (Patna: 1950), text p. 54. Here the term *ātman* does not appear, but its meaning is clearly indicated by the four epithets which—when everything is considered—point to the gradual infiltration of Hindu ideas into the mainstream of Buddhist thought.

45. Alex and Hideko Wayman, tr., op. cit., pp. 27-28. See also Takasaki, op. cit., pp. 258-61.

46. See Obermiller's translation of "The Sublime Science of Maitreya," *Acta Orientalia*, 9, pp. 95, 156-7, and also his "Doctrine of Prajñāpāramitā," Ibid., pp. 90, 99-100; quoted by T. R. V. Murti in *The Central Philosophy of Buddhism* (London: 1980), p. 257.

47. Johnston, ed., *Ratnagotravibhāga*, text citation translated by Alex and Hideko Wayman, op. cit., p. 46.

48. See the section "Synonyms and Alternate References to the Tathāgatagarbha" in Alex and Hideko Wayman, op. cit., pp. 44-46.

49. According to Takasaki, op. cit., p. 53.

50. Ibid. See also infra, ch. 2.1. on the *Mind-only* doctrine.

1.2. The Five Skandhas

1. Bhikkhu Ñyāṇamoli, tr., *The Path of Purification by Bhadantācariya Buddhaghosa*, vol. 2 (Berkeley: 1976), p. 587.

2. S. Radhakrishnan, *The Principal Upaniṣads* (London: 1978), p. 163.

3. For a detailed view of the Buddhist schools and sects, see: Nalinaksha Dutt, *Early History of the Spread of Buddhism and the Buddhist Schools* (Calcutta: 1925), followed by the *Buddhist Sects in India* (Calcutta: 1970). Also in Mrs. Rhys Davids & J. Ras, *The Sects of Buddhism* (London: 1891), pp. 409f.

4. See Dutt, *B. Sects*, p. 6 (following Tāranātha's account) and Shwe Zan Aung & Mrs. Rhys Davids, tr., *Points of Controversy* or *Subjects of Discourse (Kātha-Vatthu)* (London: PTS, 1915), p. 6.

5. See J. Bloch, *Les inscriptions d'Aśoka* (Paris: 1950), pp. 152f.

6. Shwe Zan Aung & Mrs. Rhys Davids, op. cit., p. 7; this incredibly equal division of all remembered heads of the Buddha's discourses, if anything, reveals the strength of the opposing groups: the Elders and the Personalists.

7. The book was written by many authors, or rather, compilers, as Mrs. Rhys Davids indicates in her "prefatory notes."

8. The 57 *dhammas*, which are reiterated in the *Laṅkā*, were 5 *khandhas*, 12 *āyatanas*, 18 *dhātus*, and 22 *indriyas*. See S. Z. Aung & Rhys Davids, op. cit., pp. 8, 15-16; and *Compendium of Philosophy* (*Abhidhammātha-Saṅgaha*, pt. 7.8)

(London: 1910), PTS, pp. 175f., 182.

9. Aung & Rhys Davids, *Points of Controversy*, p. 23.

10. Ibid., p. 22.

11. *Saṃyutta-Nikāya* 3.127, *Pāli Texts Society* 3, 108-9; see also Nolon Pliny Jacobson's *Buddhism, The Religion of Analysis* (London: 1966), p. 85.

12. *Abhidharmakośa* 9.271, commented by Ed. Conze in *Buddhist Thought in India* (London: 1962, repr. Ann Arbor: 1973), p. 126.

13. E. Sarachandra, *The Buddhist Psychology of Perception* (1958), also quoted by Conze, op. cit., p. 282.

14. L. Silburn, *Instant et Cause* (1955), pp. 237-43, ibid.

15. Conze, op. cit., pp. 131, 133.

16. Louis de La Vallée Poussin, tr., *L'Abhidharmakośa de Vasubandhu*, 6 vols. (Paris: 1923-31), 644.

17. Th. I. Stcherbatsky, "The Soul Theory of the Buddhists," *Bull. of the Academy of Sciences of the USSR* (Leningrad: 1919), pp. 824-25; also quoted by N. P. Jacobson, op. cit., pp. 85-86.

18. See article "Ātta(n)" in *A Critical Pāli Dictionary* (Copenhagen: 1948), p. 95; and also J. G. Jennings' commentary in *The Vedantic Buddhism of the Buddha* (London: 1948), p. 817.

19. *Alagaddupama-sutta* of the *Majjhima-Nikāya* 1.140, Lord Chalmers, tr., *Further Dialogues of the Buddha*, vol. 1 (London: 1926), p. 99. The two opposing theories regarding the survival of consciousness after death were Sannivāda and Asannivāda.

20. H. C. Warren, *Buddhism in Translations* (New York: 1977), p. 381.

21. Ibid., pp. 238-39.

22. Ibid., p. 172.

23. See Mrs. Rhys Davids in *Buddhist Psychology*, p. 21; *Compendium of Philosophy*, p. 278; and Keith in *Buddhist Philosophy*, p. 14.

24. See J. G. Jennings, op. cit., pp. 22-27, 36-55.

25. In the *Itivuttaka* of the *Khuddaka-Nikāya*, pp. 38-39, two kinds of extinction are mentioned, both in connection with the aggregates of existence (Khandhas): *sa-upādi-sesa-Nibbāna*, or *kilesa-Nibbāna* ("burning of the defilements with the Khandhas still remaining"), and *anupādi-sesa-Nibbāna*, or *khandha-Nibbāna* ("putting out of the aggregates through the extinction of grasping or clinging, *upādi*"). See Conze, Horner, et. al., *Buddhist Texts Through the Ages* (New York, 1974), p. 96, nn. 1, 2.

26. Ninian Smart, *Doctrine and Argument in Indian Philosophy* (London: 1964),

p. 48; cf. Buddhaghosa, *The Expositor 2* (tr. of the *Atthasalini* commentary) where all four possible views regarding the Tathāgata's self are rejected as "the intoxicants" (New York: 1921), 477.

27. See Th. Stcherbatsky, *The Conception of Buddhist Nirvāṇa* (Delhi: New York: 1978), ch. "Sūnyatā-not nihilism," pp. 42-43.

28. Cf. M. Sprung, et. al., tr., *Lucid Exposition of the Middle Way* (Boulder: 1979), pp. 174-77, 179-80.

29. Cf. Kenneth K. Inada, *Nāgārjuna* (Tokyo: 1970), p. 115.

30. C. A. F. Rhys Davids, *Buddhist Psychology* (London: 1914), p. 42.

31. Ibid., p. 40.

32. Cf. F. Edgerton, *Buddhist Hybrid Sanskrit Dictionary* (New Haven: 1953, Delhi reprint: 1977), p. 607. For two detailed discussions of each of the five Skandhas, the first written by an authority on the Pāli scriptures, and the second by a Japanese Buddhist, see: Rune E. A. Johansson, *The Psychology of Nirvāṇa* (London: 1969, reprint New York: 1970), pp. 65-72; Hajime Nakamura, "The Problem of Self in Buddhist Philosophy," in *Revelation in Indian Thought, A Festschrift in Honour of Professor T. R. V. Murti*, ed. by Harold Coward and Krishna Sivaraman (Emeryville, Ca.: 1977), pp. 114-15, nn. 11-16.

33. In the *Dhamma-Sanganī* of the Theravadin *Abhidhamma-Piṭaka* the five Khandhas are given in a threefold scheme: (1) physical, viz. *rūpa;* (2) sense-perception and reaction to it, viz. *vedanā, saññā,* and *saṅkhāra;* and (3) consciousness, or *viññāna.* In this case the three groups are called: *rūpa, cetasikā* (concomitants or conditioning factors of consciousness) and *citta* (state of consciousness).

34. Lord Chalmers, tr., *Further Dialogues of the Buddha,* vol. I, *Majjhima-Nikāya* (London: 1926), pp. 133f.

35. Ibid., p. 134.

36. This topic is presented at length by Alex Wayman in his article "The Intermediate-State Dispute in Buddhism," found in *Buddhist Insight,* G. R. Elder, ed. (Delhi: 1984), esp. pp. 257-8, where he quotes Vasubandhu's description of a *gandhabhuk* (*gandharva*), given in the *Abhidharmakośa* 3, 13-14.

37. I. B. Horner, tr., *The Middle Length Sayings,* Vol. 2 (London: 1957), p. 349.

38. Louis de La Vallée Poussin, *L'Abhidharmakośa de Vasubandhu,* Troisième Chapitre (Paris: 1926), p. 94.

39. Alex Wayman, "A Study of the Vedāntic and Buddhist Theory of *Nāma-Rūpa,*" *Indological and Buddhist Studies in Honour of Prof. J. W. de Jong* (Canberra: 1982), p. 617.

40. See *Mahā-Vagga* ("The Great Chapter), *Dūyatānupassanā sutta* ("Sermons on Dual viewpoints"), Bhikṣu Dharmaratna, ed. (Sarnath: 1951), p. 164; quoted by Wayman, op. cit., p. 631.

41. H. C. Warren, *Buddhism in Translations* (New York: 1977), p. 147.

42. For their outline, see Suzuki, *Studies*, p. 454 (Glossary). Together with the five aggregates, these new categories expanded the sphere of discourse from the analysis of man as object to the "understanding of the nature of conditioned existence from the point of view of the experiencing subject." Cf. Rupert Gethin, "The five Khandhas: their treatment in the Nikāyas and early Abhidhamma," *Journal of Indian Philosophy* 14 (1986): 35-53, esp. pp. 48-49.

43. For the use of *mana-* as "pride" in this specific location, see F. Edgerton's *Buddhist Hybrid Sanskrit Dictionary* (New Haven: 1953, reprint Delhi: 1977), p. 417.

44. Translated by J. G. Jennings in *The Vedāntic Buddhism of the Buddha* (London: 1948), p. 513.

45. Quoted by Ed. Conze in *Buddhist Thought in India* (Ann Arbor, Mi.: 1973), p. 128.

46. Ibid.

47. See Ananda K. Coomaraswamy & I. B. Horner, *The Living Thoughts of Gotama the Buddha* (London: 1948), p. 149.

48. Lord Chalmers, tr., *Further Dialogues of the Buddha*, vol. I, *Majjhima-Nikāya* (London: 1926), pp. 304-307.

49. This principle was unanimously accepted by all schools and was quite frequently employed throughout the scriptures. It postulated four alternatives, all denied: (1) X exists, (2) X does not exist, (3) X neither exists nor does not exist, and (4) X both exists and does not exist. All four are efficiently used in rejecting any obstinate attachment to any one metaphysical viewpoint. See A. Wayman, "Who Understands the Four Alternatives of the Buddhist Texts?" *Philosophy East and West* 27 (Jan. 1977), pp. 3-21; also Burtt, *Philosophy East and West* 5 (1955), pp. 203-205 and Conze, op. cit., 219-20. For an extensive discussion of the tetralemma logic, see below ch. 2.0.

50. Herman Oldenberg, *Buddha, his Life, his Doctrine, his Order* (London: 1928), p. 278.

51. Lord Chalmers, op. cit., vol. 1, p. 5, *Majjhima-Nikāya* 1.8.

52. Ed. Conze, for example, in *Buddhist Thought in India*, op. cit., p. 220, says that through the application of the *catuṣkoṭi* principle "at all times and everywhere, one-sided affirmation and negation have been rejected as erroneous, in favor of some 'non-dual' reality which is free from both being and non-being."

53. See Nalinaksha Dutt, *Aspects of Mahāyāna Buddhism and its Relation to Hīnayāna* (London: 1930), p. 143; also see Conze, op. cit., p. 124.

54. See Th. Stcherbatsky, *The Conception of Buddhist Nirvāṇa* (Delhi, New York: 1968, 1978), Introduction, pp. 55-57.

55. Horner's translation given in Conze, Horner, et. al., *Buddhist Texts Through the Ages* (New York: 1974), p. 93.

56. M. Eliade, *Yoga: Immortality and Freedom* (Princeton: 1973, reprint of the French edition, Paris: 1954), p. 192.

57. T. W. Rhys Davids, *Buddhist Suttas* (New York: 1969), p. 116.

58. C. A. F. Rhys Davids, *A Manual of Buddhism* (London: 1932), p. 274; and *What Was the Original Gospel in Buddhism?* (London: 1938), p. 38.

59. Stcherbatsky, op. cit., p. 55.

60. Edgerton, op. cit., p. 79.

61. Warren, op. cit., p. 122.

62. D. T. Suzuki, *The Laṅkāvatāra Sūtra* (Boulder: 1978), p. 100, n. 1.

63. Suzuki, *Studies*, p. 136.

64. For an authoritative overview regarding the paradigm shift in science, see Fritjof Capra, *The Turning Point—Science, Society, and the Rising Culture* (New York: 1982), esp. ch. 11.

65. Francis L. K. Hsu, et. al., eds., *Culture and Self—Asian and Western Perspectives* (New York: 1985), ch. 2, part 1, "The Self in Cross-cultural Perspective," pp. 24-55.

66. See Hsu, op. cit., pp. 28 & 37.

67. See Akihisa Kondo, "Illusion and Human Suffering: A Brief Comparison of Horney's Ideas with Buddhistic Understanding of Mind," in *Buddhist and Western Psychology*, Nathan Katz, ed. (Boulder: 1983), pp. 139-48, esp. p. 144.

1.3. Dharmadhātu

1. For a concise review of the various meaning of the term (Pāli, Dhammadhātu), see Louis de La Vallée Poussin,*La Siddhi de Hiuan-Tsang (Vijñaptimātratāsiddhi)*, vol. 2 (Paris: 1929), pp. 751--54.

2. The terms *objective* and *perceptual* are borrowed from Husserl's *Ideas, General Introduction to Pure Phenomenology* (London: 1931, repr. New York: 1962), p. 116, where he speaks about "objective space" and "perceptual space" in relation to the "corporeal reality" of "true Being." He adds, however, that what is given bodily may be "mere appearance," or perceived "merely subjectively," although not as an "empty illusion." Note the surprising

similarity with the Yogācāras' distinction between 'perceptual' and 'object-discriminating' knowledge, as discussed below in chapter 2.3.

3. Suzuki, *Studies*, p. 412 (Glossary).

4. See Edgerton, op. cit., p. 278.

5. Quoted by Edgerton, ibid.

6. See, Th. Stcherbatsky, *The Central Conception of Buddhism and the Meaning of the Word "Dharma"* (London: 1923, Delhi: 1979), p. 10 and n. 1 & 2.

7. Ibid., p. 73.

8. Ibid., p. 9.

9. See Suzuki, *Studies*, p. 454 (Glossary).

10. Stcherbatsky, op. cit., p. 9, n. 2.

11. Ibid.

12. See Stcherbatsky, *The Conception of Buddhist Nirvāṇa* (New York: 1968, Delhi: 1978), p. 35.

13. Ibid., p. 57.

14. For a summary of the Buddhist story of creation, see Alex Wayman's article "Buddhism" in *Historia Religionum*, C. J. Bleeker, ed. (Leiden: 1971), vol. 2, *Religions of the Present*, pp. 428-30; for a review of Buddhist cosmology, see T. O. Ling, *A Dictionary of Buddhism* (New York: 1972), pp. 78-81 and M. McGovern, *A Manual of Buddhist Philosophy* (1923), vol. 1 *Cosmology*.

15. See the succeeding section 2.1.

16. Alex Wayman, "No Time, Great Time, and Profane Time in Buddhism," in *Buddhist Insight*, G. Elder, ed. (Delhi: 1984), p. 270.

17. Quoted by A. Wayman in "Dependent Origination—The Indo-Tibetan Tradition," *Buddhist Insight*, p. 166 and n. 7.

18. See Louis de La Vallée Poussin, *Théorie des douze causes* (Gand: 1913), p. 70.

19. *Madhyānta-vibhāga* 1, 13a-b, quoted by A. Wayman, *Buddhist Insight*, p. 272.

20. By Bhavya, Candrakīrti, and Śāntarakṣita, according to Chr. Lindtner, who translated it from the Tibetan version in *Nāgārjuniana, Studies in the Writings and Philosophy of Nārgārjuna, Indiske Studier* 4 (Copenhagen: 1982), pp. 31-70. The summary of the seven divisions of the text given here loosely follows that suggested by Lindtner in his analysis of the text, op. cit., p. 33.

21. See N. A. Śastri, "Store-consciousness (Ālaya-Vijñāna)—A Grand Concept of the Yogācāra Buddhists," *Bulletin of Tibetology*, vol. 9, no. 1 (Gangtok, Sikkim: 15 Feb. 1972), p. 9.

22. Surendranath Dasgupta, *A History of Indian Philosophy*, vol. 1 (Cambridge: 1963), p. 131.

23. Noriaki Hakamaya, "The Realm of Enlightenment in *Vijñaptimātratā*: The Formulation of the 'Four Kinds of Pure Dharmas'," tr. by John Keenan in the *Jn. of the Int. Assoc. of Buddhist Studies* 3 (1980), no. 2, pp. 24-25, 28-29.

24. Ibid., p. 28, quoted from Haribhadra, *Abhisamayālaṃkārāloka* (Wogihara ed.), p. 30, 2.8-9.

25. Hakamaya, op. cit., p. 28.

26. Jikidō Takasaki, "Dharmatā, Dharmadhātu, Dharmakāya and Buddhadhātu—Structure of the Ultimate Value in Mahāyāna Buddhism," *Jn. of Indian and Buddhist Studies* vol. 14, no. 2 (Tokyo: March 1966), pp. 83-84 (English order).

27. Takasaki, op. cit., p. 83 (English order).

28. The quote from the *Madhyāntavibhāga-bhāṣya*, 3, k.3 (R. C. Pandeya's ed., p. 38) and its translation are given by Isshi Yamada in his article "Vijñaptimātratā of Vasubandhu," *Journal of the Royal Asiatic Society of Great Britain & Ireland* no. 2 (1977), pp. 167 & 173, n. 36.

29. Interestingly, in light of what we know from modern physics, the essential nature of the cosmos is indeed more voidness than anything else. What we call "atoms," the constitutive elements of the universe, are in fact 99.99% empty space between the minute nucleus and the outer sphere of electronic orbits, itself in constant vibration and movement towards and away from the center.

2.0. Epistemology and Dialectics

1. This distinction is similar to Bertrand Russell's discrimination between "absolute" and "technical" truth. The latter, he says, is a matter of degree, while the former claims "to embody eternal and absolutely certain truth" of a religious creed. Cf. B. Russell, *Religion and Science* (New York: Oxford University Press, 1935, reprint, 1962), pp. 14-15.

2. Frederick J. Strengh, "The Problem of Symbolic Structures in Religious Apprehension," *History of Religions* 4. 1 (1964): 128-30; restated in *Emptiness, A Study in Religious Meaning* (Nashville: Abingdon Press, 1967), pp. 105, 106, 122f., 148-51; cf. in J. W. de Jong, "The Problem of the Absolute in the Mādhyamaka School," *Journal of Indian Philosophy* 2 (1972): 4.

3. Chandradhar Sharma, *A Critical Survey of Indian Philosophy* (Delhi: Motilal Banarsidass, 1960, reprint: 1976), pp. 52-53.

4. Sharma, op. cit., p. 53, note 2.

5. *Āptamīmāṃsā*, I. 7, quoted by Sharma, op. cit., p. 53, note 5.

6. Sharma, op. cit., pp. 53-55.

7. Sharma, op. cit., p. 56 and notes 1 and 2.

8. Ibid., p. 55 and note 4.

9. Ninian Smart, *Doctrine and Argument in Indian Philosophy* (London: George Allen and Unwin, Ltd., 1964), pp. 179-80.

10. For a comparison between the Jain and Buddhist schemas, see K. N. Jayatilleke, *Early Buddhist Theory of Knowledge* (London: G. Allen and Unwin, Ltd., 1963, Delhi: 1980), pp. 338f.

11. It is precisely on account of his substantial conceptual borrowing from his rivals' logical arsenal (i.e., the Śūnyavāda Buddhists) that the greatest Hindu philosopher, Śaṅkara, the founder of Advaita Vedānta, was called a "crypto-Buddhist."

12. For a history of the concept in Indian philosophy, see: P. T. Raju, "The principle of four-cornered negation in Indian philosophy," *Review of Metaphysics* 7.4 (June 1954): 694-713; also for a review of its possible interpretations, see: Frits Staal, *Exploring Mysticism* (Berkeley: 1975), pp. 32-46.

13. Raju, op. cit., pp. 694-95. For an account of the historical background of the Buddhist theory of knowledge, see Jayatilleke, op. cit., pp. 121-39 and 337-38.

14. J. G. Jennings, *The Vedāntic Buddhism of the Buddha* (London: Oxford University Press, 1948), p. 43.

15. H. C. Warren, *Buddhism in Translations* (Cambridge: Harvard University Press, 1896; reprint: New York, 1977), p. 165.

16. Ibid., p. 166.

17. Ibid., p. 167.

18. Lord Chalmers, tr., *Further Dialogues of the Buddha*, Vol. 1 *Majjhima-Nikāya* (London: Oxford University Press, 1926), p. 342. For similar passages in the *Anguttara-Nikāya*, see *Pāli Texts Society* 2.25; and in the *Dighā-Nikāya*, op. cit., 1.23, 31 & 32.

19. Ibid., 1, pp. 43-44.

20. Ibid., 1, pp. 43-44.

21. Ibid., Vol. 2, pp. 131-36.

22. Ibid., 2, p. 136.

23. A. Coomaraswamy & I. B. Horner, *The Living Thoughts of Gotama the Buddha* (London: Morrison & Gibb, Ltd., 1948), p. 149.

24. H. Oldenberg, *Buddha, his Life, his Doctrine, his Order* (London: Luzac & Co., 1928), p. 278.

25. *Majjhima-Nikāya* 1.8, in Lord Chalmers, op. cit., Vol. 1, p. 5.

26. *Majjhima-Nikāya* 1.427f., ibid., Vol. 1, p. 305.

27. David J. Kalupahana, *Nāgārjuna, The Philosophy of the Middle Way* (Albany: State University of New York Press, 1986), p. 5.

28. L. de La Vallée Poussin, *The Way to Nirvana* (Cambridge: Cambridge University Press, 1917), p. 111. Could it be that the Western, Aristotelian bias made it too difficult for him to see the practical usefulness of the tetralemma within the Buddhist universe of discourse? See F. J. Hoffman's conclusion to his article "Rationality in early Buddhist four fold logic," in the *Journal of Indian Philosophy* 10 (1982): 309-337.

29. McClure, in his lecture on Epicureanism at the Philosophy Colloquium, University of Illinois, Urbana (Dec. 15, 1952), quoted by Raju, op. cit., p. 695. More recently, a number of authoritative opinions on the possible confluence of the Mādhyamika and Greek dialectical systems have been critically summarized by Prof. Thomas McEvilley from Rice University, in his remarkable article "Early Greek philosophy and Mādhyamika," *Philosophy East and West* 31. 2 (April 1981): 141-64. Needless to say, it would be difficult to establish, due to an equally balanced scholarly evidence on both sides of the matter, who influenced whom, in respect to the specific use of dialectics for the purpose of rejecting all conceptualizations with pretenses of absolute truths. Without discarding either possibility, one feels inclined, however, to take this fascinating cultural parallelism *in toto*, as Prof. Ed. Conze did in his book *Buddhism, Its Essence and Development* (New York: Harper & Row, Pub., 1975), pp. 142-43, as a *de facto* illustration of the striking similitude of the way in which the mind operates, when confronted with the difficult task of interpreting itself and the world.

30. A. E. Wardman and J. L. Creed, tr., *The Philosophy of Aristotle* (New York, London: The New American Library, Inc., 1963), pp. 71-73. For an in-depth comparative study of the dialectics of Aristotle and Nāgārjuna, see Guy Bugault's article: "Logic and dialectics in the *Mādhyamakakārikās*," *Journal of Indian Philosophy* 11 (1983): 7-76, esp. pp. 13-14, "Aristotle and the Tetralemma."

31. A. E. Wardman & J. L. Creed, tr., op. cit., p. 74. Reading these lines, one is irresistibly reminded of Aristotle's idea of the good as the golden mean between two equally vicious extremes, as expounded in his *Nicomachean Ethics*, Book 2, 5-9.

32. R. H. Robinson, *Early Mādhyamika in India and China* (Madison, Wis.: University of Wisconsin Press, 1967, reprint Delhi: 1976), pp. 50-57.

33. Ibid. Robinson selected and translated these examples from the Sanskrit original, edited by Louis de La Vallée Poussin as the *Mūlamadhyamakakārikās de Nāgārjuna avec la Prasannapadā de Candrakīrti* (*Bibliotheca Buddhica*, vol. 4). St. Petersburg: Imperial Academy of Sciences, 1913.

34. K. N. Jayatilleke, "The logic of four alternatives," *Philosophy East and West*, 17, 1-4 (Jan.-Oct., 1967): 81.

35. See, for example: A. S. Hanson, "Buddhism and logic," *Middle Way* 45.70-72 (1970); also Ed. Conze, *Buddhist Thought in India* (London, Ann Arbor: University of Michigan Press, 1973), p. 219.

36. Alex Wayman, "Who understands the four alternatives of the Buddhist texts?" in *Philosophy East and West* 27.1 (Jan. 1977), pp. 3, 18; also, Tsoṅ-kha-pa's "Lam rim chen mo," the 'Discerning the Real' section of the *Calming the Mind and Discerning the Real* (New York: Columbia University Press, 1978), A. Wayman, tr.

37. Jayatilleke, op. cit., p. 82.

38. Jacques May, "On Mādhyamika Philosophy," *Journal of Indian Philosophy* 6 (1978): 233.

39. Quoted by T. R. V. Murti in *The Central Philosophy of Buddhism* (London: George Allen & Unwin, Ltd., 1980), p. 51.

40. Stcherbatsky also adheres to this view in his analysis of *The Conception of the Buddhist Nirvāṇa* (Delhi: 1978), p. 214. Other authors interpret the tetralemma as a technique intended to defeat an opponent through *reductio ad absurdum* (*prāsaṅgāpādana*). See Ramchandranath Ghose, *The Dialectics of Nāgārjuna* (Allahabad: 1987), p. 309.

41. E. H. Johnston and A. Kunst, "Vigrahavyāvartanī of Nāgārjuna," *Melanges chinois et bouddhiques* 9 (1948-51): 151, quoted by Alex Wayman in "The Buddhist 'Not this, Not this'," *Philosophy East and West* 11. 3 (April 1961): 102.

42. Unless otherwise indicated, all translations from the *Mūla-mādhyamika-kārikās* are mine. A number of reliable studies of the text are available, including the original Sanskrit. See: Th. Stcherbatsky, op. cit.; Kenneth K. Inada, *Nāgārjuna, A Translation of his MMK with an Introductory Essay* (Tokyo: The Hokuseido Press, 1970); and more recently, Kalupahana, op. cit. For an anthology of Nāgārjuna's works, see Chr. Lindtner, *Nāgārjuniana, Studies in the Writings and Philosophy of Nāgārjuna,* (Copenhagen: Akademisk Forlag, 1982). Indiske Studier IV.

43. See Stcherbatsky, op. cit., p. 217, note 9.

44. Candrakīrti's commentary on the *MMK* 22.12, quoted by Stcherbatsky, op. cit., pp. 14-15.

45. See Stcherbatsky, "Scientific achievements in ancient India," in *Papers of Stcherbatsky* (Calcutta: R. D. Press, 1969), p. 68.

46. Raju, op. cit., p. 702. For a succint review of several interpretations of tetralemma and voidness, read: Richard H. Robinson, "Some logical aspects of Nāgārjuna's system," *Philosophy East and West* 6.4 (Jan. 1957): 294, 301-307; also J. W. de Jong, "Emptiness," *J.I.P.* 2 (1972): 7-13.

47. See Wayman, "Who understands . . . ?" (as above), p. 8.

48. Robinson, *Early Mādhyamika*, etc. . . . (as above), p. 56.

49. Robinson, "Some logical aspects . . ." (as above), p. 305.

50. Ibid.

51. Wayman, "Who understands . . .? (as above), pp. 11-12.

52. Murti, op. cit., pp. 131, 133-36.

53. K. Venkata Ramanan, *Nāgārjuna's Philosophy* (Delhi: Motilal Banarsidass, 1978), pp. 160-70.

54. David J. Kalupahana, *Causality, The Central Philosophy of Buddhism* (Honolulu: University of Hawaii Press, 1975), pp. 97, 143, 157.

55. Robert W. Clark & Acharya Lozang Jamspal, tr., *Skhalitapramathana-yukti-hetu-siddhi* V by Acharya Āryadeva, in the *Glory of India*, Vol. 3, No. 1 (March 1978); see also the Appendix: "A Summary of the Sixty-two types of wrong views" (reprint).

56. Wayman, "Who understands . . .? (as above), p. 15.

57. If Stcherbatsky is right in tracing down the original meaning of *śūnya* = zero, then A. Bharati's intuitive extrapolation of this notion from the metaphysical domain to the psychological field, appears historically justifiable within the Buddhist tradition (to which he claims to belong as a spokesman). I am referring here to his formula "the zero experience," meaning the abolishment of the notional activity of the mind, or—in his words—indicating the "zero content of a cognitive sort" that characterizes the ultimate mystical experience. Vide: Agehananda Bharati, *The Light at the Center, Context and Pretext of Modern Mysticism* (Santa Barbara: Ross-Erikson Press, 1976), p. 48.

However, nowhere in his book does Bharati give any hint that his use of the term "Zero experience" is, or was consciously related to the ancient (mathematical) usage of the term *śūnya*, as pointed out by Stcherbatsky in his study (vide supra: "Scientific achievements in ancient India," as above, p. 68).

58. Robert F. Olson, "Aspects of the Middle Way—A Study of Mūla-mādhyamika-kārikā of Nāgārjuna in the light of the Perfection of Wisdom," an unpublished *Ph.D. Dissertation* (New York: Columbia University, 1967), p. 168.

59. Jacques May, op. cit., p. 236.

60. Ibid., pp. 234, 236.

61. Ibid., pp. 235-6.

62. See Stcherbatsky, *Nirvāṇa* (as above), pp. 48-50.

63. See above, ch. 1.1. for a more complete translation on the meaning of the Tathāgata-garbha.

64. Bertrand Russell, *Human Knowledge, Its Scope and Limits* (New York: Simon and Schuster, 1948; reprint, 1976), p. 256.

65. For an excellent study of the "Theory of Language in Yogācāra," based mainly on Chinese sources, see Diana Y. Paul, *Philosophy of Mind in Sixth-Century China, Paramārtha's 'Evolution of Consciousness'* (Stanford: Stanford University Press, 1984), Ch. 3, pp. 72-92. Also see Edward Hamlin's text-specific article: "Discourse in the *Laṅkāvatāra-sūtra*," *Journal of Indian Philosophy* 11 (1983): 267-313, where the sūtra's critique of language is analyzed from the standpoint of two key Buddhist concepts: *upāya* (skill in means) and *māyā* (dream-like reality).

66. For an in-depth discussion of these terms, see ch. 2.2, the subsection on the meaning and the means of achievement of the Noble Wisdom (*ārya-jñāna*).

67. The word "dialectic" is taken here in the most generic sense, given by its Greek origin (*dialektikē*), meaning an argumentative art, technique, or mode of reasoning which includes, indeed mandates, the opposite, negative viewpoint in its presentation which, most frequently, is based upon questions and answers. "Because of this method, which he employed with masterly skill, Zeno was called by Aristotle the inventor of Dialectic and Plato says that he could make one and the same appear to his hearers, as like and unlike, as one and many, as in motion and at rest." See Ed. Zeller, *A History of Greek Philosophy* (London: 1881), Vol. 1, p. 613.

68. The most thorough investigation to date, covering historical, philosophical, as well as comparative analysis of Mādhyamika dialectic with both Eastern and Western related systems, in T. R. V. Murti's *The Central Philosophy of Buddhism* (London: George Allen & Unwin, 1955; reprint, 1980), especially chs. V-VII & XII-XIII.

69. M. Eliade, *Occultism, Witchcraft and Cultural Fashions, Essays in Comparative Religion* (Chicago: University Press, 1976), p. 45.

70. See Murti, op. cit., p. 124, note 2, on the beginnings of Western dialectic.

71. See Murti, op. cit., pp. 40-41, 124 and note 2; also Streng, op. cit., pp. 242-43, where other interpreters' views are cited.

72. In that he is in agreement with the three-valued and many-valued modern logical systems, such as the indeterminate, intuitionistic logic, based on the multi-set, intuitionistic mathematics of L. E. J. Brouwer (See Staal, op. cit., pp. 39-40, 42-3, 46), where the need to reject, or rather transcend, the principle of the excluded middle, or of the double negation, is acknowledged.

The inadequacy of language in the study of subatomic physical phenomena is also well known: Heisenberg in his elaboration of the 'Uncertainty Principle,' and Einstein in his explanation of the 'Quantum physics,' have pointed this out (See for a brief review of their conclusions, along with pertinent comments and bibliography: Michael Talbot, *Mysticism and The New Physics* (New York: Bantam Books, Inc., 1981), pp. 70-73, 199-204).

73. See for instance: Ninian Smart, *Doctrine and Argument in Indian Philosophy* (London: 1964, reprint: 1969), p. 58; Stefan Anacker, *Seven Works of Vasubandhu, The Buddhist Psychological Doctor* (Delhi: 1984), p. 62; and Thomas A. Kochumuttom, *A Buddhist Doctrine of Experience: A New Translation and Interpretation of the Works of Vasubandhu, the Yogācārin* (Delhi: 1982), p. 222.

2.1. Citta-mātra

1. See, for instance, Stephen Beyer, who in his book *The Cult of Tārā: Magic and Ritual in Tibet* (Berkeley: 1973), p. 92, says the following: "Much of Buddhist 'ontological psychology' is an attempt to explain in historical terms why we make a systematic epistemological error in our apprehension of the world, why we attribute to it a solidity that in fact it does not possess."

2. Janice Dean Willis, *On Knowing Reality, The Tattvārtha Chapter of Asaṅga's Bodhisattvabhūmi* (New York: 1979), pp. 24-25.

3. Louis de La Vallée Poussin, *Nirvana* (Paris: 1925), p. 64; *l'Abhidharmakośa de Vasubandhu*, ch. VI (Paris, Louvain: 1925), p. 299; *Vijñaptimatratāsiddhi* (Paris: 1928-29), pp. 109-113, 215, 530.

4. "Precanonical Buddhism," *Archiv Orientalni*, VII (1935), p. 131.

5. *Beiträge zur Indischen Philologie und Altertumskunde* (Hamburg: 1951), p. 152.

6. Quoted by J. W. de Jong in *Buddhist Studies*, Gregory Schopen, ed. (Berkeley, CA.: 1979), pp. 48-49.

7. For a detailed presentation of the various *kleśas* as held by both Northern and Southern schools, see Wm. M. McGovern, *A Manual of Buddhist Philosophy*, Vol. I (London: 1923), pp. 145-49.

8. See J. W. de Jong, op. cit., p. 49.

9. Cf. Nalinaksha Dutt, *Aspects of Mahāyāna Buddhism* (London: 1930), p. 148; see also Schayer, op. cit., p. 131 and C. Regamey, *Roczik Orientalistyczny*, 21 (1957), p. 48.

10. For a review of the relevant texts and commentaries, see La Vallée Poussin, *Vijñaptimatratāsiddhi*, vol. 1, pp. 420-23.

11. See chapter 1.1. on the triple meaning of the Tathāgata-garbha and its relation with the Ālaya-vijñāna.

12. For a systematic analysis of the usage of the word *manas* in the *Laṅkā*, see J. Takasaki "The concept of *manas* in the *Laṅkāvatāra*," *Journal of Indian and Buddhist Studies* 39, 2 (1981), 1-8.

13. For an extensive discussion of the significance of the term *vijñaptimātra* and its correlates: *prajñaptimātra*, *nāmamātra*, *vikalpamātra* and *vijñānamātra*,

see Suzuki's *Studies*, pp. 181f., and 278-82. For its various interpretations in the secondary literature, see Thomas A. Kochumuttom's *A Buddhist Doctrine of Experience* (Delhi: 1982), pp. 198-200, "The Meaning of Vijñāpti-mātra."

14. Monier Monier-Williams, *A Sanskrit-English Dictionary* (Oxford: 1964), p. 395.

15. Ibid., p. 394; see also Suzuki's "Introduction" to *LAS*, p. XXI, and F. Edgerton's *Buddhist Hybrid Sanskrit Dictionary* (Delhi: 1977), p. 229. Stefan Anacker in his study, *Seven Works of Vasubandhu, The Buddhist Psychological Doctor* (Delhi: 1984), indicates that both meanings of the word *citta* can be found in the writings of Vasubandhu, as well. Thus, on p. 161, he translates *citta-mātra* as "All this is perception-only . . . the equivalent of an optical disorder," while on p. 290, he equates *citta* with *citatvāt* ("becoming accumulated"), as having virtually the same meaning.

16. *Laṅkā*, pp. XXI-XXII.

17. Monier-Williams, loc. cit., gives only the past participle *cita* for the root *ci*, but the sense could have easily been expanded to include the meaning usually associated with the Ālaya-vijñāna, the Repository of Impressions, although this would not necessarily imply its derivation from *ci*, but rather a semantic transference, or slippage.

18. *Studies*, p. 254, note 3.

19. Alex Wayman, "The Yogācāra Idealism," review article in the *Philosophy East and West*, vol. 15, no. 1 (Jan. 1965), p. 66.

20. Monier-Williams, op. cit., p. 804.

21. Sylvain Lévi, *Vijñaptimātratāsiddhi par Vasubandhu* (Paris: 1925), pp. 20-1.

22. Th. Stcherbatsky, *The Central Conception of Buddhism and the Meaning of the Word "Dharma"* (Delhi: 1979), Appendix II, pp. 100-4. See also Étienne Lamotte, *Histoire du Bouddhisme Indien, Des Origins à l'ére Śaka*, Bibl. de Muséon, Vol. 43 (Louvain: 1958), pp. 659-70.

23. The complete list is found in Nyanatiloka, *Guide through the Abhidhammapiṭaka* (Colombo), p. 12 (table). See also the list in the *Abhidhammatthasangaha*, S. Z. Aung, tr., *Compendium of Philosophy* (London: 1929), summarized in H. von Glasenapp, *Die Philosophie der Inder* (Stuttgart: 1949), p. 326-332.

24. See Vasubandhu's *Triṃśika* IX, in S. Radhakrishnan and Ch. Moore, ed., *A Sourcebook in Indian Philosophy* (Princeton: 1957), p. 335; also, E. Lamotte, op. cit., pp. 659-60. For a detailed commentary, see A. K. Chatterjee, *The Yogācāra Idealism* (Varanasi: 1962), pp. 150f.

25. Quoted by Stcherbatsky, op. cit., pp. 18-19.

26. C. A. F. Rhys Davids, *A Buddhist Manual of Psychological Ethics* (New Delhi: 1975), pp. 265, 318; see also notes no. 4, loc. cit.

27. In Radhakrishnan and Moore, op. cit., p. 337.

28. Suzuki, *Studies*, p. 277.

29. Ibid., p. 407 and Edgerton (op. cit., pp. 258, 259) agree on the rendition of these two terms as the "triple universe" of the *kāma-*, *rūpa*, and *arūpa-* states of existence.

30. See P. D. Shastri, *The Docrine of Māyā in the Philosophy of the Vedānta* (Luzac: 1911), pp. 30f.; and Teun Goudriaan, *Māyā Divine and Human* (Delhi: 1978), pp. 243f. Radhakrishnan defines *māyā* as "the principle which accounts for the apparent conditioning of the unconditioned Absolute," *History of Philosophy*, vol. 1, p. 66.

31. See K. N. Jayatileke, *Early Buddhist Theory of Knowledge* (London: 1963, Delhi: 1980), pp. 359f.

32. See chapter 1.1. on the Tathāgata-garbha and the rejection of the Ātman doctrine. For a general account of the philosophical debates which the Yogācāra thought provoked in India, see J. Sinha's *Indian Realism* (Delhi: 1938) and Stcherbatsky's examples in *Buddhist Logic* (New York: 1962), vol. 2, pp. 360f.

33. See Alex Wayman, "Yogācāra and the Buddhist Logicians," *JIABS*, Vol. 2, no. 1, 1979, p. 75.

34. Ibid., p. 73.

35. In Wayman, op. cit., p. 76.

36. Ibid.

37. Alex Wayman, "The Yogācāra Idealism," review article of Ashok Kumar Chatterjee, *The Yogācāra Idealism* (Varanasi: 1962), in *Philosophy East and West*, Vol. 15, no. 1, Jan. 1965, p. 67.

38. Lambert Schmithausen, as given in *German Scholars on India, Contributions to Indian Studies*, vol. 2 (Bombay: 1976).

39. Ibid., p. 246.

40. Ibid., p. 247.

41. Quoted by Conze in the Introduction to Suzuki's *On Indian Mahāyāna Buddhism* (New York: 1968), p. 26.

42. Ibid., note 83.

43. Loc. cit., and p. 27. See also the *Indo-Iranian Journal*, vol. 2 (1963), p. 74.

44. Cited by Wayman in the "Yogācāra and the Buddhist Logicians," *Jn. of the Int. Assoc. of Buddhist Studies*, vol. 2, no. 1 (1979), 72.

45. See Ed. Conze, I. B. Horner, et. al., *Buddhist Texts Through the Ages* (New York: 1964), p. 98, n. 1.

46. Suzuki's *Studies*, p. 267.

47. Ibid., p. 273.

48. Suzuki's *Studies*, p. 273.

49. For instance, the solid appearance of a table is utterly deceiving. When our visual ability is enhanced by microscopic devices, the table looks more like a structured energy field than as a continuous, solid mass.

50. See M. Monier-Williams, *English-Sanskrit Dictionary*, p. 804.

51. According to G. Lakoff and M. Jahnson in *Metaphors We Live By* (Chicago: 1980), p. 5, where they also state that "human thought processes are largely metaphorical" and "the human conceptual system is metaphorically structured and defined."

52. See Heinrich Dumoulin, *A History of Zen Buddhism* (Boston: 1963), pp. 151ff.

53. See Suzuki's *Zen and Japanese Culture* (New York: 1959), p. 150ff. See also Dumoulin, op. cit., pp. 227-78 and 264-68.

54. H. Dumoulin, *Zen Enlightenment, Origins and Meaning* (New York, Tokyo: 1979; orig. 1976), pp. 50-52.

55. See Suzuki's *The Zen Doctrine of No Mind* (London: 1969), p. 57.

56. P. B. Yampolsky, tr., *The Platform Sūtra of the Sixth Patriarch (New York: 1971)*, pp. 137ff.

57. Suzuki, *Essays in Zen Buddhism*, 1 (London: 1927, 1958), pp. 233ff.

2.2. From Mind to No-mind

1. Reason: if *citta* = *vijñāna* = "Mind," and *āryajñāna* = *Jñāna* = "No-mind," then the eight Vijñānas system = *both* "Mind *and* No-mind").

2. E.g., *saddharma*, "the true, good Law," *dharmakāya*, the "body of Law," *dharmacakra*, "the Wheel of Law, *dharmaparyāya*, the "practice of religion," etc.

3. Such as *sarvadharmaśūnyatā*, "the Voidness of all things," or *dharmanairātmya*, "the Selflessness of objects," for instance.

4. See, for instance, Akira Sugunuma, "The Five Dharmas in the *Laṅkāvatāra*," *Indo-Gaku Bukkhyo-Gaku Kenkyu* 15, no. 2 (29-30), March 1967, pp. 32-39 (English order).

5. M. Monier-Williams, *A Sanskrit-English Dictionary* (Oxford: 1964), p. 551.

6. See the following section 2.3. on the eight Vijñānas.

7. *Tathatā* is frequently related in the *Laṅkā* to the twofold ego-lessness (of things and persons, the two *nairātmyas*), which is always mentioned along

with the five Dharmas, the three Svabhāvas and the eight Vijñānas (vide *Laṅkā* VI: 224).

8. A. Wayman, "Buddhism," in *Historia Religionum, Handbook for the History of Religions*, C. Jouco Bleeker & Geo Widengren, eds. (Leiden: 1971), vol. 2, pp. 440-41. For a detailed presentation of the 'five paths' theory, see Eugen Obermiller, "The Doctrine of Prajñā-pāramitā as exposed in the *Abhisamayālaṃkāra* of Maitreya," *Acta Orientalia*, vol. 11, 1932. Wayman also points out that Asaṅga used the term *bhūmi* instead of *mārga*, in "Nescience and Insight According to Asaṅga's *Yogācārabhūmi*," see *Buddhist Studies in Honour of Walpola Rahula* (London, Vimamsa: 1980), p. 260.

9. See, for instance, the discussions of the *tri-kāya* doctrine by D. T. Suzuki in his *Studies in the Laṅkāvatāra Sūtra* (London: 1930, reprint: 1968), pp. 308-338; and by T. R. V. Murti, in *The Central Philosophy of Buddhism* (London: 1955, 1980), pp. 184-7.

10. Suzuki, op. cit., p. 331.

11. M. Monier-Williams, op. cit., p. 274.

12. Mircea Eliade, *Yoga: Immortality and Freedom* (Princeton: 1973), p. 361.

13. See T. R. V. Murti's outline of the dispute op. cit., pp. 317-20; and also the preceding section 2.1. dealing with the Citta-mātra doctrine in the *Laṅkāvatāra-sūtra*.

14. See *jñāna* in the glossary appended to Suzuki's *Studies*, p. 397; see also the next chapter 2.3. on Vijñānas, in the present work.

15. The former in relation to the abstracting and synthesizing faculties of the mind, the latter vis-à-vis the ability to see the world in its totality, beyond the contradictory points of view, as indicated previously in this chapter. For a more comprehensive synopsis on the various epistemic structures developed in the *Laṅkā*, see the subsection "*Jñāna* and *vijñāna* . . ." of the following ch. 2.3.

16. Suzuki, *Studies*, pp. 158-59.

17. Suzuki, *Studies*, p. 159.

18. See Chr. Lindtner, *Nāgārjuniana, Studies in the Writings and Philosophy of Nāgārjuna* (Copenhagen: 1982), p. 193. For a discussion of the three Modes of Cognition in the writings of Vasubandhu, see: Fernando Tola and Carmen Dragonetti, "The *Trisvabhāvakārikā* of Vasubandhu," *Journal of Indian Philosophy* 11 (1983): 225-266, esp. pp. 232-235 and pp. 230-231, where an extensive bibliography of modern studies on this interesting subject can be found.

19. Suzuki, *The Laṅkāvatāra Sūtra* (Boulder: 1978), pp. 243-44, n. 8.

20. For a summary of this early debate among Ch'an Buddhists, see Heinrich Dumoulin, *Zen Enlightenment, Origins and Meaning* (New York, Tokyo: 1979; German original: 1976), pp. 39 & 46-50.

21. Quoted and translated by Heinrich Dumoulin in *A History of Zen Buddhism* (Boston: 1963; orginal German version by A. Francke AG Verlag: 1959), p. 49 (Paul Peachey's English translation).

22. Cf. H. Dumoulin, *Zen Enlightenment* (as above), p. 39.

23. For various accounts and interpretations of the experience of Buddhist enlightenment (Chinese: *wu;* Japanese: *satori*), see: Heinrich Dumoulin, *Zen Enlightenment, Origins and Meaning* (New York & Tokyo: 1979), especially chs.: 11 & 12; *A History of Zen Buddhism* (Boston: 1963), pp. 276-81; also Suzuki's *Essays in Zen Buddhism,* First Series (New York: 1949, 1961), pp. 260-66; and H. Benoit, *The Supreme Doctrine: Psychological Studies in Zen Thought,* with a Forword by Aldous Huxley (New York: 1955, 1959; French original, Paris: 1952), pp. 72-78 & 134.

2.3. The Eight Vijñānas

1. Quoted by Edgerton, op. cit., p. 486.

2. Ibid.

3. One should note, however, that the supreme Wisdom of the Buddhas and the Bodhisattvas (Āryajñāna), is already present in all sentient beings, albeit in potentiality only, as the Germ-of-Buddhahood (Tathāgata-garbha). See Suzuki, *Studies,* p. 140, and the preceding chapter of this thesis (1.1.).

4. See previous ch. 2.2. on the three Epistemic States (*svabhāvas*).

5. Cf. Nalinaksha Dutt, *Aspects of Mahāyāna Buddhism and its Relation to Hīnayāna* (London: 1930), ch. 2, "Points of agreement between the two Yānas mentioned in the Mahāyānic texts," pp. 54-57.

6. These two types of knowledge developed by the Yogācāras differ from Husserl's similar categories of "perceptual" and "objective" space (*Ideas,* p. 116), in that they are subject to errors of *both* perception and judgment (vide supra, ch. 1.3.).

7. This Repository-of-impressions (sometimes known as the *mūla-* or *bīja-vijñāna*) is contrasted in the *Laṅkā* with the seven dynamic *vijñānas* (*pravṛtti-vijñānas*). See L. de La Vallée Poussin, *Vijñaptimātratāsiddhi* (Paris: 1928-29), vol. 1, p. 398.

8. Ibid., pp. 1.41, and 1.289f. For the variety of alternate names for *ālaya-vijñāna* in the Yogācāra literature, see ibid., p. 1.166.

9. Ibid., p. I.398f. Cf. Edward Hamlin, "Discourse in the *Laṅkāvatāra-sūtra,*" *Journal of Indian Philosophy* 11 (1983): 267-313, where he interprets *manas* as the clinging force which "develops attachments and aversions to the 'things' which *manovijñāna* isolates" (p. 281).

10. Yoshifumi Ueda, "Two Main Streams of Thought in Yogācāra Philosophy," *Philosophy East and West,* vol. 17, No. 1-4 (Jan.-Oct. 1967), p. 162 and also note 2 for further reference.

11. Louis de La Vallée Poussin, op. cit., p. 1.297. ("The perceptive consciousness discerns the general character of the object," n.n.)

12. This cognitive paradox is beautifully illustrated in the metaphorical work of the Dutch artist M. C. Escher. One of his lithographs (the 1935 *Self-portrait*) is reproduced here on the cover of this book, showing the artist holding a mirrored sphere which reflects a curiously distorted image of himself and of his world.

13. Since the *vāsanā* is stored in the *ālaya*, it is here, too, that the revulsion (*parāvṛtti*) takes place; Mind-only, also, ultimately refers to the eighth *vijñāna*, the *ālaya*. Cf. Suzuki, *Studies*, p. 362, note 3, and Alex and Hideko Wayman, *The Lion's Roar of Queen Śrīmālā* (New York: 1974), p. 55, who point out that the term used for the Buddha Stage in the *Ratnagotravibhāga* is *āśraya-parivṛtti* ("reversion of the basis"), referring to the Tathāgata-garbha. Also, I should add, it is our contention that it was precisely this idea of sudden psychological transmutation which provided the doctrinal basis to the Northern Ch'an (or Zen) school of sudden Enlightenment (Japanese, *satori*), althought it was not advocated as such in the text itself (see conclusions to ch. 2.2. above).

14. Alex Wayman, "The Sacittikā and Acittikā Bhūmi, Text and Translation," in *Buddhist Insight*, G. R. Elder, editor (Delhi: 1984), pp. 330-31. Originally published in the *Journal of Indian and Buddhist Studies* (Tokyo), 7:1 (1960), pp. 375-79. For an extensive bibliography of the Yogācāra sources discussing the topic of the Ālaya-vijñāna and its derivatives, see Fernando Tola and Carmen Dragonetti, "The *Trisvabhāvakārikā* of Vasubandhu," *Journal of Indian Philosophy* 11 (1983): 225-266, esp. pp. 259-260, note 21.

15. The four principal poisonous outflows are: lust (*kāma*), clinging to life (*bhāva*), speculation (*dṛṣṭi*) and ignorance (*avidyā*).

16. Here lies yet another connecting link between the *Laṅkāvatāra* and the teachings of Zen Buddhism, namely the accessibility of Enlightenment to people of all sorts, along with the disdain of intellectualism for its own sake.

17. See Conze, *Buddhist Thought in India* (Ann Arbor: 1973), pp. 251f.; also P. T. Raju, *Idealistic Thought in India* (London: 1953), pp. 277-78.

18. Ibid., p. 277.

19. See Georg Feuerstein, *The Yoga-Sūtra of Patañjali* (Folkestone, Kent, England: 1979), p. 194.

20. Quoted by Padmasiri De Silva in his *Buddhist and Freudian Psychology* (Colombo: 1973), p. 122.

21. See, for instance, the valuable anthology *Buddhist and Western Psychology*, edited by Nathan Katz (Boulder: 1983), which includes comparative articles written by scholars of Buddhism and by mental health practitioners from both East and West. See also Edwina Pio, *Buddhist Psychology: A Modern*

Perspective (New Delhi: 1988), esp. ch. 5, pp. 125-153 ("Psychopathology in Buddhism"), and ch. 6, pp. 155-158 ("Summary"). Indeed, Eastern psychology at last is earning respect among Western intellectuals.

2.4. The Theory of Causation

1. See Ed. J. Thomas, *The History of Buddhist Thought* (London: 1933, 1971), the chapter on causation: pp. 58-70; A. B. Keith, *Buddhist Philosophy in India and Ceylon* (India reprint), pp. 105-109; A. Wayman, *Buddhist Insight* (Delhi: 1984), pp. 163-92.

2. D. J. Kalupahana, *Causality, The Central Philosophy of Buddhism* (Honolulu: 1975), pp. 163-76.

3. His own mistranslation of the passage ("The Great Recluse says that the Tathāgata has spoken . . . etc.") befuddles the issue even more; see K. N. Jayatilleke, *Early Buddhist Theory of Knowledge* (London: 1963, Delhi: 1980 reprint), p. 454.

4. Jayatilleke, op. cit., p. 449.

5. See, for instance, the list of the twelve causal links (*nidāna*), or conditions (*pratyaya*) given by Wayman in op. cit., p. 164, thus: 1) nescience (*avidyā*), 2) motivations (*saṃskāra*), 3) perception (*vijñāna*), 4) name-and-form (*nāma-rūpa*), 5) six sense-bases (*saḍāyatanāni*), 6) sense-contact (*sparsa*), 7) feelings (*vedanā*), 8) craving (*tṛṣṇā*), 9) indulgence (*upādāna*), 10) gestation (*bhāva*), 11) birth (*jāti*), and 12) old age and death (*jarā-maraṇa*).

These are pictorially represented along the rim of the well-known Tibetan Wheel-of-Becoming (*bhavacakra*), reproduced, for instance, in Thomas, op. cit., opposite p. 68.

6. See, for instance, the numerous passages describing the immortality of the Self in the *Bṛhadāranyaka Upaniṣad* 1.4.1; 4.5.14-15; 3.9.26; 4.2.4; 4.4.22; 2.3.5; and in *Chāndogya Upaniṣad* 8.8.3, 14, etc. Cf. Louis de La Vallée Poussin, *Vijñaptimātratāsiddhi* (Paris: 1928, 1929), Tome 1, p. 32 and ff.

7. Cf. La Vallée Poussin, op. cit., 1. 72f.; 2. 534f.

8. Cf. Th. Stcherbatsky, *The Conception of Buddhist Nirvāṇa* (Delhi, New York: 1968, 1978), pp. 1.70, 78-88; 2.48-51. By contrast, Kochumuttom's interpretation of the Yogācāra as a form of realistic pluralism, identical to the Theravāda atomism, cannot seriously be sustained in light of such essential concepts as Śūnyatā (Voidness), Tathatā (Suchness), Buddhatā (Buddhahood), or even the Buddha's own rejection of Eternalism, as one of the extreme philosophical views. See Thomas A. Kochumuttom, *A Buddhist Doctrine of Experience (A New Translation and Interpretation of the Works of Vasubandhu the Yogācārin)* (Delhi: 1982), pp. 1-4, 227-228.

9. Quoted by A. Wayman in *Buddhist Insight* (Delhi: 1984), pp. 175-76 and note 22, p. 176.

10. Photo ed. of Tibetan Tanjur, vol. 23, p. 19-5-2, q. by Wayman, op. cit. p. 176.

11. Photo ed. of Tibetan canons, vol. 154, pp. 71.4 to 72.1, ibid., p. 177. For the orig. Sanskrit, see J. Rahder, ed., *Daśabhūmika et Bodhisattvabhūmi*, pp. 48-49.

12. See David J. Kalupahana, *Causality: the Central Philosophy of Buddhism* (Honolulu: 1975), especially chapters 1 & 2.

13. Ibid., pp. 60-22.

14. Ibid., pp. 23-44.

15. Ibid., pp. 44-53.

16. Ibid., pp. 45, 53. See also K. N. Jayatilleke, *Early Buddhist Theory of Knowledge* (London: 1963, Delhi: 1980), pp. 67, 261.

17. Kalupahana, op. cit., p. 53; see also note 152, p. 202.

18. Jayatilleka, op. cit., p. 261; Kalupahana, loc. cit.

19. Kenneth K. Inada, tr., *Nāgārjuna, A Translation of his Mūlamadhyamaka-kārikā with an Introductory Essay* (Tokyo: 1970), p. 39 (Chapter 1, verse 1).

20. For a review of the various causal theories and lists of terms, with special emphasis on the Yogācāra literature, see Ch. 7: "Causal Correlations: Another Facet of Development," in Kalupahana, op. cit., pp. 163-76.

21. Ibid., Ch. 3: "Clarification of Terminology," pp. 54-66. See also La Vallée Poussin, op. cit., Tome 2, pp. 454, 467.

22. See Jayatilleke, op. cit., pp. 213-15, 256, 275, 357n, 431-2.

23. See the description of *paticca-samuppada* in the *Kaccāyana-gotta-sutta* of the *Samyutta-Nikāya*, and for references to European writings on this topic, see Nyanatiloka, *Guide through the Abhidhamma-Piṭaka* (Colombo: 1957), 2nd ed., pp. 157-73.

24. For a textual illustration of the Abhidharmists' position, see Bhadantācariya Buddhaghosa, *The Path of Purification (Visuddhi-magga)*, bhikkhu Nyānamoli, tr. (Berkeley, London: 1976), vol. 2, pp. 592f.

25. Louis de La Vallée Poussin, ed., *Mādhyamikavṛtti (Mādhyamika-kārikās)*, Biblioteca Buddhica 4 (St. Petersburg: 1903-1913); tr. by Frederick J. Streng, *Emptiness: A Study in Religious Meaning* (New York: 1967), Appendix A. pp. 183-219.

26. According to Kenneth K. Inada, *Nāgārjuna* (Tokyo: 1970), p. 38.

27. Vidhushekhara Bhattacharya, ed. and tr., *Mahāyānaviṃśaka of Nāgārjuna* (Calcutta: 1931).

28. This mistake is still being made today as it has been in the past;

for a review and discussion of various scholarly opinions on the notion that the world is "nothing but the mind," supposedly held by the Yogācāra Buddhists, see the preceding Citta-mātra section of this work (ch. 2.1.).

29. See Vasubandhu's *Triṃśika*, stanzas 7 and 28, in Radhakrishnan and Moore, *A Sourcebook in Indian Philosophy* (Princeton: 1973), pp. 336-37, where he speaks of a "state of mind" only, and not of a denial of the external world.

30. For a complete list of synonyms, with their textual location, see Suzuki's *Studies*, p. 273 and notes 2 through 9.

31. The second line of verse 96 reads: *cittamātravyavasthānam anutpādam*, that is "the non-origination is the (state of) abiding in nothing but the mind," or the "Mind-only" state.

32. Being essentially a practical "philosophy," Yogācāra (like Zen, its distant brain-child) defies clear-cut designations, favored in the West. For, any such categorization (i.e., an object upon which to fix one's thought) would be a strangling snare to the freedom of the spirit, the ultimate goal of the Yogācāra practitioner.

3.0. Final Overview

1. See J. L. Austin, *How to Do Things with Words* (Cambridge: Harvard University Press, 1977), p. 3. For an essential summary of the analytical and logical positivism as a method, see Bertrand Russell, *A History of Western Philosophy* (New York: Simon and Schuster, 1945), pp. 828-36. For an in-depth presentation of its *modus operandi*, see A. J. Ayer, *Language, Truth, and Logic* (New York: Dover Pub., Inc., 1952), chs. 2, 3 and 5.

Also, see Wittgenstein's *Philosophical Investigations* (New York: Macmillan Press Pub., Co., Inc., 1968), pp. 5e-21e; and for its limitations, consult Russell's Introduction to E. Gellner's *Words and Things* (London: Victor Gollancz, Ltd., 1959), p. 13.

2. This is, of course, a much simplified view of these very complex Buddhist metaphysical concepts, done here for the sake of clarity only.

3. The precise nature of Buddhism, whether religious or philosophical, has been debated for the past 150 years without a clear answer in sight. Indeed, as Th. Stcherbatsky the great Russian Buddhologist put it, in *The Conception of Buddhist Nirvāṇa* (Leningrad: 1927), p. 1, "no other religion has proved so refractory to clear formulation."

For a review of the various arguments and a systematic attempt to clarify the adequacy of Western philosophical categories within Buddhist, as well as global context, see George Chatalian's article "Early Indian Buddhism and the nature of philosophy: a philosophical investigation," in the *Journal of Indian Philosophy* 11 (1983): 167-222.

Bibliography

Agrawala, V. S. "The Thirty-two Marks of the Buddha-Body," *Journal of the Oriental Institute,* M. S. University of Baroda, vol. 1, no. 1 (Sept. 1951): 20-22.

Anacker, Stefan. *Seven Works of Vasubandhu, The Buddhist Psychological Doctor.* Delhi: 1984.

"Ātta(n)," *A Critical Pāli Dictionary.* Copenhagen, 1948.

Asaṅga. *Mahāyāna-Sūtrālaṃkāra,* Sylvain Lévi, ed. Paris, 1907 and 1911.

Asvaghosha. *The Buddha-karita of Asvaghosha,* E. B. Cowell, ed. Oxford, 1893.

Bareau, André. *Les Sectes Bouddhiques du Petit Véhicule.* Saigon, 1955.

Beyer, Stephen. *The Cult of Tārā: Magic and Ritual in Tibet.* Berkeley, 1973.

Bhadantācariya Buddhaghosa. *The Expositor 2* (tr. of the *Atthasalini* Commentary). New York, 1921.

———. *Visuddhi-Māgga (The Path of Purification),* Bhikkhu Ñyanamoli, tr. Berkeley, Ca., 1976.

Bloch, J. *Les Inscriptions d'Aśoka.* Paris, 1950.

Bugault, Guy. "Logic and Dialectics in the *Mādhyamakakārikās,*" *Journal of Indian Philosophy* 11 (1983): 7-76.

Burtt, E. A. "What Can Western Philosophy Learn from India?" *Philosophy East and West* 5, no. 3 (Oct. 1955): 195-210.

Chatterjee, Aśok Kumar. *The Yogācāra Idealism.* Varanasi, 1962.

Conze, Edward. *The Prajñāpāramitā Literature* (Indo-Iranian Monographs). The Hague, 1960.

———. *Buddhist Thought in India. Three Phases of Buddhist Philosophy.* London, 1962; reprint Ann Arbor, 1973.

———. *Buddhism: Its Essence and Development.* New York, 1975.

Conze, Ed., Horner, I. B. et. al., eds. *Buddhist Texts through the Ages.* Oxford, 1954; reprint New York, 1964.

Coomaraswamy, A. K. & Horner, I. B. *The Living Thoughts of Gotama the Buddha.* London, 1948.

Daśabhūmikasūtra et Bodhisattvabhūmi: Chapitres Vihāra et Bhūmi. J. Rahder, ed. Paris and Louvain, 1926.

Dasgupta, Surendranath. *Indian Idealism.* Cambridge, 1933; 1969.

———. *A History of Indian Philosophy,* vol. 1. Cambridge, 1963.

Dayal, Har. *The Bodhisattva Doctrine in Buddhist Sanskrit Literature.* London, 1932; reprint Delhi, 1978.

de Jong, J. W. *Buddhist Studies,* Gregory Schopen, ed. Berkeley, 1979.

Demiéville, Paul. "Saṅdhinirmocanasūtra," *Bulletin d'École Francaise des Études Orientales,* 24, 1-2, 53.

de Silva, P. *Buddhist and Freudian Psychology.* Colombo, 1973.

Deussen, Paul. *The Philosopy of the Upanishads.* Edinburgh, 1906; New York, 1908.

Dumoulin, Heinrich. *A History of Zen Buddhism.* New York, 1969.

———. *Zen Enlightenment, Origins and Meaning.* New York, 1979.

Dutt, Nalinaksha. *Early History of the Spread of Buddhism and the Buddhist Schools.* Calcutta, 1925.

———. *Aspects of Mahāyāna Buddhism and its Relation with Hīnayāna.* London, 1930.

———. *Buddhist Sects in India.* Calcutta, 1970.

Edgerton, Franklin. *Buddhist Hybrid Sanskrit Dictionary.* New Haven, 1953; reprint Delhi, 1977.

Eisler, R. *Kant Lexicon.* Berlin, 1930.

Eliade, Mircea. *Yoga: Immortality and Freedom.* Paris, 1954; reprint Princeton, 1973.

Faure, Bernard. "La Volonté d'Orthodoxie," unpublished *Ph.D. Dissertation,* Tome I. Paris: Collége de France, 1984.

———. "Bodhidharma as Textual and Religious Paradigm," *History of Religions* 25, no. 3 (Feb. 1986): 187-98.

Frauwallner, E. *Beiträge zur Indischen Philologie und Altertumskunde.* Hamburg, 1951.

———. "On the Date of the Buddhist Master of the Law, Vasubandhu," *Serie Orientale Roma,* 3 (1951).

——. *Die Philosophie des Buddhismus.* Hamburg, 1956.

Geiger, Wilhelm, tr. *Mahāvaṃsa,* or *The Great Chronicle of Ceylon,* vol. 3. London, 1912.

Ghose, Ramchandranath. *The Dialectics of Nāgārjuna.* Allahabad, 1987.

Goudriaan, Teun. *Māyā Divine and Human.* Delhi, 1978.

Hakamaya, Noriaki. "The Realm of Enlightenment in *Vijñaptimātratā:* The Formulation of the 'Four Kinds of Pure Dharmas'," tr. by John Keenan in the *Journal of the International Association of Buddhist Studies* 3 (1980), no. 2, 21-41.

Hamlin, Edward. "Discourse in the *Laṅkāvatāra-sūtra,*" *Journal of Indian Philosophy* 11 (1983): 267-313.

Hauer, J. W. "Das *Laṅkāvatāra-Sūtra* und das Sāṃkhya," *Beiträge zur Indischen Sprachwissenschaft und Religionsgeschichte.* Stuttgart, 1927.

Hegel, G. W. F. *The Science of Logic.* London, 1969.

Heidegger, Martin. *Being and Time,* Macquarrie, J. & Robinson, E., trs. Oxford, 1967.

Hoffman, F. J. "Rationality in Early Buddhist Four Fold Logic," *Journal of Indian Philosophy* 10 (1982): 309-337.

Hopkins, E. W. *Epic Mythology.* Varanasi, 1968.

Horner, I. B., tr. *The Middle Length Sayings,* vol. 2. London, 1957.

Husserl, Edmund. *Ideas, General Introduction to Pure Phenomenology,* Boyce Gibson, W. R., tr. London, 1931; reprint New York, 1962.

Inada, Kenneth K. *Nāgārjuna.* Tokyo, 1970.

Ingarden, R. *Der Streit um die Existenz der Welt,* 2 vols. Tübingen, 1964/65, reprint of Kraków, 1947/48 and Warszawa, 1960; reprinted in English only partially (vol. 1) as *Time and Modes of Being,* Michejda, H. R., ed. Springfield, Ill., 1960.

Jacobson, Nolon Pliny. *Buddhism, The Religion of Analysis.* London, 1966.

Jayattileke, K. N. *Early Buddhist Theory of Knowledge.* London, 1963; reprint Delhi, 1980.

———. *The Message of the Buddha,* a posthumous work edited by Ninian Smart. London, 1975.

Jennings, J. G. *The Vedāntic Buddhism of the Buddha.* London, 1948.

Johansson, Rune E. A. *The Psychology of Nirvāṇa.* London, 1948; reprint New York, 1970.

Kalupahana, David J. *Causality; The Central Philosophy of Buddhism.* Honolulu, 1975.

———. *Buddhist Philosophy, A Historical Analysis.* Honolulu, 1976; reprint, 1982.

———. *Nāgārjuna, The Philosophy of the Middle Way.* Albany, 1986.

———. *The Principles of Buddhist Psychology.* Albany, 1987.

Katz, Nathan, ed. *Buddhist and Western Psychology.* Boulder, 1983.

Keith, A. B. *Buddhist Philosophy in India and Ceylon,* 4th ed. Varanasi, 1963.

Kirk, G. S. "Natural Change in Heraclitus," in *The Pre-Socratics,* Mourelatos, A. P. D., ed. New York, 1974; 189-96.

Kochumuttom, Thomas A. *A Buddhist Doctrine of Experience (A New Translation and Interpretation of the Works of Vasubandhu the Yogācārin).* Delhi, 1982.

Kunst, Arnold. "Some of the Polemics in the *Laṅkāvatārasūtra,*" in *Buddhist Studies in Honour of Walpola Rahula.* London, 1980: 103-112.

Küng, Guido. *Ontology and the Logical Analysis of Language, An Enquiry into the Contemporary Views on Universals.* Wien, 1963; reprint Dordrecht, Holland, 1967.

La Vallée Poussin, Louis de. Théorie des douze causes. Gand, 1913.

———. *Nirvāṇa*. Paris, 1925.

———. *Vijñaptimātratāsiddhi, La Siddhi de Hiuan-Tsang*. Paris, 1929.

Lamotte, Étienne. *Histoire du Buddhisme Indien, Des Origins à l'ére Śaka*, Bibliothèque de Muséon, vol. 43. Louvain, 1958.

Lewis, Todd Thornton. "The Tuladhars of Kathmandu: A Study of Buddhist Tradition in a Newar Merchant Community," unpublished *Ph.D. dissertation* at Columbia University. New York, 1984.

Lindtner, Chr. *Nāgārjuniana, Studies in the Writings and Philosophy of Nāgārjuna, Indiske Studier 4*. Copenhagen, 1982.

Ling, T. O. *A Dictionary of Buddhism*. New York, 1972.

Mādhyamikavṛtti (Mādhyamikakārikās), Louis de La Vallée Poussin, ed. Biblioteca Buddhica 4. St. Petersburg, 1903-1913.

Madhyānta-Vibhāga-Śāstra, Ramchandra Pandeya, ed. Delhi, 1971.

Mahāyānaviṃśaka of Nāgārjuna, Vidhushekhara Bhattacharya, ed. and tr. Calcutta, 1931.

Masson-Oursel, Paul. "Tathāgatagarbha et Ālayavijñāna," *Journal Asiatique* 210 (Paris, 1927): 297-98.

Matilal, Bimal Krishna. "A Critique of Buddhist Idealism," in *Buddhist Studies in Honour of I. B. Horner*, Cousins, L. et al., eds. Dordrecht, Holland, 1974.

McGovern Wm. M. *A Manual of Buddhist Philosophy*, vol. 1, "Cosmology." London, 1923.

McRae, John Robert. "The Northern School of Chinese Ch'an Buddhism," unpublished *Ph.D. dissertation* at Yale University. New Haven, 1983.

Monier-Williams, Sir M. *A Sanskrit-English Dictionary*. Oxford, 1899; reprint, 1964.

Murti, T. R. V. *The Central Philosophy of Buddhism*. London, 1955; reprint, 1980.

Nakamura, Hajime. "The Problem of Self in Buddhist Philosophy," in *Revelation in Indian Thought, A Festschrift in Honour of Professor T. R. V. Murti*, Coward, Harold & Sivaraman, Krishna, eds. Emeryville, Ca., 1977.

Nanjio, Bunyiu, ed. *The Laṅkāvatāra Sūtra*. Kyoto, 1923.

Nyanatiloka, *Guide through the Abhidhamma Piṭaka*, 2nd edition. Colombo, Śri Lanka, 1957.

Obermiller, Eugen. *History of Buddhism (Chos-hbyung)* by Bu-ston. Heidelberg: 1931; reprint 1965.

———. "The Doctrine of Prajñā-pāramitā as exposed in the *Abhisamayālaṃkāra* of Maitreya," in *Acta Orientalia*, vol. 11 (1932): 1-133 & 334-54 ("Additional indices").

Oldenberg, Herman. *Buddha—His Life, his Doctrine, his Order*. London,

1928.
Paramārtha. "The Life of Vasu-bandhu by Paramārtha (499-569)," in *T'oung Pao*, ser. 2, 5 (1904): 269-96.
Paul, Diana Mary. *The Buddhist Feminine Ideal: Queen Srīmālā and the Tathāgatagarbha*, AAR Dissertation Series no. 30. Ann Arbor, 1980.
Paul, Diana Y. *Philosophy of Mind in Sixth-Century China*—Paramārtha's 'Evolution of Consciousness.' Stanford, 1984.
Pio, Edwina. *Buddhist Psychology: A Modern Perspective*. New Delhi, 1988.
Radhakrishnan, Sarvepalli. (gen. ed.), *The Cultural Heritage of India*, vol. 1: *The Early Phases: Prehistoric, Vedic, and Upanishadic, Jaina, and Buddhist*. Calcutta, 1937.
———. *The Principal Upaniṣads*. London, 1953; reprint New York, 1978.
——— and Moore, Charles, eds. *A Sourcebook in Indian Philosophy*. Princeton, 1957; reprint 1973.
Rahula, Walpola. *What the Buddha Taught*. New York, 1959.
———. "Vijñaptimātratā Philosophy in the Yogācāra System and Some Wrong Notions," in the *Middle Way: Journal of the Buddhist Society*, 47, no. 3 (1972).
Raju, P. T. *Idealistic Thought of India*. London, 1953.
Regamey, C. "Le problème du bouddhisme primitif et les derniers travaux de S. Schayer," *Roczik Orientalistyczny* 21 (1957): 37-58.
Rhys Davids, C. A. F. and Ras, J. *The Sects of Buddhism*. London, 1891.
———. *Compendium of Philosophy (Abhidhammātha-Saṅgaha)*. London, 1910.
———. *Buddhist Psychology*. London, 1914, 1924.
——— and Aung, Shwe Zan, trs. *Points of Controversy* or *Subjects of Discourse (Kātha-Vatthu)*. London, 1915.
———. *The Milinda-Questions*. London, 1930.
———. *A Manual of Buddhism*. London, 1932.
———. *What was the Original Gospel in Buddhism?* London, 1938.
———. *A Buddhist Manual of Psychological Ethics*. New Delhi, 1975.
Rhys Davids, T. W. *Buddhist Suttas (Sacred Books of the East)*. London, 1881; reprint New York, 1969.
Ruegg, David Seyfort. *La Théorie du Tathāgatagarbha et du Gotra, Études sur la Sotériologie et la Gnoséologie du Bouddhisme*. Paris, 1969.
———. *Le Traité du Tathāgatagarbha de Bu Ston Rin Chen Grub*. Paris, 1973.
Sangharakshita, Bhikshu. *A Survey of Buddhism*. Bangalore, 1957.
Sarachandra, E. R. *The Buddhist Psychology of Perception*. Colombo, 1958.
Śastri, N. A. "Store-consciousness (Ālaya-Vijñāna)—A Grand Concept of the Yogācāra Buddhists," *Bulletin of Tibetology* vol. 9, no. 1 (Gangtok, Sikkim, 15 Feb. 1972): 5-16.
Śastri, P. S. *Indian Idealism: Epistemology and Ontology*, 2 vols. Delhi,

1975/76.

Schayer, Stanislaw. "Precanonical Buddhism," *Archiv Orientalni* 7 (Prague, 1935): 121-32.

Schmithausen, Lambert. "On the Problem of the Relation of Spiritual Practice and Philosophical Theory in Buddhism," in *German Scholars on India, Contributions to Indian Studies*, vol. 2. Bombay, 1976.

Sharma, Chandradhar. *A Critical Survey of Indian Philosophy*. Delhi, 1960; 1976.

Shastri, P. D. *The Doctrine of Māyā in the Philosophy of the Vedānta*. Luzac, 1911.

Silburn, Lilian. *Instant et Cause*. Paris, 1955.

Sinha, J. *Indian Realism*. Delhi, 1938.

Smart, Ninian. *Doctrine and Argument in Indian Philosophy*. London, 1964; 1969.

Sprung, Mervyn. *Lucid Exposition of the Middle Way. The Essential Chapters from the Prasannapadā of Candrakīrti*. Boulder, 1979.

Stcherbatsky, F. Th. *The Central Conception of Buddhism and the Meaning of the Word 'Dharma.'* London, 1923; reprint Delhi, 1979.

———. *The Conception of Buddhist Nirvāṇa*. Leningrad, 1927; Delhi, 1978.

———. *Buddhist Logic*, 2 vols. Leningrad, 1930; reprint New York, 1962.

Streng, Frederick J. *Emptiness: A Study in Religious Meaning*. New York, 1967.

Sugunuma, Akira. "The Five Dharmas in the *Laṅkāvatārasūtra*," *Indo-Gaku Bukkhyō-Gaku Kenkyū* 15, no. 2 (29-30), March 1967: 32-39 (English order).

Suzuki, Daisetz Teitaro. *Essays in Zen Buddhism*, 3 vols. London, 1927; 1933.

———. *Studies in the Laṅkāvatāra Sūtra*. London, 1930, 1968.

———. *The Laṅkāvatāra Sūtra, A Mahāyāna Text* (translation with an Introduction). London, 1932; reprint Boulder, 1978.

———. *An Index to the Laṅkāvatāra Sūtra (Nanjio Ed.) with the Chinese and Tibetan Equivalents*. Kyoto, 1933.

———. *Zen and Japanese Culture*. New York, 1959.

———. *On Indian Mahāyāna Buddhism*, Conze, Edward, ed. New York, Evanston, and London, 1968.

———. *The Zen Doctrine of No Mind*. London, 1969.

Takakusu, Junjirō. *The Essentials of Buddhist Philosophy*. Honolulu, 1947; reprints: Bombay, 1956; Delhi, 1975, 1978.

Takasaki, Jikidō. "Dharmatā, Dharmadhātu, Dharmakāya and Buddhadhātu—Structure of the Ultimate Value in Mahāyāna Buddhism," *Journal of Indian and Buddhist Studies (Indo-Gaku Bukkhyō-Gaku Kenkyū)* 14, no. 2 (28), March 1966; 78-94 (Engl.).

———. *A Study on the Ratnagotravibhāga (Uttaratantra)*. Roma, 1966.

———. "Analysis of the *Laṅkāvatāra*—in search of its original form," *Indianisme et Bouddhisme, Mélanges offerts à Mgr. Étienne Lamotte*. Louvain-La-Neuve, 1980: 339-52.

———. "The Concept of *manas* in the *Laṅkāvatāra*," *Journal of Indian and Buddhist Studies (Indo-Gaku Bukkhyō-Gaku Kenkyū)* 29, no. 2 (58), March 1981: 1-8 (English order).

———. "Sources of the *Laṅkāvatāra* and its Position in Mahāyāna Buddhism," in *Indological and Buddhist Studies, Volume in Honour of Professor J. W. de Jong on his Sixtieth Birthday*. Canberra, 1982.

Takata, N. "On the *Āryacandrottaradārikāvyākaraṇa-nāma-mahāyāna-sūtra*," *Journal of Indian and Buddhist Studies*, vol. 5, no. 1 (1957): 83-86.

Tāranātha. *History of Buddhism in India*. Chattopadhyaya, A. and Lama Chimpa, trs. Simla, 1970.

Thatcher, Adrian. *The Ontology of Paul Tillich*. Oxford, 1978.

Thomas, Edward J. *The History of Buddhist Thought*. London, 1933; 1971.

Thurman, Robert A. F. "Buddhist Hermeneutics," *Journal of the American Academy of Religion* 47, no. 1 (1978).

Tokiwa, Gishin. "Tathāgata Garbha," *Journal of Indian and Buddhist Studies* 22, no. 1 (Dec. 1973): 10-19 (English order).

———. "*svacittamātra*—The Basic Standpoint of the *Laṅkāvatāra sūtra*," *Journal of Indian and Buddhist Studies* 26, no. 1 (Dec. 1977): 34-39 (English order).

———. "The Tathāgata Entering the Womb (Garbha)," *Journal of Indian and Buddhist Studies* 30, no. 1 (Dec. 1981): 1-5 (English order).

Tola, Fernando and Dragonetti, Carmen. "The *Trisvabhāvakārikā* of Vasubandhu," *Journal of Indian Philosophy* 11 (1983): 225-266.

Tripathi, C. L. *The Problems of Knowledge in Yogācāra Buddhism*. Varanasi, 1972.

Tucci, Giuseppe. *On Some Aspects of the Doctrine of Maitreya (-nātha) and Asaṅga*. Calcutta, 1930.

Ueda, Yoshifumi. "Two Main Streams of Thought in Yogācāra Philosophy," *Philosophy East and West* 17 (January-October 1967): 155-65.

Ui, H. "Maitreya as a Historical Personage," in *Indian Studies in Honour of Charles Rockwell Lanman*. Cambridge, Ma., 1929.

Vasubandhu. *L'Abhidharmakośa de Vasubandhu*, Louis de La Vallée Poussin, tr., 6 vols. Paris, 1923-31.

———. *Vijñaptimātratāsiddhi par Vasubandhu*, Sylvain Lévi, tr. Paris, 1925.

von Glasenapp, H. *Die Philosophie der Inder*. Stuttgart, 1949.

Warder, A. K. *Indian Buddhism*. Delhi, 1970.

Warren, H. C. *Buddhism in Translations*. Cambridge, Ma., 1896; reprint New York, 1977.

Wayman, Alex. *Analysis of the Śrāvakabhūmi Manuscript*. Berkeley, Ca., 1961.

———. "The Yogācāra Idealism," (review article) in *Philosophy East and West* 15, no. 1 (Jan. 1965): 65-73.

———. "Buddhism," in *Historia Religionum*, vol. 2: *Religions of the Present*. Leiden, 1971: 372-462.

——— and Hideko Wayman. *The Lion's Roar of Queen Śrī-Mālā, A Buddhist Scripture on the Tathāgatagarbha Theory*. New York and London, 1974.

———. "Who Understands the Four Alternatives of the Buddhist Texts?" *Philosophy East and West* 27 (Jan. 1977): 3-21.

———. "Yogācāra and the Buddhist Logicians," *Journal of the International Association of Buddhist Studies* 2, no. 1 (1979): 65-78.

———. "Nescience and Insight According to Asaṃga's *Yogācārabhūmi*," in *Buddhist Studies in Honour of Walpola Rahula*. London, 1980.

———. "The Title and Textual Affiliation of the *Guhyagarbhatantra*," in *Daijō Bukkyō kara Mikkyō e (From Mahāyāna Buddhism to Tantra)*, Honorary Volume for Dr. Shunkyo Katsumata. Tokyo, Sept. 20, 1981: 1-15 (English order).

———. "A Study of the Vedāntic and Buddhist Theory of *Nāma-Rūpa*," *Indological and Buddhist Studies in Honour of Professor J. W. de Jong*. Canberra, 1982.

———. *Buddhist Insight*, George Elder, ed. Delhi, 1984.

Willis, Janice Dean. *On Knowing Reality, The Tattvārtha Chapter of Asaṅga's Bodhisattvabhūmi*. New York, 1979.

Yamada, Isshi. "*Vijñaptimātratā* of Vasubandhu," *Journal of the Royal Asiatic Society of Great Britain and Ireland* 2 (1977): 167-75.

Yampolsky, Philip B. *The Platform Sūtra of the Sixth Patriarch, The Text of the Tun-Huang Manuscript, translated, wih notes*. New York, 1967.

Yuichi, Kajiyama, "Hannya-gyō" ('Prajñā literature') in *Nihon no buten* ('Buddhist Literature of Japan'), ed. by Takeuchi, Toshinori and Umehara, Takeshi (Chūkō shinshō No. 179 in a series). Tokyo, 1969.

Index